Foundational Perspectives in Multicultural Education

Eduardo Manuel Duarte
Hofstra University

Stacy Smith
Bates College

An imprint of Addison Wesley Longman, Inc.

New York • Reading, Massachusetts • Menlo Park, California • Harlow, England
Don Mills, Ontario • Sydney • Mexico City • Madrid • Amsterdam

Editor-in-Chief: Priscilla McGeehon
Supplements Editor: Joy Hilgendorf
Marketing Manager: Marilyn Borysek
Project Manager: Dora Rizzuto
Design Manager: John Callahan
Cover Designer: Kay Petronio
Cover Photo: EyeWire
Senior Print Buyer: Hugh Crawford
Electronic Production Specialist and Electronic Page Makeup: Sarah Johnson
Printer and Binder: The Maple-Vail Book Manufacturing Group
Cover Printer: Coral Graphic Services, Inc.

For permission to use copyrighted material, grateful acknowledgment is made to the copyright holders on pp. 361–362, which are hereby made part of this copyright page.

Library of Congress Cataloging-in-Publication Data
Foundational perspectives in multicultural education / [edited by]
    Eduardo Manuel Duarte, Stacy Smith.
        p.   cm.
    Includes bibliographical references (p.   ) and index.
    ISBN 0-321-02345-5
    1. Multicultural education—United States.   I. Duarte, Eduardo
Manuel.   II. Smith, Stacy, (date)–   .
    LC1099.3.F68   2000
    370.117—dc21   99–36610
                                                            CIP

Please visit our website at http://www.awlonline.com

ISBN 0-321-02345-5

1 2 3 4 5 6 7 8 9 10   MA   01 00 99

Contents

Preface

National standards documents, curriculum materials, and scholarly treatises extolling the goals of multicultural education abound. In these materials, educators are encouraged to respect the diverse perspectives of their students, to promote understanding between students from various cultural groups, and to ensure that students from all cultural backgrounds are guaranteed equal educational opportunities. These goals appear laudable, but it is important to ask "why?" The rhetoric surrounding any educational goal needs to be evaluated to determine its merit. Broad objectives are endorsed without adequate accompanying arguments that explain, justify, or defend why such educational objectives are worthy of pursuit. Many proclamations that fall under the rubric of multiculturalism are espoused in such vague language that their message appears generic and directions for implementation remain uncertain.

This volume is intended to provide educators—especially pre-service and in-service teachers and higher education faculty—with opportunities to reflect on questions such as "what educational goals are desirable in response to the 'multicultural condition' of our democratic society?" and "what specific goals are more important than others?" We believe that this sort of reflective, foundational thinking is an integral part of effective educational practice. In order to make reasoned, principled decisions about our practice, and consequently to pursue directed and justifiable courses of action, educators need access to historical and theoretical contexts surrounding particular educational issues. Without a sense of how we orient ourselves in relation to these contexts and issues, educators cannot develop and implement coherent agendas that link our overarching educational goals with consistent curricular objectives, instructional methods, and modes of assessment.

Accordingly, this is not a "*how to*" book on multicultural education. There are plenty of these types of books available to educators. This book is based on the premise that educators need to be able to answer the question "*what for?*" before deciding upon a given practice or considering "how to" implement it. We offer this text as a "*what for?*" book that links a critical exploration of the concept of multiculturalism with various articulations of the imperatives of a multicultural education. *Foundational Perspectives in Multicultural Education* guides the course of this exploration in a few different ways. First, by explicating four distinct perspectives on multiculturalism, the text encourages reflection on divergent priorities and points of emphasis between each perspective. By including a wide range of selections alongside one another, the text serves as a forum for dialogue among prominent voices responding to our "multicultural condition." Second, careful elucidation of the differences between perspectives allows readers to consider the distinct implications of each strand for educational practice. Third, a variety of questions—guiding questions to frame each section and discussion questions that follow each section—provide multiple opportunities for readers to participate in this dialogue surrounding the meanings of multiculturalism and multicultural education within their own specific contexts. Finally, suggestions for further readings allow readers to explore each perspective in more depth.

EDUARDO MANUEL DUARTE
STACY SMITH

Introduction: Multicultural Education—What For?

Which passage best describes your understanding of the term *multiculturalism?*

1. Multiculturalism is just the latest in [a] sequence of terms describing how American society, particularly American education, should respond to its diversity. . . . But no word can be constrained. Multiculturalism, for its advocates, becomes a new image of a better America, without prejudice and discrimination, in which no cultural theme linked to any racial or ethnic group has priority, and in which American culture is seen as the product of a complex intermingling of themes from every minority ethnic and racial group, and from indeed the whole world. To those who oppose multiculturalism's thrust, and in particular fear that it is fostering an education that emphasizes the faults and failures of America, multiculturalism has become a term describing all that has gone wrong in American education—indeed, more than that, in American public life in general. It has become an epithet denouncing those who do not appreciate what is good and decent about our society. (Nathan Glazer, *We Are All Multiculturalists Now,* 1997.)

2. Because [two distinct projects]—one of opening young people to the variety of social identities in the world, the other of closing them off into identities already ascribed to them—have been defended in the name of multiculturalism, we need to distinguish them. Once they are distinguished, we can claim the good one, and repudiate the bad one, and declare a victory for multiculturalism. (K. Anthony Appiah, "The Multiculturalist Misunderstanding," *New York Review of Books,* 1997.)

3. Multiculturalism seems such an engaging idea and yet, somehow, threatening. Why do I, like many people, feel so ambivalent about

it? The explanation is not, after all, so hard to find: the term "multiculturalism" is multiply ambiguous. (Susan Haack, "Multiculturalism and Objectivity," *Partisan Review*, 1995.)

What Is *"Multiculturalism"*?

Many educators, from a broad spectrum of grade levels and disciplines, would agree that "multiculturalism" has something to do with promoting an understanding and appreciation of cultural diversity. Such aims are commonly associated with a movement generally referred to as *multicultural education*. The diversity of views presented in the passages just cited, however, shows that there is no general agreement among educators, or so-called multiculturalists, as to what precisely is to be appreciated or understood about cultural diversity. How are educators to determine what multicultural education should look like in practice if we are unclear as to what multiculturalism is striving to attain? Since multiculturalism is such a foggy concept, educators can be lost in their attempts to practice multicultural education. Our aim in this volume is to enable educators to clarify the aims of multiculturalism. Clarity will then enhance educators' capacities to translate multicultural aims into effective educational practices.

Nathan Glazer claims that the term *multiculturalism* is applied to so many concepts, in so many contexts, that it lacks clear meaning. He writes: "the word [multiculturalism] has emerged and spread so rapidly, has been applied to so many phenomena in so many contexts, has been used in attack and in defense so often to cover such very different developments, that it is no easy task to describe what one means by multiculturalism" (Glazer, 1997, 7). We agree with his account of the term's ambiguous meaning. Glazer's concern points to a central purpose of *Foundational Perspectives in Multicultured Education:* to encourage educators to reflect on some of the most influential definitions of multiculturalism, and to derive for themselves meaningful uses of the term *multiculturalism*. This book is intended to assist educators in identifying which aspects of their work raise challenges that are multicultural in nature, and what types of responses are appropriate. With such clarity of purpose, educators will be more fully equipped to bring their practice in line with their espoused goals.

Because multiculturalism is both a confusing and a contested concept, we think that it is important to explain our purposes for and orientation to editing this volume. We will begin by making three major claims about multiculturalism and multicultural education. These claims express our fundamental premises and assumptions, and the thinking that led us to identify four foundational perspectives in multicultural education. Each of these perspectives is described later in this introduction, and then represented through selected readings in the following sections of the book.

Distinguishing the Multicultural Condition and Multiculturalisms

First, multiculturalism is much more than a demographic phenomenon. It is a way of seeing the world and one's place in it. For this reason, we think that it is important to understand the difference between the "multicultural condition" and "multiculturalism." The phrase *multicultural condition* describes the demographic presence of different ethnic groups within a population along with related factors surrounding particular groups' historical experiences, cultural beliefs, values, and social status within the society at large.[1] By contrast, the phrase *multiculturalism* denotes a response to this condition. In other words, multiculturalism has to do with how an individual *interprets* or *sees the world* and *perceives his/her place in it*—the world being a place characterized by the "multicultural condition." In addition, multiculturalism has to do with how one *evaluates this sense of place,* for oneself and for others, *and what one proposes to do in response* to the multicultural condition.

Second, and consequently, there is no one "multiculturalism," but rather a variety of "multiculturalisms." As the passages at the beginning of this introduction suggest, there is no single response to the multicultural condition. This is because different people interpret the multicultural condition differently. Indeed, there are likely as many responses as there are people.[2] And some of these responses are not usefully thought of as multicultural in nature. When educational theorists develop responses to the multicultural condition, however, the proposals are not so radically plural. Rather, the responses put forward by a wide variety of individual scholars and educators can be clustered into four distinct perspectives. Each foundational perspective exhibits unique, yet similar understandings of the challenges posed by the multicultural condition in contemporary U.S. society, and of how political and educational institutions should respond to those challenges.

Third, as the concept of *multiculturalisms* suggests, most debates in the arena of education are not simply arguments between two opposing intellectual camps, as Anthony Appiah asserts in the passage at the beginning of this introduction. Rather, a multiplicity of conversations and arguments occur at the same time and mutually influence one another. When transported into the arena of education, these multiculturalisms represent hotly contested approaches to educational practice with implications at many levels: curriculum, teaching methodology, administration, and policy making to name a few. Ac-

---

[1]Many people interpret the terms *multicultural* and *multiculturalism* to include reference to categories of social identity including race, ethnicity, gender, class, sexual orientation, and disability, among other things. We constrain our usage of these terms to refer to phenomena surrounding ethnicity, race, and culture. We emphasize the ethnicity/race/culture matrix in order to narrow the scope of our focus and thus allow for depth, rather than breadth, in our investigation of various meanings and implications of the terms. In addition, we use the term "ethnic group" rather than "race" throughout the text not to ignore the concepts of race and racism, but because we believe that race is a socially constructed, rather than a biologically driven, category. Accordingly, there are no "races." Ethnic groups, however, certainly are subject to "racialized experiences" based upon differences in skin color.

[2]This reflects the "radical plurality" that Hannah Arendt describes as characteristic of the human condition (Arendt, 1958, 8).

cordingly, debates surrounding multicultural education are wide ranging and complex. Taken together, these responses to the multicultural condition are polyphonic in that they express many independent, yet juxtaposed voices. This book is designed specifically to represent the polyphony of four perspectives, to illuminate areas of harmony and dissonance, and to illustrate the implications of each perspective for educational policies and practices.

In order to clarify further the thinking that has led to the organization of this book, we think that it is important to delineate: (1) what makes certain responses to the multicultural condition count as one of the four multiculturalisms we label as *foundational*, and (2) what we mean by the term *perspective* on multicultural education. We take up both of these questions in the next two sections and thereby explain why the readings included in this book represent foundational perspectives in multicultural education. We then go on to elucidate each of the four foundational perspectives presented in this volume: *Ethnic Studies Multiculturalism, Antiracist Multiculturalism, Critical Multiculturalism,* and *Liberal Democratic Multiculturalism.*

Foundational Perspectives in Multicultural Education

What counts as a "foundational perspective" in multicultural education? In order to answer this question, we must first determine what points of view should be labeled *multicultural.* This is a very difficult determination to make, not only because the concept of multiculturalism is so confusing, but also because self-described "multiculturalists" have different definitions about the meaning of the label. Moreover, many theorists who write about multiculturalism—including some of the authors included in this book—would not refer to themselves as *multiculturalists.* Many of them vehemently reject the label and propose something else in its place.

Despite this difficulty, we believe that it is possible to distinguish between those perspectives that represent a multiculturalist response to the multicultural condition and those that do not. So far we have defined a *multiculturalism* as an interpretive response to the multicultural condition. At this point it is necessary to extend this definition in order to identify responses to the multicultural condition that are or are not multicultural in nature.

We identify a *multiculturalist position* as one that exhibits two broadly defined features. First and foremost, multiculturalist positions are based, at least in part, on a rejection of the United States as a cultural "melting pot." Multiculturalists value the United States as a democracy with diversity in ethnicity, language, lifestyle, and tradition. As a result, multiculturalists reject an ideal of America as a "melting pot" where such diversity is *assimilated* into a common culture. Second, because cultural assimilationism has been the dominant political force in the United States, multiculturalist positions have taken on an *oppositional* role. In this oppositional role, multiculturalists question, and often reject, those ideas and institutions that have been dismissive or repressive of the pluralism that characterizes the multicultural condition.

Views on Assimilation: America as a Melting Pot or Salad Bowl?

The cultural pluralism that characterizes the multicultural condition poses specific challenges to liberal democratic societies such as the United States, Canada, and the United Kingdom. In a liberal democracy, ideals such as individual freedom and equality are highly valued and provide principles that guide actions within public institutions such as schools. The democratic tradition is characterized by interest in government "by, for, and of the people." Within this tradition, societies in the United States, Canada and the United Kingdom can be described as ongoing experiments to institutionalize, or make real, ideals such as liberty and equality. One example is the practice of "majority rule." Another example is the practice of compulsory schooling. This practice is based, in part, on the belief that a publicly supported education ensures that schooling will be "equally in the interests of all" and will prepare children for their future roles as democratic citizens.

Inventing and implementing practices of self-governance that are fair and equally in the interests of all citizens is never an easy task. But the task appears to face additional hurdles in pluralistic liberal democratic societies. Pluralism complicates the application of principles of equality in institutional contexts. Thus, within the realm of education, such societies are persistently faced with the question: in a pluralistic democracy, how can we invent and implement educational structures and practices that measure up to the ideals of equality and freedom for all?

In the United States, one particular response to this set of challenges and questions held sway for much of the history of the nation. Many politicians and educators alike adhered to the image of "America" as a "melting pot" where the unique attributes of particular ethnic or cultural groups would be melded together into a common American culture. This melting process was referred to as assimilation and was identified as a primary goal of public education, also referred to as common schooling, throughout the first half of this century. But this century has also witnessed the rise of divergent responses to the challenges and questions that arise from our multicultural condition. Taken together, these responses reject assimilationism or the ideal of America as a melting pot.

Multiculturalists reject assimilationism because it emphasizes cultural sameness rather than cultural diversity. Depending upon their particular perspective, multiculturalists are wary of sameness for a variety of reasons. Ethnic studies proponents, for example, resist assimilation as an ideal that has historically degraded the attributes of minority and colonized cultural groups in favor of the attributes of majority and colonizing cultural groups. Liberal multiculturalists voice another concern; they are suspicious of sameness because of their firm belief that a diversity of ideas and values is necessary for moral and social progress. A marketplace of ideas is only as rich as the number and quality of ideas at its disposal.

Despite their varying reasons for distrusting an emphasis on cultural sameness, multiculturalists share a concern to preserve, if not promote, cultural distinctiveness. In the United States, multiculturalists add cultural diversity to the list of democratic ideals and offer up a new image for U.S. democracy within the multicultural condition. In place of the assimilationist vision of the melting pot, multiculturalists offer the vision of a salad bowl. In a salad, each ingredient retains its unique appearance and integrity as a separate and distinct entity while simultaneously contributing to the overall flavor of the dish. At the same time, all of the ingredients share their location within the bowl, similar to the shared locale of diverse peoples who live within the United States.

Opposition to assimilationism, particularly within the cultural context of the United States, is a primary marker for identifying a position as multicultural. Accordingly, this marker is evident in each of the four "multiculturalisms" presented in this volume. We contend that one's stance toward assimilationism and the "melting pot" are defining features of one's perspective on the multicultural condition and, accordingly, determine whether one is a *critic* or an *advocate* of multiculturalism. Before describing the four perspectives that advocate particular multiculturalisms, a few examples of critics of multiculturalism will help to illustrate this point.

Critics of Multiculturalism

According to historian Arthur Schlesinger:

> The vision of America as melted into one people prevailed through most of the two centuries of the history of the Unites States. But the twentieth century has brought forth a new and opposing vision. . . . A cult of ethnicity has arisen both among non-Anglo whites and among nonwhite minorities to denounce the idea of a melting pot, to challenge the concept of "one people," and to protect, promote, and perpetuate separate ethnic and racial communities. (Schlesinger, 1991, 14–15)

Although we agree with Schlesinger that "the twentieth century has brought forth a new and opposing vision" of multicultural America that rejects the melting pot ideal, we disagree with his characterization of multiculturalism as a "cult of ethnicity." First, the term *cult* suggests that the response is dogmatic and spurious, based more on zealous faith than reasoned thinking. We view this choice of terminology as indicative of Schlesinger's disagreement with those responses to the multicultural condition that emphasize ethnic or racial identity. Moreover, we argue that twentieth century responses to the multicultural condition are widely variant. While some responses may seek to "protect, promote, and perpetuate separate ethnic and racial communities," others would reject this option as vehemently as does Schlesinger.

Schlesinger's language suggests that he is concerned about twentieth century responses to the multicultural condition that emphasize particular ethnic or cultural identities. Schlesinger is concerned that attention to particular ethnic identities will result in a fragmentation of the American populace and, hence, a "disuniting of America." Thus, his text reads as something of an alarm cry for a sense of united American identity; an identity that is to be achieved by adhering to assimilationism and promoting this ideal within our educational institutions. For Schlesinger, the term *multiculturalism* implies a rejection of the possibility of a common culture within America, and is therefore to be rejected. In light of this position, we suggest that Schlesinger might be usefully referred to as a "hard critic" of multiculturalism.

By contrast, other scholars and educators fall into the category of "soft critics" of multiculturalism. These critics are "soft" because they refer to themselves as multiculturalists, but retain a commitment to assimilationism. For example, Diane Ravitch is a scholar who calls herself a multiculturalist but whom we nonetheless label a "soft critic" of multiculturalism. Ravitch believes that "we" in America *already have* a "multicultural common culture" (Ravitch, 1992). Therefore, through her eyes, the contemporary multicultural condition poses no problems to be solved and no responses are required. The perspectives included in this volume reject as simplistic Ravitch's response to the multicultural condition on one of two grounds. First, some of the perspectives view any existing "common American culture" as the result of monoculturalism or the repression of diversity. Other perspectives believe that a multicultural common culture is desirable and possible to achieve. Nevertheless, they note that this goal has historically proven to be complex and difficult to achieve, and remains something to be worked toward. Some of that work, these multiculturalists insist, involves opposition to educational policies and practices that appeal to assimilationism.

In sum, we have excluded from this volume responses to the multicultural condition that draw upon assimilationism and/or insist that the United States already shares a common culture that is "multicultural." We have included those responses that: (1) reject assimilationism, largely based upon a critique of existing American culture as monocultural or, (2) at the very least, acknowledge and are concerned with giving sustained attention to the difficulties and complexities of forging a "multicultural common culture."

Oppositional Views

David Theo Goldberg succinctly captures the traditional vision of America that multiculturalists are opposing:

> [The] history of monoculturalism is contemporaneous with melting pot assimilationism as the prevailing standard underlying policies concerning ethnoracial immigration and relations in the United States. The United States was taken in its dominant self-representation to have a core set of cultural and political values, and assimilation meant giving up all those "un-American" values to be able to assume those that would fashion one American subject to the warrant of monocultural interpretation. The core values were those of the class and racial culture that historically had become hegemonic. Blending into the mainstream

melting pot meant renouncing—often in clearly public ways—one's subjectivity, who one literally was: in name, in culture, and, as far as possible, in color. (Goldberg, 1994, 4–5)

Thus, multiculturalists are not against assimilationism simply because they support diversity over sameness. Rather, multiculturalists are against assimilationism because of the historical ramifications of how ideals of universal citizenship and national identity have been sought after and institutionalized. Multiculturalists argue that the "core values" of some cultural groups have gained *hegemony*, more influence or authority, over "American culture" at the expense of values held by other cultural groups. Therefore, multiculturalists are those who argue that relationships of inequality have grown up around these political ideas. Consequently, these ideas and their attainment need to be reconsidered, and possibly even rejected, in light of challenges posed by the multicultural condition.

Historically, two responses to the multicultural condition in the United States—racism and Eurocentrism—have hindered the realization of the democratic ideals of individual freedom and political equality. Both of these responses are grounded in the undemocratic assumption that human beings are not equal. Both insist that some groups are superior, by nature or by tradition, and therefore have the right or privilege to retain the majority of economic and political power. Racist doctrines have identified some peoples as inferior based upon skin color, and consequently excluded them from exercising rights of universal citizenship. Eurocentrism, while insisting that humans are by nature equally endowed, also insists that cultural groups have used these natural endowments in more or less superior ways. Moreover, Eurocentrism defines commonality and worth in terms of the standards of peoples descending from the European continent, and excludes or diminishes the standards of peoples outside of this tradition.

Multiculturalists share a sense of opposition toward the unequal access to political power and institutional resources that result from racism and Eurocentrism. In many respects, the four distinct multiculturalist positions included in this volume are similar to forms of "oppositional consciousness" that Chela Sandoval identifies within feminist liberation movements. Sandoval describes forms of "consciousness in opposition to the dominant social order in terms of a 'topography'." Drawing from the Greek word "topos" or place, she develops a conceptual topography that resembles a map of places in that it charts "realities that occupy a specific kind of cultural region" (Sandoval, 1991, 11). According to Sandoval, her topography of oppositional consciousness:

delineates the set of critical points around which individuals and groups seeking to transform oppressive powers constitute themselves as resistant and oppositional subjects. These points are orientations deployed by those subordinated classes which have sought subjective forms of resistance other than those forms determined by the social order itself. (Sandoval, 1991, 11)

Although multiculturalists are not all members of subordinated classes (nor are all self-described feminists), Sandoval's concept of oppositional consciousness is useful in that it demonstrates a shared sense of critique of the dominant social order and a shared sense of opposition to this perceived state of affairs. Among multiculturalists, as well as feminists, the shared agreement often ends here. Various groups "in opposition" do not agree on why things are as they are, how they should be, or how to get from here to there.

As with the feminist movement, the various forms of multicultural oppositional consciousness manifest themselves in quite distinctive ways. In response to a racist doctrine of white supremacy, for example, some Afrocentrists want to claim the superiority of peoples of African descent and the inferiority of peoples of Caucasian descent based upon degrees of melanin in the skin pigment. In this scenario, racist ideology is not transcended; instead, the historical power differential is displaced with the previously subordinated group taking the position of dominance. This is similar to feminist ideologies that promote the superiority of "feminine" over "masculine" attributes. Other forms of oppositional consciousness emphasize exploding, rather than merely displacing, the power differential inherent in relations of domination and subordination. Some strands of modern liberalism, for instance, propose to overcome racial discrimination against African Americans by guaranteeing all individuals equal rights and equal treatment under the law. In this contrasting example, both forms of oppositional consciousness reject racial discrimination against African Americans, but the proposed remedies are quite different.

Each of the four multiculturalisms presented in *Foundational Perspectives in Multicultural Education* grows out of a particular oppositional stance and, consequently, congeals around distinct sets of questions with particular implications for educational practice. Apart from the shared features— critical stances toward assimilation and stances in opposition to the dominant social order— the four perspectives on the multicultural condition offered in this volume vary widely. The next section draws upon Sandoval's "topographical" approach to "oppositional consciousness" in order to provide a conceptual framework for understanding how these four stances toward the multicultural condition both intersect with and differ from one another. After this framework is explained, and we describe more specifically the four multiculturalisms that it informs, we will conclude by drawing upon another of Sandoval's concepts, that of "differential consciousness." Differential consciousness "enables movement 'between and among'" the various perspectives that comprise the landscape of multiculturalism (Sandoval, 1991, 14). In this respect, consciousness is consistent with our ideal of reflective educators who are able to consider the specificity of unique situations and localized contexts. Thus, educators with a differential consciousness can adeptly navigate between the four foundational perspectives presented in this volume in order to translate multicultural aims into educational practices. Reflective scholar-practitioners are able to critically reflect on the four multiculturalisms, possible implications of each, and, ultimately, to create their own brands of multicultural education.

A Conceptual Framework for Organizing Multiculturalisms[3]

In the preceding section we explained that *multiculturalisms* denote particular types of responses to what we termed the *multicultural condition*. We explained that it is possible to identify a radical plurality of multiculturalisms. This radical plurality is the source for much of the foggy thinking about the multicultural condition. As Susan Haack writes: "the term 'multiculturalism' is multiply ambiguous" (Haack, 1995, 397). Yet, we also suggested that a topographical "skyline view" of this bazaar of responses begins to clear the fog by revealing four distinguishable clusters of responses that coalesce around distinct sets of questions and priorities. Each of these four clusters, or locations within the topography, has in its own way evolved into a foundational perspective on multicultural education. In this section, the development of these four foundational perspectives is addressed by explaining our use of the term *perspective*. Each of the four perspectives is then discussed.

There are several key characteristics that define a *perspective*. These characteristics are: (1) a mode of consciousness which signifies a distinct topographical "location" for the scholar-practitioners to inhabit, (2) an evolving network of shared commitments expressed in distinct vocabularies, or "language games," and (3) a common intellectual heritage that has congealed into a philosophical tradition. While all three of these characteristics overlap to a certain degree, they represent distinct "markers" to outside observers who seek to dialogue with or locate themselves within the perspective. Together, these characteristics mark the parameters of the perspective in the same way the lines on a surface identify a "field of competition" for both the participants and the spectators of an athletic event. Each foundational perspective on multicultural education expresses these characteristics in its own unique way.

Perspectives as Locations

Using Sandoval's language, our explanation of the four foundational perspectives can be described as a "topography," or the charting of specific positions from which we can view the general landscape called the multicultural condition. A foundational perspective is, first and foremost, an intellectual place where a particular mode of consciousness emerges. Put another way, a foundational perspective on multicultural education is one of several locations with its own distinct mode of consciousness. By particular *mode of consciousness* we

---

[3]A number of scholars have offered typologies for delineating specific approaches to multiculturalism (Haack, 1995; Tamir, 1995) and multicultural education (Gibson, 1976; Pratte, 1983; Sleeter and Grant, 1988; Banks, 1995). Our approach to multiculturalism and multicultural education is distinct from each of these in that we offer a philosophical justification for the features that characterize the conceptual framework that we label a perspective. Our approach is thus *foundational* in a dual sense: (1) we provide the historical and theoretical foundations that define a unique approach to viewing the multicultural condition, i.e. the notion of "perspectives"; and (2) we offer foundational texts that provide the grist for understanding the thrust of each perspective.

mean something akin to what the philosopher Edmund Husserl (1969) suggested when he described perception as a "singling out" of a specific object in the world. A particular mode of consciousness is what happens to a human being when she/he becomes captivated by, or significantly interested in, a phenomenon. Thus, when a subject locates her/himself within a foundational perspective she/he is granted a distinct vantage point on the multicultural condition that frames, apprehends, or perceptually grasps the subject's consciousness within a finite field of perception. Although one can speak of perspective as a form of "captive-ation," this limitation is an intensification of perception rather than a imprisonment. In other words, having one's consciousness apprehended by a foundational perspective is not unlike using a telescope to survey a panorama.

Perspectives as Research Communities

A second characteristic of a foundational perspective is its community structure. We can speak of foundational perspectives as "locations" with particular modes of consciousness because we can identify a network of shared commitments expressed in a set of technical terms. Not unlike a region whose inhabitants speak with a local dialect, foundational perspectives possess distinct "vocabularies" that constitute equally distinct "language games." In this regard, the foundational perspective is analogous to a research community.[4]

First, as a specific location, the parameters of a foundational perspective are constituted by the scholar-practitioners who identify themselves with a particular research discourse. What makes the foundational perspective on multicultural education particularly unique is the fact that the discourse is expressive of a shared *normative* response to the multicultural condition. In other words, those who subscribe to a particular multiculturalism share views about what *should be done* in response to the multicultural condition. Thus, as opposed to natural scientists who simply agree about the "correct" descriptions of natural phenomenon, the scholar-practitioners who establish a foundational perspective are always working with and within ideology or contested ethical and political terrain. Ideologies always involve normative prescriptions as to how the condition of humans in the world *ought to be*.

An important characteristic of a foundational perspective is the particular language used by the theorists and researchers; the way they "talk" about the world. This theoretic vocabulary helps us to define the borders of a research community. A foundational perspective is essentially a discursive or linguistic cohort, or what the philosopher Ludwig Wittgenstein (1953) called a "language game." According to Wittgenstein, a language game is the particular context or the "surroundings" within which a term or phrase takes on a certain, particular meaning. The very term *multiculturalism* has a particular meaning, depending on whether it is being used by members of one of the four foundational

---

[4]See Thomas Kuhn, *The Structure of Scientific Revolutions*, 2nd ed., 1970.

perspectives or another. Antiracist educators, for example, will use the term *multiculturalism* with a negative connotation to describe pedagogical practices that fall short of fighting racism in schools. This example illustrates how a particular research community, in this case "antiracist" scholars and practitioners, emerges around a common vocabulary.

In sum, analogous to a research community, a foundational perspective is organized around common responses to the multicultural condition. However, as we mentioned earlier, the scholar-practitioner using the vocabulary of a foundational perspective is self-consciously aware of its status as a prescriptive lexicon: a way of understanding one's world and one's ideals for that world. Yet, a foundational perspective should not be mistaken for dogma or a set of unquestioned principles. On the contrary, the inhabitants of a foundational perspective often express the philosophic spirit of pragmatism.[5] In other words, they recognize that while a theory is more or less conducive to certain kinds of ethical or political commitments and action, no theory guarantees any particular ethical or political outcomes, nor transcends the particular historical conditions and agents which produce them. Thus, inhabitants within a particular foundational perspective recognize the historical limits of their location. They understand these borders as framing a tradition. In turn, they are neither concerned with establishing "foundations" for ethical or political life which would cut across time and space, nor in arbitrarily or capriciously replacing or redefining their common vocabulary.

Perspectives as Traditions

As Thomas Kuhn suggests, a clear way of identifying the existence of a research community is to locate a common set of historic theoretical achievements that a group of contemporary researchers identify as part of their intellectual genealogy. When a group of researchers shares with one another theoretic examples that it "already recognizes as among its established achievements" (Kuhn, 1970, 45–46) it is safe to term this cohort a research community. In the same way, we understand that an acknowledged representation of important achievements is one of the principal characteristics of a foundational perspective on multicultural education. What is crucial is that members of a research community acknowledge or recognize a common heritage of important achievement so that these function as precedents and/or models for further research.

This third characteristic signifies a foundational perspective as historically evolving. It names what the philosopher Hans Georg Gadamer (1989) would call the hermeneutic situation of the perspective: the determinateness of heritage coupled with the openness of current and future interpretations and uses of this past. This third characteristic represents the evolution of the vocabulary or the history of those basic descriptive terms that represent the current lexicon of the research community. The third characteristic thus marks the foundational perspective as a *tradition*: the handing down of statements, beliefs, cus-

---

[5]See Cornel West, "The Ethical Dimensions of Marxist Thought," 1991.

toms, and so on from generation to generation of scholar-practitioners, by word of mouth or through practice.

To understand the foundational perspective as a "tradition" is to call attention to the fact that the uniqueness of the location—its particular mode of consciousness—is related to a number of significant "events" which have occurred over time within that particular location. These "events" are simply those major accomplishments that are "canonical" for the members of the research community. Unlike a so-called "great text," however, which is understood to be both timeless and universal, these notable achievements indicate the historical development of the foundational perspective. They provide generational signposts that help those within and outside the community to understand the tradition. Through such events, the rules of language games emerge and evolve, yet ultimately define the scope of a research community.

To summarize, a foundational perspective's significance in the present is partially related to its significance in the past. The present is shaped by the rethinking of that significant past. As the political theorist Chantal Mouffe (1988) suggests, the movement of tradition is constituted by the life of the past in the present, a present that is constituted by language. Following Mouffe, we suggest that participation within a foundational perspective on multicultural education "can be understood as the creation of new usages for the key terms of a given tradition." More importantly, it is this use of "new language games that make new forms of life possible" (Mouffe, 1988, 40). We return to this idea of creating new usages for traditional terms, and of playing aspects of traditions against one another, when we advocate Sandoval's idea of differential consciousness to readers of this text. But, first, we need to discuss the substantive content of each of our four perspectives.

The Historical and Theoretical Substance of Our Four Perspectives

This volume presents four perspectives that represent distinguishable, fairly coherent strands of responses to the multicultural condition, responses that raise particular possibilities and challenges in the educational arena. The four perspectives are distinct from one another in that each raises different questions, draws upon specific theoretical principles, and translates these principles into practice—or compels action—in unique ways. In turn, each perspective uniquely problematizes the other, so as to establish a dialogic and dialectical relationship between them. The organization of this volume aims to provide a fruitful context for such dialogue. Before launching into this dialogue among authors, we will briefly describe the thrust of each perspective, its historical antecedents, and key implications for translating its theoretical imperatives into educational practice.

Ethnic Studies Multiculturalism

Ethnic studies is an approach to the study of particular ethnic groups that arose in the United States as a reaction and "alternative to the existing ethnocentric curriculum of the schools" (Suzuki, 1979, 44). Some scholars of multicultural education date this movement to the late 1960s and early 1970s, but others look further back to the early years of the twentieth century. Modes of consciousness within the Ethnic Studies perspective approach the multicultural condition in terms of the concerns of distinct cultural groups—namely African Americans, Asian Americans, Native Americans, and Latinos/as. Often, advocates within this tradition emphasize the cultivation of a sense of collective group identity and pride around a particular cultural heritage. Sometimes these group-based aims are translated into an educational focus on students who are members of the cultural group in question. Other approaches to Ethnic Studies are concerned with educating all members of U.S. society about the history and culture of their particular group.

Contemporary approaches to ethnic studies are preceded by at least two historical stages of development. Taken together, these historical moments comprise the tradition that frames current scholarship and activism in the field. According to prominent advocate of multicultural education James Banks, ethnic studies has witnessed two pivotal, and developmental, stages during this century. He refers to the first stage as the "Early Ethnic Studies Movement."[6]

Banks uses Black studies as a paradigmatic case study for the development of the ethnic studies tradition. He explains that early ethnic studies scholars within this tradition, including Carter G. Woodson and W.E.B. DuBois, "were concerned that African Americans develop knowledge of Black history and culture, and a commitment to the empowerment and enhancement of the African American community" (Banks, 1995, 7). Woodson's *The Mis-education of the Negro* (1933) was one of the exemplary works of this early Ethnic Studies movement among African Americans. In this well-known text Woodson argued that schools and colleges in the United States were miseducating African Americans by teaching about European civilization but not about great African civilizations and the cultures of African peoples. He argued that this curricular neglect led to harmful effects on the thinking and self-esteem of African American youth (Banks, 1995, 7).

Woodson's critique set the stage for a few key features of Ethnic Studies Multiculturalism that remain integral to the perspective through the present day. First, he highlights the cultural hegemony that is promoted through school curricula that emphasize "European civilization" and culture. Second, he asserts that African American children are harmed by this curricular exclusion; in particular, their self-esteem is harmed. Each of these emphases—the critique of

---

[6]We are drawing upon Banks's description of "stages" in ethnic studies in a different manner than that which he employs. Banks describes "The Early Ethnic Studies Movement" and "The Ethnic Studies Movement of the 1960s and 1970s." But he does not refer to these as "stages" within the ethnic studies tradition, as we do. Instead, Banks fits these movements into the evolutionary schemata that he offers on the development of "multicultural education" by referring to "ethnic studies" as the "first phase of multicultural education" (Banks, 1995). Our notion of four distinct perspectives, or multiculturalisms, differs from his evolutionary, developmental, chronological portrayal in that our perspectives are more fluid and dynamic. Yet each of the four perspectives shares some of the descriptive aspects of each of his phases in multicultural education.

school curricula as perpetuating cultural hegemony and the claim that such curricula harm African American children—has specific practical implications for the types of educational policies and programs that would remedy the perceived problems.

W.E.B. DuBois agreed with Woodson's critique of U.S. education, but also extended the argument to include a critique of the social, political, and economic status of African Americans within a racist U.S. society. In a speech addressed to Fisk University in 1933, the same year that Woodson's *Mis-education of the Negro* was published, DuBois linked the segregated, caste-like status of African Americans with a call for separate Negro colleges. He proclaimed:

> the American Negro problem is and must be the center of the Negro university. It has got to be. . . . You are teaching American Negroes in 1933, and they are the subjects of a caste system in the republic of the United States of America and their life problem is primarily the problem of caste. (DuBois, 1933, 92)

DuBois recognized that many people would criticize his call for all-Black colleges on the grounds that he was stressing the cultural history and identity of a specific group as primary to a shared history and identity as American citizens. Thus, he was careful to explain that this cultural separation in the field of higher education was not voluntary, but necessary. In the face of racial discrimination and inequality in the United States, African Americans would be best prepared to achieve ideals of universal citizenship and equality through a program of separate higher education in which the "Negro problem" was at the crux of intellectual investigation (DuBois, 1933, 99–100).

DuBois contended that it was only within institutions that were controlled and populated by African Americans that the curriculum could focus on rectifying the abysmal condition of African Americans in the United States in 1933. Thus, his insistence on the need for separate universities heralds a third feature of Ethnic Studies Multiculturalism—an emphasis on separate institutions, or separate programs within mixed institutions, as a remedy to the racism, ethnocentricity, and discrimination prevalent within mainstream institutions.

Each of these three features—critique of curricular hegemony, concern for the self-esteem of students from particular cultural groups, and calls for separate institutions—carried over into the second stage of Ethnic Studies Multiculturalism—the Ethnic Studies Movement of the 1960s and 1970s. James Banks proposes that this stage of ethnic studies arose largely in response to impatience with the pace of desegregation in the wake of the *Brown* vs. *Board of Education* Supreme Court decision. According to Banks, this impatience resulted in demands for various forms of representation and control in educational institutions ranging from community control of schools, to increased hiring of African American teachers and administrators, to an infusion of Black history into the curriculum (Banks, 1995, 9–10). One of the immediate results of such demands was the institutionalization of Black studies centers and programs in a handful of colleges and universities around the nation.

In the wake of the institutionalization of Black studies and other ethnic studies programs beginning in the late 1960s and early 1970s, higher education has become the primary stage for playing out the imperatives of Ethnic Studies Multiculturalism. Apart from curricular reform at all educational levels, much of the current energy in Ethnic Studies is focused around specific programs within colleges and universities. In this arena, Woodson's critique of curricular neglect and harm to students, and DuBois's call for specific attention to the problems faced by members of a particular group, are shared among virtually all approaches to Ethnic Studies. However, ideas as to how these problems should be addressed differ.

Collectively, as the Ethnic Studies movement approaches, or perhaps experiences, its third wave, scholars and advocates of the tradition grapple with such questions as: (1) What are the primary purposes of Ethnic Studies? (2) How should Ethnic Studies be situated within the wider educational establishment (e.g., the university)? and (3) Whom should Ethnic Studies serve? Various scholars offer specific responses to these questions that are often at odds with one another. Some scholars, for example, tout the benefits of separate ethnic studies programs and single group studies while others criticize these practices as isolationist. Nevertheless, Ethnic Studies Multiculturalists share a critique of existent inequitable power relations among groups based on race/ethnicity. And they are committed to addressing such inequities among groups through equalizing access to resources such as knowledge and status at the institutional level, and educational opportunities and self esteem for individual students. The open question remains how these shared ideals are to be achieved.

Antiracist Multiculturalism

The location of antiracism as a mode of consciousness is precisely what it states: a specific antiracist posture. The fundamental premise of this perspective asserts that racism is an institutional and not an attitudinal problem; the problem of racism is not prejudice but domination (hooks, 1989). Accordingly, antiracism does not seek to develop pedagogical practices that are designed for prejudice reduction. Instead, this location produces an oppositional critique of racism in its systemic and institutional form. Antiracist Multiculturalism also seeks to inspire collective political action across race, class, and gender differences. The foundational perspective of antiracism responds to the call issued by Christine Sleeter when she wrote, "multicultural education needs to develop vocabulary and action strategies for addressing white racism and other forms of oppression. . . . Educators in general don't usually think in terms of collective political action to make changes . . ." (Sleeter, 1996, 153). This drive to build solidarity amongst ALL willing parties distinguishes Antiracist Multiculturalism from the Ethnic Studies and Liberal Democratic perspectives.

In order for one to describe this perspective as a location for the building of solidarity against racism, it is necessary to understand the distinct vocabulary and language games of antiracism as articulating a critique of systemic racism and oppression. It is, as Christine Sleeter suggests, to understand it "as part of a larger quest for redistribution of power and economic resources" (Sleeter, 1996, 138). Scholar-practitioners within the antiracist perspective offer critiques of racism as systemic inequality. Thus, as a location of opppositionality and critical consciousness, antiracism attempts to undermine the normalized racist order of social relations by problematizing the political and economic systems that thrive within racist society.

A brief overview of the antiracist language game(s) highlights three points. First, antiracism calls attention to the hegemonic ideology of monocultural white supremacy that legitimizes systemic exploitation of people of color. This critique of cultural hegemony forms the basis of an oppositional language game which represents a "rejection of the existing socioeconomic system and its power relationships" (Grinter, 1992, 101). Second, antiracism understands itself to be the starting point for initiating a political movement in opposition to systemic discrimination. This activist vocabulary reflects a critical humanism that is grounded in the belief that racism is "an organizing principle of the social and political structure, closely linked to a system of class and other forms of discrimination that deny human rights" (Grinter, 1992, 102). Third, antiracism aims to achieve its goals by developing educational programs that are specifically antiassimilation. "Antiracist education aims, through learning processes that question the social structure and its basic assumptions, to produce activists against social injustice. . . . This is the very reverse of assimilation. The White consensus is the problem. . . ." (Grinter, 1992, 103).

Historically speaking, the tradition of antiracism, particularly as a form of oppositional intellectual activism, was initiated by the abolitionist movements in the United Kingdom and the United States. One could, perhaps, trace the tradition back to the earliest critiques offered up by Jesuits against the Spanish and Portuguese colonial genocide against the indigenous peoples of the Americas. The humanist basis of the Jesuit critique focused on the injustice of the ideology of racial superiority. The Spanish and Portuguese had used such an ideology to rationalize their dehumanization of the indigenous peoples and the plundering of their fertile lands. This critique was later echoed in the northern states of the United States with the abolitionist movement to dismantle slavery through legislative institutional reform. The abolitionist-organized political opposition culminated in the emancipation acts of the British parliament in the 1830s, which abolished slavery in the Caribbean, and, finally, with the Thirteenth Amendment (1865) to the U.S. constitution, which outlawed slavery. Of course, these official legal documents did not erase the pervasive white supremacist ideology that was imbedded within the fabric of everyday life.

The limits of the critique in its earliest phases were its inability to articulate an internal critique that would effectively unmask the veiled hegemonic presumptions of Christian humanism. Thus, the Jesuits were incapable of recognizing the assimilationist hegemony of their humanism, which presumed to speak for all peoples, or to have catholic applicability. This limitation is overcome when the critique, first, emerges within the secular parliamentary discourse of liberal democracy and, second, when the critique is appropriated by the oppressed who were now in the position to offer the strongest opposition to racism.

Hence, the contemporary antiracist perspective can trace its roots to the U.S. movement that was led by Frederick Douglass and other African American abolitionists whose struggle can itself be traced back to militant opposition leaders like Nat Turner. These postcolonial critics and activists are the progenitors of the contemporary antiracist discourse which, from its inception, was a strident critique and a collective democratic oppositional movement against the ideology and systems of white supremacy. bell hooks (1989) explains that it was Douglass who in the nineteenth century "made the crucial point that 'power accedes nothing without demand'" (hooks, 1989). Douglass's call set the tone for a movement that would consistently appeal to the ethicopolitical foundations of constitutional democracy and "demand of white people, of black people, of all people that we eradicate white supremacy . . ." As Sleeter notes, Douglass's call to the white community did not fall upon deaf ears. "History," she insists to her fellow white educational activists, "contains numerous examples of white people who have worked collaboratively with oppressed racial groups to combat racist policies and practices. We are not starting from scratch; we have a history to guide us" (Sleeter, 1996, 153).

Critical Multiculturalism

Critical Multiculturalism has emerged as an oppositional educational discourse and is an example of what Peter McLaren (1997) calls "Revolutionary Pedagogy." This distinct perspective, however, combines a wide variety of theoretic traditions. Like antiracism, Critical Multiculturalism attempts to dismantle the hegemony of the bourgeois "white-anglo-American" worldview in education. Moreover, it has roots in the liberatory educational praxis of Paulo Freire. Indeed, Critical Multiculturalists attempt to emulate Freire's provisional utopianism, which he expressed as "the possibility to go beyond tomorrow without being naively idealistic. This is utopianism as a dialectical relationship between denouncing the present and announcing the future. To anticipate tomorrow by dreaming today" (Freire and Shor, 1987, 186). This foundational perspective is also following in the tradition of John Dewey, and thereby represents an effort to confront antidemocratic practices and ideology by politicizing the educational sphere. However, it contemporizes Dewey by addressing what Cornel West calls the problem of "democracy in postmodern times" (1995).

Critical Multiculturalism maintains a desire to establish the school as an oppositional site, as a space where pacifying and assimilationist pedagogical practices can be undermined. The work of Michel Foucault has strengthened Critical Multiculturalism's commitment to the project of radical democracy. Critical Multiculturalism has employed Foucault to complement Freire's dialogics. Indeed, a Freire/Foucault synthesis enables the Critical Multiculturalist to recognize that while it may have the potential to be liberatory, dialogue also has the potential to be a vehicle for enforcing norms and rules of communication; while it has the capacity to liberate, dialogue is often a mechanism for disciplining consensus and silencing differences. In summary, the perspective of Critical Multiculturalism is, as McLaren has noted, "a nascent disciplinary trajectory within education that has its roots in Marxian class analyses of class but which has recently made efforts at appropriating deconstructive reading of discursive formations and certain strands of poststructuralist and postmodern critique" (McLaren, 1994, 319).

Critical Multiculturalism's intriguing hybrid is the basis from which it mounts a critique of liberal democratic theory. The critique suggests that multiculturalism's attention to difference goes well beyond expanding the parameters of liberalism, and is suspicious of any attempt to "fit" difference into the liberal democratic framework. The critique argues that liberalism's inhospitability toward difference is a permanent fixture of liberalism's model of society as "one big family." Liberal democracy, it is argued, dilutes real difference (dissimilarity) by requiring "family resemblances among its diverse populations. It is bound, therefore, by its nature to seek and maintain consensus and sameness. The liberal society's civil and political mechanism begins to falter when family resemblances among its diverse population either break down or become tenuous" (Kazmi, 1994, 67). The suspicion expressed here insists, again, that multiculturalism is not simply "affirming diversity" as an ideal (indeed, classic liberalism's notion of tolerance has always argued for the protection of religious and civil liberty) but contesting assimilation, or disrupting the "family resemblances" within the populace that "would fashion one American subject" (Goldberg, 1994, 4).

The synthesis of various twentieth century continental philosophical movements is also seen most clearly in the antimodern language game of Critical Multiculturalism. Providing the basis for an alternative democratic theory, the antimodern language game emphasizes and most often celebrates the fact that we "live in a decentered, polycentric world in which there is no possibility of a unifying interpretation" (Bernstein, 1988). In addition to developing a critique similar in form to Jacques Derrida's deconstructionism, antimodernism also recovers the early Frankfurt School's antifascist critical theory which was developed by Adorno and Horkheimer (1972). Antimodernism incorporates a style of negative dialectics in an attempt to defend difference and resist reason's tendency to pass over plurality and heterogeneity in favor of a metaphysics of finality, essentialism, and universality. Thus, using a critique that is a curious hybrid of the Frankfurt School negative dialectics and French poststructuralist critique, antimodernism defends difference by deconstructing language and communication. This strategy leads the antimodernist to articulate an antidialogic political philosophy that entails a decentered normative landscape and a disengaged form of agency. By insisting that the words we read, write, and speak are saturated with hidden meanings and veiled desires, which are motivated by economies of power, the antimodern multiculturalist warns that engaging in dialogue across differences involves the risk of silencing marginal speech acts that fall outside the parameters of "official" discourses.

When translated into a perspective of Critical Multiculturalism, antimodernism champions difference by admonishing unity or community, and the possibility of achieving solidarity through dialogue. Antimodernists "agree" that the best defense of difference is located within anti-dialogue, dissent, and/or counter-hegemonic discourses. Through various forms of negative dialectics, antimodernism is interested in disrupting the dialogue across difference. Within the context of Critical Multiculturalism, antimodernism abandons as dangerous any calls for a unifying dialogue, and limits political freedom to freedom from the dominant discourses of the public sphere. In conclusion, against liberal democratic theory antimodernism emphasizes the importance of what Isaiah Berlin (1969) called *negative liberty.* This idea of freedom abandons the conviction that different cultural forms of life are, in the end, compatible with or entailing each other. Negative freedom emphasizes the incommensurabilities among cultures, traditions, and groups; the untranslatability of the cultural and/or ethnic language games; and the unbridgeable gap between people and peoples. It protects the rights of people, particularly minority groups, from the "tyranny" of the public sphere. (As such, it represents the basis from which indigenous peoples mount their claims for cultural survival.) Negative liberty safeguards the individual from having to legitimize his/her lifestyle practices (i.e., linguistic, religious, sexual, etc.). It provides the freedom from having to prove that one's language game is acceptable to the community or mainstream/dominant cultural framework. According to antimodernism, negative liberty creates the possibility for a genuinely multicultural political space, and leaves political actors in the position where, as Jean-Francis Lyotard wrote, "all we can do is gaze in wonderment at the diversity of discursive species, just as we do at the diversity of plant or animal species" (1984, 26).

Finally, the perspective of Critical Multiculturalism is defined by the idea of *borderland* and the *mestizo* (hybrid) mode of consciousness. Within the multicultural borderland the individual agent is one who can occupy a multiplicity of subject positions. To be a subject within the cultural borderland is to be at the nexus of many cultural and sociopolitical currents. This definition of agency possesses characteristics associated with Richard Rorty's contingent self who is able to appreciate "her" vocabulary as a sociohistorical construction that is constantly transformed, expanded, and/or "edited" (Rorty, 1989). This understanding of the subject is also defined by Mouffe:

> as a decentered, detotalized agent, a subject constructed at the point of intersection of a multiplicity of subject-positions between which there exists no a priori or necessary relation. . . . Consequently, no identity is ever definitively established, there always being a certain degree of openness and ambiguity in the way the different subject-positions are articulated. (Mouffe, 1988, 35)

From a macro point of view, the multicultural borderland defines cultural experience as the crisscrossing of the lives of diverse people(s) and expresses an understanding of self and society as processual, dynamic, open ended, or *mestizo.* As a stance in opposition, Critical Multiculturalism aims to undermine monocultural ideology by embracing Rosaldo's borderland category which defines the U.S. cultural experience as a "porous array of intersections where distinct processes crisscross from within and beyond its borders" (Rosaldo, 1993, 208).

Liberal Democratic Multiculturalism

As stated earlier, democratic societies—including the United States, Canada, and the United Kingdom, to name only a few—place a premium on political principles such as individual rights and equal citizenship. As *democratic* societies, these countries are concerned with making collective decisions that represent the consent of all citizens. Equal sovereignty among citizens is deemed essential to reaching political agreements that reflect the common interests of the population. When understood as *liberal* societies, these countries are concerned with protecting the autonomy and freedom of individuals. This is often accomplished by the state granting a set of universal political rights to all adult citizens.

Multiculturalism, or cultural pluralism, across the citizenry of a liberal democratic country complicates the realization of such political ideals. How are rights to be applied to every citizen universally if citizens are different from one another? How are citizens to be treated as equal individuals if they belong to groups that have been historically treated unequally? What political values will unify a diverse, or even disparate, citizenry? Currently, a large number of political theorists are grappling with these types of questions. In light of the increasing cultural pluralism within many countries, as well as debates over the roles of specific cultural groups within such countries, theorists of Liberal Democratic Multiculturalism are concerned with finding ways to create a common political culture that equally represents the interests of all.

Liberal Democratic Multiculturalism is situated within a tradition of modern liberalism that takes as its paradigmatic case the example of religious toleration. Put another way, modern liberal theory is interested in supporting principles and institutions that allow people with widely divergent values, beliefs, and opinions to live together in a stable society and according to ideals of individual equality and fairness. In light of this tradition, Liberal Democratic Multiculturalism tends to emphasize potential conflicts between diverse *values* rather than implications of diverse cultural *identities* that have grown out of ethnic and racialized differences and attendant historical, social, and political experiences of *institutionalized inequities.*

Much of Liberal Democratic Multiculturalism's contemporary concern over what values and institutions liberal democracies need to share in common is in response to issues raised by Ethnic Studies and Critical Multiculturalists. The thrust of Ethnic Studies, for instance, emphasizes the concerns of distinct cultural groups and the cultivation of collective identities. Sometimes these collective aims are interpreted as requiring separatism of one cultural group from the rest of the polity or asserting the primacy of a group over its individual members. For Liberal Democratic Multiculturalists these types of claims raise questions surrounding whether groups have rights (as opposed to only individuals bearing political rights), the importance of individual autonomy versus collective identity, and how to balance the survival of minority cultures against the requirements of a common political culture.

A parallel set of questions arises in response to issues of power relations between groups that are emphasized by Antiracists and Critical Multiculturalists. Whereas antiracist and critical approaches to multiculturalism focus upon countering discrimination and equalizing power relations, Liberal Democratic Multiculturalists are concerned with what distinct groups need to share in common in order to function as a political unit. In terms of countering discrimination, a Liberal Democratic Multiculturalist might ask: is "equal opportunity" granted to individuals or groups? Should we be focusing upon equal opportunity or equal outcomes? In terms of analyzing unequal power relations between groups, liberal theorists often ask of critical theories: Can we only criticize dominance or should we also endorse positive ideals such as equality and liberty for all?

Navigating the Perspectives

Throughout this chapter we have relied upon Chela Sandoval's language to describe a foundational perspective on multicultural education as one of several "locations" with its own distinct mode of consciousness. To talk about a foundational perspective is already to insist that a scholar-practitioner who locates oneself within a perspective has situated her/himself within a unique way of seeing the multicultural condition. Each perspective is thus, first and foremost, a specific intellectual location, or a mode of consciousness, that poses specific, often normative, questions of and responses to the multicultural condition.

In concluding this introduction we would like to draw upon Sandoval's concept of "differential consciousness" in order to encourage educators to embrace the four foundational perspectives presented in this volume in an active and engaged manner. Drawing upon Sandoval's idea of differential consciousness enables us to stress that each of the foundational perspectives represents a unique view of the landscape upon which scholar-practitioners embark when they journey into the multicultural condition of the United States, Canada, and the United Kingdom, or other pluralistic democracies. The journey is and should be unique for all who embark upon it, and the framework offered in this book is one of many "maps" that can guide. As editors of *Foundational Perspectives in Multicultural Education,* we can perhaps best describe ourselves as cartographers of a much-traveled yet uncharted landscape. When we describe ourselves in this manner, we do so with the understanding that the foundational perspectives represent a continuum of options with respect to the appreciation, recognition and/or respect of cultural, ethnic, and linguistic diversity.

Sandoval's concept of differential consciousness reflects our belief that the four foundational perspectives are not incommensurable positionalities that one must choose between. On the contrary, the idea of differential consciousness suggests that the scholar-practitioner can move from one perspective to another in a "kinetic motion that maneuvers" back-and-forth amongst them.

Thus, a differential mode of consciousness serves as a conceptual tool with which one can weave "between and among" the foundational perspectives. Put another way, differential consciousness "operates like the clutch of an automobile: the mechanism that permits the driver to select, engage, and disengage gears in a system for the transmission of power" (Sandoval, 1991, 14).

We advocate a notion of differential consciousness—or the idea that one can smoothly shift between rather than remaining stuck within a perspective—as an invitation to scholar-practitioners of multicultural education to create and experiment with their own hybrid theories of multiculturalism. Understanding and navigating foundational perspectives on multicultural education should be understood as occasions to ask new questions and to create new usages for key terms that one identifies within each foundational perspective. For, as Mouffe suggests, it is this use of "new language games that make new forms of life possible" (1988). Finally, this volume is meant to invite scholar-practitioners to rewrite the vocabulary that articulates their work in education, and thereby to engage themselves with others in the reflective practices of policy-making, curriculum construction, and pedagogical experimentation.

~

Ethnic Studies Multiculturalism

According to Evelyn Hu-DeHart, professor of history and director of the Center for Studies of Ethnicity and Race in America at the University of Colorado, Boulder:

> Ethnic studies seeks to recover and reconstruct the histories of those Americans whom history has neglected; to identify and credit their contributions to the making of U.S. society and culture; to chronicle protest and resistance; and to establish alternative values and visions, institutions and cultures. Ethnic studies scholarship has become a new discipline in and of itself. It is continuously defining and clarifying its own unique methodology and epistemology. (1993, 52)

The authors represented in this section are part of the processes of recovery and reconstruction that Hu-DeHart describes. However, these writers pose a variety of alternatives as to which educational practices and policies, including institutional structures, will best achieve these broad ends.

In the first selection, Ramon Gutierrez outlines the evolution of ethnic studies in American colleges and universities from the mid-1960s through the mid-1990s. He points out that different decades have witnessed shifting imperatives in terms of how the theoretical commitments of ethnic studies are put into practice. During the early years of the movement, for example, many proponents of ethnic studies called for the creation of separate programs or departments in colleges and universities. Over the next two decades, some ethnic studies scholars began to call into question this tactic of separation. Fears of isolation or concerns that non-minority students were not being served have led to criticisms of separate programming and calls for practices such as interdisciplinarity and whole-school requirements that are intended to integrate ethnic studies perspectives throughout colleges and universities.

Molefi Asante's essay entitled "The Afrocentric Idea in Education" lays out one of the central arguments that drives calls for separate ethnic studies programming. Asante offers his concept of "Afrocentricity" as a conceptual tool for highlighting the specific historical and cultural experiences of African American students. Drawing upon the critique put forward by Carter G. Woodson earlier this century, which we discussed in the introduction, Asante argues that "African Americans have been educated away from their own culture and traditions and attached to the fringes of European culture; thus dislocated from themselves . . ." In response to this "mis-education," and the resulting cultural dislocation, Asante wants to "center" African American students within "a frame of reference wherein phenomena are viewed from the perspective of the African person."

Asante's desire to promote centricity in education is consonant with Hu-DeHart's description of the "culturally nationalistic vantage point" of many early ethnic studies programs. She explains, "[t]his perspective still has enormous resonance in the Afrocentrism of some black studies programs" (1993, p. 52). Despite the continuing appeal of this approach, other ethnic studies scholars reject it in favor of integrating ethnic studies throughout mainstream curricula. Ward Churchill, for instance, warns that separate "Minority Studies Programs" allow the status quo that he and Asante both criticize to remain in place. In his essay "White Studies: The Intellectual Imperialism of Contemporary U.S. Higher Education," Churchill disagrees with the hegemony of what he calls "White Studies," and what Asante calls "Eurocentricity," for many of the same reasons that Asante finds problematic. But Churchill reaches a different practical solution; he calls for approaches such as "Interdisciplinary Studies," where members of different groups jointly pool knowledge, resources, and effort.

Pragmatic calls by ethnic studies scholars for separate, autonomous programming on one hand versus integrated, interdisciplinary programming on the other demonstrate the key points of contention within the perspective. Different answers to the questions: (1) What are the main purposes of ethnic studies? (2) Who comprises the primary audience? and (3) What forms should ethnic studies take at the institutional level? lead to distinct realizations of a similar overarching vision—that of recovery and reconstruction that Hu-DeHart describes. A more recent pragmatic response to these questions has come in the form of calls for an "ethnic studies requirement" that all students attending a particular college or university are required to take.

California is a state in which the "ethnic studies requirement" has proven popular, and has become mandated policy on a number of campuses. It was within this context—particularly on the campuses of Sonoma State University, UC Berkeley, and UC Santa Cruz—that Sucheng Chan has grappled with questions surrounding an ethnic studies requirement in her role as a professor of Asian American Studies. Chan, in her article "On the Ethnic Studies Requirement," describes her own ambivalence surrounding the question: "who should ethnic studies serve?" Although she avidly supported an ethnic studies requirement for all students, Chan found herself lamenting some shifts in perspectives and classroom climate that accompanied an increase of non-Asian American students in her courses. She lays out a few of the corresponding advantages and disadvantages of ethnic studies courses that serve as ethnic enclaves versus forums where students from a diverse assortment of ethnic backgrounds can interact.

Finally, this section ends with a selection that challenges Asante's vision of Afrocentricity and offers in its place a vision of "transnational multiculturalism." Angie Dernersesian's "'Chicana! Rican? No, Chicana-Riqueña!' Refashioning the Transnational Connection" calls into question one of the tenets underlying Asante's concept of "centricity"—namely, the presumption that there is a unitary perspective on the world based upon an individual's membership within a particular cultural group. Dernersesian highlights her identity as both a Chicana and a Puerto Rican to advocate a "hybrid" notion of cultural identity that blurs and disrupts cultural borders. Ultimately, she argues for a refashioning of transnational connections across borders; a refashioning that allows neglected histories and territorial connections to be reclaimed, and that expands the concept of multiculturalism into one capable of migrating beyond the national borders of the United States.

Guiding Questions for Section One

- What are the primary purposes of ethnic studies?
- How should ethnic studies be situated within the wider educational establishment (e.g., the university)?
- Who should ethnic studies serve?

Ethnic Studies: Its Evolution in American Colleges and Universities

Ramon A. Gutierrez

Ethnic studies has recently emerged as a discrete discipline at institutions of higher education in the United States, Canada, and Europe. This development has been largely a response to heightened levels of political awareness regarding ethnic, racial, and religious conflict worldwide and as a program for the recognition of multiculturalism. In the most optimistic scenarios, ethnic studies offers a path for the peaceful management of differences over time; at worst, it is seen as exacerbating the importance of identity politics over time. This essay traces some of the important historical lineages that led to the creation of ethnic studies in the United States, outlines how the discipline is currently defined, charts the direction of contemporary scholarship, and lists the sites at which this scholarship is being generated.

Some thirty years ago in the mid-1960s, in the midst of the escalation of the war in Vietnam and the movement for civil rights in the United States, many colleges and universities created programs, centers, and departments devoted to the study of particular racial and ethnic groups. This development was motivated primarily by a crashing of the universities' gates by a popular challenge from below to what were imagined then as bastions of white Euro-American male ideals and privilege. As part of the democratizing project of the civil rights movement, young women and men of African, Mexican, Native American, and Asian ancestry started to arrive in unprecedented numbers on American campuses. As they did, they taxed the former habits and attitudes of institutions of higher education. Minority students demanded that the curriculum reflect their presence and that safe havens exist for them in what they rightly perceived as alien and hostile environs. They demanded that scholars from minority communities be hired to teach the culture and history of minorities in the United States. And they demanded that the study of race and ethnicity be removed from the disciplinary homes they had long occupied in departments of sociology and anthropology, where race and ethnicity were pathologized, problematized, or exoticized.

This demand for a separate space on college campuses devoted to the recognition of racial and ethnic differences in the United States mirrored larger political debates in the public realm. During the 1940s and 1950s civil rights movement, activists had sought slow, peaceful, change through assimilation, through petitions for governmental beneficence, and through appeals to white liberal guilt; trends that were reflected in scholarship as well. Talcott Parsons, for example, whose theories influenced not only the sociology of deviance, but also cultural anthropology, saw ethnicity as a social problem to be explained through careful study of the barriers preventing full assimilation into the mainstream of society.[1] Thus consensus historians such as Oscar Handlin[2] and Stanley Elkins[3] looked respectively at how immigrants had assimilated over time and how the institutional legacies of slavery slowly were being eroded. Scholars from marginalized communities responded to such perspectives in the 1950s by lauding the resourcefulness and ingenuity of racial and ethnic groups, noting their accomplishments and contribution to society, even in the face of overwhelming discrimination. John Hope Franklin's *From Slavery to Freedom: A History of Negro Americans,* Americo Paredes' *With His Pistol in His Hand: A Border Ballad and its Hero,* and Kenneth M. Stampp's *The Peculiar Institution* were illustrative of this perspective.

The political turn in the mid-1960s from a movement for civil rights to nationalism was accompanied by a rejection of assimilation and a demand for cultural autonomy and national self-determination. In the public realm, black nationalists declared the creation of the Nation of Islam. Others called for the Black Belt Nation's independence. Chicanos declared that they wanted nation-state status for their ancestral land, Aztlan. And Native Americans militated for greater sovereignty rights over their own affairs. On college campuses, students translated self-determination as meaning the need for separate centers, programs, and departments devoted to the study of African, Asian, American Indian, and Mexican culture and history; a development that was quickly expressed in the production of a scholarship that chronicled the protest and resistance of the powerless to their domination and exploitation in the United States. Examples of this perspective abound: Vine Deloria's *Custer Died for Your Sins,* Rudolfo Acuna's *Occupied America: The Chicano's Struggle Toward Liberation,* Vincent Harding's *This Is a River: The Black Struggle for Freedom in America,* and Herbert Gutman's *The Black Family in Slavery and Freedom.* This scholarship concluded by elaborating distinctive values, institutions, and semiautonomous cultural realms generated internally by ethnic and racial communities, but constrained and shaped by external social forces.

The demography and cultural geography of constituencies generally dictated the ways faculty and college administrators responded to the programmatic and curricular demands raised by minority students. In areas of large African-American population density and at schools that had recruited large numbers of African-American students, the pressure for black studies and its more global analogue, Africana studies, dominated. In the southwestern and midwestern parts of the United States, in states where there was a large number of Mexican immigrants, the call for Mexican-American and Chicano studies was raised and addressed. Similar demographic pressures explain much of the spatial distribution of Asian-American and Native American studies programs throughout the United States.

If one surveys the degree of institutionalization that these ethnic and racial studies programs were able to attain in the 1960s and early 1970s, without a doubt, the movement for black studies, broadly defined, was by far the most successful. While a few academic departments of Chicano studies were created at the community college level, numerous black studies, Afro-American, and Africana studies programs blossomed as independent, autonomous, degree-granting departments. *The Directory of Afrikanamerican Research Centers* by 1980 listed 103 major departments with associated research institutes. The *Hispanic Resource Directory*, published in 1988, counted well over 100 programs in Chicano studies, Latino studies, Boricua studies, and Puerto Rican studies, but few academic departments.[4] The emergence of professional associations such as the National Council on Black Studies, the National Association of Interdisciplinary Ethnic Studies, the National Association of Chicano Studies, and the Association for Asian-American Studies further attested to the increasing permanence and professionalization of the study of race and ethnicity in the United States by the late 1970s.

The reason black studies programs were able to establish themselves on many campuses as independent departments undoubtedly was due to the strong moral and political arguments that the larger public was then willing to endorse regarding the history of slavery and the legacy of racial discrimination in the United States. Chicano studies and Asian-American studies activists tried to advance moral arguments for their curricular cause by imagining themselves as internal colonies dominated by white America. But in the end, the arguments that were most persuasive on their behalf were political. Educational institutions, particularly public ones, had to address the educational needs of the entire citizenry.

As was to be expected, programs in black studies and Chicano studies that began as formally recognized departments were the most successful and long-lasting. This was so because of the structural and organizational location that departments occupy in the business of colleges and universities. Resources are doled out by department, courses are listed by department, faculty are recruited and promoted by departmental criteria, and the degrees departments grant are largely governed by departmentally defined requirements.

By contrast, the multidepartmental program was the model most black, Chicano, Native American, and Asian-American studies programs created in the early 1970s took. These programs relied almost exclusively on the resources of established departments for their courses and personnel. Programs were pieced together by offering a hodgepodge curriculum: a course here and there on history, a sociology of race relations course, a course on deviance in minority communities, and perhaps a smattering of literature courses drawn from

English and foreign-language departments. In the heat of the moment, the educational objectives of very few programs were carefully articulated and, instead, what they reflected was the curricular colonialism that had previously characterized the academic study of minorities. Many in the academy believed that professional upward mobility and national prominence was achieved by studying major problems as opposed to the minor problems of minorities. In the minds of skeptics and agnostics these programs had been created to deal with the "minority problem"; that is, with campus unrest and remedial education for the ill-prepared immigrants in the university.[5]

For the faculty who gave their skills and services to such minority studies programs, the work proved difficult, primarily because of the structural problem most programs face on university campuses—programs are usually dependent on the generosity of established departments. If departments did not deem the faculty who staffed the various ethnic studies programs' course offering as essential to their particular departmental curriculum, or judged the whole area of scholarship as deficient, job vacancies went unfilled for years. Departments expected faculty working with the black studies, Chicano studies, or Asian-American studies programs to fulfill all of their departmental responsibilities. Programs expected just as much, thus requiring two full-time jobs instead of just one. Given that programs devoted to American racial and ethnic minorities included a large component of student remedial education, faculty in these programs also were asked to do the support services that few faculty in mainstream disciplines did. All of this further guaranteed that tenure would be even more difficult for faculty persons in these programs to attain. The end result of faculty vacancies that were not immediately filled by departments were course listings that were not taught, demoralized and overtaxed faculty, and programmatic curricula that were uneven and fragmented.

The creation of programs and departments of black, Chicano, Asian-American, and Native American studies naturally had mixed results. On the positive side, if any conclusion can be drawn from the educational research on the social and psychological effects of such educational programs on student learning and retention, it is that they significantly improved minority student self-image and identity, enhanced academic skills, and by making universities less alienating environments, led to greater retention and higher graduation rates.[6]

On the negative side, programs devoted to the study of race and ethnicity were particularly fragile and unpredictable. To begin with, the faculty members who were recruited initially into these programs in the early 1970s were young assistant professors working in heterodox and experimental topics that did not fit clearly into established disciplinary boundaries. Many of these scholars left university settings. They did so for a variety of reasons: for some, potently perceived social and political commitments kept them from producing the scholarship necessary to obtain tenure; for others, private industry and government employment offered better pay and demanded less; and others, particularly the better researchers, were lured away to more prestigious institutions where they entered into Afro-American, black, and Chicano studies departments. They chose moves into such departments because they had felt isolated in traditional departments as the sole minority member doing research colleagues often deemed "minor." In departments focused on the study of race and ethnicity, they found a critical mass of kindred intellects, and a more nurturing environment in which no one would question the validity or importance of their work.

If the 1960s and 1970s were the heydays for the genesis and maturation of programs and departments devoted to the study of American racial and ethnic groups, the 1980s proved to be the decade of retrenchment. In these years, under the presidencies of Ronald Reagan and George Bush, the ideal of fair access to housing, education, and employment was actively attacked by conservative Republicans and political forces on the Right. Affirmative action programs were caricatured as reverse discrimination, as reparations for slavery, and as racial quotas. Whereas in the previous decade affirmative action had been used to recruit faculty of color, now the program was used cynically to subvert governmental intent. Upper class Argentines and Peruvians, for example, were recruited to satisfy "Hispanic" hiring goals, as were West Indians in lieu of African-Americans. These were all recruitment and hiring practices that created a backlash against affirmative action policies. Discussions of Eurocentrism in the curriculum and the need to expand the range of voices represented in university courses fell largely on deaf, if not hostile, ears. Economically, these were years of dwindling resources for programs that studied race and ethnicity, matched attitudinally by apathy, and reflected in lower course enrollments and a decreasing number of majors in such programs.

The end of the 1980s saw attempts to rehabilitate, reorganize, and reinvigorate what had become moribund programs in black, Chicano, Native American, and Asian-American studies. This movement was a result of numerous developments at the international, national, and local levels. At the international level, the decolonialization of most areas of the world, save South Africa, led to an examination of the legacy that colonialism had wrecked on the nation state. What invariably was found was that when independence came to former colonies in the Third World and power was transferred to national elites, the old ethnic tensions and rivalries that had long been held in abeyance by the force of the imperial state, suddenly exploded in open conflicts. Such latent tensions also increasingly came to light as cracks started to appear in the Berlin Wall and as the Soviet empire fragmented into warring nations.

The move to reimagine the structure and function of academic programs devoted to the study of race and ethnic relations in the United States created in the 1960s was rooted in these larger global concerns and accelerated by a renewed educational concern to articulate the theoretical intersections among the epistemologies of black studies, Chicano studies, Asian-American studies, and Native American studies. What united the study of these groups? How were the experiences of these groups different? Was there a sufficiently distinct and well articulated knowledge base to define these programs as a discipline?

Several institutions of higher education in the United States entered the conversation. The University of California, Berkeley, initiated what is now regarded as the first conceptualization of ethnic studies as a distinct discipline-based department. Founded in 1969 at the end of several months of student protest, the autonomous department of ethnic studies at UC–Berkeley encompassed under its umbrella four independent and vertically separate programs devoted to Afro-American studies, Asian-American studies, Chicano studies, and Native American studies. According to Ling-chi Wang, one of the early chairs of the UC–Berkeley department of ethnic studies, "the early advocates of ethnic studies deliberately rejected the notion of curricular 'mainstreaming' or 'integration', favoring instead, autonomous academic programs built on the principles of solidarity among racial minorities, interdisciplinary approach, 'self-determination', and 'educational relevance', unencumbered by failed paradigms and biased scholarship of the past."[7]

The vertical structure that the UC–Berkeley department of ethnic studies chose was particularly problem-prone, primarily because of the competition for resources that each of the vertical components (that is, Chicano studies, Native American studies, etc.) had to engage in. Resources won by one program in the department were resented by the others, thus eventually leading to the secession of Afro-American studies which eventually became an independent department. In 1994, Native American studies similarly declared its independence and currently is seeking departmental status. However, it was not until 1980 that the ethnic studies department at Berkeley developed a more comprehensive vision of what it could be when it established a Ph.D. granting program explicitly devoted to comparative ethnic studies. Here the emphasis was to tie the department's concerns about domestic minorities with Third World peoples, thus giving an international component to the curriculum.

The desire to merge the various and distinct ethnic programs into one larger unit was already well in the air of higher-education circles. By the mid-1970s, scholars such as James A. Banks and Jack Bass had proposed the consolidation of single-group ethnic programs into larger aggregations that could explore commonalities and divergences in the experiences of racial and ethnic groups domestically and worldwide.[8] Bowling Green State University took up this challenge in 1979, creating an ethnic studies department that was a hybrid between the older organizational model and the newer one imagined, thus integrating general ethnic studies with black studies and Latino studies.[9]

Despite these initial curricular transformations of older models for the study of race and ethnicity, little thought was given to an articulation of a more complicated model for ethnic studies, one that attempted to define the parameters of the discipline and its main propositions. In 1988, several faculty members in the Chicano studies, Asian-American studies, and black performing arts programs at the University of California, San Diego, were brought together by this author to propose the formation of an ethnic studies department that incorporated the best of the ethnic studies movement, but avoided the problems that had plagued the UC–Berkeley ethnic studies department. We did this with a clear realization that the nature of knowledge and its use as a tool to understand the physical world and the human condition was then in radical flux. As new social and scientific discoveries were made every day, so too new fields and disciplines were being born. Clifford Geertz, the eminent cultural anthropologist, referred to this refiguration of knowledge as the "blurring of genres . . . a phenomenon general enough and distinctive enough to suggest that what we are seeing is not just another drawing of the cultural map—the moving of a few disputed borders, the making of some more picturesque mountain lakes—but an alteration of the principles of mapping."[10] As a result of these changes, hybrid disciplines in the natural sciences codified as disciplines and departments of geophysics and biochemistry had emerged. In the sciences, the growth of transdisciplinary or supradisciplinary fields had led to the creation at the University of Chicago in 1984 of new departments of microbiology, biochemistry, and biophysics and theoretical biology which replaced the old departments of biochemistry and molecular biology and the department of molecular genetics and cell biology. The chair of the University of Chicago's committee charged with this reorganization stated that the change would "more accurately reflect . . . the current principal areas of biological research."[11] There were many other relevant examples of the refigurations of social and scientific knowledge that were then taking place, but the rationale for the creation of departments of cognitive science worldwide sufficiently and spectacularly illustrated this trend.

It was in the light of these larger developments that the faculty at the University of California, San Diego, began to imagine ethnic studies as a distinct discipline. By our assessment, ethnic studies as a discipline had been born in the 1960s out of the cultural conflicts that occurred when blacks, Chicanos, American Indians, and Asian-Americans protested that their contributions to American society had been sorely ignored in the texts that Eurocentric middle-class white males historically had articulated. Ethnic studies scholars objected that the claims these men had advanced regarding the universalism of their perspectives and their freedom from particularistic commitments, claims that gave them a detached objectivity and a monopoly on truth, were actually strong reflections of the value the dominant culture gave to a rigid distinction between the mind and body, and the presumed advantages of detachment and distance from the object of study. Claims to objectivity had to be founded not on transcendent universalisms or sharp dichotomies between subjectivity and objectivity, but in the recognition of the importance of perspective; perspectives that were always partial and situated in relationship to power.

The perspectives that ethnic studies scholars brought to the debate on the meaning of America's past, and which uniquely defined the method and discipline of ethnic studies, looked at social relations from the bottom up, from the vantage point of those who were powerless or marginalized, and were rooted in the lived historical memories of slavery, racism, victimization, and physical and psychological damage.

Though ethnic studies scholarship had begun as "contributionism" aimed at overcoming historical neglect, it quickly had moved on to chronicle protest and resistance, finally elaborating distinctive values, institutions, and semiautonomous cultural realms generated internally by ethnic and racial communities, but constrained and shaped by external forces. Ethnic studies scholarship revealed the ways in which people gave meaning to their lives under even the most brutal conditions, thus in being, or becoming more than mere victims. Since so much of ethnic studies scholarship required the mining of unused empirical sources that had been ignored for generations, the discipline by necessity became cross-disciplinary, taking methods of intensive investigation from the social sciences, and enriching them with vantage points from the humanities, particularly with a concern for change over time.

The enduring methodological principles that had emerged from the study of racial and ethnic groups in the United States were: (1) all knowledge claims had to be viewed as situated and recognized as partial; (2) culture was not a unified system of shared meanings, but a system of multivocal symbols, the meanings of which were frequently contested, becoming a complex product of competition and negotiation between various social groups, such as between males and females, between masters and slaves, between blacks and whites, and between rich and poor; and (3) the study of race and ethnicity was best understood by using comparative interdisciplinary methods.

The 1989 proposal for the creation of an ethnic studies department at the University of California, San Diego (UCSD), approved in 1990, began by rejecting the vertical model of single ethnic-based programs and, instead, proposed a horizontal model that focused on common trends and experiences among social groups. Ethnic studies was thus the study of the social, cultural, and historical forces that have shaped the development of America's diverse ethnic peoples. Focusing on immigration, slavery, and genocide, the three social processes that combined to create in the United States a nation of nations, the ethnic studies department at UCSD was organized to examine intensively the histories, languages, and cultures of America's racial and ethnic groups in and of themselves, in their relationships to each other, and particularly, in structural contexts of power.

The goal of the ethnic studies department at the University of California, San Diego, was to promote research, teaching, and community service in ethnic studies that: (1) focused intensively on the histories of different ethnic and racial groups, particularly on intragroup stratification, (2) drew larger theoretical lessons from comparisons among these groups, (3) sought to articulate general principles that shaped racial and ethnic relations presently and historically, and (4) explored how ethnic identity was constructed and reconstructed over time, internally and externally.

In the past, most ethnic studies scholarship focused on African-Americans, Asian-Americans, Chicanos/Latinos, and Native Americans. The numerous ethnic groups encompassed in these broad categories were studied as largely autonomous, as if their particular experiences were isolated and unique in American history. The ethnic studies department at UCSD expanded the scope of the study of race and ethnicity in the United States in two ways. First, comparative analysis was made a fundamental component of ethnic studies research and teaching. Second, to understand fully the power dynamics that had shaped relationships between dominant groups and minorities in the United States, the European-American immigrant experience would also be explored, thus making the department's focus comparative and relational.

Since the creation of the ethnic studies department at UC–San Diego, other colleges and universities have attempted to consolidate and reimagine their single-group ethnic programs into units that study the dynamics of race and ethnicity in global and comparative context. In 1991, for example, the University of Washington's department of American ethnic studies which grew out of their Afro-American studies program, began offering a degree in American ethnic studies.[12] Brown University's Center for the Study of Race and Ethnicity in America, a research center closely affiliated with the American studies program, has recently proposed a similar focus, moving from the study of American exceptionalism to the comparative study of the dynamics of race and ethnicity in the United States.[13] At a moment when nationalism is reemerging powerfully among students in the United States as well as many other nations and states around the globe, it seems imperative that we see that glorification of local systems of knowledge which are rooted in racial, religious, and ethnic distinctions, as fundamentally tied to the globalization, commodification, and massification of social life.

Notes

1. The influence of Talcott Parsons can be found in Robert E. Park, *Race and Culture* (Glencoe, IL: The Free Press, 1950); Louis Wirth, "The Problem of Minority Groups," in Ralph Linton, ed., *The Science of Man in the World Crisis* (New York: Columbia University Press, 1945); Milton Gordon, *Assimilation in American Life* (New York: Oxford University Press, 1964).
2. Oscar Handlin, *Boston's Immigrants* (Cambridge: Harvard University Press, 1941).
3. Stanley M. Elkins, *Slavery: A Problem in American Institutional and Intellectual Life* (Chicago: University of Chicago Press, 1959).
4. Bill Foster, *The Directory of Afrikanamerican Research Centers* (New York: Institute of AfriKan Research, 1980); Alan Edward Schorr, *Hispanic Resources Directory* (Juneau, AK: Denali Press, 1988), pp. 327–30.
5. The field of women's studies underwent rather similar developments on many American college campuses. On the similarities between ethnic studies and women's studies programs, see Johnella E. Butler and Betty Schmitz, "Ethnic Studies, Women's Studies, and Multiculturalism," in *Change* (January/February 1992), pp. 36–41; and Johnella E. Butler and John C. Walter, *Transforming the Curriculum: Ethnic Studies and Women's Studies* (Albany, NY: SUNY Press, 1991).
6. Henry L. Gates Jr, "Academe Must Give Black Studies Programs their Due," *The Chronicle of Higher Education*, 36, 3 (September 20, 1989), p. 56; Wilson Reed, "Some Implications of the Black Studies Movement for Higher Education in the 1970s," *Journal of Higher Education*, 44 (1973), pp. 191–216; Henry Sioux Johnson and William J. Hernandez-Martines, *Educating the Mexican American* (Valley Forge, PA: Judson Press, 1970), p. 2; Roberto Jesus Garza, "Chicano Studies: A New Curricular Dimension for Higher Education in the Southwest" (Ed.D. diss., Oklahoma State University, 1975), esp. pp. 75–6; Charles V. Willie and Arline Sakuma McCord, *Black Students at White Colleges* (New York: Praeger, 1972), p. 109; Winnie Bengelsdorf, *Ethnic Studies in Higher Education* (Washington, DC: American Association of State Colleges and Universities, 1972); Larry A. Braskamp and Robert D. Brown, "Evaluation of Programs on Blacks," *Educational Record*, 53 (1972), pp. 51–8; Allen H. Frerichs, "Relationship of Self-Esteem of the Disadvantaged to School Success," *Journal of Negro Education*, 40 (1971), pp. 117–20; Edmund W. Gordon and Doxey A. Wilkerson, *Compensatory Education for the Disadvantaged* (New York: College Entrance Examination Board, 1966); Harriet P. Lefley, "Effects of a Cultural Heritage

Program on the Self-Concept of Micerosulcee Indian Children," *The Journal of Educational Research,* 67 (1974), pp. 462–6; Margo K. McCormick and Juanita H. Williams, "Effects of a Compensatory Program on Self-Report, Achievement and Aspiration Level of 'Disadvantaged' High School Students," *Journal of Negro Education,* 43 (1974), pp. 47–52; Roger W. Buffalohead, "Native American Studies Programs: Review and Evaluation," in Convocation of American Indian Scholars, *Indian Voices* (San Francisco: Indian Historian Press, 1970), pp. 161–90; Vine Deloria Jr, "Indian Studies: The Orphan of Academia," *Wicazo Sa Review,* 2 (1986), pp. 1–7; Annette M. Jaimes, "American Indian Studies: Toward an Indigenous Model," *American Indian Culture and Research Journal,* 11 (1987), pp. 1–16.

7. Ling-chi Wang, "Ethnic Studies and Curriculum Transformation at UC Berkeley: Our Past, Present, and Future" (unpublished paper), p. 2.

8. James A. Banks, *Teaching Strategies for Ethnic Studies* (Boston: Allyn and Bacon, 1975); Jack Bass, *Widening the Mainstream of American Culture: A Ford Foundation Report on Ethnic Studies* (New York: Ford Foundation, 1978).

9. Robert L. Perry and Susan May Pauly, "Crossroads to the 21st Century: The Evolution of Ethnic Studies at Bowling Green State University," *Explorations in Ethnic Studies,* 11, 1 (January 1988), pp. 13–22.

10. Clifford Geertz, "Blurred Genres: The Refiguration of Social Thought," in his *Local Knowledge: Further Essays in Interpretive Anthropology* (New York: BasicBooks, 1983), p. 34.

11. "Biological Sciences Reorganization Reflects Current Areas of Study," *University of Chicago Magazine,* 76 (Summer 1984), pp. 3–4.

12. Johnella E. Butler, "Ethnic Studies: A Matrix Model for the Major," *Liberal Education,* 77 (1991), pp. 26–32.

13. Rhett S. Jones, "Ethnic Studies: Beyond Myths and Into Some Realities (A Working Paper)" (unpublished paper, March 12, 1993).

Questions

1. How were broader political demands for cultural autonomy and self-determination played out on college campuses at the inception of the Ethnic Studies Movement of the late 1960s to early 1970s?

2. How do the reasons for establishing Black studies programs differ from reasons for programs that target the study of other ethnic groups?

3. Why does Gutierrez describe the 1980s as "the decade of retrenchment"?

4. What are some of the relative merits of autonomous programs for single-group studies versus integrating the mainstream curriculum with ethnic studies content?

5. In your view, is ethnic studies a distinct discipline? Explain.

The Afrocentric Idea in Education

Molefi Kete Asante

Introduction

Many of the principles that govern the development of the Afrocentric idea in education were first established by Carter G. Woodson in *The Mis-education of the Negro* (1933). Indeed, Woodson's classic reveals the fundamental problems pertaining to the education of the African person in America. As Woodson contends, African Americans have been educated away from their own culture and traditions and attached to the fringes of European culture; thus dislocated from themselves, Woodson asserts that African Americans often valorize European culture to the detriment of their own heritage (p. 7). Although Woodson does not advocate rejection of American citizenship or nationality, he believed that assuming African Americans hold the same position as European Americans vis-à-vis the realities of America would lead to the psychological and cultural death of the African American population. Furthermore, if education is ever to be substantive and meaningful within the context of American society, Woodson argues, it must first address the African's historical experiences, both in Africa and America (p. 7). That is why he places on education, and particularly on the traditionally African American colleges, the burden of teaching the African American to be responsive to the long traditions and history of Africa as well as America. Woodson's alert recognition, more than 50 years ago, that something is severely wrong with the way African Americans are educated provides the principal impetus for the Afrocentric approach to American education.

In this article I will examine the nature and scope of this approach, establish its necessity, and suggest ways to develop and disseminate it throughout all levels of education. Two propositions stand in the background of the theoretical and philosophical issues I will present. These ideas represent the core presuppositions on which I have based most of my work in the field of education, and they suggest the direction of my own thinking about what education is capable of doing to and for an already politically and economically marginalized people—African Americans:

1. Education is fundamentally a social phenomenon whose ultimate purpose is to socialize the learner; to send a child to school is to prepare that child to become part of a social group.
2. Schools are reflective of the societies that develop them (i.e., a White supremacist-dominated society will develop a White supremacist educational system).

Definitions

An alternative framework suggests that other definitional assumptions can provide a new paradigm for the examination of education within the American society. For example, in education, *centricity* refers to a perspective that involves locating students within the context of their own cultural references so that they can relate socially and psychologically to other cultural perspectives. Centricity is a concept that can be applied to any culture. The centrist paradigm is supported by research showing that the most productive method of teaching any student is to place his or her group within the center of the context of knowledge (Asante, 1990). For White students in America this is easy because almost all the experiences discussed in American classrooms are approached from the standpoint of White perspectives and history. American education, however, is not centric; it is Eurocentric. Consequently, non-White students are also made to see themselves and their groups as the "acted upon." Only rarely do they read or hear of non-White people as active participants in history. This is as true for a discussion of the American Revolution as it is for a discussion of Dante's *Inferno;* for instance, most classroom discussions of the European slave trade concentrate on the activities of Whites rather than on the resistance efforts of Africans. A person educated in a truly centric fashion comes to view all groups' contributions as significant and useful. Even a White person educated in such a system does not assume superiority based upon racist notions. Thus, a truly centric education is different from a Eurocentric, racist (that is, White supremacist) education.

Afrocentricity is a frame of reference wherein phenomena are viewed from the perspective of the African person. The Afrocentric approach seeks in every situation the appropriate centrality of the African person (Asante, 1987). In education this means that teachers provide students the opportunity to study the world and its people, concepts, and history from an African world view. In most classrooms, whatever the subject, Whites are located in the center perspective position. How alien the African American child must feel, how like an outsider! The little African American child who sits in a classroom and is taught to accept as heroes and heroines individuals who defamed African peo-ple is being actively de-centered, dislocated, and made into a nonperson, one whose aim in life might be to one day shed that "badge of inferiority": his or her Blackness. In Afrocentric educational settings, however, teachers do not marginalize African American children by causing them to question their own self-worth because their people's story is seldom told. By seeing themselves as the subjects rather than the objects of education—be the discipline biology, medicine, literature, or social studies—African American students come to see themselves not merely as seekers of knowledge but as integral participants in it. Because all content areas are adaptable to an Afrocentric approach, African American students can be made to see themselves as centered in the reality of any discipline.

It must be emphasized that Afrocentricity is *not* a Black version of Eurocen-tricity (Asante, 1987). Eurocentricity is based on White supremacist notions whose purposes are to protect White privilege and advantage in education, economics, politics, and so forth. Unlike Eurocentricity, Afrocentricity does not condone ethnocentric valorization at the expense of degrading other groups' perspectives. Moreover, Eurocentricity presents the particular historical reality of Europeans as the sum total of the human experience (Asante, 1987). It im-poses Eurocentric realities as "universal"; i.e., that which is White is presented as applying to the human condition in general, while that which is non-White is viewed as group-specific and therefore not "human." This explains why some scholars and artists of African descent rush to deny their Blackness; they believe that to exist as a Black person is not to exist as a universal human being. They are the individuals Woodson identified as preferring European art, lan-guage, and culture over African art, language, and culture; they believe that anything of European origin is inherently better than anything produced by or issuing from their own people. Naturally, the person of African descent should be centered in his or her historical experiences as an African, but Eurocentric curricula produce such aberrations of perspective among persons of color.

Multiculturalism in education is a nonhierarchical approach that respects and celebrates a variety of cultural perspectives on world phenomena (Asante, 1991). The multicultural approach holds that although European culture is the majority culture in the United States, that is not sufficient reason for it to be im-posed on diverse student populations as "universal." Multiculturalists assert that education, to have integrity, must begin with the proposition that all hu-mans have contributed to world development and the flow of knowledge and information, and that most human achievements are the result of mutually in-teractive, international effort. Without a multicultural education, students re-main essentially ignorant of the contributions of a major portion of the world's people. A multicultural education is thus a fundamental necessity for anyone who wishes to achieve competency in almost any subject.

The Afrocentric idea must be the stepping-stone from which the multicul-tural idea is launched. A truly authentic multicultural education, therefore, must be based upon the Afrocentric initiative. If this step is skipped, multicul-tural curricula, as they are increasingly being defined by White "resisters" (to be discussed below) will evolve without any substantive infusion of African American content, and the African American child will continue to be lost in the Eurocentric framework of education. In other words, the African American child will neither be confirmed nor affirmed in his or her own cultural information. For the mutual benefit of all Americans, this tragedy, which leads to the psychological and cultural dislocation of African American children, can and should be avoided.

The Revolutionary Challenge

Because it centers African American students inside history, culture, science, and so forth rather than outside these subjects, the Afrocentric idea presents the most revolutionary challenge to the ideology of White supremacy in education during the past decade. No other theoretical position stated by African Americans has ever captured the imagination of such a wide range of scholars and students of history, sociology, communications, anthropology, and psychology. The Afrocentric challenge has been posed in three critical ways:

1. It questions the imposition of the White supremacist view as universal and/or classical (Asante, 1990).
2. It demonstrates the indefensibility of racist theories that assault multiculturalism and pluralism.
3. It projects a humanistic and pluralistic viewpoint by articulating Afrocentricity as a valid, nonhegemonic perspective.

Suppression and Distortion: Symbols of Resistance

The forces of resistance to the Afrocentric, multicultural transformation of the curriculum and teaching practices began to assemble their wagons almost as quickly as word got out about the need for equality in education (Ravitch, 1990). Recently, the renowned historian Arthur Schlesinger and others formed a group called the Committee for the Defense of History. This is a paradoxical development because only lies, untruths, and inaccurate information need defending. In their arguments against the Afrocentric perspective, these proponents of Eurocentrism often clothe their arguments in false categories and fake terms (i.e., "pluralistic" and "particularistic" multiculturalism) (Keto, 1990; Asante, 1991). Besides, as the late African scholar Cheikh Anta Diop (1980) maintained: "African history and Africa need no defense." Afrocentric education is not against history. It is *for* history—correct, accurate history—and if it is against anything, it is against the marginalization of African American, Hispanic American, Asian American, Native American, and other non-White children. The Committee for the Defense of History is nothing more than a futile attempt to buttress the crumbling pillars of a White supremacist system that conceals its true motives behind the cloak of American liberalism. It was created in the same spirit that generated Bloom's *The Closing of the American Mind* (1987) and Hirsch's *Cultural Literacy: What Every American Needs to Know* (1987), both of which were placed at the service of the White hegemony in education, particularly its curricular hegemony. This committee and other evidences of White backlash are a predictable challenge to the contemporary thrust for an Afrocentric, multicultural approach to education.

Naturally, different adherents to a theory will have different views on its meaning. While two discourses presently are circulating about multiculturalism, only one is relevant to the liberation of the minds of African and White people in the United States. That discourse is Afrocentricity: the acceptance of Africa as central to African people. Yet, rather than getting on board with Afrocentrists to fight against White hegemonic education, some Whites (and some Blacks as well) have opted to plead for a return to the educational plantation. Unfortunately for them, however, those days are gone, and such misinformation can never be packaged as accurate, correct education again.

Ravitch (1990), who argues that there are two kinds of multiculturalism—*pluralist multiculturalism* and *particularist multiculturalism*—is the leader of those professors whom I call "resisters" or opponents to Afrocentricity and multiculturalism. Indeed, Ravitch advances the imaginary divisions in multicultural perspectives to conceal her true identity as a defender of White supremacy. Her tactics are the tactics of those who prefer Africans and other non-Whites to remain on the mental and psychological plantation of Western civilization. In their arrogance the resisters accuse Afrocentrists and multiculturalists of creating "fantasy history" and "bizarre theories" of non-White people's contributions to civilization. What they prove, however, is their own ignorance. Additionally, Ravitch and others (Nicholson, 1990) assert that multiculturalism will bring about the "tribalization" of America, but in reality America has always been a nation of ethnic diversity. When one reads their works on multiculturalism, one realizes that they are really advocating the imposition of a White perspective on everybody else's culture. Believing that the Eurocentric position is indisputable, they attempt to resist and impede the progressive transformation of the monoethnic curriculum. Indeed, the closets of bigotry have opened to reveal various attempts by White scholars (joined by some Blacks) to defend White privilege in the curriculum in much the same way as it has been so staunchly defended in the larger society. It was perhaps inevitable that the introduction of the Afrocentric idea would open up the discussion of the American school curriculum in a profound way.

Why has Afrocentricity created so much of a controversy in educational circles? The idea that an African American child is placed in a stronger position to learn if he or she is centered—that is, if the child sees himself or herself within the content of the curriculum rather than at its margins—is not novel (Asante, 1980). What is revolutionary is the movement from the idea (conceptual stage) to its implementation in practice, when we begin to teach teachers how to put African American youth at the center of instruction. In effect, students are shown how to see with new eyes and hear with new ears. African

American children learn to interpret and center phenomena in the context of African heritage, while White students are taught to see that their own centers are not threatened by the presence or contributions of African Americans and others.

The Condition of Eurocentric Education

Institutions such as schools are conditioned by the character of the nation in which they are developed. Just as crime and politics are different in different nations, so, too, is education. In the United States a "Whites-only" orientation has predominated in education. This has had a profound impact on the quality of education for children of all races and ethnic groups. The African American child has suffered disproportionately, but White children are also the victims of monoculturally diseased curricula.

The Tragedy of Ignorance

During the past five years many White students and parents have approached me after presentations with tears in their eyes or expressing their anger about the absence of information about African Americans in the schools. A recent comment from a young White man at a major university in the Northeast was especially striking. As he said to me: "My teacher told us that Martin Luther King was a commie and went on with the class." Because this student's teacher made no effort to discuss King's ideas, the student maliciously had been kept ignorant. The vast majority of White Americans are likewise ignorant about the bountiful reservoirs of African and African American history, culture, and contributions. For example, few Americans of any color have heard the names of Cheikh Anta Diop, Anna Julia Cooper, C. L. R. James, or J. A. Rogers. All were historians who contributed greatly to our understanding of the African world. Indeed, very few teachers have ever taken a course in African American Studies; therefore, most are unable to provide systematic information about African Americans.

Afrocentricity and History

Most of America's teaching force are victims of the same system that victimizes today's young. Thus, American children are not taught the names of the African ethnic groups from which the majority of the African American population are derived; few are taught the names of any of the sacred sites in Africa. Few teachers can discuss with their students the significance of the Middle Passage or describe what it meant or means to Africans. Little mention is made in American classrooms of either the brutality of slavery or the ex-slaves' celebration of freedom. American children have little or no understanding of the nature of the capture, transport, and enslavement of Africans. Few have been taught the true horrors of being taken, shipped naked across 25 days of ocean, broken by abuse and indignities of all kinds, and dehumanized into a beast of burden, a thing without a name. If our students only knew the truth, if they were taught the Afrocentric perspective on the Great Enslavement, and if they knew the full story about the events since slavery that have served to constantly dislocate African Americans, their behavior would perhaps be different. Among these events are: the infamous constitutional compromise of 1787, which decreed that African Americans were, by law, the equivalent of but three-fifths of a person (see Franklin, 1974); the 1857 Dred Scott decision in which the Supreme Court avowed that African Americans had no rights Whites were obliged to respect (Howard, 1857); the complete dismissal and nonenforcement of Section 2 of the Fourteenth Amendment to the Constitution (this amendment, passed in 1868, stipulated as one of its provisions a penalty against any state that denied African Americans the right to vote, and called for the reduction of a state's delegates to the House of Representatives in proportion to the number of disenfranchised African American males therein); and the much-mentioned, as-yet-unreceived 40 acres and a mule, reparation for enslavement, promised to each African American family after the Civil War by Union General William T. Sherman and Secretary of War Edwin Stanton (Oubre, 1978, pp. 18–19, 182–183; see also Smith, 1987, pp. 106–107). If the curriculum were enhanced to include readings from the slave narratives; the diaries of slave ship captains; the journals of slaveowners; the abolitionist newspapers; the writings of the freedmen and freedwomen; the accounts of African American civil rights, civic, and social organizations; and numerous others, African American children would be different, White children would be different—indeed, America would be a different nation today.

America's classrooms should resound with the story of the barbaric treatment of the Africans, of how their dignity was stolen and their cultures destroyed. The recorded experiences of escaped slaves provide the substance for such learning units. For example, the narrative of Jacob and Ruth Weldon presents a detailed account of the Middle Passage (Feldstein, 1971). The Weldons noted that Africans, having been captured and brought onto the slave ships, were chained to the deck, made to bend over, and "branded with a red hot iron in the form of letters or signs dipped in an oily preparation and pressed against the naked flesh till it burnt a deep and ineffaceable scar, to show who was the owner" (pp. 33–37). They also recalled that those who screamed were lashed on the face, breast, thighs, and backs with a "cat-o'-nine tails" wielded by White sailors: "Every blow brought the returning lash pieces of grieving flesh" (p. 44). They saw "mothers with babies at their breasts basely branded and lashed, hewed and scarred, till it would seem as if the very heavens must smite the infernal tormentors with the doom they so richly merited" (p. 44). Children and infants were not spared from this terror. The Weldons tell of a nine-month-old baby on board a slave ship being flogged because it would not eat. The ship's captain ordered the child's feet placed in boiling water, which dissolved the skin and nails, then ordered the child whipped again; still the child refused to eat. Eventually the captain killed the baby with his own hands and commanded the child's mother to throw the dead baby overboard. When the mother refused, she, too, was beaten, then forced to the ship's side, where "with her head averted so she might not see it, she dropped the body into the sea" (p. 44). In a similar vein a captain of a ship with 440 Africans on board noted that 132 had to be thrown overboard to save water (Feldstein, 1971, p. 47). As another wrote, the "groans and soffocating [sic] cries for air and water coming from below the deck sickened the soul of humanity" (Feldstein, 1971, p. 44).

Upon landing in America the situation was often worse. The brutality of the slavocracy is unequalled for the psychological and spiritual destruction it wrought upon African Americans. Slave mothers were often forced to leave their children unattended while they worked in the fields. Unable to nurse their children or to properly care for them, they often returned from work at night to find their children dead (Feldstein, 1971, p. 49). The testimony of Henry Bibb also sheds light on the bleakness of the slave experience:

> I was born May 1815, of a slave mother . . . and was claimed as the property of David White, Esq. . . . I was flogged up; for where I should have received moral, mental, and religious instructions, I received stripes without number, the object of which was to degrade and keep me in subordination. I can truly say that I drank deeply of the bitter cup of suffering and woe. I have been dragged down to the lowest depths of human degradation and wretchedness, by slaveholders. (Feldstein, 1971, p. 60)

Enslavement was truly a living death. While the ontological onslaught caused some Africans to opt for suicide, the most widespread results were dislocation, disorientation, and misorientation—all of which are the consequences of the African person being actively de-centered. The "Jim Crow" period of second-class citizenship, from 1877 to 1954, saw only slight improvement in the lot of African Americans. This era was characterized by the sharecropper system, disenfranchisement, enforced segregation, internal migration, lynchings, unemployment, poor housing conditions, and separate and unequal educational facilities. Inequitable policies and practices veritably plagued the race.

No wonder many persons of African descent attempt to shed their race and become "raceless." One's basic identity is one's self-identity, which is ultimately one's cultural identity; without a strong cultural identity, one is lost. Black children do not know their people's story and White children do not know the story, but remembrance is a vital requisite for understanding and humility. This is why the Jews have campaigned (and rightly so) to have the story of the European Holocaust taught in schools and colleges. Teaching about such a monstrous human brutality should forever remind the world of the ways in which humans have often violated each other. Teaching about the African Holocaust is just as important for many of the same reasons. Additionally, it underscores the enormity of the effects of physical, psychological, and economic dislocation on the African population in America and throughout the African diaspora. Without an understanding of the historical experiences of

African people, American children cannot make any real headway in addressing the problems of the present.

Certainly, if African American children were taught to be fully aware of the struggles of our African forebears they would find a renewed sense of purpose and vision in their own lives. They would cease acting as if they have no past and no future. For instance, if they were taught about the historical relationship of Africans to the cotton industry—how African American men, women, and children were forced to pick cotton from "can't see in the morning 'til can't see at night," until the blood ran from the tips of their fingers where they were pricked by the hard boll; or if they were made to visualize their ancestors in the burning sun, bent double with constant stooping, and dragging rough, heavy croaker sacks behind them—or picture them bringing those sacks trembling to the scale, fearful of a sure flogging if they did not pick enough, perhaps our African American youth would develop a stronger entrepreneurial spirit. If White children were taught the same information rather than that normally fed them about American slavery, they would probably view our society differently and work to transform it into a better place.

Correcting Distorted Information

Hegemonic education can exist only so long as true and accurate information is withheld. Hegemonic Eurocentric education can exist only so long as Whites maintain that Africans and other non-Whites have never contributed to world civilization. It is largely upon such false ideas that invidious distinctions are made. The truth, however, gives one insight into the real reasons behind human actions, whether one chooses to follow the paths of others or not. For example, one cannot remain comfortable teaching that art and philosophy originated in Greece if one learns that the Greeks themselves taught that the study of these subjects originated in Africa, specifically ancient Kemet (Herodotus, 1987). The first philosophers were the Egyptians Kagemni, Khun-anup, Ptah-hotep, Kete, and Seti; but Eurocentric education is so disjointed that students have no way of discovering this and other knowledge of the organic relationship of Africa to the rest of human history. Not only did Africa contribute to human history, African civilizations predate all other civilizations. Indeed, the human species originated on the continent of Africa—this is true whether one looks at either archaeological or biological evidence.

Two other notions must be refuted. There are those who say that African American history should begin with the arrival of Africans as slaves in 1619, but it has been shown that Africans visited and inhabited North and South America long before European settlers "discovered" the "New World" (Van Sertima, 1976). Secondly, although America became something of a home for those Africans who survived the horrors of the Middle Passage, their experiences on the slave ships and during slavery resulted in their having an entirely different (and often tainted) perspective about America from that of the Europeans and others who came, for the most part, of their own free will seeking opportunities not available to them in their native lands. Afrocentricity therefore seeks to recognize this divergence in perspective and create centeredness for African American students.

Conclusion

The reigning initiative for total curricular change is the movement that is being proposed and led by Africans, namely, the Afrocentric idea. When I wrote the first book on Afrocentricity (Asante, 1980), now in its fifth printing, I had no idea that in 10 years the idea would both shake up and shape discussions in education, art, fashion, and politics. Since the publication of my subsequent works, *The Afrocentric Idea* (Asante, 1987) and *Kemet, Afrocentricity, and Knowledge* (Asante, 1990), the debate has been joined in earnest. Still, for many White Americans (and some African Americans) the most unsettling aspect of the discussion about Afrocentricity is that its intellectual source lies in the research and writings of African American scholars. Whites are accustomed to being in charge of the major ideas circulating in the American academy. Deconstructionism, Gestalt psychology, Marxism, structuralism, Piagetian theory, and so forth have all been developed, articulated, and elaborated upon at length, generally by White scholars. On the other hand, Afrocentricity is the product of scholars such as Nobles (1986), Hilliard (1978), Karenga (1986), Keto (1990), Richards (1991), and Myers (1989). There are also increasing numbers of young, impressively credentialled African American scholars who have begun to write in the Afrocentric vein (Jean, 1991). They, and even some young White scholars, have emerged with ideas about how to change the curriculum Afrocentrically.

Afrocentricity provides all Americans an opportunity to examine the perspective of the African person in this society and the world. The resisters claim that Afrocentricity is anti-White; yet, if Afrocentricity as a theory is against anything it is against racism, ignorance, and monoethnic hegemony in the curriculum. Afrocentricity is not anti-White; it is, however, pro-human. Further, the aim of the Afrocentric curriculum is not to divide America, it is to make America flourish as it ought to flourish. This nation has long been divided with regard to the educational opportunities afforded to children. By virtue of the protection provided by society and reinforced by the Eurocentric curriculum, the White child is already ahead of the African American child by first grade. Our efforts thus must concentrate on giving the African American child greater opportunities for learning at the kindergarten level. However, the kind of assistance the African American child needs is as much cultural as it is academic. If the proper cultural information is provided, the academic performance will surely follow suit.

When it comes to educating African American children, the American educational system does not need a tune-up, it needs an overhaul. Black children have been maligned by this system. Black teachers have been maligned. Black history has been maligned. Africa has been maligned. Nonetheless, two truisms can be stated about education in America. First, some teachers *can and do* effectively teach African American children; secondly, if some teachers can do it, others can, too. We must learn all we can about what makes these teachers' attitudes and approaches successful, and then work diligently to see that their successes are replicated on a broad scale. By raising the same questions that Woodson posed more than 50 years ago, Afrocentric education, along with a significant reorientation of the American educational enterprise, seeks to respond to the African person's psychological and cultural dislocation. By providing philosophical and theoretical guidelines and criteria that are centered in an African perception of reality and by placing the African American child in his or her proper historical context and setting, Afrocentricity may be just the "escape hatch" African Americans so desperately need to facilitate academic success and "steal away" from the cycle of miseducation and dislocation.

References

Asante, M. K. (1980). *Afrocentricity: The theory of social change.* Buffalo, NY: Amulefi.

Asante, M. K. (1987). *The Afrocentric idea.* Philadelphia: Temple University Press.

Asante, M. K. (1990). *Kemet, Afrocentricity, and knowledge.* Trenton, NJ: Africa World Press.

Bloom, A. (1987). *The closing of the American mind.* New York: Simon & Schuster.

Feldstein, S. (1971). *Once a slave: The slave's view of slavery.* New York: William Morrow.

Franklin, J. H. (1974). *From slavery to freedom.* New York: Knopf.

Herodotus. (1987). *The history.* Chicago: University of Illinois Press.

Hilliard, A. G., III. (1978, June 20). *Anatomy and dynamics of oppression.* Speech delivered at the National Conference on Human Relations in Education, Minneapolis, MN.

Hirsch, E. D. (1987). *Cultural literacy: What every American needs to know.* New York: Houghton Mifflin.

Howard, B. C. (1857). *Report of the decision of the Supreme Court of the United States and the opinions of the justices thereof in the case of Dred Scott versus John F. A. Sandford, December term, 1856.* New York: D. Appleton & Co.

Jean, C. (1991). *Beyond the Eurocentric veils.* Amherst, MA: University of Massachusetts Press.

Karenga, M. R. (1986). *Introduction to Black studies.* Los Angeles: University of Sankore Press.

Keto, C. T. (1990). *Africa-centered perspective of history.* Blackwood, NJ: C. A. Associates.

Nicholson, D. (1990, September 23). Afrocentrism and the tribalization of America. *The Washington Post,* p. B–1.

Nobles, W. (1986). *African psychology.* Oakland, CA: Black Family Institute.

Oubre, C. F. (1978). *Forty acres and a mule: The Freedman's Bureau and Black land ownership.* Baton Rouge, LA: Louisiana State University Press.

Ravitch, D. (1990, Summer). Multiculturalism: E pluribus plures. *The American Scholar,* pp. 337–354.

Richards, D. (1991). *Let the circle be unbroken.* Trenton, NJ: Africa World Press.

Smith, J. O. (1987). *The politics of racial inequality: A systematic comparative macro-analysis from the colonial period to 1970.* New York: Greenwood Press.

Van Sertima, I. (1976). *They came before Columbus.* New York: Random House.

Woodson, C. G. (1915). *The education of the Negro prior to 1861: A history of the education of the colored people of the U.S. from the beginning of slavery.* New York: G. P. Putnam's Sons.

Woodson, C. G. (1933). *The mis-education of the Negro.* Washington, DC: Associated Publishers.

Woodson, C. G. (1936). *African background outlined.* Washington, DC: Association for the Study of Afro-American Life and History.

Questions

1. According to Carter G. Woodson, how have students of African descent been "mis-educated" in American schools?

2. How does Asante define *centricity*?

3. What might it look like to apply the concept of *centricity* in educational practice?

4. Asante defines *Afrocentricity* as "a frame of reference wherein phenomena are viewed from the perspective of the African person." Do you agree with his premise that "the perspective of the African person" exists? Why? Why not?

5. How does Asante distinguish Afrocentricity from Eurocentricity? Do you find this distinction valid? Do you find it useful? Why? Why not?

6. In Asante's view, what is the relationship between Afrocentricity and multiculturalism?

7. When Asante claims that "[a] truly multicultural education, therefore, must be based upon the Afrocentric initiative" do you think that he is referring to a multicultural education for *African American students* or to a multicultural education for *all students*? Explain.

8. According to Asante, what are some of the negative repercussions of "de-centeredness"?

9. Do you endorse Asante's "Afrocentric Idea in Education"? Explain.

White Studies:
The Intellectual Imperialism
of U.S. Higher Education

Ward Churchill

> Education should be adapted to the mentality, attitudes, occupation, and traditions of various peoples, conserving as far as possible all the sound and healthy elements in the fabric of their social life.
>
> David Abernathy, *The Dilemma of Popular Education*

> Since schooling was brought to non-Europeans as a part of empire . . . it was integrated into the effort to bring indigenous peoples into imperial/colonial structures. . . . After all, did not the European teacher and the school built on the European capitalist model transmit European values and norms and begin to transform traditional societies into "modern" ones?
>
> Martin Carnoy, *Education as Cultural Imperialism*

Over the past decade, the nature and adequacy of educational content has been a matter of increasingly vociferous debate among everyone from academics to policymakers to lay preachers in the United States. The American educational system as a whole has been amply demonstrated to be locked firmly into a paradigm of Eurocentrism, not only in terms of its focus, but also its discernable heritage, methodologies, and conceptual structure. Among people of non-European cultural derivation, the kind of "learning" inculcated through such a model is broadly seen as insulting, degrading, and functionally subordinative. More and more, these themes have found echoes among the more enlightened and progressive sectors of the dominant Euroamerican society itself.[1]

Such sentiments are born of an ever-widening cognition that, within any multicultural setting, this sort of monolithic pedagogical reliance upon a single cultural tradition constitutes a rather transparent form of intellectual domination, achievable only within the context of parallel forms of domination. This is meant in precisely the sense intended by David Landes when he observed, "It seems to me that one has to look at imperialism as a multifarious response to a common opportunity that consists simply as a disparity of power."[2] In this connection, it is often pointed out that, while education in America has existed for some time, by law, as a "common opportunity," its shape has all along been defined exclusively via the "disparity of power" exercised by members of the ruling Euroamerican elite.[3]

Responses to this circumstance have, to date, concentrated primarily upon what might be best described as a "contributionist" approach to remedy. This is to say they seek to bring about the inclusion of non-Europeans and/or non-European achievements in canonical subject matters, while leaving the methodological and conceptual parameters of the canon itself essentially intact.[4] The present essay represents an attempt to go a bit further, sketching out to some degree the preliminary requisites in challenging methods and concepts as well. It should be noted before proceeding that while my own grounding in American Indian Studies leads me to anchor my various alternatives in that particular perspective, the principles postulated should prove readily adaptable to other "minority" venues.

1: White Studies

As currently established, the university system in the United States offers little more than the presentation of "White Studies" to students, "general population" and minority alike.[5] The curriculum is virtually totalizing in its emphasis, not simply upon an imagined superiority of Western endeavors and accomplishments, but upon the notion that the currents of European thinking comprise the only really "natural"—or at least truly useful—formation of knowledge/means of perceiving reality. In the vast bulk of curriculum content, Europe is not only the subject (in its conceptual mode, the very process of "learning to think"), but the object (subject matter) of investigation as well.

Consider a typical introductory level philosophy course. Students will in all probability explore the works of the ancient Greek philosophers,[6] the fundamentals of Cartesian logic and Spinoza, stop off for a visit with Hobbes, Hume, and John Locke, cover a chapter or two of Kant's aesthetics, dabble a bit in Hegelian dialectics, and review Nietzsche's assorted rantings. A good Leftist professor may add a dash of Marx's famous "inversion" of Hegel and, on a good day, his commentaries on the frailties of Feuerbach. In an exemplary class, things will end up in the twentieth century with discussions of Schopenhauer, Heidegger, and Husserl, Bertrand Russell and Alfred North Whitehead, perhaps an "adventurous" summarization of the existentialism of Sartre and Camus.

Advanced undergraduate courses typically delve into the same topics, with additive instruction in matters such as "Late Medieval Philosophy,"

"Monism," "Rousseau and Revolution," "The Morality of John Stuart Mill," "Einstein and the Generations of Science," "The Phenomenology of Merleau-Ponty," "Popper's Philosophy of Science," "Benjamin, Adorno, and the Frankfurt School," "Meaning and Marcuse," "Structuralism/Poststructuralism," even "The Critical Theory of Jürgen Habermas."[7] Graduate work usually consists of effecting a coherent synthesis of some combination of these elements.

Thus, from first-semester surveys through the Ph.D., philosophy majors—and non-majors fulfilling elective requirements, for that matter—are fed a consistent stream of data defining and presumably reproducing Western thought at its highest level of refinement, as well as inculcating insight into what is packaged as its historical evolution and line(s) of probable future development. Note that this is construed, for all practical intents and purposes, as being representative of philosophy *in toto* rather than of Western European thought per se.

It seems reasonable to pose the question as to what consideration is typically accorded the non-European remainder of the human species in such a format. The answer is often that coursework does in fact exist, most usually in the form of upper-division undergraduate "broadening" curriculum: surveys of "Oriental Philosophy" are not unpopular,[8] "The Philosophy of Black Africa" exists as a catalogue entry at a number of institutions,[9] even "Native-American Philosophical Traditions" (more casually titled "Black Elk Speaks," from time-to-time) makes its appearance here and there.[10] But nothing remotely approaching the depth and comprehensiveness with which Western thought is treated can be located at any quarter.

Clearly, the student who graduates, at whatever level, from a philosophy program constructed in this fashion—and all of them are—walks away with a concentrated knowledge of the European intellectual schema rather than any genuine appreciation of the philosophical attainments of humanity. Yet, equally clearly, a degree in "Philosophy" implies, or at least should imply, the latter.

Nor is the phenomenon in any way restricted to the study of philosophy. One may search the catalogues of every college and university in the country, and undoubtedly the search will be in vain, for the department of history which accords the elaborate oral/pictorial "prehistories" of American Indians anything approximating the weight given to the semiliterate efforts at self-justification scrawled by early European colonists in this hemisphere.[11] Even the rich codigraphic records of cultures like the Mayas, Incas, and Mexicanos (Aztecs) are uniformly ignored by the "historical mainstream." Such matters are more properly the purview of anthropology than of history, or so it is said by those representing "responsible" scholarship in the U.S.[12]

As a result, most introductory courses on "American History" still begin for all practical intents and purposes in 1492, with only the most perfunctory acknowledgment that people existed in the Americas in pre-Columbian times. Predictably, any consideration accorded to pre-Columbian times typically revolves around anthropological rather than historical preoccupations, such as the point at which people were supposed to have first migrated across the Beringian Land Bridge to populate the hemisphere,[13] or whether native horticulturalists ever managed to discover fertilizer.[14] Another major classroom topic centers on the extent to which cannibalism may have prevailed among the proliferation of "nomadic Stone Age tribes" presumed to have wandered about America's endless reaches, perpetually hunting and gathering their way to the margin of raw subsistence.[15] Then again, there are the countless expositions on how few indigenous people there really were in North America prior to 1500,[16] and how genocide is an "inappropriate" term by which to explain why there were almost none by 1900.[17]

From there, many things begin to fall into place. Nowhere in the modern American academe will one find the math course acknowledging, along with the importance of Archimedes and Prothagerus, the truly marvelous qualities of pre-Columbian mathematics: that which allowed the Mayas to invent the concept of zero, for example, and, absent computers, to work with multidigit prime numbers.[18] Nor is there mention of the Mexicano mathematics which allowed that culture to develop a calendrical system several decimal places more accurate than that commonly used today.[19] And again, the rich mathematical understandings which went into Mesoamerica's development of what may well have been the world's most advanced system of astronomy are typically ignored by mainstream mathematicians and astronomers alike.[20]

Similarly, departments of architecture and engineering do not teach that the Incas invented the suspension bridge, or that their 2,500 mile Royal Road—paved, leveled, graded, guttered, and complete with rest areas—was perhaps the world's first genuine superhighway, or that portions of it are still used by motorized transport in Peru.[21] No mention is made of the passive solar temperature control characteristics carefully designed by the Anasazi into the apartment complexes of their cities at Chaco Canyon, Mesa Verde, and elsewhere.[22] Nor are students drawn to examine the incorporation of thermal mass into Mandan and Hidatsa construction techniques,[23] the vast north Sonoran irrigation systems built by the Hohokam,[24] or the implications of the fact that, at the time of Cortez's arrival, Tenochtitlán (now Mexico City) accommodated a population of 350,000, making it one of the largest cities on earth, at least five times the size of London or Seville.[25]

In political science, readers are invited—no, defied—to locate the course acknowledging, as John Adams, Benjamin Franklin, and others among the U.S. "Founding Fathers" did, that the form of the American Republic and the framing of its constitution were heavily influenced by the pre-existing model of the Haudenosaunee (Six Nations Iroquois Confederacy of present-day New York and Quebec).[26] Nor is mention made of the influence exerted by the workings of the "Iroquois League" in shaping the thinking of theorists such as Karl Marx and Friedrich Engels.[27] Even less discussion can be found on the comparably sophisticated political systems conceived and established by other indigenous peoples—the Creek Confederation, for example, or the Cherokees or Yaquis—long before the first European invader ever set foot on American soil.[28]

Where agriculture or the botanical sciences are concerned, one will not find the conventional department which wishes to "make anything special" of the fact that fully two-thirds of the vegetal foodstuffs now commonly consumed by all of humanity were under cultivation in the Americas, and nowhere else, in 1492.[29] Also unmentioned is the hybridization by Incan scientists of more than 3,000 varieties of potato,[30] or the vast herbal cornucopia discovered and deployed by native pharmacologists long before that.[31] In biology, pre-med and medicine, nothing is said of the American Indian invention of surgical tubing and the syringe, or the fact that the Incas were successfully practicing brain surgery at a time when European physicians were still seeking to cure their patients by applying leeches to "draw off bad blood."[32]

To the contrary, from matters of governance, where the Greek and Roman democracies are habitually cited as being sole antecedents of "the American experiment,"[33] to agriculture, with its "Irish" potatoes, "Swiss" chocolate, "Italian" tomatoes, "French" vanilla, and "English" walnuts,[34] the accomplishments of American Indian cultures are quite simply expropriated and recast in the curriculum as if they had been European in origin.[35] Concomitantly, the native traditions which produced such things are themselves deculturated and negated, consigned to the status of being "people without history."[36]

Such grotesque distortion is, of course, fed to indigenous students right along with Euroamericans,[37] and by supposedly radical professors as readily as more conservative ones.[38] Moreover, as was noted above, essentially the same set of circumstances prevails with regard to the traditions and attainments of all non-Western cultures.[39] Overall, the situation virtually demands to be viewed from a perspective best articulated by Albert Memmi:

> In order for the colonizer to be a complete master, it is not enough for him to be so in actual fact, but he must also believe in [the colonial system's] legitimacy. In order for that legitimacy to be complete, it is not enough for the colonized to be a slave, he must also accept his role. The bond between colonizer and colonized is thus destructive and creative. It destroys and recreates the two partners in colonization into colonizer and colonized. One is disfigured into an oppressor, a partial, unpatriotic and treacherous being, worrying only about his privileges and their defense; the other into an oppressed creature, whose development is broken and who compromises by his defeat.[40]

In effect, the intellectual sophistry which goes into arguing the "radical" and "conservative" content options available within the prevailing monocultural paradigm, a paradigm which predictably corresponds to the culture of the colonizer, amounts to little more than a diversionary mechanism through which power relations are reinforced, the status quo maintained.[41] The monolithic White Studies configuration of U.S. higher education—a content heading which, unlike American Indian, Afroamerican, Asian American and Chicano Studies, has yet to find its way into a single college or university catalogue—thus serves to underpin the hegemony of white supremacism in its other, more literal manifestations: economic, political, military, and so on.[42]

Those of non-European background are integral to such a system. While consciousness of their own heritages is obliterated through falsehood and omission, they are indoctrinated to believe that legitimacy itself is something derived from European tradition, a tradition which can never be truly shared by non-Westerners despite—or perhaps because of—their assimilation into Eurocentrism's doctrinal value structure. By and large, the "educated" American Indian or black thereby becomes the aspect of "broken development" who "compromises [through the defeat]" of his or her people, aspiring only to serve the interests of the order he or she has been trained to see as his or her "natural" master.[43]

As Frantz Fanon and others have observed long-since, such psychological jujitsu can never be directly admitted, much less articulated, by its principal victims. Instead, they are compelled by illusions of sanity to deny their circumstance and the process which induced it. Their condition sublimated, they function as colonialism's covert hedge against the necessity of perpetual engagement in more overt and costly sorts of repression against its colonial subjects.[44] Put another way, the purpose of White Studies in this connection is to trick the colonized into materially supporting her/his colonization through the mechanisms of his/her own though processes.[45]

There can be no reasonable or "value-neutral" explanation for this situation. Those, regardless of race or ethnicity, who endeavor to apologize for or defend its prevalence in institutions of higher education on "scholarly" grounds, do so without a shred of honesty or academic integrity.[46] Rather, whatever their intentions, they define themselves as accepting of the colonial order. In Memmi's terms, they accept the role of colonizer, which means "agreeing to be a . . . usurper. To be sure a usurper claims his place and, if need be, will defend it with every means at his disposal. . . . He endeavors to falsify history, he rewrites laws, he would extinguish memories—anything to succeed in transforming his usurpation into legitimacy."[47] They are, to borrow and slightly modify a term, "intellectual imperialists."[48]

2: An Indigenist Alternative

From the preceding observations as to what White Studies is, the extraordinary pervasiveness and corresponding secrecy of its practice, and the reasons underlying its existence, certain questions necessarily arise. For instance, the query might be posed as to whether a simple expansion of curriculum content to include material on non-Western contexts might be sufficient to redress matters. It follows that we should ask whether something beyond data or content is fundamentally at issue. Finally, there are structural considerations concerning how any genuinely corrective and liberatory curriculum or pedagogy might actually be inducted into academia. The first two questions dovetail rather nicely, and will be addressed in a single response. The third will be dealt with in the next section.

In response to the first question, the answer must be an unequivocal "no." Content is, of course, highly important, but, in and of itself, can never be sufficient to offset the cumulative effects of White Studies indoctrination. Non-

Western content injected into the White Studies format can be—and, historically, has been—filtered through the lens of Eurocentric conceptualization, taking on meanings entirely alien to itself along the way.[49] The result is inevitably
the reinforcement rather than the diminishment of colonialist hegemony. As
Vine Deloria, Jr. has noted relative to just one aspect of this process:

> Therein lies the meaning of the white's fantasy about Indians—the prob-
> lem of the Indian image. Underneath all the conflicting images of the In-
> dian one fundamental truth emerges—the white man knows that he is
> an alien and he knows that North America is Indian—and he will never
> let go of the Indian image because he thinks that by some clever manip-
> ulation he can achieve an authenticity that cannot ever be his.[50]

Plainly, more is needed that the simple introduction of raw data for handling within the parameters of Eurocentric acceptability. The conceptual mode
of intellectuality itself must be called into question. Perhaps a bit of "picto-
graphic" communication will prove helpful in clarifying what is meant in this
respect. The following schematic represents the manner in which two areas of
inquiry, science and religion (spirituality), have been approached in the European tradition.

Diagram I: European Conceptual Model

In this model, "knowledge" is divided into discrete content areas arranged
in a linear structure. This division is permanent and culturally enforced; witness
the Spanish Inquisition and "Scopes Monkey Trial" as but two historical illustra-
tions.[51] In the cases of science and religion (as theology), the mutual opposition
of their core assumptions has given rise to a third category, speculative philosophy, which is informed by both, and, in turn, informs them. Speculative philosophy, in this sense at least, serves to mediate and sometimes synthesize the lin-
early isolated components, science and religion, allowing them to communicate
and "progress." Speculative philosophy is not, in itself, intended to apprehend
reality, but rather to create an abstract reality in its place. Both religion and science, on the other hand, are, each according to its own internal dynamics,
meant to effect a concrete understanding of and action upon "the real world."[52]
Such compartmentalization of knowledge is replicated in the departmental-
ization of the Eurocentric education itself. Sociology, theology, psychology, phys-
iology, kinesiology, biology, cartography, anthropology, archeology, geology,
pharmacology, astronomy, agronomy, historiography, geography, demography—the whole vast proliferation of Western "ologies," "onomies," and "ogra-

phies"—are necessarily viewed as separate or at least separable areas of inquiry within the university. Indeed, the Western social structure both echoes and is echoed by the same sort of linear fragmentation, dividing itself into discrete organizational spheres: church, state, business, family, education, art, and so forth.[53] The structure involved readily lends itself to—perhaps demands—the sort of hierarchical ordering of things, both intellectually and physically, which is most clearly manifested in racism, militarism, and colonial domination, class and gender oppression, and the systematic ravaging of the natural world.[54]

The obvious problems involved are greatly amplified when our schematic of the Eurocentric intellectual paradigm is contrasted to one of non-Western, in this case Native American, origin:

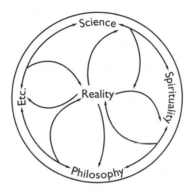

Diagram II: Native American Conceptual Model

Within such a conceptual model, there is really no tangible delineation of compartmentalized "spheres of knowledge." All components or categories of intellectuality (by Eurocentric definition) tend to be mutually and perpetually informing. All tend to constantly concretize the human experience of reality (nature) while all are simultaneously and continuously informed by that reality. This is the "Hoop" or "Wheel" or "Circle" of Life—an organic rather than synthesizing or synthetic view holding that all things are equally and indispensably interrelated—which forms the core of the native worldview.[55] Here, reality is not something "above" the human mind or being, but an integral aspect of the living/knowing process itself. The mode through which native thought devolves is thus inherently anti-hierarchical, incapable of manifesting the extreme forms of domination so pervasively evident in Eurocentric tradition.[56]

The crux of the White Studies problem, then, cannot be located amidst the mere omission or distortion of matters of fact, no matter how blatantly ignorant or culturally chauvinistic these omissions and distortions may be. Far more importantly, the system of Eurosupremacist domination depends for its continued maintenance and expansion, even its survival, upon the reproduction of its own intellectual paradigm—its approved way of thinking, seeing, understanding, and being—to the ultimate exclusion of all others. Consequently, White

Studies simply cannot admit to the existence of viable conceptual structures other than its own.[57]

To introduce the facts of precolonial American Indian civilizations to the curriculum is to open the door to confronting the utterly different ways of knowing which caused such facts to be actualized in the first place.[58] It is thoroughly appreciated in ruling circles that any widespread and genuine understanding of such alternatives to the intrinsic oppressiveness of Eurocentrism could well unleash a liberatory dynamic among the oppressed resulting in the evaporation of Eurosupremacist hegemony and a corresponding collapse of the entire structure of domination and elite privilege which attends it.[59] The academic "battle lines" have therefore been drawn, not so much across the tactical terrain of fact and data as along the strategic high ground of Western versus non-Western conceptualization. It follows that if the latter is what proponents of the White Studies status quo find it most imperative to bar from academic inclusion, then it is precisely that area upon which those committed to liberatory education must place our greatest emphasis.

3: A Strategy to Win

Given the scope and depth of the formal problem outlined in the preceding section, the question of the means through which to address it takes on a crucial importance. If the objective in grappling with White Studies is to bring about conceptual—as opposed to merely contentual—inclusion of non-Western traditions in academia, then appropriate and effective methods must be employed. As was noted earlier, resorting to inappropriate "remedies" leads only to cooptation and a reinforcement of White Studies as the prevailing educational norm.

One such false direction has concerned attempts to establish, essentially from scratch, whole new educational institutions, even systems, while leaving the institutional structure of the status quo very much intact.[60] Although sometimes evidencing a strong showing at the outset, these perpetually underfunded, understaffed, and unaccredited "community-based"—often actually separatist—schools have almost universally ended up drifting and floundering before going out of existence altogether.[61] Alternately, more than a few have abandoned their original reason for being, accommodating themselves to the "standards" and other requirements of the mainstream system as an expedient to survival.[62] Either way, the outcome has been a considerable bolstering of the carefully nurtured public impression that "the system works" while alternatives don't.

A variation on this theme has been to establish separatist centers or programs, even whole departments, within existing colleges and universities. While this approach has alleviated to some extent (though not entirely) difficulties in securing funding, faculty, and accreditation, it has accomplished little if anything in terms of altering the delivery of White Studies instruction in the broader institutional context.[63] Instead, intentionally self-contained "Ethnic

Studies" efforts have ended up "ghetto-ized"—that is, marginalized to the point of isolation and left talking only to themselves and the few majors they are able to attract—bitter, frustrated, and stalemated.[64] Worse, they serve to re-inforce the perception, so desired by the status quo, that White Studies is valid and important while non-Western subject matters are invalid and irrelevant.

To effect the sort of transformation of institutional realities envisioned in this essay, it is necessary *not* to seek to create parallel structures as such, but instead to penetrate and subvert the existing structures themselves, both pedagogically and canonically. The strategy is one which was once described quite aptly by Rudi Deutschke, the German activist/theorist, as amounting to a "long march through the institutions."[65] In this, Ethnic Studies entities, rather than constituting ends in themselves, serve as "enclaves" or "staging areas" from which forays into the mainstream arena can be launched with ever-increasing frequency and vitality, and to which non-Western academic guerrillas can withdraw when needed to rest and regroup among themselves.[66]

As with any campaign of guerrilla warfare, however metaphorical, it is important to concentrate initially upon opponents' point(s) of greatest vulnerability. Here, three prospects for action come immediately to mind, the basis for each of which already exists within most university settings in a form readily lending itself to utilization in undermining the rigid curricular compartmentalization and pedagogical constraints inhering in White Studies institutions. The key is to recognize and seize such tools, and then to apply them properly.

1. While tenure-track faculty must almost invariably be "credentialed"—i.e. hold the Ph.D. in a Western discipline, have a few publications in the "right" journals, etc.—to be hired into the academy, the same isn't necessarily true for guest professors, lecturers, and the like.[67] Every effort can and should be expended by the regular faculty—"cadre," if you will—of Ethnic Studies units to bring in guest instructors lacking in Western academic pedigree (the more conspicuously, the better), but who are in some way exemplary of non-Western intellectual traditions (especially oral form). The initial purpose is to enhance cadre articulations with practical demonstrations of intellectual alternatives by consistently exposing students to "the real thing." Goals further on down the line should include incorporation of such individuals directly into the core faculty, and, eventually, challenging the current notion of academic credentialing in its entirety.[68]

2. There has been a good deal of interest over the past twenty years in what has come to be loosely termed "Interdisciplinary Studies." Insofar as there is a mainstream correspondent to the way in which American Indians and other non-Westerners conceive of and relate to the world, this is it. Ethnic Studies practitioners would do well to push hard in the Interdisciplinary Studies arena, expanding it whenever and wherever possible at the direct expense of customary Western disciplinary boundaries. The object, of course, is to steep students in the knowledge that nothing can be understood other than in its relationship to everything

else; that economics, for example, can never really make sense if arbitrarily divorced from history, politics, sociology, and geography. Eventually, the goal should be to dissolve the orthodox parameters of disciplines altogether, replacing them with something more akin to "areas of interest, inclination and emphasis."[69]

3. For a variety of reasons, virtually all colleges and universities award tenure to certain faculty members in more than one discipline or department. Ethnic Studies cadres should insist that this be the case with them. Restricting their tenure and rostering exclusively to Ethnic Studies is not only a certain recipe for leaving them in a "last hired, first fired" situation during times of budget exigency, it is a standard institutional maneuver to preserve the sanctity of White Studies instruction elsewhere on campus. The fact is that an Ethnic Studies professor teaching American Indian or Afroamerican history is just as much a historian as a specialist in nineteenth-century British history; the Indian and the black should therefore be rostered to and tenured in History, *as well as* in Ethnic Studies. This "foot in the door" is important, not only in terms of cadre longevity and the institutional dignity such appointments signify *vis-à-vis* Ethnic Studies, but it offers important advantages by way of allowing cadres to reach a greater breadth of students, participate in departmental policy formation and hiring decisions, claim additional resources, and so forth. On balance, success in this area can only enhance efforts in the two above.[70]

The objective is to begin to develop a critical mass, first in given spheres of campuses where opportunities present themselves—later throughout the academy as a whole—which is eventually capable of discrediting and supplanting the hegemony of White Studies. In this, the process can be accelerated, perhaps greatly, by identifying and allying with sectors of the professorate with whom a genuine affinity and commonality of interest may be said to exist at some level. These might include those from the environmental sciences who have achieved, or begun to achieve, a degree of serious ecological understanding.[71] It might include occasional mavericks from other fields, various applied anthropologists,[72] for instance, and certain of the better and more engaged literary and artistic deconstructionists,[73] as well as the anarchists like Murray Bookchin who pop up more-or-less randomly in a number of disciplines.[74]

By-and-large, however, it may well be that the largest reservoir or pool of potential allies will be found among the relatively many faculty who profess to consider themselves, "philosophically" at least, to be Marxian in their orientation. This is not said because Marxists tend habitually to see themselves as being in opposition to the existing order (fascists express the same view of themselves, after all, and for equally valid reasons).[75] Nor is it because, where it has succeeded in overthrowing capitalism, Marxism has amassed an especially sterling record where indigenous peoples are concerned.[76] In fact, it has been argued with some cogency that, in the latter connection, Marxist practice has proven even more virulently Eurocentric than has capitalism in many cases.[77]

Nonetheless, one is drawn to conclude that there may still be a basis for constructive alliance, given Marx's positing of dialectics—a truly nonlinear and relational mode of analysis and understanding—as his central methodology. That he himself consistently violated his professed method,[78] and that subsequent generations of his adherents have proven themselves increasingly unable to distinguish between dialectics and such strictly linear propositions as cause/effect progressions,[79] does not inherently invalidate the whole of his project or its premises. If some significant proportion of today's self-proclaimed Marxian intelligentsia can be convinced to actually learn and apply dialectical method, it stands to reason that they will finally think their way in to a posture not unlike that elaborated herein (that they will in the process have transcended what has come to be known as "Marxism" is another story).[80]

4: Conclusion

This essay presents only the barest glimpse of its subject matter. It is plainly, its author hopes, not intended to be anything approximating an exhaustive or definitive exposition on its topics. To the contrary, it is meant only to act as, paraphrasing Marcuse, the Archimedian point upon which false consciousness may be breached en route to "a more comprehensive emancipation."[81] By this, we mean not only a generalized change in perspective which leads to the abolition of Eurocentrism's legacy of colonialist, racist, sexist, and classist domination, but the replacement of White Studies' Eurosupremacism with an educational context in which we can all, jointly and with true parity, "seek to expand our knowledge of the world" in full realization that,

> The signposts point to a reconciliation of the two approaches to experience. Western science must reintegrate human emotions and intuitions into its interpretation of phenomena; [non-Western] peoples must confront . . . the effects of [Western] technology . . . [We must] come to an integrated conception of how our species came to be, what it has accomplished, and where it can expect to go in the millennia ahead . . . [Then we will come to] understand as these traditionally opposing views seek a unity that the world of historical experience is far more mysterious and eventful than previously expected. . . . Our next immediate task is the unification of human knowledge.[82]

There is, to be sure, much work to be done, both practically and cerebrally. The struggle will be long and difficult, frustrating many times to the point of sheer exasperation. It will require stamina and perseverance, a preparedness to incur risk, often a willingness to absorb the consequences of revolt, whether overt or covert. Many will be required to give up or forego aspects of a comfort-zone academic existence, both mentally and materially.[83] But the pay-off may be found in freedom of the intellect, the pursuit of knowledge in a manner more proximate to truth, unfettered by the threats and constraints of narrow vested interest and imperial ideology. The reward, in effect, is participation in the process of human liberation, including our own. One can only assume that this is worth the fight.

Notes

1. For an overview of the evolution of the current conflict, see Ira Shore, *Culture Wars: School and Society in the Conservative Restoration, 1969–1984* (Boston: Routledge & Kegan Paul, 1986), for reactionary analysis, see Roger Kimball, *Tenured Radicals: How Politics Has Corrupted Our Higher Education* (New York: Harper & Row, 1990).
2. David S. Landes, "The Nature of Economic Imperialism," *Journal of Economic History* 21 (December 1961), as quoted in Harry Magdoff, *The Age of Imperialism* (New York: Monthly Review Press, 1969) p. 13.
3. Gerald Jayne and Robbin Williams (eds.) *A Common Destiny: Blacks and American Society* (Washington, DC: National Academy Press, 1989).
4. One solid summary of the contributionist trend will be found in Troy Duster, *The Diversity Project: Final Report* (Berkeley: University of California Institute for Social Change, 1991); for complaints, see Robert Alter, "The Revolt Against Tradition," *Partisan Review* vol. 58, no. 2, 1991.
5. General population, or "G-Pop" as it is often put, is the standard institutional euphemism for white students.
6. A good case can be made that there is a great disjuncture between the Greek philosophers and the philosophies later arising in Western Europe; see Martin Bernal, *Black Athena: The Afro-Asiatic Roots of Ancient Greece Vol. 1* (Princeton, NJ: Princeton University Press, 1987).
7. Marxian academics make another appearance here, insofar as they do tend to teach courses, or parts of courses, based in the thinking of non-Europeans. It should be noted, however, that those selected for exposition—Mao, Ho Chi Minh, Vo Nguyen Giap, Kim El Sung, et al.—are uniformly those who have most thoroughly assimilated Western doctrines in displacement of their own intellectual traditions.
8. Probably the most stunning example of this I've ever encountered came when Will Durant casually attributed the thought of the East Indian philosopher Shankara to a "preplagiarism" (!!!) of Kant: "To Shankara the existence of God is no problem, for he defines God as existence, and identifies all real being with God. But the existence of a personal God, creator or redeemer, there may, he thinks, be some question; such a deity, says this *pre-plagarist* of Kant, cannot be proved by reason, he can only be postulated as a practical necessity" (emphasis added); Will Durant, *The History of Civilization, Vol 1: Our Oriental Heritage* (New York: Simon & Schuster, 1954) p. 549. It should be remarked that Durant was not a reactionary of the stripe conventionally associated with white supremacism, but rather an intellectual of the Marxian progressive variety. Yet, in this single book on the philosophical tradition of Asia, he makes no less than ten references to Kant, all of them implying that the earlier philosophers of the East acted "precisely as if [they] were Immanual Kant" (p. 538), never that Kant might have predicated his own subsequent philosophical articulations in a reading of Asian texts. The point is raised to demonstrate the all but unbelievable lengths even the more dissident Western scholars have been prepared to go in reinforcing the mythos of Eurocentrism, and thus how such reinforcement transcends ideological divisions within the Eurocentric paradigm.
9. It should be noted, however, that the recent emergence of an "Afrocentric" philosophy and pedagogy, natural counterbalances to the persistence of Eurocentric orthodoxy, has met with fierce condemnation by defenders of the status quo; see David Nicholson, "Afrocentrism and the Tribalization of America," *Washington Post National Weekly Edition*, October 8–14, 1990.
10. A big question, frequently mentioned, is whether American Indians ever acquired the epistemological sensibilities necessary for their thought to be correctly understood as having amounted to "philosophical inquiry." Given that epistemology simply means "investigation of

the limits of human comprehension," one can only wonder what the gate-keepers of philosophy departments make of the American Indian conception, prevalent in myriad traditions, of there being a "Great Mystery" into which the human mind is incapable of penetrating; see, for example John G. Neihardt (ed.) *Black Elk Speaks* (New York: William Morrow Publisher, 1932) also see J. R. Walker, *Lakota Belief and Ritual* (Lincoln: University of Nebraska Press, 1980). For an unconsciously comparable Western articulation, see Noam Chomsky's discussions of accessible and inaccessible knowledge in the chapters entitled "A Philosophy of Language?" and "Empiricism and Rationalism," in *Language and Responsibility: An Interview by Mitsou Ronat* (New York: Pantheon Books, 1977).

11. As illustration, see Wilcomb E. Washburn, "Distinguishing History for Moral Philosophy and Public Advocacy," in Calvin Martin (ed.), *The American Indian and the Problem of History* (New York: Oxford University Press, 1987), pp. 91–7.

12. For a veritable case study of this mentality, see James Axtell, *After Columbus: Essays in the Ethnohistory of Colonial North America* (New York: Oxford University Press, 1988).

13. For a solid critique of the Beringia Theory, see Jeffrey Goodman, *American Genesis: The American Indian and the Origins of Modern Man* (New York: Summit Books, 1981); also see Jonathan E. Ericson, R. E. Taylor, and Rainier Berger (eds.), *The Peopling of the New World* (Los Altos, Calif.: Ballena Press, 1982).

14. For an exhaustive enunciation of the "fertilizer dilemma," see James C. Hurt, *American Indian Agriculture* (Lawrence: University Press of Kansas, 1991).

15. An excellent analysis of this standard description of indigenous American realities may be found in Jack Weatherford, *Indian Givers: How the Indians of the Americas Transformed the World* (New York: Crown, 1988). On cannibalism specifically, see W. Arens, *The Man-Eating Myth: Anthropology and Anthropophagy* (New York: Oxford University Press, 1979).

16. The manipulation of data undertaken by succeeding generations of Euroamerican historians and anthropologists in arriving at the official twentieth-century falsehood that there were "not more than one million Indians living north of the Rio Grande in 1492, including Greenland" is laid out very clearly by Francis Jennings in his *The Invasion of America: Indians, Colonialism and the Cant of Conquest* (Chapel Hill: University of North Carolina Press, 1975). For a far more honest estimate, deriving from the evidence rather than ideological preoccupations, see Henty F. Dobyns, *Their Number Become Thinned: Native American Population Dynamics in Eastern North America* (Knoxville: University of Tennessee Press, 1983); also see Russell Thornton, *American Indian Holocaust and Survival: A Population History Since 1492* (Norman: University of Oklahoma Press, 1987). Dobyns places the actual number as high as 18.5 million; Thornton, more conservative, places it at 12.5 million.

17. During a keynote presentation at the annual meeting of the American History Association in 1992, James Axtell, one of the emergent "deans" of the field, actually argued that genocide was an "inaccurate and highly polemical descriptor" for what had happened. His reasoning? That he could find only five instances in the history of colonial North America in which genocides "indisputably" occurred. Leaving aside the obvious—that this in itself makes genocide an appropriate term by which to describe the obliteration of American Indians—a vastly more accurate chronicle of the process of extermination will be found in David E. Stannard, *American Holocaust: Columbus and the Conquest of the New World* (New York: Oxford University Press, 1992).

18. Syvanus G. Morely and George W. Bainerd, *The Ancient Maya* (Stanford, Calif.: Stanford University Press, 1983); Robert M. Carmack, *Quichean Civilization* (Berkeley: University of California Press, 1973).

19. Anthony Aveni, *Empires of Time: Calendars, Clocks and Cultures* (New York: Basic Books, 1989).

20. Mexicano astronomy is discussed in D. Durán, *Book of Gods and Rites and the Ancient Calendar* (Norman: University of Oklahoma Press, 1971); also see Paul Radin, *The Sources and Authenticity of the History of Ancient Mexico* (Berkeley: University of California Publications in American Archeology and Ethnology, vol. 17, no. 1, 1920).

21. Victor Wolfgang Von Hagen, *The Royal Road of the Inca* (London: Gordon and Cremonesi, 1976).

22. Robert H. Lister and Florence C. Lister, *Chaco Canyon: Archeology and Archaeologists* (Albuquerque: University of New Mexico Press, 1981); also see Buddy Mays, *Ancient Cities of the Southwest* (San Francisco: Chronicle Books, 1962).

23. Peter Nabokov and Robert Easton, *American Indian Architecture* (New York: Oxford University Press, 1988); the "submerged" building principles developed by the Mandan and Hidatsa, ideal for the plains environment but long disparaged by the Euroamericans who displaced them, are now considered the "cutting edge" in some architectural circles. The Indians, of course, are not credited with having perfected such techniques more than a thousand years ago.

24. Emil W. Haury, *The Hohokam: Desert Farmers and Craftsmen* (Tucson: University of Arizona Press, 1976), pp. 120–51; the City of Phoenix and its suburbs still use portions of the several thousand miles of extraordinarily well-engineered Hohokam canals, constructed nearly a thousand years ago, to move their own water supplies around.

25. Cortez was effusive in his descriptions of Tenochtitlán as being, in terms of its design and architecture, "the most beautiful city on earth"; Bernal Díaz del Castillo, *The Discovery and Conquest of Mexico 1519–1810* (London: George Routledge & Sons, 1928) p. 268. On the size of Tenochtitlán, see Rudolph van Zantwijk, *The Aztec Arrangement: The Social History of Pre-Spanish Mexico* (Norman: University of Oklahoma Press, 1985, p. 281; on the size of London in 1500, Lawrence Stone, *The Family, Sex and Marriage in England, 1500–1800* (New York: Harper & Row, 1977), p. 147; for Seville, J. H. Elliott, *Imperial Spain 1469–1716* (New York: St Martin's Press, 1964), p. 177.

26. Donald A. Grinde, Jr, and Bruce E. Johansen, *Exemplar of Liberty: Native America and the Evolution of Democracy* (Los Angeles: UCLA American Indian Studies Center, 1992).

27. Between December 1880 and March 1881, Marx read anthropologist Lewis Henry Morgan's 1871 book, *Ancient Society*, based in large part on his 1851 classic *The League of the Hau-dernosau-nee or Iroquois*. Marx took at least ninety-eight pages of dense notes during the reading, and after his death, his collaborator, Friedrich Engels, expanded these into a short book entitled *The Origin of the Family, Private Property and the State: In Light of the Researches of Lewis Henry Morgan*. The latter, minus its subtitle, appears in *Marx and Engels: Selected Works* (New York: International Publishers, 1968).

28. Weatherford, *Indian Givers*.

29. Alfred W. Crosby, Jr. *The Columbian Exchange: Biological and Cultural Consequences of 1492* (Westport, Conn.: Greenwood Press, 1972); Carol A. Bryant, Anita Courtney, Barbara A. Markesbery and Kathleen M. DeWalt, *The Cultural Feast* (St Paul, Minn.: West, 1985).

30. Redcliffe N. Salaman, *The History and Social Influence of the Potato* (Cambridge: Cambridge University Press, 1949).

31. Clark Wissler, Wilton M. Krogman and Walter Krickerberg, *Medicine Among the American Indians* (Ramona, Calif.: Acoma Press, 1939); Norman Taylor, *Plant Drugs That Changed the World* (New York: Dodd, Meade, 1965).

32. Virgil Vogel, *American Indian Medicine* (Norman: University of Oklahoma Press, 1970); Peredo Guzman, *Medical Practices in Ancient America* (Mexico City: Ediciones Euroamericana, 1985). On contemporaneous European medical practices, see William H. McNeill, *Plagues and Peoples* (Garden City, NY: Anchor/Doubleday, 1976).

33. For good efforts at debunking such nonsense, see German Arciniegas, *America in Europe: A History of the New World in Reverse* (New York: Harcourt Brace Jovanovich, 1986), and William Brandon, *New Worlds for Old: Reports from the New World and Their Effect on Social Thought in Europe, 1500–1800* (Athens: Ohio University Press, 1986).

34. Carl O. Sauer, "The March of Agriculture Across the Western World," in his *Selected Essays, 1963–1975* (Berkeley: Turtle Island Foundation, 1981); also see Weatherford, *Indian Givers*.

35. This is nothing new, or unique to the treatment of American Indians Indeed, the West has comported itself in similar fashion *vis-à-vis* all non-Westerners since at least as early as the inception of "Europe"; see Philippe Wolf, *The Awakening of Europe: The Growth of European Culture from the Ninth Century to the Twelfth* (London: Cox & Wyman, 1968).

36. For a much broader excursus on this phenomenon, see Eric R. Wolf, *Europe and the People Without History* (Berkeley: University of California Press, 1982).

37. For surveys of the effects, see Thomas Thompson (ed.) *The Schooling of Native America* (Washington, DC: American Association of Colleges for Teacher Education, 1978); James R, Young (ed.) *Multicultural Education and the American Indian* (Los Angeles: UCLA American Indian

Studies Center, 1979), and Charlotte Heath and Susan Guyette, *Issues for the Future of American Indian Studies* (Los Angeles: UCLA American Indian Studies Center, 1985).

38. Consider, for example, the "Sixteen Thesis" advanced by the non-Marxist intellectual Alvin Gouldner as alternatives through which to transform the educational status quo. It will be noted that the result, if Gouldner's pedagogical plan were implemented, would be tucked as neatly into the paradigm of Eurocentrism as the status quo itself. See Alvin W. Gouldner, *The Future of Intellectuals and the Rise of the New Class* (New York: Seabury Press, 1979). For Marxian views falling in the same category, see Theodore Mills Norton and Bertell Ollman (eds.), *Studies in Socialist Pedagogy* (New York: Monthly Review Press, 1978).

39. See generally, Edward W. Said, *Orientalism* (New York: Oxford University Press, 1987).

40. Albert Mernmi, *Colonizer and Colonized* (Boston: Beacon Press, 1965), p. 89.

41. The procedure corresponds well in some ways with the kind of technique described by Herbert Marcuse as being applicable to broader social contexts in his essay "Repressive Tolerance," in Robert Paul Wolff, Barrington Moore, Jr, and Herbert Marcuse, *A Critique of Pure Tolerance* (Boston: Beacon Press, 1969).

42. The theme is handled well in Vine Deloria, Jr, "Education and Imperialism," *Integrateducation*, vol. xix, nos. 1–2, January 1982. For structural analysis, see Giovanni Arrighi, *The Geometry of Imperialism* (London: Verso, 1978).

43. Memmi develops these ideas further in his *Dominated Man* (Boston: Beacon Press, 1969).

44. See especially, Fanon's *Wretched of the Earth* (New York: Grove Press, 1965) and *Black Skin/White Masks: The Experiences of a Black Man in a White World* (New York: Grove Press, 1967).

45. Probably the classic example of this, albeit in a somewhat different dimension, were the Gurkas, who forged a legendary reputation fighting in behalf of their British colonizers, usually against other colonized peoples; see Patrick McCrory, *The Fierce Pawns* (Philadelphia: J. B. Lippincott, 1966).

46. See, for example, Allan Bloom, *The Closing of the American Mind* (New York: Simon & Schuster, 1988); Dinesh D'Sousa, *Illiberal Education: The Politics of Race and Sex on Campus* (New York: Free Press, 1991); Arthur Schlesinger, Jr., *The Disuniting of America* (New York: W. W. Norton, 1992).

47. *Colonizer and Colonized*, Memmi, pp. 52–3.

48. Martin Carnoy, *Education as Cultural Imperialism* (New York: David McKay, 1974); also see Laurie Anne Whitt, "Cultural Imperialism and the Marketing of Native America," in *Historical Reflections*, 1995.

49. A fascinating analysis of how this works, distorting the perspectives of perpetrator and victim alike, may be found in Richard James Blackburn, *The Vampire of Reason: An Essay in the Philosophy of History* (London: Verso, 1990).

50. Vine Deloria, Jr, "Forward: American Fantasy," in Gretchen M. Bataille and Charles L. P. Silet (eds.), *The Pretend Indians: Images of Native Americans in the Movies* (Ames: Iowa State University Press, 1980), p. xvi.

51. On the Inquisition, see Mary Elizabeth Perry and Anne J. Cruz (eds.), *Cultural Encounters: The Impact of the Inquisition in Spain and the New World* (Berkeley: University of California Press, 1991). On the context of the Scopes trial, see Stephan Jay Gould, *The Mismeasure of Man* (New York: W. W. Norton, 1981).

52. For a sort of capstone rendering of this schema, see Karl Popper, *Objective Knowledge: An Evolutionary Approach* (New York: Oxford University Press, 1975).

53. Useful analysis of this dialectic will be found in David Reed, *Education for Building a People's Movement* (Boston: South End Press, 1981).

54. For an interesting analysis of many of these cause/effect relations, see Jerry Mander, *In the Absence of the Sacred: The Failure of Technology and the Survival of Indian Nations* (San Francisco: Sierra Club Books, 1991). Also see William H. McNeill (ed.) *Pursuit of Power: Technology, Armed Force and Society Since A.D. 1000* (Chicago: University of Chicago Press, 1982).

55. For elaboration, see Vine Deloria, Jr., *God Is Red* (New York: Grosset & Dunlap, 1973). Also see John Mohawk, *A Basic Call to Consciousnes* (Rooseveltown, NY: *Akwesasne Notes*, 1978).

56. A Westerner's solid apprehension of this point may be found in Stanley Diamond, *In Search of the Primitive: A. Critique of Civilization* (New Brunswick, NJ: Transaction Books, 1974); also see

Keith Thomas, *Man and the Natural World: A History of Modern Sensibility* (New York: Pantheon Books, 1983).

57. The matter has been explored tangentially, from a number of angles. Some of the best, for purposes of this essay, include Tala Asad (ed.) *Anthropology and the Colonial Encounter* (New York: Humanities Press, 1973); Robert Berkhofer, *The White Man's Indian: Images of the American Indian from Columbus to the Present* (New York: Alfred A. Knopf, 1978); Tzvetan Todorov, *The Conquest of America: The Question of the Other* (New York: Harper & Row, 1984); and Robert Young, *White Mythologies: Writing History and the West* (London: Routledge, 1990).

58. More broadly, the thrust of this negation has always pertained in the interactions between European/Euroamerican colonists and native cultures; see Richard Drinnon, *Facing West: The Metaphysics of Indian Hating and Empire Building* (Minneapolis: University of Minnesota Press, 1980).

59. Aside from the paradigmatic shift, culturally speaking, embedded in this observation, it shares much with the insights into the function of higher education achieved by New Left theorists during the 1960s; see Carl Davidson, *The New Student Radicals in the Multiversity and Other Writings on Student Syndicalism* (Chicago: Charles Kerr, 1990).

60. In essence, this approach is the equivalent of Mao Tse-Tung's having declared the Chinese revolution victorious at the point it liberated and secured the Caves of Hunan.

61. One salient example is the system of "survival schools" started by AIM during the mid–1970s, only two of which still exist in any form; see Susan Braudy, "We Will Remember Survival School: The Women and Children of the American Indian Movement," *Ms. Magazine*, no. 5, July 1976.

62. For a case study of one initially separatist effort turned accommodationist, see Maryls Duchene, "A Profile of American Indian Community Colleges"; more broadly, see Gerald Wilkenson, "Educational Problems in the Indian Community: A Comment on Learning as Colonialism"; both essays will be found in *Integrateducation*, vol. xix, nos. 1–2, January–April 1982.

63. Ward Churchill and Norbert S. Hill Jr, "Indian Education at the University Level: An Historical Survey," *Journal of Ethnic Studies*, vol. 7, no. 3, 1979.

64. Further elaboration of this theme will be found in Ward Churchill, "White Studies or Isolation: An Alternative. Model for American Indian Studies Programs," in James R. Young (ed.), *American Indian Issues in Higher Education* (Los Angeles: UCLA American Indian Studies Center, 1981).

65. So far as is known, Deutschke, head of the German SDS, first publicly issued a call for such a strategy during an address of a mass demonstration in Berlin during January 1968.

66. Mao Tse Tung, *On Protracted War* (Peking: Foreign Language Press, 1967); Che Guevara, *Guerrilla Warfare* (New York: Vintage Books, 1961).

67. For an excellent and succinct examination of the implications of this point, see Jurgen Herget, *And Sadly Teach; Teacher Education and Professionalization in American Culture* (Madison: University of Wisconsin Press, 1991).

68. The concept is elaborated much more fully and eloquently in Paulo Freire's *Pedagogy of the Oppressed* (New York: Continuum Books, 1981).

69. Again, one can turn to Preire for development of the themes; see his *Education for Critical Consciousness* (New York: Continuum Books, 1982). For the results of a practical—and very successful—application of these principles in the United States, see *TRIBES 1989: Final Report and Evaluation* (Boulder: University of Colorado University Learning Center, August 1989).

70. For overall analysis, see Vine Deloria, Jr, "Indian Studies—The Orphan of Academia," *Wicazo Sa Review*, vol. II, no. 2, 1986; also see José Bacriero, "The Dilemma of American Indian Education," *Indian Studies Quarterly*, vol. 1, no. 1, 1984.

71. As examples, Bill Devall and George Sessions; see their *Deep Ecology: Living as if Nature Mattered* (Salt Lake City: Perigrine Smith Books; 1985). Also see André Gorz, *Ecology as Politics* (Boston: South End Press, 1981).

72. The matter is well-handled in Edward W. Said, "Representing the Colonized: Anthropology's Interlocutors," *Critical Inquiry*, no. 15, 1989.

73. See, for instance, Lucy Lippard, *Mixed Blessings: New Art in Multicultural America* (New York: Pantheon, 1990).

74. Murray Bookchin, *The Ecology of Freedom* (Palo Alto, Calif.: Cheshire Books, 1982); also see Steve Chase (ed.) *Defending the Earth: A Dialogue Between Murray Bookchin and Dave Foreman* (Boston: South End Press, 1991).
75. Fritz Stern, *The Politics of Cultural Despair: A Study in the Rise of Germanic Ideology* (Berkeley: University of California Press, 1961); also see Wilhelm Reich, *The Mass Psychology of Fascism* (New York: Farrar, Straus & Giroux, 1970).
76. See generally, Walker Connor, *The National Question in Marxist—Leninist Theory and Strategy* (Princeton, NJ: Princeton University Press, 1984).
77. Russell Means, "The Same Old Song," in Ward Churchill (ed.) *Marxism and Native Americans* (Boston: South End Press, 1983).
78. Ward Churchill and Elisabeth R. Lloyd, *Culture versus Economism: Essays on Marxism in the Multicultural Arena* (Denver: University of Colorado Center for the Study of Indigenous Law and Politics, 1990).
79. Michael Albert and Robin Hahnel, *Unorthodox Marxism* (Boston: South End Press, 1978).
80. As illustration of one who made the transition, at least in substantial part, see Rudolph Bahro, *From Red to Green* (London: Verso, 1984).
81. Marcuse, "Repressive Tolerance."
82. Vine Deloria, Jr., *The Metaphysics of Modern Existence* (New York: Harper & Row), 1979, p. 213.
83. For insights, see Ellen Schrecker, *No Ivory Tower: McCarthyism and the Universities* (New York: Oxford University Press, 1986).

Questions

1. What does Churchill mean when he uses the phrase "White Studies"?

2. Locate a copy of the course catalog for your college/university and take a look at the courses offered by the philosophy department. Does Churchill's critique that students in many departments gain "a concentrated knowledge of the European intellectual schema rather than any genuine appreciation of the philosophical attainments of humanity" apply to your institution? Explain. How do other departments fare in light of his critique?

3. Churchill argues that a monolithic "White Studies" paradigm prevails in higher education because of a dominant European tradition that systematically distorts and omits other intellectual traditions. Offer a counterargument. For instance, what other reasons might account for the disproportionate representation of the European intellectual schema in college/university curricula?

4. According to Churchill, why is "content . . . in and of itself . . . [insufficient] to offset the cumulative effects of White Studies indoctrination"?

5. How does the European Conceptual Model differ from the Native American Conceptual Model?

6. Why does Churchill warn against the creation of "Self-contained 'Ethnic Studies' efforts"? Do you agree with his analysis? In other words, would you recommend that such programs be avoided? Explain.

7. Churchill offers three suggestions for undercutting the intellectual dominance of White Studies. Which suggestion do you think is most important to his argument? Why?

On the Ethnic Studies Requirement

Sucheng Chan

Stanford University made national headlines when its faculty debated whether or not to change the core list of books that first-year students are required to read in its Western Culture Program, in response to faculty and student criticisms that works by non-Europeans and by women were not included in the "canon." Likewise, the University of California at Berkeley received widespread media coverage when its faculty postponed voting on a proposal to add an "American cultures" course to the university's list of graduation requirements. The actions garnered so much publicity because these two institutions rank among the world's leading research universities. But they are by no means the only campuses where such debates are taking place. As more and more institutions begin to grapple with various aspects of ethnic diversity in the coming years, it is important to understand why current efforts at enlarging the curriculum have generated such heated exchanges between supporters and opponents of the proposed reforms.

On the face of it, the very reasonable request that universities require their graduates to learn something about nonwhite peoples and cultures in the United States should not have aroused the intense emotions that it did. The fact that such efforts have been so controversial indicates that something far larger than curriculum reform is at stake. What is being challenged, I think, is the very structure of power within the university—the debate over whether or not to add one little course being only a sign of a more encompassing struggle.

A similar challenge had been mounted in the 1960s and 1970s, when student and faculty activists demonstrated militantly to demand that ethnic studies programs be established. Some were indeed set up, but though quite a number have survived, few have expanded in the last twenty years. The campaign to get a campus-wide ethnic studies requirement passed at various colleges across the nation marks a new stage in the growth of ethnic studies. This development is encountering stiff resistance in some places because no one can predict how the final outcome will affect existing power relations in American higher education. Like their predecessors, today's activists are asking questions about who makes decisions, based on what criteria, about curriculum, personnel, and the distribution of resources, and to whom such decision-makers should be accountable. But beyond these material concerns, they are also raising issues about who gets to define reality. By so doing, they are calling into question the ideological foundations of society in general and of the university in particular. Were this not the case, we would not be witnessing the sound and fury that have so captured public attention in recent months.

In the last three years, students and faculty at four University of California campuses—Santa Cruz, Riverside, Santa Barbara, and Berkeley—have pushed for the establishment of some kind of ethnic studies requirement. While such a requirement is already in force in Santa Cruz and Riverside, the final votes will not be taken at Santa Barbara and Berkeley until the spring of 1989.[1] I shall analyze the efforts to get such a requirement passed at these four UC campuses, as well as at Stanford University, in Part II of this article. In this first segment, I shall reflect on how the classroom dynamics in the ethnic studies courses I have taught that fulfill a campus-wide requirement differ from the situation in classes that do not fulfill one. By analyzing my own reactions to the changes, I hope to clarify some of the commonly held but not always explicitly articulated premises upon which ethnic studies—as both an academic enterprise and a political project—have been built.

I began teaching Asian American Studies at Sonoma State University in 1971. Subsequently, I spent ten years on the Asian American Studies faculty at UC Berkeley. At both institutions, Asian American students comprised at least 97 percent of the enrollment in my classes. (This represents a greater "ethnic concentration" than is found in most Afro-American, Chicano/Latino, or Native American Studies courses, according to colleagues teaching in those areas.) Quite frankly, I rather liked having such an ethnic enclave. My students, on the other hand, have reacted to the ethnic clustering in different ways. Many feel more comfortable in these Asian American Studies classes than they do in other classes. After an initial reluctance, they often learn to talk freely in discussions. Some who have grown up in primarily white neighborhoods or who have purposely avoided contact with fellow Asian Americans, on the other hand, tend to feel very uneasy when they are first surrounded by people who look like themselves. Yet others experience a virtual catharsis when given the chance to come to terms with who they are. The latter often become strongly committed to the Asian American movement. As is true of other teachers, I have been liked by some of my students and disliked by others. But regardless of how they evaluated my teaching, I always felt that teaching primarily Asian American students was a privilege: the rooms in which we held our classes became, however temporarily, *our* space; the lecture hours became *our* time. I did not realize how much this privilege meant to me until I lost it.

At UC Santa Cruz, to which I moved in 1984, the ethnic composition and the atmosphere in my classes did not differ greatly from those at Berkeley. But after the Santa Cruz Academic Senate approved an ethnic/Third World studies requirement in February 1985—a requirement that went into effect in the fall of 1986—things changed in subtle but important ways. I taught the introductory Asian American history course twice that first year. These two classes—though the same course—turned out to be vastly different experiences for me as a teacher. Even though I assigned the same readings and gave more or less the same lectures (my lectures are never *quite* the same from quarter to quarter, since I do not read from notes), the overall ambience of the class changed. The shift was probably perceptible to no one but myself, but it troubled me sufficiently to make me wonder what the difference augured.

The first time around, there were forty-six students in the class. Thirty-five were Asian American, two were Black, two Chicano, one Latino American, and six White. I had no teaching assistants, so we had no scheduled discussion sections. But the class was still small enough for spontaneous discussions to occur. At first, almost everybody was shy and I had to pull words out of many individuals. But by the third week or so, the ice had broken and several talkative students began to say more and more. In time, the class became so eager to talk that I had to set up discussion sections outside of lecture hours, so that we could get through the lecture materials.

In these conversations, the most important discovery we made was that not only do non-Asians hold biased images of Asian Americans—something we have always known and felt angry about—but that Asian Americans *also* have inaccurate perceptions of White, Black, Latino, and other Americans. Moreover, we found that among that group of students, at least, television programs seemed to be the primary source of such stereotypes. A very touching exchange took place one afternoon when several Asian American students talked about how their parents did not love them. Unlike white parents in certain television shows they had watched who hug, kiss, and say nice things to their children, they said, theirs never embraced them. As tears began to glisten in some of their eyes, one of the white students said very gently, "You know, in real life not all white parents express their affection the way you think they do . . . many of our parents are divorced, some of our moms and dads fight a lot and seldom spend time with us . . . my Mom had to work when I was very young so she was never home waiting with a jar of cookies when I came home from school . . . one of the reasons I took this class is that I have always envied Asian Americans who have such close-knit families." The Asian American students who had felt so sorry for themselves just a moment ago looked up, startled. Other students then told about their childhood, many of which were not happy. Although the discussion took time away from the lecture I had planned to give that day, I did not stop the students from talking, because the factual information they missed hearing from me seemed less important than the common bond they were discovering amongst themselves.

As the quarter progressed, I encouraged members of the class to relate the Asian American material to larger issues, particularly their own relationship to the world around them. Like other people, I pointed out, Asian Americans are connected to others through history and a complex web of social interactions in which are embedded unequal power relationships. While some of us accept our lot, others do not. But before we can transform what we do not like, I cautioned, we need to understand clearly how the present situation evolved, why some conditions are so difficult to change, and what the personal and social costs of political action may be. By getting the students to think along these lines, I hoped that even if I did not succeed in goading them to do anything significant to change their lives—much less the world—I could at least help them understand how individual psychology is linked to history and sociology, so that those who felt wounded by life's cruelties no longer suffered alone.

That class was very satisfying to teach. With Asian American students in the majority, it provided a haven in which those who were verbally reticent could slowly learn to express themselves. At the same time, having a small number of students from a variety of ethnic backgrounds made a more probing exchange of views possible. The following quarter, however, more than a hundred students crowded into a room designed to hold forty. As I looked out over the sea of faces—most of them white—my mind began tying itself into knots: "I have no T.A.s, no readers . . . we can't have this kind of class without discussions . . . the students *must* have an opportunity to talk about and 'process' the emotionally charged issues we will be dealing with . . . I cannot possibly lead five discussion sections a week and write more than a hundred narrative evaluations[2] without any help . . . certainly not when I am holding two administrative positions! . . . I *must* do something to reduce the class size . . ."

My virtual panic had nothing to do with a fear of crowds: I not only do not mind teaching large classes, I actually *enjoy* teaching them. However, when I had taught very large classes at Berkeley, I always had T.A.s to work with me. Even though the graduate assistants I hired there often had no training in Asian American Studies *per se*, they learned quickly and were indispensable to the success of the courses. At Santa Cruz, in contrast, no provision had been made for dealing with the sudden rise in the enrollment in courses fulfilling the new requirement; moreover, even if funds were available, few graduate students were to be had, since there are only a few Ph.D. programs outside of the natural sciences.

"There is no way I can accommodate so many students in this class," I began.

"You can't kick us out!" they exclaimed, before I could finish my sentence. "We *have* to get into a class that fulfills the ethnic studies requirement."

"But there are lots of other classes that do," I replied.

"That's not true—there are only five this quarter!"

"The fire marshall won't let you sit all over the aisles . . ."

"Then get a bigger classroom!" they demanded.

"I've already tried, there aren't any available at this hour. You know, there's going to be *lots,* and I mean *lots,* of reading in this course—are you *sure* you want to take this class?"

"We have to! We have no choice."

Well, neither really did I. Having worked so hard to get an ethnic studies requirement established, was I not morally obligated to take all the students who desired to enroll, with or without T.A.s?

We eventually found a larger classroom in an evening time slot. That worked out well since I had a grant that quarter to rent a lot of films. Though only four hours were scheduled for the lectures, the class actually met for six hours a week: I was able to show the films after the lectures without reserving another room for them since there was no other class scheduled in that room after mine. Furthermore, since I felt that it was mandatory that we have some discussions, I arranged voluntary discussion sections in the afternoons. I divided the class into four groups, each of which was to meet every other week. There being no T.A.s, I had to lead all the sections myself. This was a heavy burden. What helped me get through the quarter was that the class had an upbeat atmosphere: attendance was surprisingly good (even though it rained a lot that winter, and dark, wet nights in the redwoods of Santa Cruz can be scary), morale was high, and the students frequently told me how much they were enjoying the course.

But one aspect of the class really bothered me. In the discussion sections, the white students chatted amiably enough, but regardless of how hard I tried, very few of the Asian American students were willing to say anything. Although many of the T.A.s who had worked with me at Berkeley had often wrung their hands over Asian American students who would not talk, I have seldom encountered this problem myself. Somehow, I had always managed to get at least a few of the students to say something. But in this instance, being numerically overwhelmed, the Asian American students felt vulnerable: they could not very well spill their guts in public.

My colleague Wendy Ng, who has also taught at Santa Cruz, has tried heroically to carry on discussions *during lecture hours* in a class with over a hundred students—something I never found the courage to do. Despite her success, she was troubled greatly by the anger that Asian American students felt over the way white students dominated the discussions. My students did not seem particularly angry, but their silence nevertheless spoke volumes. Behind closed doors in my office, I tried to find out why, unlike the group I had the quarter before, these students did not open their mouths.

"Surely it can't be so hard to talk to or in front of white classmates . . . don't you have any non-Asian friends?" I asked.

"Yes, but those are our *friends*."

"Some of the students in this class *could* become your friends . . ."

"It's not the same."

Indeed, it was not. Although I received superb teaching evaluations that quarter—from Asian and non-Asian students—I could not help feeling an immense and inconsolable sense of loss: the circle of trust within which my Asian American students and I had ensconced ourselves in bygone years was no more.

That I should feel disconsolate requires explanation, for I am not normally a sentimental person. Why, then, in this case, in spite of the overwhelmingly positive response to my course, did I feel such nostalgia for the way things used to be? To get to the root of my vexation, I asked myself anew several old questions. First, for whose benefit are we offering ethnic studies courses? Second, what do we actually hope to accomplish in our classes? Third, what undergirds the authority of the faculty teaching such courses? With respect to each question, how does the answer change when our courses become part of a general education requirement? In thinking about these issues, much can be learned about race relations in today's American universities.

At first glance, the answer to the question, "Whom should our courses benefit?" seems simple enough. Since students of color were the primary motive force behind the establishment of the pioneer ethnic studies programs, the courses should of course benefit them. But even a cursory look at the faces in our classrooms will immediately reveal that "students of color" or "minority students" or "Asian American students" are not monolithic terms. Our students come from different national origins and socioeconomic classes. They were born in places near and far. They have been in the United States for varying lengths of time—fifth-generation Chinese Americans mingle with recently arrived refugees from Vietnam. Those who are immigrants came to this country at different ages, which means they encountered mainstream American culture at different stages in their socio-psychological development. They have also grown up in contrasting environments. Some are the children of well-off professionals and business executives, others come from families so poor that they have to send part of their financial aid checks home to help support their parents, grandparents, or siblings. Just because we use the handy label "Asian American" to refer to them collectively, it does not mean they have similar interests or that we should expect our lectures and assigned readings to touch them equally.

On the other hand, heterogeneity does not imply a lack of commonality. I have learned through my teaching that what makes "Asian American" a defensible and meaningful *analytical category* is not so much that we or our ancestors all came from somewhere in Asia, but rather, virtually all individuals of Asian ancestry in the United States know what it feels like to be a member of a minority group. I say this despite the fact that some students of Asian ancestry deny vehemently that they have ever encountered racism or discrimination of any kind. But such denial is often a protective device, a defense mechanism. When placed in a situation—such as an Asian American Studies class—where it is socially *acceptable* to discuss how Asian Americans and other minorities have been treated, the memories of such individuals seem all of a sudden to be triggered. They begin to recall little incidents or disquieting feelings they have long forgotten or repressed—experiences that reveal they *have,* after all, encountered racial and cultural subordination. Whether or not we wish to acknowledge it, we discover that in the end it is our status as members of *American-made* minority groups that binds us.

Asian American students respond well to Asian American Studies because in our courses we *do* dissect the experiences that trouble them. We do so by imparting information about historical and sociological phenomena and by analyzing and interpreting their meaning. It is this cognitive component that differentiates our courses from what goes on in counseling groups: we attempt to link personal experiences to changing social, cultural, economic, and political *structures*, while therapists focus more on *individuals* and their relationship to people closest and most significant to them.

Because I consider efforts to help Asian American students "locate" themselves in society to be so important, I felt as though the rug had been pulled out from under me when my classroom became populated largely by white students. I reacted this way not because I am a "reverse racist" but because I am conscious of the fact that my effectiveness as a teacher of Asian American Studies depends on my ability to keep my finger on the pulse of a majority of my students. I am tuned in to how most Asian American students think and feel, but I do not think the same "fit" exists between me and my non-Asian American students.

"Fit" matters because for me what kind of students are in my class and how they respond to the materials I present affect how I teach. I believe that in every course there is a "text" and a "subtext." The text is what is in our syllabuses, lectures, and readings—the body of knowledge to be transmitted. But since students are not mere receptacles, the manner in which they absorb and react to what we present becomes a subtext. Thus, though we may dish out the same text year after year, the subtext changes every time we encounter a new group of students. Teachers who care about *how* students learn take note of such changes and react to them, whether consciously or subconsciously. I, for example, prefer to lecture without notes because it allows me to sweep my eyes across the room, calibrating the amount of details I should present as well as how I should frame particular issues, depending on what my "antenna" is picking up.

When the composition of my class changed from being largely Asian American to predominately white, I told the students my purpose would remain the same—to help them understand what life has been like for Asian Americans through successive historical periods. But at the same time, I realized that instead of *articulating* the experience of the group—on its behalf, as I had always done—I now had to, instead, *translate* that experience into terms that non-Asian Americans could comprehend.

Articulation is important when some of our students have not yet found words to describe certain facets of their lives. For them, language has not yet become a tool for making the world intelligible, not because their English is inadequate or they lack intelligence, but because in their families and at school, some aspects of reality have never been talked about or are not permitted to be talked about. By helping them to express inchoate feelings and to explore suppressed ideas, I provide them with cognitive maps—in the form of a vocabulary and a set of explanations—that enable them to make better sense of their world. To the extent that my analysis reflects and resonates with their own experiences, I validate their existence and offer them a means to get a handle on whatever has vexed them. "Facts" thus become vehicles for self-discovery and empowerment, as they realize that being different is not the same as being deviant or inferior.

Having a large number of non-Asian students in my class complicates matters enormously because even though I can still articulate the Asian American experience, when I do so now I risk making my Asian American students feel self-consciously naked—as though they are in a fishbowl, for everyone to stare at and possibly to make fun of. As Asian American playwright Philip Kan Gotanda has put it, being a minority person is a real burden because it forces one to constantly "monitor" one's environment. Gotanda tells of an almost magical moment when, after residing in Japan for some years—a period long enough for him to have become fluent in spoken Japanese and to have picked up all the proper body language—he all of a sudden felt he could finally become anonymous, and consequently free.[3] For the same reason, I think many Asian American students prefer not to talk in classes where they are not in the majority because they hope silence will spare them ridicule: "If *I* don't say anything, maybe *they* won't notice that I'm different." But having a teacher express what they themselves might have said is no less disconcerting when it is done in a room full of "strangers." Thus, the very same process of self-delineation—which can be so empowering in an in-group setting—can cause profound discomfort when it occurs in a mixed milieu.

My dilemma is that I feel obligated to cover the same ground even though I know doing so might make the Asian American students embarrassed and their white peers uneasy. I believe that if I eschew talking about the more sensitive issues, I cheat both my Asian American and my non-Asian American students of the very insights they should gain by taking courses such as mine. The challenge then becomes how one can pay equal attention to both subgroups. The solution I found was to translate, instead of articulate. A translator must ensure that *both* sets of communicators understand the messages being conveyed. In this instance, even though we are all speaking English, I still play the role of translator because I am explicating a reality known by one subgroup to the other subgroup, whose members may not be privy to its secrets. However, translation is not a perfect solution. When I could no longer focus exclusively on Asian American students and their needs, the lucidity born of intimacy is lost.

My sense of loss is tied to my understanding of the different perspectives that can be used to study minority groups. I can think of at least four. The oldest approach—an attitude that permeates the scholarly literature published before the 1960s—treats minority groups as deviant or deficient. According to proponents of this view, to become "normal," members of minority groups must assimilate into the majority culture and discard the "dysfunctional" minority one. The second perspective focuses on the "contributions" of various ethnic groups. It is a celebratory stance couched in terms of multicultural enrichment, but it seldom probes the causes of inequality. The third viewpoint defines the minority groups as victims. Its theorists seek to understand how forces of exploitation and oppression are built into the fabric of society. The fourth angle of vision sees members of minority groups as agents of history— people who think and feel and who make decisions even when their lives are severely circumscribed by conditions beyond their control.

I identify most strongly with the fourth perspective. For that reason, getting quiet Asian American students to talk in class is very important to me because I believe self-expression is one means through which individuals can *externalize* their experiences. Unlike the internalization that occurs when new members of a society—be they children or immigrants—are socialized into the values and norms of the community they have to learn to call home, externalization involves an opposite social process: it allows subjective experiences to acquire communal meaning and to become a vocalized, hence tangible, element in the culture that the new members enter. Instead of being passive recipients of the host culture, new members who have a voice can play an active role in shaping that culture. Speech provides a means through which many hitherto quiet Asian American students can learn to become agents of history. But they can acquire such agency only when they overcome a double repression: Asian traditions that train the young (and especially the female) to be quiet, submissive, and obedient *and* American racism that threatens members of minority groups with harm unless they "stay in their place." Staying in their place means keeping silent. Conversely, breaking silence is an act of rebellion—a declaration that a public self now exists.

I believe that those who control decision-making in the university have opposed the growth of ethnic studies courses precisely because they contain such an element of self-discovery and empowerment for students. If all that ethnic studies courses try to do is to impart information *about* the history and "exotic" cultural practices of nonwhite groups, they would not be threatening at all. After all, cultural pluralism in and of itself is innocuous and even colorful; it only becomes ominous when it is used as the ideological justification for changing existing arrangements of privilege and power. On the level of scholarship, those academic gatekeepers who determine what kind of work is legitimate sometimes dismiss the writings of feminist scholars or minority scholars as "too shrill," "too angry," or "too bitter" precisely because our sharp words puncture the sheath that envelops the still mostly male and mostly white world of academic discourse—discourse that pretends it has the sole right to define normalcy, universality, what is human.

Ideally, for ethnic studies courses that enroll a large number of non-minority students to succeed in their purpose, they must help students of color to arrive at the same conceptual clarity about the history, contemporary manifestation, and meaning of racial inequality that all ethnic studies courses aim to achieve. Second, they must help white students to come to terms with the fact that they may unwittingly be what Kenneth Clark has called "accessories to profound injustice."[4] Third, they must provide all students with an arena in which to explore a new vision—a world where interdependent groups share a common destiny. The end we seek is mutual empathy. But we can only hope to reach this goal if we do not assume an accusatory stance. The importance of not "guilt tripping" white students was taught me by a student who had acquired a reputation for disrupting the lectures of minority faculty whenever they talked about racism. This student, however, was very well behaved in my class. One day I decided to ask him what had caused him to change his attitude.

"It's not my attitude," he explained. "I got angry in the other classes because every time the professors lectured about racism, I felt that they were accusing me *personally* of being racist. But you're very analytical—you try to explain why racism exists and how it has affected Asian Americans—so I don't feel like you are attacking *me* directly."

This observation alerted me to another dilemma: by creating analytical "distance," I avoid alienating white students, but by soft-pedaling racism, I rob my Asian American students of an important forum in which to express their confusion, hurt, and anger. In the short span of ten weeks—or even fifteen or twenty weeks—it does not seem possible to meet the needs of white and Asian American students simultaneously. There simply is not enough time to work through all the thoughts and feelings that the course material elicits. A more daunting difficulty is that even if faculty may want to help students overcome the interracial tensions that are so deeply rooted in American society, most of us are not up to the task. Which one of us can claim to be completely free of racism, sexism, homophobia, and class and religious prejudice?

Therefore, to avoid disappointment, bitterness, and cynicism, we must be modest in our goals. We should recognize that courses that fulfill an ethnic studies requirement cannot eradicate racism. All we can hope to do, if we are good teachers, is to get our students to listen to us and to each other, to learn a few unpleasant truths, to gain the insight that people who do not look like ourselves nevertheless face similar dilemmas common to the human condition. Even this will not be easy to accomplish: students who have to take a course because it is required often resent doing so.

Faced with a captive, possibly restive, audience, we may wonder if our authority as professors under such circumstances may have become more tenuous. Could the "threshold of convincibility"—the amount of evidence needed to convince our audience that this or that assertion is indeed true—now be higher?[5] I worried about such a possibility when I puzzled over why far fewer students challenged all the things I said than I had expected. It was then that I realized that several of the films I had shown contained scenes of white, male scholars discussing the discrimination Asian immigrants had faced (and continue to face). Not only that, these colleagues assert that such discrimination was clearly racist. In Stephen Okazaki's *Unfinished Business*, for example, Peter Irons and Roger Daniels expound on the racism that led to the incarceration of Japanese Americans during World War II. In Spencer Nakasako's film on Vietnamese refugee fishermen, *Monterey's Boat People,* Sandy Lydon comments on the earlier discriminatory legislation against Chinese and Japanese immigrant fishermen. In *Dollar a Day, Ten Cents a Dance,* a film about Filipino farmworkers by Mark Schwartz and Geoffrey Dunn, Howard DeWitt talks about the racism manifest in the anti-Filipino riot that took place in Watsonville, California, in the early 1930s. Although I had lectured about the same events and their meaning, I could not help but suspect that having Irons, Daniels, Lydon, and DeWitt—who *look and talk* like the white male authority figures with whom all students are familiar—validate my analysis made it easier for my students to accept what they heard. It does not flatter my ego, of course, to think that white male colleagues may have enhanced my credibility; on the other hand, since I want above all else to penetrate the wall of resistance that some students may have unconsciously erected to block out information about the dark, unpleasant "underside of American history," I do not mind using all the means at my disposal.

As we enter a new stage in our struggle for academic legitimacy and more widespread influence, our central task is to convince colleagues and nonminority students that we, too, are educators—educators competent to teach not only students of color but *all* students. Such a claim has to be made because during the last two decades we have justified the existence of ethnic studies programs primarily by arguing that we meet the special, unmet needs of students of color. Critics of such programs, meanwhile, have charged *ad nauseum* that the manner in which we have sought to meet those needs has been "nonacademic," too "political," and therefore unacceptable. But we must point out to them that what we are trying to do is but a variant of what the defenders of a liberal education argue it should do.

Faculty who believe in the importance of a liberal education try to provide an overview of the structure of knowledge and how scholars have divided it into different branches, each dealing with some segment of human experience or natural phenomena. They teach students how to think critically about the information they receive by examining the underlying values that influence the way such information is packaged. They encourage those coming of age in these times of flux to understand the constantly changing world in which we live and our relationship to it. They urge students to use the knowledge they gain to improve the quality of human life.

Faculty teaching ethnic studies, skeptics need to realize, can play a crucial role in a liberal education, though our contributions have so far not yet been recognized, much less rewarded. Our specialty is to make sense of the historical and contemporary experiences of nonwhite peoples in the United States. We broaden the university's offerings first by unearthing (through research and analysis) and then by imparting (through teaching) information not found in the regular curriculum. When we show students how to think critically, we often do so by suggesting competing perspectives on the world—points of view that have sometimes been suppressed because they challenge the status quo way of looking at things. While our stance may threaten colleagues who are insecure about their own standing in the academy, it can, and should, stimulate others to formulate dazzling new theories or promote collaborative efforts that lead to breakthroughs in the state of knowledge about certain phenomena. Hence, our presence within the university should be treated as an exciting addition, not an inconvenient political necessity. Finally, when we give students tools needed to enable them to make the world better, future generations benefit. If those of us who have taught ethnic studies for many years did not believe all this to be true, we certainly would not have devoted the best years of our lives to developing the field.

Notes

1. The University of California, one of the largest public university systems in the world, consists of nine campuses located at Berkeley, Davis, Irvine, Los Angeles, Riverside, San Diego, San Francisco, Santa Barbara, and Santa Cruz. With the exception of the San Francisco campus, which is a medical school, all the other campuses are comprehensive, research universities, offering the B.A., B.S., M.A., Ph.D. and a variety of professional degrees in a wide range of subjects.
2. The University of California, Santa Cruz, does not have grades. Rather, instructors must write a "narrative evaluation"—ranging from a few sentences to more than a page (single-spaced)—describing and assessing the work each student has done during the quarter. This is a time-consuming task that not all faculty enjoy doing.
3. Philip Kan Gotanda, "Visions of an Asian American Writer," National Asian American Telecommunications Association workshop, San Francisco, 3 December 1988.
4. Kenneth Clark, *Dark Ghetto* (New York, 1965), 75.
5. I borrow this term from Carol Nagy Jacklin, "Feminist Research and Psychology," in *The Impact of Feminist Research in the Academy*, edited by Christie Farnham (Bloomington and Indianapolis, 1988), 99.

Questions

1. What are some of the reasons that Chan appreciated her Asian American Studies courses serving as "ethnic enclaves" for Asian American students?
2. In response to a sudden rise in student enrollments, Chan wonders, "[h]aving worked so hard to get an ethnic studies requirement established, was I not morally obligated to take all the students who desired to enroll . . . ?" Do you think that Chan was morally obligated to take *all students?* Explain.
3. How does Chan make sense of "Asian American" as "a defensible and meaningful analytical category"? In other words, what does she claim that most, if not all, Asian Americans share in common?
4. How does Chan distinguish ethnic studies programs from counseling groups?
5. According to Chan, why did the influx of white students into her Asian American Studies course pose such a complex pedagogical challenge?

6. How did Chan transform her teaching in order to respond to this challenge?

7. Chan offers a few "different perspectives that can be used to study minority groups." Which of these perspectives does she endorse? Why?

8. What are Chan's goals for ethnic studies courses that enroll a large number of non-minority students?

9. According to Chan, what roles do ethnic studies programs and ethnic studies faculty play in a liberal education?

"Chicana! Rican? No, Chicana-Riqueña!" Refashioning the Transnational Connection[1]

Angie Chabram Dernersesian

Yo soy tu hij[a]/I am your daughter
de una migración . . . /from a migration . . .
ahora regreso, Puerto Rico . . . /Now I return, Puerto Rico . . .
por uno de tus/through one of your
muchos callejones./many passageways.[2]

Following in the tradition of alternative ethnographies which self-consciously reference situated knowledges, global travels, and the reflexive commentary of a socially constructed author-coproducer, I begin by explaining why I chose to speak about transnational identities within Chicana/o discourse in the manner described in the title. In reality, I must admit that the explanation became the paper, that this paper displaced another one referencing a transnational connection with México. While it could be stated that I willfully entered into a forbidden space by seriously interrogating *why* I was expending my intellectual and physical labor in a particular manner when academia leaves one so little room for doing so, I had no way of knowing that once I elaborated the rationale, I would enter another forbidden space: an unsanctioned transnational migration within Chicana/o discourse.

I am referring to a transnational migration: Chicana-Riqueña!, which intersects with México, which crisscrosses Chicanas/os in the contemporary world order, and which I believe should be engaged, at least considered, if the Eurocentric bent of multicultural paradigms is to be newly challenged. From within the field of Chicana/o studies this type of interrogation is timely because Chicanas/os are assuming their founding discourses in a critical fashion, as discourses which have "not only liberated us, but also gagged and disempowered many of us," to extend the language of Anzaldúa.[3] This endeavor is also relevant for a feminist theory which is deconstructive in character and as Barrett and Phillips point out, "seeks to destabilize,—challenge, subvert, reverse, overturn—some of the hierarchical binary oppositions . . . of western culture"[4] along the lines of the "local, the specific, the particular."

It is important to note that these thoughts on transnational identities[5] coalesced as I prepared to visit Los Angeles, an urban space known for its "Third World" extensions, glimpse of the future, and irreverent cultural and ethnic border crossings.[6] For me, the trip to "Our Lady of" Los Angeles offers more than a delicious and much awaited escape from the heart of agribusiness and the grip of the ivory tower "*al norte*" (to the North)—it is also a connection with my past, my family, and with a strategic body/*cuerpo* foregrounded in the area: Chicana/o studies. Not surprisingly, what is examined in this entrance into the field is a particular claim to representation, for it is within this slippery territory that I labor along with many others refashioning fractured identities and community linkages, retracing critical histories, and reconfiguring social and political geographies. Given this context, it should not come as a surprise that the autobiographical should be foregrounded within this consciously assumed inquiry-turned-paper, because, to a large extent, that's what Chicana/o studies claims to be, a self-representation, a conscious and strategic doubling of oneself and each other, a way of affecting not only the content but also the relations and politics of representation.[7]

In this paper I choose to register my own autobiographical impulses, the ones that complicate earlier schemes of Chicana/o identity, the ones that prefigure the kinds of transnational multicultural linkages anticipated in Chicana/o Latina/o, a problematic, yet forward looking attempt to forge semantic linkages between peoples and cultures of the Americas, here and there. Examining these kinds of transnational linkages interrupts traditional multicultural constructions, which revisit melting-pot theories of assimilation in an effort to ward off a presumed "tribalism"[8] and/or apprehend ethnic difference through simplified relations between dominant and subordinate groups without accounting for the differences between them, for the complex ways in which they negotiate these differences in daily life.[9]

*   *   *   *

The seeds that generated the thoughts for this paper were planted while I was on a postdoctoral fellowship at the Chicana/o Research Center at UCLA. Shortly after having made the acquaintance of a colleague and delivering to him the familiar Chicana/o salutation: a mode of opening up discourse around a narrative of one's origins, he responded to me: "Chicana! Riqueña? You aren't a Puerto Rican, you're a Chicana!" To be sure, this bothered me for I had voiced my plurality as a way of formulating a connection, not a disruption. Implicit in his statement is the idea that I had to be one or another, a Chicana or a Puerto Rican, but not both, certainly not a hybrid, hybrids aren't authentic, they have no claim to a fixed set of ethnic categories. Implicit in the statement is the idea that I might pass for a Puerto Rican in appearance, but no one could seriously mistake me for a Puerto Rican. At least no one who knew Puerto Ricans, no one who could really distinguish between Latinas/os, no one who could identify specific Latina/o roots.

I didn't talk like a Puerto Rican, I had never lived in New York or on the Island, *everything* about me spoke Chicana! That is a particular rendering, a refashioning of Chicanas/os along singular Mexican/American lines. The fact that I was raised single-handedly by a Chicana from El Paso, Texas, grew up in La Puente, California, lived in Occupied México and not Occupied Boriquen. . . . The fact that I had reconstituted myself through strategic Chicana revisions of the nineties. . . . The fact that I taught Chicana/o studies at Davis. . . . All of this only served to reframe my identity within this unitary mode of Chicana/o.

Since by this I was made akin to a card-carrying Chicana, there was no question about my Chicana*ness,* no dispute about this being a problem, about being on the *inside* of that representation, hence the exclamation point. The problem was with the selected ethnic equation, the particular framing of Chicana, the Rican who intersected it, the Rican who spoke to a continuity and a difference simultaneously, the Rican who interrupted the socially acceptable polarity, the mode of writing Chicana/o history, the mode of experiencing Chicana subjectivity, the mode of drawing "American" relations. In retrospect, I know I was being challenged like other Chicanas/os know they are being challenged when we are called *pochas* (half-breeds) and not *Méxicanas, marxistas y feministas* and not Chicanas, and inhabitants of the *United States* of America instead of inhabitants of the other America. The one José Martí termed, *"Nuestra América"*/*"Our America"* to retain the plural character of this geopolitical space.

Yes, I had been administered the acid test which would confirm a particular claim to authenticity, and in all honesty, this type of ethnic containment was commonplace. However, I wasn't about to masquerade as a Puerto Rican national or a Nuyorican, to engage in the business of inventing ready made identities the way Chicano nationalists did when they celebrated a glorious Aztec past with questionable relations to the present, but neglected to map vital relations with contemporary *indígenas* and other local underrepresented groups. I was, after all, a Chicana-Riqueña, a particular type of Chicana-Riqueña, a West Coast one with a Chicana-Méxicana foundation. I had no patent on the identity or the multiple ways of assuming this identity delivered by histories, social experiences, and human subjects. And to be fair, I wasn't being singled out, it was not as if I hadn't heard similar things about being Mexican—that I wasn't really a Mexican either because I was a second-generation Chicana, because my mother had grown up in El Paso and lived through the aftermath of her parents' migration into the United States as a result of the violence associated with the Mexican Revolution.

For years I had witnessed Central Americans, Latinas/os, even Spaniards/ *Españoles* joining the ranks of the Chicana/o movement, consciously assuming a Chicano political identity and strategically glossing over their ethnic and cultural distinctions, and being expected to do so for a chance to join in a forge an alliance, *una relación con la causa chicana/o* relationship with the Chicana/o cause. But they were not alone in this endeavor, there was already a blueprint for containing ethnic differences engraved in important documents such as in the epic poem/book *I am Joaquín/yo soy joaquín*,[10] where the speaking subject infers that *la raza:* Méxicanos, Españoles, Latinos, Hispanos, and Chicanos; Yaquis, Tarahumaras, Chamulas, Zapotecs, Mestizos, and indios, are all the same because of *his* authenticating universal discourse of the Chicano.[11] This masculine construction in and around whose body and social location and ideological purview these particular multiethnic constructions converge and are diluted, can be read as a "Chicano" rendition of pluralism although it is framed within a nationalist perspective that opposes assimilation and white "melting-potism." Artistic representations of *mestizaje,* in which the Chicano/ male/*mestizo* is framed on the one side by the conquistador and on the other by the *indígena,* making *mestizaje* the preferred ethnic construction, have furnished a way also of containing ethnic pluralities within brown masculinities.

Even today this model of *mestizaje* presupposes a confluence, based on equal mixtures, with the Chicano as the confluence and the other two, the indians and the *españoles,* as the tributaries. This type of *mestizaje* is the age-old political embodiment of the Mexican national who has traditionally occupied this central space and is the subject of contention by many *indígenas* for whom *mestizaje* means inequality, a concerted dilution of indianness, and partnership with the Mexican State. Yet, this "native" multiculturalism has gained much currency among Chicana/o and Méxicana/o writers because, as Rosaura Sánchez points out, "writers such as Octavio Paz and Carlos Fuentes have made a fetish of *mestizaje,* attributing to this notion essentialist monocausality to explain Mexican identity and history." She explains that:

> [F]rom this we are to understand that the struggle between warring Spanish conquistadores and hermetic, stoic Indians is ongoing in the blood of all Mexicans, a mixture that explains not only the contradictory national character but even problems in socioeconomic development. *Mestizaje* then serves all too conveniently to explain away a multitude of economic, political, and social sins. The manipulation of essentialist discourses like *mestizaje* is thus another hegemonic strategy which we need to disarticulate and reject, just as in the United States, notions such as the "melting pot" of American culture need to be debunked.[12]

Yet as Sánchez points out, far from rejecting these ideas around *mestizaje,* Chicana/o writers have privileged them within essentialist discourses, "unwittingly perhaps repeating Mexican hegemonic discourses which have become, to a degree at least, part of the dominant political rhetoric there and served to distort and obfuscate the oppression and exploitation of thousands of Mexican Indians."[13]

For those seeking to reference the contemporary social realities and new ethnicities that mark a fully transculturated context, this type of native multi-culturalism has little to offer. Given the prevailing ethnic absolutism which marked so much of the thinking around issues of identity and subjectivity within Chicana/o discourse, it is not then surprising that aside from the unsat-isfactory discourse of *la raza,* there are so few possibilities for referencing the kind of "local" transnational plurality with which I was contending at UCLA within an already constituted body of Chicana/o discourse.[14] In its authorita-tive renditions, this discourse is largely fashioned around a Mexican-American binary, only disrupting this model occasionally with cultural productions reg-istering Latino metanarratives: border crossings in other geographical direc-tions that often maintain the interpellated ethnicities at a comfortable distance from one another.[15] Within dominant productions, the situation is worse since these groups are either artificially polarized or else blended into an unrecog-nizable mass.

It is ironic that while we live in a period which prizes the multiplicity of identities and charts border crossings with borderless critics, there should be such a marked silence around the kinds of divergent ethnic pluralities that cross gender and classed subjects within the semantic orbit of Chicana/o. So powerful is the hegemonic reach of dominant culture that fixed categories of race and ethnicity continue to be the foundation, the structuring axis around which Chicana/o identities are found. Few are those who have cut through the nationalist or pluralist registers which promote an "all-or-nothing approach" to writing the intersections between underrepresented transnational ethnic groups and their heterogeneous social movements towards one another.

I am the first to admit that to modify this scenario in ways that do not sig-nal complicity with the nullifying gestures of the dominant culture is to enter a territory where strategic maneuvers are required at every turn, especially given the different kinds of multicultural scenarios that are present within the na-tional context and implicate Chicanas/os in competing ways. Yet the cost of not confronting the new ethnicities that frame Chicana/o in 1994 is very high, for it is to accept what is seemingly unacceptable from a Chicana/o studies viewpoint: that we are not only unable, but also *unwilling* to engage the social panorama, the community, the *reason* for Chicana/o representation. For even though an academic Chicana/o discourse may lag far behind the continual re-furbishing of global transnational identities in fashioning particular ethnic sub-jects, social reality has not; it is speeding ahead as the geopolitical boundaries of this territory extend north and south in an unrelentless march towards the twenty first century. And Los Angeles has led the way in this regard. There, if anywhere, the binary structure which manages distinct cultural and ethnic groups is destabilized within the social formation by a series of mixed racial and ethnic identities that speak to the wide range of possibilities that frame Chicana/o:

Chicana/o African-American; Chicana/o Asian-American; Chicana/o Native American; Chicana/o Central-American; Chicana/o Latin-

American; Chicana/o white; Chicana/o Middle Eastern; and the list goes on, breaking down the familiar blocks that follow the term, Chicana/o here, expanding beyond them with such configurations as Chicana/o Ukrainian, Chicana/o Armenian, Chicana/o Indian.[16]

I am referring to the new ethnicities of this generation,
to our relatives,
to our forebears,
to ourselves, *a nos otros*
to the *human panorama* across which we experience and socially construct our identities,
to the *unacknowledged* generations silenced by ethnic absolutism of the Mexican-American binary.

Can we afford to keep us/them within an ethnic closet? How will we/they write our/their herstories and histories and draw a connection to the past? To an alternative tradition of resistance and contestation? It seems to me that we/they have no choice: we/they must break out of the prisonhouse of nationalism if we/they are to engage our/their socially intersected ethnicities "on the inside." And this is, of course, only a narrow reference to "ethnicities," a category which itself is problematic if not recoded in a critical fashion because, historically, this term does not address any number of other pluralities at work in the formation of socially constructed identities. Instead it tends to subsume them into an essentialist frame that promotes a notion of Americanness that survives by an imaginary notion of the nation as a unified cultural community, "by marginalizing, dispossessing, displacing and forgetting other ethnicities."[17]

I do not recall this context as a way of reinscribing racialized ethnic categories as primary, nor as a way of reinventing the primacy of race through an acknowledgment of another hybridity: Chicana-Riqueña. Neither do I seek to expand the circumference of an oppressive nationalistic mode of writing Chicana/o identity, by unproblematically adding Caribbean or Central American or Latin American linkages to it, by making the fatal move into an unmarked collectivity. This Chicana-Riqueña frame is a social identity constructed through any number of experiences and discursive practices that extend beyond what is illustrated here by way of an introduction; it intersects with Chicana/o in any number of ways implicating not only race and ethnicity but also gender and class. Thus it is susceptible to competing modes of interpretation, themselves changing and intersected. Rather than inscribing monocausality, a one-dimensional view of oppression, it forecasts an articulation of other intersected and overlapping categories.

I appeal to this framing of social identity as a way of opening up a discussion around "the diversity of identities within ourselves and our communities,"[18] and as a way of acknowledging the transnational perspectives which must be figured into a more "diverse concept of ethnicity" which "is theorized through differences: the relations among and between different social groups" and which *does* recognize the role that an alternative reframing of the discourses of national origin can play in contesting the dominant notion of ethnicity which has coupled itself "with nationalism, imperialism, racism, and the state."[19] Instead of seeking recognition of Chicana-Riqueña identity through a logic of exceptionalism, one appeals to unique circumstances: the important struggles for self- determination within the "belly of the monster" which bring Chicanas/os and Puerto Ricans into an important political convergence, I appeal to the Chicana-Riqueña modality because of its significance for an alternative mode of writing social identities and agencies within the larger context in which we live as we approach the year 2000 in the purview of the so-called "New World Order."

Within this fully transculturated reality, where newspapers forecast an unprecedented browning of California (according to the U.S. Census Bureau, 36 percent of the ten million immigrants estimated in California in the next quarter century will be Latino[20]) and where even the governor has launched his infamous anti-immigrant rights campaign, doubling his forces with liberal democrats and an angry constituency and creating hysteria over *their* borders and *our* numbers, there is little doubt that the subordinated ethnic pluralities to which we are being partnered are *here* in unprecedented numbers. There is little doubt that these socially constructed identities are being worked out in ways that beg for a rethinking of the politics of one's location and one's contestation/*una respuesta* as well as a refashioning, perhaps even the coding of a new critical language to reference alongside, between, and through Chicana/o.[21] Compared to the current scenario, the largely simplified Mexican-American dilemma that was the staple of a nationalist ideology which combatted Anglo-Saxon purism might seem manageable enough, easily referenced and consumed, and not at all like the complex relations inscribed through the hyphens above. However, that is until we begin to deconstruct a state generated *Mexican* identity, claim its absented presences: the underrepresented multiethnic communities *en México,* and voice the other intersected ethnic pluralities that link us to the *American of the Americas.* And that is until we attempt to forge our complex historical relationships to both sides of the deconstructed binary.

In my own case, I was motivated along this line of thinking, not only by the heterogeneous social panorama and my unspoken circumstance, but also by the children, the ones who are well on their way to adulthood and to forging cultural and political identities. I am referring to those who live well out of the limits proscribed by Chicana/o discourse and its traditional notions of "*mestizaje.*" In particular, I am motivated by my nieces and nephews, the sons and daughters of my brothers and sister,[22] who, like me, have counterparts with Mexican Puerto Rican linkages. I am referring to siblings who *did* grow up on the island, who *do* speak like Puerto Ricans, and who are rarely mistaken as Mexicans or Chicanas/os. This situation is not all that unique; it may well be the norm. While these types of social identities have not occupied a strategic place within Chicana/o discourse, there is no reason why they should not.

Given this context, there is no reason why the Puerto Rican, for instance, should be othered as *another* within this space, where historic social and ethnic intersections have been prominent at least at the symbolic level, where even the Spanish and Yankee colonizers have earned recognition amidst a critique of the violence that their conquests incurred. Within Chicana/o discourse, assuming a claim to representation means staking out a territory based on historical and political entitlements. This claim involves a strategy of reversal commonly activated by Chicanas who contest exclusion within mainstream and alternative sectors. From this vantage point, the counterposition: Chicana-Riqueña is a response to those who would silence the pluralities marking alternative subject positions and histories. It is a counterposition to those who would suggest that the intersected Riqueña (and by extension, the African-American or the Native American or the Asian-American) was/were not there: *aquí* (here), and that therefore their/our intersected herstories and histories—local or global—should not be written within, throughout, or across Chicana/o.

This position involves a passionate form of "talking back," "*lanzando la palabra*," throwing the word back like you would throw a rock. This speech intersects with a tradition of defiance that extends beyond the dualistic limits of resistance inscribed by the ballad of the border hero who negotiates a political boundary between México and the United States, and it entails an interrogation of socially-accepted subject positions that do not script the relations between underrepresented ethnic groups. To throw the word back in this particular case (Chicana-Riqueña) can be construed as a response to the original ethnic dislocation and absolutism contained in the violent phrase: "You're not a Puerto Rican!,"[23] a response with an alternative mapping of an ethnic ancestry, one that I refashion on the basis of a partial life story rendered in the tradition of the *testimonio*/testimony with the *contestación* (answer and contestation): Who?

Who has the right to deny me this ethnicity, a particular history, mediated by the contemporary experiences of rupture, conquest, migratory cycles, and divorce? Who dare tell me that my first and most formative experiences with collectivity didn't constitute a cultural identity worthy of a presence and a place within a Chicana/o genealogy of difference? Who could dispute the fact that my *abuelos*/grandfathers, the one who cut lawns in El Paso and the one who taught women on the island, weren't both my *abuelos?* Who could dispute the fact that María, who migrated from Arecibo to Monterey, California, and Chavela, who migrated from Chihuahua to El Paso, Texas, would not anticipate a kind of transnational migration that their granddaughters would consciously assume generations later as a way of tracing different subordinated ethnic ancestries and cultural identities denied to them through the state-sanctioned borders of t.v. and public education? Those identities that complicate the Chicana-Riqueña frame many times over with other hyphenated spaces filled with four or five transnational migrations through nation states and occupied territories that share an uneven distribution of the wealth of the globe.

Who would erase my *tía,* my wonderful Puerto Rican aunt turned Chicana-Riqueña in the seventies, she who modeled a Chicana/o studies identity for me and provided a much-needed path from literature to Chicana/o studies? Who would censure the life histories of all of those Central Americans, Puerto Ricans, and Latinas/os who are in Chicana/o studies classes, calling themselves Chicanas/os in the tradition of my *tía*?[24] Those students who live a strategic connection between different histories and peoples, a connection that is often relegated to the private realm or the back burner as exclusionary and ready made notions of Chicana/o are consumed within the academy.

Will these transnational migrations through Chicana/o be written? Or will they be perceived as ripping away at the core of Chicana/o studies, a domain being contested under the deconstructive insights of gender and cultural studies and where the glue that is generally accepted as "holding it all together in spite of it all" is often a specific notion of race or ethnicity? Will the tensions that mediate political alliances and/or ruptures between Chicanas/os, Méxicanos and other Central and Latin American groups be silenced within the age-old multicultural discourse of Chicanas/os? Will we disseminate the impression that the inherited notion of "*mestizaje*" is a "natural" phenomenon and not a discourse? That this framing of the mixture is at all desirable—that it should not give way to others—just because there exist shared histories among Chicanas/os, Latinas/os, and *indígenas* referencing colonialism and imperialism and which also inscribe important differences that are often repressed by native multiculturalisms.

Will we insist that this type of multiculturalism is enough to usher away the tensions between Chicanas/os and any other Latinos or Hispanos? Especially between Chicanas/os and their hyphenated Latina/o-*indígena* coalitions, and those who dispense with this intersected group because of its problematic relationship to Spanish-speaking communities and linkage to colonized nations or tribes, because the Chicana/o denomination deliberately strays from the Hispanic ethnic flock by attaching specific political conditions and ideological sequences to the notion of ethnic identity. Or, finally, because Chicanas/os, Méxicanas/os and the rest are a majority of working poor to be contended with locally, to be assisted and joined in alliances and life-long commitments?

These kinds of problematic situations emerge when native multiculturalisms fail to account for how Chicanas/os are impugned because of their bilingual expressions, their filial relationship to a territory annexed by the United States, and are accused of being alingual or illiterate because their particular code of Spanish is not the official language in this region and is not reaccentuated by the dominant form of linguistic capital: Euro/Their-American. Reinscribing a brown smorgasbord is a risky business, not only when Central Americans, Latin Americans, or Cubanos are added to the equation; multiple tensions also emerge when Chicanas/os are unproblematically partnered with Méxicanos along an essentialist transnational route, without consideration for the disruptive influences of history, class, race, or gender. As Rosaura Sánchez points out, "representation on the basis of national origin alone continues nonetheless to be unidimensional and to bracket other forms of oppression and exploitation in society." She continues:

> There is an excellent antidote to this essentialist discourse, a practice that shatters all notions of collectivity or identity purely on the basis of

national origin. And that practice is interactional, requiring only that one come in contact with upper-class Mexicans. It is then that the myth of a shared cultural identity goes up in smoke for Chicanos, who at that moment experience the same class-based rejection to which they are subject in the US.[25]

This is not to suggest that, for example, the children of those who most vehemently promote linguistic purism (in terms of Spanish or English) and other class-based attitudes from a position of social and economic privilege aren't also capable of partaking in the type of racial discrimination launched at Chicanas/os once they cross the border. It is this type of a convergence that has often led Chicanas/os into multicultural paradigms that only promise to exclude them down the road along with many others. As a way of censuring the native element over here, institutions of dominant culture frequently anchor transnational "hegemonic" multiculturalisms under the leadership of a foreign-born and socially-privileged Spanish-speaking elite.

By invoking these examples, I do not wish to undermine the histories of those working-class Central Americans, Puerto Ricans, and Latinas/os whose life histories and social conditions converge strategically with Chicanas/os and who bring important lessons of resistance that are often ignored by Chicana/o nationalists who walk a more separatist and exclusionary path even while appealing to global notions of *"la raza."* I offer these examples as a way of demonstrating the complex relations that are to be negotiated between those whom government documents loosely refer to as "Hispanic," "Spanish," or "Latino," as if they all shared the same social, cultural, and ethnic characteristics, and as if they all sought natural coalitions with one another. All too often predominant multicultural paradigms sin by virtue of casting these social constituencies as homogeneous elements which only encounter difference when relating to other subordinated ethnic groups (that are not Spanish-speaking) or when coming into contact with dominant ethnic groups in the United States. This kind of faulty thinking has important repercussions because, without accounting for their differences, it is impossible to comprehend, for instance, why some Chicana-Riqueña coalitions are desirable within an alternative subject position recording intersected political agencies while others are not. The same holds true for other Chicana/o Latina/o, Latina/o Chicana/o connections. Marking these types of positionalities within identities is not entirely new to Chicana/o discourse where, from the very beginning, lines were drawn between Chicanas/os and Mexican-Americans, those who claimed the subordinated ethnicity and the benefits to be reaped from Chicana/o struggles and Chicana/o sufferings but not the politics inscribed in these divergent identities or the controversial mode of self-naming that still raises eyebrows. The difference is that native multiculturalisms have rarely been scrutinized, thus these amorphous essentialist constructions of race and national identity prevail.

If it is true that the differences among and between Chicanas/os and Latinas/os are commonly factored out of predominant multicultural paradigms, it is also true that within these paradigms, the different subordinated social and ethnic groups are often cut off from the *trans*national context so that crucial relations between competing nation states are factored out of the social panorama. The result is that these groups are deprived of the vital connections that make diverse ethnic communities part of a local as well as globalized cultures in contact. Forging the connections outside of the proscribed limits of national culture (at home and abroad) offers the possibility of apprehending viable transnational and multicultural linkages that have generally gone unexplored. This approach also promises to shed light on the complexity of the unconventional narrative of ethnic ancestry contained in Paul Gilroy's eye catching title: "It Ain't Where You're From, It's Where You're At."[26] "Where You're At" involves a necessary and oftentimes continuous reconfiguration of "Where You're From" or, as I see it, "Where You've Been." In the case of Chicanas/os, Méxicanas/os, and Puerto Ricans, for instance, this is particularly relevant, especially since the notion of the nation—"Where You've Been"—is itself under dispute. Thus, it is not only a question of navigating across water and borders and joining multiethnic communities over there, it is not only a question of charting immigration or reverse migrations towards México or Puerto Rico or other parts of "Aztlán." This type of recovery also involves contending with the realities of conquest; with having state-sanctioned borders being crossed over you and your ancestors; and with being labelled a legal or an illegal alien; and retaining a viable memory of another type of political geography, one that is sustained through strategic multicultural and multiethnic linkages.

Forging viable transnational linkages that operate in a dynamic manner also involves acknowledging the various forms of multiculturalism that coexist within a global culture outside of the U.S. national context and addressing a series of competing notions of what constitutes "multiculturalism." Most "multicultural" readers offer little insight into these "other worlds" and even within ethnic studies there is a tendency to focus on how multiethnic populations here experience their dislocations, their strategic relocations, instead of focusing on how these human movements are also inscribed at their points of origin, the local communities and nation states from which migration takes place. Within Chicana/o studies, a much needed project involves looking at how different Mexican and indigenous communities have incorporated Chicana/o political agencies and modes of writing culture, how multiculturalism takes place through a transnational Mexican register that also "talks back" to Chicanas/os through a Méxicana/o Chicana/o dialogue.

Recently, an important novel, *Paletitas de Guayaba* (*Guayaba Suckers*) by Erlinda Gonzalez Berry, staged some of these complexities around a female protagonist who repatriates herself to Mexico City through memory, journey, and sexual desire.[27] She travels as a way of reclaiming her connection to her past and making sense of her present. Rather than encountering the ready made, unproblematic, mimetic identities furnished by Movement narratives, her identity is contested at every turn. She struggles with the stigma of being called a *"pocha"* or a *"pochita"* (a female half-breed/outsider in its diminutive form, "little") by Mexican males who would deny her partnership with a national identity; she struggles with the stigma of being *"manita"* with Chicano nationalists who interrogate her Chicananess because of regionalism: her New Mexican affiliation; and she challenges received notions of New Mexican identity for being Spanish-centered and for ignoring the necessary Mexican-Chicana/o working-class connection.

In addition, she explores the sexual nuances that are attached to any number of these terms by competing masculinities (white, Méxicano, Chicano) who would rob her of her agency and reify her as a sex object. Assuming social relations within a world fractured by split identities means that she negotiates her relations with others through different subject positions, acquiring power over discourse through extensive monologues and definitions that must be rendered as a kind of pedagogy of resistance in light of the rampant ignorance about her mode of living out a Chicana/o Méxicana/o transnational experience. This also involves reformulating a number of heterosexual displacements moving from their space into her own space and connecting to other Méxicana subjects and icons.

While the novel does threaten to reinscribe a *mujer*/woman-centered essentialism and only tangentially deals with class, it reverses the strategy of multicultural paradigms that speak to a Mexican ancestry only as a way of figuring a distant past from the position of the United States. In fact, all too often the Mexican disappears quickly once the Chicana/o emerges within the annals of Chicana/o history. This does not occur in *Paletitas*, for the scene of the multicultural encounter is *there*, in México, and the protagonist does not leave her baggage behind once she arrives—she does not instantaneously receive a new fictitious identity and it isn't presumed that she'll be nourished in spirit automatically. She negotiates from the *inside* of a Chicana representation and these negotiations are often painful, ironic, sarcastic, and humorous. She travels through layers of contestation: this means responding to national dynamics, to regional dynamics, to gender dynamics, to racial dynamics, to sexual dynamics, to the politics of the Movement, and it means confronting the discourse of the brown female other: *"pochita"* at the point of origin.

A point where one is susceptible to insult, a point where one is disrupting another hegemonic construction of national identity, from the inside, as someone who carries different traces of Mexicanness that are foreign to accepted notions of *mestizaje*. This is a radically different location than that offered Joaquín, in the movement poem "I Am Joaquín," for his immersion is an adaptation of a ready-made epic of México's official history—it does not offer the possibility of a Mexican rejection, of someone else (*otro Méxicano*, for instance) talking back to him as he claims a Mexican space through various levels of *mestizaje*. Nor does it offer the possibility of someone offering a rampant distortion of who he is. This poem lacks the kinds of tensions involved in making coalitions that we see in *Paletitas* because Joaquín's act of poetic self-constitution involves identifying with the conquerors *and* the conquered and he is spared the kind of gender objectification experienced by Chicanas/os and Méxicanas within the national space and its masculinist orientation. By relocating the Chicana/o subject positions into México, *Paletitas* offers a kind of forum, a limited possibility of a multicultural paradigm that seeks to be participatory at many levels, at least to talk back, and where speaking across difference does involve risks, contradictory processes of reterritorialization, and where dialogues and even coalitions are temporarily imagined.

Berry's novel offers a glimpse of the types of transnational complexities that mark a Chicana Méxicano border crossing, and yet this is only one location from which such a transnational connection can be made. Multiple border crossings are possible outside of the text in every day life, where local transnational migrations from Chicana/o to Méxicana/o and back again take place all over the Southwest, in Michigan, Chicago, and other places as well. In the greater Sacramento area, for example, it is common to see Mexican farmworkers from specific regions in México settled in Chicana/o communities, marking out separate as well as shared terrains of coexistence, of difference and similarity. The kinds of transnational linkages which they refashion in daily life in the factories, in the fields, on the street corners, and in the schools, are rich but they are a far cry from the epic narratives that are commonplace in Chicana/o discourse. Suffice it to say these local connections rarely make their way into multicultural paradigms even when Mexican linkages are actively sought across transnational lines. It is even rarer to encounter alternative narratives of ethnic ancestry in Chicana/o discourse that chart transnational migrations towards two or more points of ethnic origin and geopolitical spaces.

The transnational migration through *Paletitas* offers an example of how one aspect of a transculturated connection can be written from Chicana/o to Méxicanas/os through an international register that reverses the terms of the old-style multiculturalism. An admittedly partial and highly interpretative glimpse of my own transnational connection to Puerto Rico offers a different example, a local example, of how another side of these connections can be traced through a narrative of ethnic ancestry which intentionally deviates from quantifiable bilingual constructs, pretending to measure how much one is one thing and not another and naively assuming that hybrid identities necessarily operate from stable or "equal mixtures" of two ethnic groups.

Drawing partially on Kobena Mercer's reinterpretation of Walter Benjamin's phrase, "I seek not so much as to rearticulate the past the way it really was," but "to seize hold of a memory as it flashes up at a moment of danger."[28] I do so at this moment where Chicanas/os are being interpellated by hegemonic discourses urging them to reject immigrants (their families), at a time when defensive nationalistic frameworks reemerge in the alternative sector, inscribing once again unsatisfactory multiculturalisms with which to counter the effects of capitalists and racism. However, in contrast to Mercer's articulation, this memory is woven through a representation of a family history, one of the many starting points for a critical elaboration of our imagined communities, and for rethinking the terms of the counter hegemonic struggles that have prevailed within Chicana/o.

I newly assume the term *retomo la palabra* in the manner familiarized in the Chicana/o oral tradition by stating that in my childhood I crossed the border many times, but not only the border to México. I never travelled to Puerto Rico, but it was there, *here,* it was all around me although he, the Puerto Rican national, my father, he was not there/here. I experienced Puerto Rico from a Chicana-centered household on Eldon Street, from a Chicana/o barrio of household and domestic workers and of commuters who worked in downtown Los Angeles and "made ends meet" to send their children to Catholic school.[29] At home, the connection was there in our *"platicas"* as we revisited the historical and economic junctions that brought our parents together that fateful day in the *parque* in El Paso, Texas, and later in Fort Bliss; the connection was there as we rotated *frijoles* with *habichuelas, arroz blanco con sopa de arroz, sofrito* with *salsa méxicana,* and the connection was there as we listened to Javier Solís sing *"En mi viejo San Juan,"* ("In my Old San Juan"), transporting us once again from Mexicanness to Puerto Ricanness with somber, passionate tunes, with the nostalgic desire of the immigrant who has left to "a strange nation" but dreams of the return, of the day he will search for his love, of the day he will dream once again there, in his "Old San Juan."[30]

Javier's refashioning of an island, vibrant in memory is nourished by a contradictory *despedida* (*me voy, adiós, adiós,*) and a return (*pero algún dia solveré,* but one day I'll return), one that I experienced, not as a Puerto Rican immigrant, but as a member of an extended family of Méxicana/o and Puerto Rican immigrants. For me the song was a return, a way of contending with historical, geographical, and emotional displacements, it was a way of making Puerto Rico present. And it *was* present beyond the nostalgia of the song, but it was present in an unusual form. It was there, coexisting, at times interrupting and intermingling, and it was spoken from the interstices of Chicana/o, irreverently recreating itself through a family narrative of Chicana/o discourse that would do for me what the Chicano movement discourse had not done and would not do. The Puerto Rican and the Chicana were partnered in the contrasting narratives of how my *papás* negotiated their ethnic and political differences, in how the linguistic imaginations of a first-generation bilingual Chicana and a Puerto Rican migrant, whose tongue was primarily Spanish, converged, many times only to diverge.[31] The Chicana and the Riqueña were partnered in the rest home where *mis abuelos*/grandparents worked in La Puente. There grandpa, Rafael Chabrán, gave *mi hermano*/my brother by the same name, his first lessons *en literatura* by recounting the necessary *declamaciones y repeticiones* and all the while smoking his *puro* (cigar) *cubano* and *saboreando* (tasting) the day he would return to Puerto Rico. Grandpa got his wish, he returned to Arecibo, but not before instilling in us grandchildren the desire to teach, something that we would instill in other *Chicana/o* subjects.

And, the Chicana-Riqueña narrative was reinscribed again, indelibly marked on my imagination through the narratives of divorce, the ones that are rarely talked about even as the gates of sexuality are opened wide and rupture is now preferred to continuity. I am referring to the narratives around *"la ruptura"*/the rupture *y "la sobrevivencia"*/survival, around how we would pull together and around how the *vecinos*/neighbors were an integral part of the process.[32] And, I am referring to all of the *mujer*-centered theories that were born at home about what this meant for a mother of four in the late 1950s and early 1960s. A mother who was indisputably on her own and the first in her family bravely to assume the Texas–California migration by then already in full swing, to make her own life work on her own terms before there was a socially acceptable feminism to legitimate her path. Through her cluster of narratives, she anticipated poststructuralist dynamics, carefully marking the absence/presence dynamic, a movement of continuity and discontinuity, which marked complex negotiations with this gendered Puerto Rican ethnicity. She did so through her narrative that framed *her* cry *"Si se puede"* within a Chicana–Tejana imaginary which insisted that it was *necessary* for women to work outside the home, that one need not be married to survive, that one (women) could do without men if that's what one wanted to do, and that the children of divorced parents need not be juvenile delinquents as was commonly assumed in those days.[33]

The first lesson in Chicana resistance, the most important lesson in self-fashioning, was framed around a dialogue between a Chicana and a Puerto Rican body, a body that encapsulated an individual and a collective. There she framed the contested identity with her own self-styled positioning, offering a daring and forward-looking conscious assumption of masculine and feminine roles and rendering an account of those aspects of Puerto Rican culture which she would pass on to her children. There the working class origins, her unforgettable heroic struggle for survival and historic entrance into the labor force as a factory worker were counterposed with another Puerto Rican's ascending middle-class lifestyle and privilege. Yes, class and gender are definitely a part of this ethnic equation, an inescapable part of this transnational ethnic connection, and this is, of course, not the only way of encountering them within a Chicana-Riqueña frame.

It does not cease to amaze me that it was *she* who nurtured a sense of Puerto Ricanness in me—she who had all the right to be a nationalist following the purist dictates associated with this politics, for she was a Chicana, she was not mixed in my way with the Riqueña.[34] In retrospect, it occurs to me that what she presented me with throughout one of the trajectories of our lives as mother and daughter was a pedagogy of Chicanas/os, a mode of knowing Puerto Rico from the inside of Chicana/o, a way of speaking across fractured ethnicities, a way[35] of initiating a dialogue among and between different ethnic groups. As an astute community theorist, she furnished a way of giving Puerto Rico and México another decisive connection, another border crossing beyond those which are naturally assumed when ethnic and cultural identities are automatically derived from the contexts of rapidly diminishing two-parent households, where intersected and subordinated ethnicities are believed to be represented equally within the immediate geopolitical space, and outside of the socioeconomic constraints of gender. While this narrative of ethnic ancestry cannot begin to approach the kinds of political negotiations that are required when these intersections (the hyphens) are marked by political identities: collective histories, specific programs for social change, and diverse subject positions enlisted in such a struggle, it does open a window into the kinds of irreverent ways in which people disrupt prevailing ethnic absolutions, stray from the chauvinistic gateways of racial and ethnic dominance, the ones Chicana/o discourse is theoretically committed to eradicating for ourselves and for others.

If it is true, as Stuart Hall has suggested, that we live in a period of a new cultural politics which engages rather than suppresses difference and which depends, in part, on the construction of new ethnic identities, then writing the repressed within Chicana/o discourse in terms that far exceed the bordered ethnicity described here by means of a personal illustration, is entirely appropriate at this period in time. A contemporary refashioning of subordinated and underrepresented transnational subjects from the inside of another politics of Chicana/o offers the opportunity to renegotiate the other pluralities silenced by the Mexican-American binary; to begin really to acknowledge the Indians who are contained by the PRI's[36] ideology of *mestizo* nationalism; to offer another ideological contestation to the state-generated metaphysics of Americanness; to activate dynamic ways of speaking across culturally and ethnically subordinated groups, particularly African-Americans, Asian-Americans, Native Americans, etc.—across those groups and their subgroups. The ones that cannot be so easily avoided now that they are on the inside of representation, *a diestra* and *siniestra*/on the right and on the left, and not divided by walls separating the major ethnic studies departments. These walls are there to remind us that if we really engage each other, we'll be fused together and all lose. Unfortunately, all too often the warning is heeded: It is not uncommon that individual ethnic studies programs have more to say to Spanish, English, history, or French departments than they do to each other.

Encountering the new ethnicities that frame Chicana/o can also be border crossings in the positive sense. Now that these ethnicities are intersecting Chicanas/os in a variety of ways, we have the opportunity to reconfigure *una relación* with our América, *desde a dentro*/from the inside, *desde afuera*/from the outside, *de otra manera*/in a different way, and to begin to problematize the pan-ethnic Latino essentialist identity which proposes an undifferentiated collectivity. This configuration stresses the Latin and not indigenous identities and nonchalantly fuses the political claim of Chicanas/os by constructing it along a singular ethnic axis. Without a linguistic path to guide the strategic relations within Latino, and to a much needed changing transnational project of Chicana/o, this configuration: Latino can offer little more than a dose of brown brotherhood, and this is a highly questionable effect.

However, by examining specific intersections, we can begin to answer crucial questions such as how Chicana/o Latino expresses itself in relation to particular social and historical movements. Engaging in this form of multiculturalism not only involves naming a collectivity, but marks its strategic relations and a connection with our América, *con nuestras historias chicanas*/with our Chicana/o herstories/histories, *con otras historias de Américas*/with other herstories and histories of the Américas, *que a veces se acompanan*/that at times accompany one another, *y otras veces se cruzan*/and at other times cross one another/*y se mezclan*/and mix with one another, *y a veces se separaran para el bien de todos*/and that at times separate from one another for everyone's good.

In encouraging the refashioning of unregistered transnational migrations through Chicana/o, I appeal to the idea of *un movimiento*/a movement, since the idea is central to Chicana/o discourse, which effects a number of strategic relocations through contested territories that are coded in the word *Chicana/o*. However, unlike many of my predecessors who are claimed as cultural gurus, I dispute the claim that says we can be anywhere or anyone we want be, that we can speak for anyone, acritically usurp anyone's position, because our ancestors traveled transnationally, because we cross the border with México both ways, because we cross the border internally in any number of different ways and with any variety of cultural and ethnic groups. To admit our *cuerpos*/bodies are actually crossed with multiple histories of domination that are not restricted to an original indigenous-Spanish/or a Mexican-Anglo *encontronazo*/crash[37] is positive, because, after all, there are many historical and political contexts which mark our borders and because there are international borders at every corner, and the corner has moved down to Central America.

The question is how do we encounter these borders within Chicana/o discourse. It is doubtful that we can encounter the new socially constructed ethnicities inscribed in Chicana/o from the founding narratives of Chicano or Latino which tend to be universal in scope and shadow a privileged selection. It is more likely that these identities will be encountered from particular social and historical locations, from situated knowledges, from ethnographic experiences of rupture and continuity, and from a complex web of political negotiations with which people inscribe their social and historical experiences and deliver their self-styled counter narratives. I do not think we need to celebrate the transnational movement for its own sake. Just having a transnational identity is not something to be romanticized or something only we have: *everyone* in the world has one, thanks to the global culture of communications and the far reaching grip of capitalist formations.

So the crucial question is: Whose transnational movements will we narrativize in Chicana/o discourse, and why? All the while remembering what happened with the North American Free Trade Agreement (NAFTA), remembering how the borders were crossed by two dominant cultures without regard for many on either side of the border. Maybe upon reflecting on the symbolic value of how NAFTA was countered by the *indígena* women who got their own informal economy going by using the Zapatista movement to sell their own wares (thus evading the U.S. corporate move to usurp most of the benefits by displacing Japan), it will be possible to gain insight into the kinds of limits and possibilities that can be afforded by transnational movements and identities. We might begin to see that transnational movements function along contrary axes of resistance and subordination, and thus choose a path of transnational resistance that is destined to fortify us, not disempower us. For after all, like many other theorists who walk a public path among our borders, we are in the purview of forging a counter discourse.

I am referring to a counter discourse that is capable of contesting *many* dominant cultures, including the ones that are supported by upper-class Latinas/os, who resist being interpellated by Chicanas and the new ethnicities they partner, who contest being made to share in the linguistic, social, and economic conditions of *campesinos, indocumentados,* and factory workers and their children who abhor the presence of a newly hyphenated Chicana/o Latina/o and its forecasting of solidarity. Until Latina/o is intersected by a political mediation inscribing resistance, it will continue to promote confusion and unexpected border disputes and it will deprive Puerto Ricans, Central Americans, Latin Americans, and Chicanas/os of a much-needed social agency that interrogates relations of power within systems that breed oppression, at home and abroad, through a number of social intersections.

Insofar as Chicana/o studies is concerned, this is *not* to suggest that we displace the idea of having a Chicana/o discourse or area of study, even when it appears that the job is too big and too complex and even when it is now common knowledge that Chicana/o studies can never be a home to us in the same old unproblematic mimetic way many naively once thought it was when it was written, Chicano. However, Chicana/o studies must be interrogated, it cannot remain the same. Chicana/o studies has oftentimes unwittingly reinforced an insular attitude by constructing its object of analysis: Chicana/o identity, Chicanas/os, on the basis of differences between dominant and subordinated cultures with little in the way of mapping the vital relations to other subordinated ethnic communities. It goes without saying that this is an artificial rendition of Chicana/o subjects; in reality people don't live in these types of compartments.

To be sure, these trends in Chicana/o studies are part of an overall strategic reaction to the way in which dominant culture has diluted ethnic cultural and racial difference or else privileged particular socioethnic identities, overlooking others in the construction of national episodes and historical events which inscribe the national body or community. For a recent example of this we can turn to representations of the L.A. riots which continue to be constructed through a black/white overdetermination which suggests that this difference is the *difference* which counts, even when the visual images revealed something else.

The academic context has also had its impact on this particular construction of Chicana/o subjects. Historically, Chicana/o studies programs have been intentionally subverted by watered-down ethnic studies requirements, garden-variety multicultural programs, mainstream "Spanish for Native Speakers Programs" that edit the voices of the natives to suit the tastes of colonial masters, and even postmodern frameworks that divorce Chicana/o studies of its political content as well as its relationship to lived Chicana/o Latina/o communities. Or, in the worst of cases, this procedure has led to tokenism or to editing out the Chicano subject altogether in favor of a Hispanic construction with the assistance of Spanish-speaking groups vying for institutional power from the position of economic privilege and a brown rendition of whiteness.[38] Here, the promise of plurality has been revealed to be the reality not of difference, but of absence, invisibility, and repeated marginality. While the effort to reinscribe a racial, ethnic opposition to dominant culture along nationalist lines may be constructed as an act of resistance to hegemonic discourse, this is destined to fail since this approach doesn't apprehend the nature of the pluralities that frame Chicana/o. In fact, this approach assumes that you need to confront a plurality: them, the dominant culture, with a singularity: us.[39] If the Chicana/o Movement has taught anything, it is that this is just not the case.[40] We should also be "wary of any attempt to seduce us to one identity" because, as Sánchez points out, "no single subject position defines us."[41]

Within Chicana/o studies it is not uncommon to hear that one of the greatest threats to this area of studies and praxis comes from *their* brand of multiculturalism, the one that circulates within the institutions of dominant culture. If this is true, then there is no doubt that a political refashioning of our own viable pluralities on the inside and next door is one of the most valuable and most important endeavors that can be undertaken. For what we would be doing is none other than providing the basis for a counterhegemonic mode of plurality and difference, one that doesn't cancel us out, one that engages us from every corner, and one that can settle the score with those who would deprive us of a global representation.

One of the ideas or premises behind multiculturalism is the notion that this configuration involves a mixture on the outside of us, that it is something that is not inside. Therefore it is not uncommon to hear university administrators counterpose their culturally-dominant multiculturalism with particular ethnic studies programs and even to assume an attitude while doing so, an arrogant attitude, accompanied by a desire for an expanse of territory. The territory of these programs is claimed under the erroneous assumption that because they don't have the plural inside them, and because they won't relinquish their singular underrepresented ethnic identity, then they need someone else to come in and do it for them, to forge global relations that look like the world does: intersected and not polarized.[42]

This line of thinking is plagued with faulty assumptions, although the maneuvers are skillful and this U.S. construction of multiculturalism does target weak spots. To begin with, Chicana/o does engage pluralities, it engages them at the very core within the social formation, even though this worldliness has never been able fully to achieve its potential as a counterhegemonic force within Chicana/o discourse and displace the real subtext of the hegemonic multicultural discourse. I am referring to the subtext that says that "we are all the same" so it doesn't matter if we are fused into "them." Inscribing an alternative type of transnational multiculturalism within the core of Chicana/o studies means fortifying these sites of study and practice in ways that are unusual, for it means further extending the scope of one's analysis, countering our presumed singularity with our historically verifiable pluralities, the ones that are intersected, and do engage positions from diverse fields of contestation. And, as I pointed out before, this counterhegemonic multiculturalism won't be encountered readily, nor in a vacuum, but from somewhere, from the social, political, and historical contexts in which we live, from the diverse subject positions and linguistic markers we have developed in our progressive movement toward self-representation and social reform.[43] This not only entails looking forward to an ethnically transformed California/America, but looking backward, too.

Seeing what happened to the subordinated ethnic pluralities within Chicana/o discourse, asking whether the Mexican-American binary really ever had the power to make our/their other social identities fully disappear. Armed with the idea that they hadn't, I returned to early Chicana/o texts and I found many references to other subordinated groups, even among the most national-istic of documents.[44] But these texts also framed a discourse of Chicana/o dif-ference which negatively marked relations to these groups, creating a distance from Chicana/o. Other social groups were there alright, but they had been can-celled out through a language of difference that stressed racial, cultural, and ethnic similarities between Chicanos and differences between this group and all others. There was no way to cross this "unbridgeable binary."[45] Within such a structure, how could we encounter the differences between Chicanas/os and the similarities they shared with other subordinate groups whose lives they would affect? It was impossible to do so.

This is why the project of critical cultural studies must be complemented with a timely and much-needed rearticulation of the varied social relations which mark the subordinated ethnic groups who are intersected through com-peting social registers and modes of political subjectivity that have only been tangentially explored here. This endeavor is not marginal to Chicana/o stud-ies, it is fundamental to this area, for at this historic juncture, Chicana/o stud-ies need not be "bound by fixed categories or histories, by the fictitious cate-gories of oneself and others, by the limits of traditional disciplines, by unchanging intellectual requirements. . . ."[46]

As many of us see it, "C.S. breaks with the equivalence between the disci-pline and the nation state, especially insofar *as it draws its object of analysis from diverse national settings.* . . . C.S. views *shifting social and ethnic borders as being central to its mode of apprehending divergent communities that refurbish and frame Chicana/o populations.*" Chicana/o studies can be a border crossing between Chicana/o and other underrepresented groups, a way of speaking about the internal and transnational connections between Chicanas/os and other peo-ples of the Americas.

Arriving at this type of an approach involves a significant complication of the current attempts "to recognize the plurality and diversity of actors and identities" at play in contemporary politics, in a period in which many of our cultural studies practitioners are also working against what Kobena Mercer calls "the race, class, and gender mantra."[47] According to Mercer, this mantra posits that "serial acknowledgment of various sources of identity is sufficient for an understanding of how different identities get articulated into a common project or don't."[48]

We also face the effective limitations of the current rhetorical strategies in which identities are articulated and "the challenge . . . to go beyond the atom-istic and essentialist logic of 'identity politics' in which differences are dealt with only one at a time and which therefore ignores the conflicts and contradic-tions that arise in the relations within and between the various movements, agents, and actors in the contemporary forms of democratic antagonism."[49] However partial our responses are to this incredible challenge at this point in time, we nevertheless count with a powerful legacy that inscribes a notion of dramatic change and intellectual growth; with community linkages that are fashioning our paths where academic and nationalistic roadblocks prevail; and with an area studies that has managed to retain the notion of intellectual growth premised on collaborative perspectives of thinkers, students, communities, and binational frameworks.

At this point in time, it is ludicrous to imagine that these challenges will be assumed only through Chicana/o studies, that our transnational identities also won't be refashioned through women's studies, Native American studies, Latin American studies, Latina/o studies, Puerto Rican studies, cultural studies, Asian-American studies, African-American studies, and gay and lesbian studies, and/or other geopolitical sites where alternative knowledges have emerged and promise to emerge. Considering the impact which the cultural and ethnic discourses of Chicana/o studies have had on the "politics of Chicana/o representation," considering the rhetorical and practical frames which have *re*limited many of the grass-roots struggles for Chicana/o studies departments and programs in California and the movements against the immigration backlash, this is a strategic location from which to refashion a transnational connection to ourselves and one another, and to contribute to a widening of imagined communities and spheres of contestation.

It is in this vein I posit that expanding the horizons of Chicana/o studies can subvert the question mark after the Rican and replace it with an exclamation point, a marker signalling "how it is possible to struggle" *beyond* the quandary of biculturalism, *beyond* the crossroads of two discordant cultures and arrive at "yet another border generation and a different pattern of migration and settlement,"[50] to the point of the repressed: the silenced and the discarded "we's" that we are.

Juan Flores suggests that Puerto Rican culture today is a culture of commuting a back-and-forth transfer. Chicana-Riqueña is then a refashioning of a transnational connection. It takes us from the Mexican to the Chicana/o; from the Puerto Rican to the Nuyorican to the L.A. Rican and back again through other sites of "mutually intruding differences."[51] To those sites occupied by people whose lives hang on the hooks of the question marks *¿allá, acá?* /there? here?[52] This is but a rearticulation of the other territories that are there to reclaim, for these are spaces between us, from where we draw borders, from where we speak to one another and struggle, and from where we migrate, commuting across transnationtional and multiethnic communities and cultural frameworks *de éste y del otro lada,* from this side of the political spectrum, from where we refashion a connection to Our/*Nuestra* América.

Notes

1. *A mi mamá:* Angeliña "Lita" Gonzalez Chabram, *a quien se lo debo todo, incluso esta etnicidad; a mi abuelo, Rafael C., que en paz descanse, que se conserve su memoria; y a mi comadre y amiga, Inés H. y a los que viven las otras caras de México desde estos callejones.*
2. This is inspired by a poem entitled "Nuyorican" by José Luis Gonzáles, quoted by Juan Flores in "Cortijo's Revenge: New Mappings of Puerto Rican Culture," in *On Edge,* eds. George

Yúdice, Jean Franco, and Juan Flores (Minneapolis: University of Minnesota Press, 1992), pp. 198–9, as a way of appealing to a third space of political and ethnic identification which marks a *mujer*'s/woman's counter discourse.

3. See Gloria Anzaldúa, "Haciendo caras, una entrada," in *Making Face, Making Soul*, ed. Gloria Anzaldúa (San Francisco: Aunt Lute Books, 1990). For another example of these trends in Chicana/o studies, see "Chicana/o Cultural Representations: Reframing Alternative Critical Discourses," special issue of *Cultural Studies*, eds. Rosa Linda Fregoso and Angie Chabram, 4, 3 (1990).

4. Michèle Barrett and Anne Phillips, "Preface," *Destabilizing Theory*, eds. Michèle Barrett and Anne Phillips, (Cambridge: Polity Press, 1992), p. 1.

5. Cultural studies critics have called for "transnational perspectives" from different contexts and intellectual traditions. See Kobena Mercer, "1968: Periodizing Politics and Identity," in *Cultural Studies*, eds. Lawrence Grossberg, Carey Nelson, and Paula Treichler (New York: Routledge, 1992), pp. 424–37 for an example of the usage of this concept in the black context; George Yúdice, Jean Franco, and Juan Flores, eds., *On Edge* (Minneapolis: University of Minnesota Press, 1992) for the Latin American context; and a forthcoming version of Rosaura Sánchez's pivotal essay, "The Politics of Representation in Chicana/o Literature," in *Chicana/o Cultural Studies: New Directions*, eds. Marío Garcia and Ellen McCraken (forthcoming).

6. I would like to thank Raymond Rocco for offering me the opportunity to present these ideas at UCLA and to offer the Chicana/o Research Center a belated thank you for supporting the production of the above-mentioned special issue of *Cultural Studies* and other projects.

7. I am indebted to Stuart Hall for this type of framing. See "The New Ethnicities," in *'Race', Culture and Difference*, eds. James Donald and Ali Rattansi (London: Sage Publications in association with the Open University, 1992), pp. 252–9.

8. For a discussion of the multicultural debate, see Wahnemma Lubiano, "Multiculturalism: Negotiating Politics and Knowledge," *Concerns* 2, 3 (1992), pp. 11–21.

9. Chandra Talpade Mohanty has argued for this type of cross-cultural work in her wonderful essay, "Feminist Encounters: Locating the Politics of Experience," in *Destabilizing Theory*, eds. Michele Barrett and Anne Phillips, pp. 74–92.

10. Rodolfo Gonzalez, *I am Joaquín* (New York: Bantam, 1972), p. 39.

11. Ibid., p. 98.

12. Sánchez, "The Politics of Representation in Chicana/o Literature," p. 17.

13. Sánchez posits this in relation to the essentialist discourse that prevails around *mestizaje*, continuing later on: "It is the discourse of mestizaje that is fetishistic because it posits the existence of a particular identity, a particular human nature based as much on blood lines as on posited cultural practices of past modes of production. Blood is posited as a carrier of cultural material which allows one to view the world in a particular way. . . ." But she also posits that: "[s]elf-representation on the basis of *mestizaje* and language, if viewed historically and dialectically rather than in an essentialist fashion, can undoubtedly play a counterhegemonic role in a country where the discourses of color and origin have been instrumental in our oppression and exploitation." Sánchez, ibid., pp. 17–18. Unfortunately, this dialectical view of *mestizaje* is rare in Chicana/o discourse where revisionist notions of José Vasconcelos' *La Raza Cósmica* dominate.

14. It is important to note that other types of transnational perspectives, other than the ones examined here, inscribed resistance through a political contestation aimed at curbing the effects of capitalism and racism. I am referring to the grass-roots movements which incorporated political philosophies from Fidel, Ché, and Fanon, in an effort to formulate alliances with Third-World liberation movements. This political current in Chicana/o representation did break away from the ethnic absolutism of nationalism, but it did not emerge as the authoritative discourse and it rarely incorporated issues of gender or the reality of local ethnic intersections in its purview.

15. One of the few journals to initiate a move against this grain and to popularize the Chicano Riqueña connection was the journal *Revista Chicano Riqueña* which offered an important comparative approach, fashioning a transnational objective across "Latino" borders: "a cross section of opinion through poetry, prose, and graphics of Latinos throughout the country who

proclaim their cultural heritage, examine their lives in the cities, and towns where they reside, and further enliven the telling of our historical presence." In an important issue, the editors clarify that the journal looks at the United States "from the perspective of the literature of the Latino minorities," taking positions "on our status in the U.S.A." They explicitly mention the heterogeneous populations affected by this circumstance, groups such as Chicanos, Méxicanos, Puerto Ricans, Cubans, Dominicans, and other Latinos living in the United States. As a response to mainstream celebrations of the bicentennial, the editors elaborate that the Revista Chicano-Riqueña serve as a forum "for clarifying the historical past, for proclaiming our cultural heritage," in a context where "our ancestors experienced the loss of their lands and patrimony, the invasion of their islands, massive forced migrations and even the flagrant imposition of colonial rule. . . ." See Nicolás Kanellos and Luis Dávila, "Preface," in *Revista Chicano Riqueña*, 4, 4 (1971), pp. 1–2. While *Revista Chicano Riqueña* anticipates an important coalition and did offer a forum from which a cross-cultural dialogue could be forged, this type of articulation does not inscribe the hybrid identities of today that are intersected not only by histories of colonialism but also by the dictates of gender and work in the so-called New World Order. However, analyzing the way the journal promotes multiculturalism is an important part of formulating an alternative vision of our cultural and ethnic relations.

16. It is not my intention to furnish a comprehensive list of the mixtures nor to suggest that all of these mixtures will be equally represented in a contested Chicana/o Latina/o *Indígena* identity that counters the hegemonic practices of dominant culture. Undoubtedly the diverse social, historical, and geographical contexts in which these identities are produced will determine how these new ethnicities are refashioned across different social registers. However, it is important to call attention to the problematic nature of these intersected identities as they are commonly scripted through the denominations: Chicana/o Asian-American; Chicana/o Latin American; Chicana/o African-American, according to the familiar groupings. As Hollinger has argued elsewhere, this move threatens to reinscribe an essentialist frame in that it refers to blocks of people and these blocks erase the diversity between the subgroups that comprise the block. By appealing to the Chicana Riqueña frame in this paper, I am targeting an internal diversity, offering a breakdown of the block Hollinger offers a conservative approach to the topic in "Postethnic America," *Contention*, 2, 1 (1992), pp. 79–96.

17. I have elaborated my critique on the basis of the insights delivered by Stuart Hall, Rosaura Sánchez, and Paul Gilroy. Hall explains: "I am familiar with all of the dangers of 'ethnicity' as a concept and have written myself about the fact that ethnicity, in the form of a culturally constructed sense of Englishness and a particularly closed, exclusive and regressive form of English national identity, is one of the core characteristics of British racism today." Hall, "The New Ethnicities," p. 256. Sánchez points out how "the discourse of ethnicity may in some cases be a way of sidestepping the more problematic discourses of race and class since the term is all-encompassing, used now as much to refer to European immigrant groups as to all underrepresented minorities." Sánchez, "The Politics of Representation in Chicana/o Literature," p. 16. Paul Gilroy adds another viewpoint by discussing how certain absolutist notions of ethnicity mask racism: "We increasingly face a racism which avoids being recognized as such because it is able to link 'race' with nationhood, patriotism and nationalism, a racism which has taken a necessary distance from crude ideas of biological inferiority and superiority and now seeks to present an imaginary definition of the nation as a unified cultural community." Paul Gilroy, "The End of Antiracism," in *Race, Culture and Difference*, eds. James Donald and Ali Rattansi (London: Sage, 1992), p. 53.

Notwithstanding his critique, Hall calls for a new contestation over the term "ethnicity," a contestation that involves "a retheorizing of difference, a more diverse concept of ethnicity, an ethnicity of the margins, of the periphery, which is not doomed to survive by marginalizing." He advocates a splitting away from the dominant notion which connects it to nation and race. Hall, "The New Ethnicities," pp. 257–8. Sánchez responds to this second characterization thus: "Hall suggests contestation on the basis of ethnicity, devoid of its connections to race and nation and linked to the concept of marginality or peripheralization, a discourse that would build on diversity and difference. . . . Hall's proposal then for 'freeing' ethnicity of its racial and

Third-World connotations fits in well with other models ... which advocate positing constructs of difference, otherness, diversity and pluralism as the basis for the creation of counter-hegemonic affinity groups. My problem with these proposals is that they displace exploitation and cleverly conceal class stratification. In fact these spatial models of periphery and marginality do not really constitute a threat to hegemonic discourses or to the dominant social and political structures of society . . . ." Sánchez, "The Politics of Representation in Chicana/o Literature," pp. 20–1. Sánchez's discussion of Hall deserves further attention than I can render here and it is not limited to a critique of this notion of ethnicity.

18. I am recasting Sánchez here.

19. I have revised Stuart Hall here according to the conditions of the context in which I work.

20. Cited in "Increasing Diversity in California," *The Sacramento Bee* (April 20, 1994), p. B4.

21. Raymond Rocco's description of the communities surrounding the urban core of Los Angeles is, in this sense, instructive: "in the area immediately surrounding the urban core . . . to the west, only a few blocks from the financial district, the Pico-Union area has been completely transformed into a Central American environment. Further to the south, around Figueroa and Martin Luther King Boulevards, neighborhoods have entire blocks populated by Mexican and Central American families. To the southeast are the cities of Huntington Park and South Gate, which went from being four per-cent Latino in 1960 to 90 per-cent in 1990. And, of course, to the east is the oldest and largest barrio of East Los Angeles, and to the northeast the Lincoln Heights and Highland Park areas which are over 70 per-cent Latino. Colombian communities have been established in neighborhoods around the corners of Third Street and Vermont Avenue as well as in South Gate, Long Beach, Huntington Park, Glendale. Cubans, Puerto Ricans, and Colombians have established a sizeable presence in the Echo Park and Silverlake area as well as immediately adjacent to Pico-Union. . . ." Fregoso and Chabram eds., *Cultural Studies*, p. 324.

22. You know who you are, Missy, Rhonda, Marissa, Rafael, Paco, and Gabriel.

23. I am very well aware that many Nuyoricans hear this upon returning to the island.

24. Or subverting the essentialist framing of Chicano with other hypenated intersections.

25. Sánchez, "The Politics of Representation in Chicana/o Literature," p. 16.

26. Paul Gilroy, "It Ain't Where You're From . . . It's Where You're At . . . : The Dialectics of Diasporic Identification," *Third Text*, 13 (1991), pp. 3–16.

27. Erlinda Gonzales Berry, *Paletitas de Guayaba* (Albuquerque: El Norte Publications, 1991).

28. Mercer quotes Walter Benjamin's phrase [1940], in "1968: Periodizing Politics and Identity," p. 427.

29. This is my interpretation of the order of things and it is but one of my interpretations. My account does not necessarily apply to anyone else and I do not pretend to speak for any other family members in recognition of the fact that they have their own memories of our imagined communities and their own rich ways of giving these communities style within discourse.

30. Javier Solís, "*En mi viejo San Juan*," *Sombras*. Audiotape. 1049, Caytonics, CBS International, n.d. The song was written by Noel Estrada.

31. Such as the times my *amá* would say "hi there" to her male friends and my *papa* would hear "hi dear."

32. I take this opportunity to thank these neighbors on Eldon Street for their support.

33. This page was discussed with her, but this is my construction and any economic gain that comes from this essay will go to her. There are many twists to this narrative that I will keep to ourselves in the tradition of Rigoberta.

34. It was as much a question of solidarity with her as it was the constraints of Chicana/o discourse that delayed my arrival into this type of a Chicana-Riqueña interrogation. But she taught me as she has always taught me that I could transgress that particular Puerto Rican border, that I could encounter a collective not bound by the same decisive ruptures, and that to do so was not a betrayal of my Mexicanness: my Chicananess, but rather an affirmation of its permeable borders. And, she paved the way for me at age 65 plus, when she finally boarded a plane and reclaimed *her* Puerto Rican relatives, met the extended family, and gave her received memories of Puerto Rico definitive forms, visual images. She even began her own self-styled

migration to Puerto Rico. Without my mother's historic revisions, my own subsequent trips to Puerto Rico would have been something quite different than what they turned out to be: part of a life-long and culturally-decisive experience.

35. Certainly this is not the only way to dialogue across ethnic borders and I do not mean to suggest that it is *the way* for all of us to do it.

36. The *Partido Revolucionario Institucional,* México's dominant political party.

37. *Encontronazo* is a term which contests the friendly multicultural encounter that is often used to describe Columbus and his conquest.

38. Kobena Mercer's proposal that "cultural difference was used as a means of fragmenting the emergence of a collective black identity" is valid for Chicanas/os even today, especially in Chicana/o studies, where it is not uncommon that university administrators deconstruct nationalist paradigms as a way of collapsing these programs and underfunding them. Kobena Mercer, "1968: Periodizing Politics and Identity," p. 39.

39. By using the plural "us" I wish to point out the contradiction in these terms.

40. It is common knowledge that it was the pluralities that gave the struggle its power, the strategically placed alliances with other political movements: Third-World liberation movements, the black civil rights movements, and the feminist movements, for example. However, the "pluralities" within Chicana/o bodies were often repressed as race took precedence over class and gender and Chicanas/os were constructed along the purviews of masculine collectives.

41. Sánchez, "The Politics of Representation in Chicana/o Literature," p. 29.

42. The *encargado*/one in charge to do this is generally someone who proposes to create an identity: a mode of multiculturalism, that no one can identify as being uniquely anyone's.

43. I have taken this idea of what I see as a critical genealogy from Mercer's retrospective discussion of 1968 ("1968: Periodizing Politics and Identity").

44. See, for example, Armando Rendon's, *The Chicano Manifesto* (New York: MacMillan, 1972). I discuss this topic in an essay entitled, "Out of the Labyrinth, into the Race," which will appear in a subsequent issue of *Cultural Studies* featuring Latinas/os in the United States.

45. For a discussion of how these binaries are constructed through the black context, see Mercer's essay, "1968: Periodizing Politics and Identity."

46. These quotes are extracted from our working document for departmental status of Chicana/o studies at UC Davis.

47. See Mercer, "1968: Periodizing Politics and Identity," pp. 425–6.

48. Ibid., p. 442.

49. Ibid., p. 425.

50. I am rephrasing a point made by Juan Flores, "Cortijo's Revenge: New Mappings of Puerto Rican Culture," p. 201, to accommodate this third space of ethnic identification.

51. Ibid., p. 201.

52. This is a point quoted by Flores from Luis Rafael Sánchez's "Air Bus," ibid., p. 201.

Questions

1. Why was Dernersesian bothered when her colleague said "You aren't a Puerto Rican, you're a Chicana!"?

2. What does Dernersesian mean by "hybridity"?

3. In what ways does Dernersesian consider her emphasis on hybridity a challenge to "predominant multicultural paradigms"? Do you agree with her analysis? Explain.

4. How does Dernersesian propose to forge "viable transnational linkages"?

5. Do you endorse Dernersesian's brand of "transnational multiculturalism?" Explain.

Section One: Suggestions for Further Reading

Asante, M. K. (1988). *Afrocentricity.* Trenton, NJ: Africa World Press, Inc.

Banks, J. (1995). Multicultural Education: Historical Development, Dimensions, and Practice. In J. Banks and C. M. Banks (Eds.), *The Handbook of Research on Multicultural Education* (pp. 3–24). New York: Macmillan.

Butler, J., and Walter, J. C. (Eds.) (1991). *Transforming the Curriculum: Ethnic Studies and Women's Studies:* Albany: SUNY Press,

Carnoy, M. (1988). *Education as Cultural Imperialism.* New York: David McKay.

Darder, Antonia (1991).*Culture and Power in the Classroom.* South Hadley, MA: Bergin and Garvey.

Deloria, Vine, Jr. (1973). "The Rise and Fall of Ethnic Studies." In M. D. Stent, W. R. Hazard, and H. N. Rivlin (Eds.), *Cultural Pluralism In Education: A Mandate for Change.* New York: Appleton-Century-Crofts, pp. 131–140.

Hu-DeHart, Evelyn (1993). "The History, Development, and Future of Ethnic Studies." *Phi Delta Kappan* (September): 50–54.

Schmitz, B. (1988). "Cultural Pluralism and Core Curricula." *New Directions for Teaching and Learning* 52: 61–69. University of Minnesota Press.

Vasquez, Jesse (1998). "The Co-opting of Ethnic Studies in the American University: A Critical View." *Explorations in Ethnic Studies* (January).

Section Two

Antiracist Multiculturalism

As noted in the introduction, antiracist educators work from the premise that racism is a systemic problem, and not simply the practice of bigotry, jingoism, or xenophobia by individuals. For antiracist educators, racism is not prejudice but oppression. In turn, as the selections in this section will indicate, the aim of antiracist pedagogy is to effect fundamental institutional change. Antiracism seeks to inspire collective political action and resistance to institutional racism.

In the first selection, "Overcoming White Supremacy: A Comment," bell hooks underlines antiracism's desire to generate collective political action. She writes: "While it is important that individuals work to transform their consciousness, striving to be antiracist, it is important for us to remember that the struggle to end white supremacy is a struggle to change a system, a structure. . . . For our efforts to end white supremacy to be truly effective, individual struggle to change consciousness must be fundamentally linked to collective effort to transform those structures that reinforce and perpetuate white supremacy." hooks' contribution also demonstrates the link between antiracism's goal of building solidarity and the liberatory pedagogy of Paulo Freire (whose influence on critical multiculturalism has been noted earlier in the introduction). hooks identifies antiracism's aim as expressing Paulo Freire's (1994) idea of education as the practice of freedom through the mutual development of critical consciousness. Like the Freirean philosophy of education, antiracism offers a view of education as the intersubjective unveiling and transformation of oppressive sociopolitical conditions. This effort can be described as a *critical humanist* agenda, because it enlists "all willing parties" regardless of race, class, and gender. hooks emphasizes this humanist thrust of antiracism by recalling the oft repeated story of Malcolm X who once told a young white college student activist that she had nothing to offer to the black power movement. Toward the end of his life, upon returning from his pilgrimage to Mecca, Malcolm

X recanted his response and called upon all activists to unite against racism and white supremacy. This is a significant parable insofar as it distinguishes antiracism from the more narrowly and internally focused oppositional pedagogy which emerges from Ethnic Studies Multiculturalism. Antiracism's critical humanism is expressed by hooks when she declares "If I commit myself politically . . . to the struggle to end white supremacy, I am not making a commitment to working only for and with black people, I must engage in struggle with all willing comrades to strengthen our awareness and our resistance."

As Christine Sleeter's contribution emphasizes, antiracism fulfills the need for multicultural education "to develop vocabulary and action strategies for addressing white racism and other forms of oppression. . . . Educators in general don't usually think in terms of collective political action to make changes . . . ." Sleeter argues that antiracism has the goal of destabilizing the normalized racist order of social relations by problematizing the political and economic systems that thrive within racist society. This is accomplished by identifying multicultural education "as part of a larger quest for redistribution of power and economic resources." Sleeter's contribution also offers a compelling criticism of those forms of "diversity education" that predominate within teacher preparation programs and, hence, in most schools. Sleeter shows that these "safe" initiatives offered by most teacher education programs stand in diametric opposition to those flowing from the foundational perspective of antiracism. Sleeter's critique indicates that these programs legitimize the tendency of white teachers to mute critique of racism by developing multicultural education practices that focus on (so-called) "global perspectives." While this approach may have its merits, it is often used as a veil to hide students from examining the deeply embedded racism that is at work in their everyday lives. For Sleeter, because they have been developed and implemented for and by white, middle-class, female teachers, these "safe" multicultural pedagogies are an example of the "white solidarity and silence about racism." This solidarity around white hegemony is akin to what contributor Robin Grinter calls the "White consensus." Sleeter sees this political "union" as a force to be contended with, given the fact that the teaching force remains overwhelmingly white (female) while "minority students" currently represent a majority in all but 2 of the 25 largest cities. Finally, Sleeter's unveiling of *white racial bonding* calls attention to the need for antiracist teacher education which "should be advancing strategies to address white racism: white control of most wealth, land and power in the nation." This move, Sleeter argues, would counter the tendency in teacher preparation to reduce racism to interpersonal relations rather than seeing these relationships as contextualized and defined by larger sociopolitical forces.

In his contribution, Robin Grinter also emphasizes the need to undergird teacher education with the goals of antiracism. For Grinter, this would empower teachers to effectively implement an antiracist education which involves "students in analysis of the whole school ethos and power structure, and in work to identify and remove racism from their educational institution." Grinter argues that effective antiracist education in schools will, in effect, trickle down from teacher preparation which exposes educators to those skills "that can enable students to recognize and dismantle stereotypes, deconstruct the ethnic studies view of the world, and reconstruct a more just view of society." Grinter, moreover, highlights the sense in which racism can best be described as an interrelationship between individual attitudes and systemic ideology: an interplay between the racist attitudes of individual members of a society and that society's ideology of white supremacy which legitimizes systemic exploitation of people of color. This context of racism explains why, on an individual basis, people tend to understand the devaluation of non-White lifestyles as natural. In his discussion Grinter is echoing the insight of bell hooks who suggests that the naturalness of racism shows "how all pervasive white supremacy is in this society, both as ideology and as behavior."

Grinter's contribution offers the most concise discussion of antiracism. He highlights the three central objectives of antiracism. First, Grinter writes, antiracism calls attention to the hegemonic ideology of monocultural white supremacy which legitimizes systemic exploitation of people of color. This critique of cultural hegemony forms the basis of an oppositional language game which represents a "rejection of the existing socioeconomic system and its power relationships." Second, Grinter confirms, antiracism understands itself to be the starting point for initiating a political movement in opposition to systemic discrimination. Again, this activist vocabulary reflects antiracism as a type of critical humanism, or a political philosophy that is grounded in the belief that racism is "an organizing principle of the social and political structure, closely linked to a system of class and other forms of discrimination that deny human rights." Finally, Grinter demonstrates, antiracism aims to achieve its goals by developing educational programs which are specifically antiassimilation. "Antiracist education aims, through learning processes that question the social structure and its basic assumptions, to produce activists against social justice. . . . This is the very reverse of assimilation. The White consensus is the problem. . . ."

In addition to offering a concise overview of antiracism, Grinter's contribution also highlights the extent to which antiracist education and multicultural education within the United Kingdom have been viewed as separate and distinct. While Sleeter's contribution makes it clear that "safe" forms of diversity education need to be infused with the more critical thrust of antiracism, Grinter's piece offers an even stronger challenge to educators. For Grinter, they must choose between multicultural and antiracist forms of education.

Grinter's challenge is taken up by Geoffrey Short. In his contribution Short, like Grinter, reviews the United Kingdom debate between multiculturalists and antiracist educators. However, as opposed to Grinter, Short is committed to working for a reconciliation between the two movements. Taking a cue from the premise that racism is, in fact, the interplay between institutions thriving under the ideology white supremacy and individuals who are acting within these institutions, Short insists that there is no reason to focus exclusively on one or the other. On the contrary, there is every reason to believe that the effort to focus education on combating cultural ignorance will establish "the psychological conditions necessary for children to benefit from an antiracist education."

Short's attempt to bring about some reconciliation between prejudice reduction and system analysis allows the reader to rethink some of the basic claims that are made by bell hooks, Sleeter, and Grinter. Short's attempt to make peace between these two separate but ideologically equivalent educational agendas is compelled by a "new racism" which has dramatically shifted the field of struggle. Indeed, for Short, this "new racism"—as an insidious regeneration of the ancient problem of xenophobia—requires that antiracist educators struggle "on a number of fronts simultaneously." According to Short, "The new racism is distinguished not just by its lack of interest in notions of racial or cultural superiority but also by its failure to blame 'immigrants' for any of the economic or social problems currently facing the country. . . . Its emphasis is on the allegedly destabilising impact on national cohesion of an alien culture." In sum, Short's contribution offers a significant challenge to those scholar-practitioners of antiracism who are committed to generating collective political response to racism.

Guiding Questions for Section Two

- What are the primary concerns and aims of antiracism?
- How does the drive to build solidarity amongst ALL willing parties distinguish antiracism from ethnic studies?
- Should guiding students toward political activism be a goal of education?

Overcoming White Supremacy: A Comment

bell hooks

Black people in the United States share with black people in South Africa and with people of color globally both the pain of white-supremacist oppression and exploitation and the pain that comes from resistance and struggle. The first pain wounds us, the second pain helps heal our wounds. It often troubles me that black people in the United States have not risen *en masse* to declare solidarity with our black sisters and brothers in South Africa. Perhaps one day soon—say Martin Luther King's birthday—we will enter the streets at a certain hour, wherever we are, to stand for a moment, naming and affirming the primacy of black liberation.

As I write, I try to remember when the word racism ceased to be the term which best expressed for me exploitation of black people and other people of color in this society and when I began to understand that the most useful term was white supremacy. It was certainly a necessary term when confronted with the liberal attitudes of white women active in the feminist movement who were unlike their racist ancestors—white women in the early woman's rights movement who did not wish to be caught dead in fellowship with black women. In fact, these women often requested and longed for the presence of black women. Yet when present, what we saw was that they wished to exercise control over our bodies and thoughts as their racist ancestors had—that this need to exercise power over us expressed how much they had internalized the values and attitudes of white supremacy.

It may have been this contact or contact with fellow white English professors who want very much to have "a" black person in "their" department as long as that person thinks and acts like them, shares their values and beliefs, is in no way different, that first compelled me to use the term white supremacy to identify the ideology that most determines how white people in this society (irrespective of their political leanings to the right or left) perceive and relate to black people and other people of color. It is the very small but highly visible liberal movement away from the perpetuation of overtly racist discrimination, exploitation, and oppression of black people which often masks how all-pervasive white supremacy is in this society, both as ideology and as behavior. When liberal whites fail to understand how they can and/or do embody white-supremacist values and beliefs even though they may not embrace racism as prejudice or domination (especially domination that involves coercive control), they cannot recognize the ways their actions support and affirm the very structure of racist domination and oppression that they profess to wish to see eradicated.

Likewise, "white supremacy" is a much more useful term for understanding the complicity of people of color in upholding and maintaining racial hierarchies that do not involve force (i.e. slavery, apartheid) than the term "internalized racism"—a term most often used to suggest that black people have absorbed negative feelings and attitudes about blackness held by white people. The term "white supremacy" enables us to recognize not only that black people are socialized to embody the values and attitudes of white supremacy, but that we can exercise "white-supremacist control" over other black people. This is important, for unlike the term "uncle tom," which carried with it the recognition of complicity and internalized racism, a new terminology must accurately name the way we as black people directly exercise power over one another when we perpetuate white-supremacist beliefs. Speaking about changing perspectives on black identity, writer Toni Morrison said in a recent interview: "Now people choose their identities. Now people choose to be Black." At this historical moment, when a few black people no longer experience the racial apartheid and brutal racism that still determine the lot of many black people, it is easier for that few to ally themselves politically with the dominant racist white group.

Assimilation is the strategy that has provided social legitimation for this shift in allegiance. It is a strategy deeply rooted in the ideology of white supremacy and its advocates urge black people to negate blackness, to imitate racist white people so as to better absorb their values, their way of life. Ironically, many changes in social policy and social attitudes that were once seen as ways to end racial domination have served to reinforce and perpetuate white supremacy. This is especially true of social policy that has encouraged and promoted racial integration. Given the continued force of racism, racial integration translated into assimilation ultimately serves to reinforce and maintain white supremacy. Without an ongoing active movement to end white supremacy, without ongoing black liberation struggle, no social environment can exist in the United States that truly supports integration. When black people enter social contexts that remain unchanged, unaltered, in no way stripped of the framework of white supremacy, we are pressured to assimilate. We are rewarded for assimilation. Black people working or socializing in predominately white settings whose very structures are informed by the principles of white supremacy who dare to affirm blackness, love of black culture and identity, do so at great risk. We must continually challenge, protest, resist while working to leave no gaps in our defense that will allow us to be crushed. This is especially true in work settings where we risk being fired or not receiving deserved promotions. Resisting the pressure to assimilate is a part of our struggle to end white supremacy.

When I talk with audiences around the United States about feminist issues of race and gender, my use of the term "white supremacy" always sparks a reaction, usually of a critical or hostile nature. Individual white people and even some non-whites insist that this is not a white-supremacist society, that racism is not nearly the problem it used to be (it is downright frightening to hear people argue vehemently that the problem of racism has been solved), that there has been change. While it is true that the nature of racist oppression and exploitation has changed as slavery has ended and the apartheid structure of Jim Crow has legally changed, white supremacy continues to shape perspectives on reality and to inform the social status of black people and all people of color. Nowhere is this more evident than in university settings. And often it is the liberal folks in those settings who are unwilling to acknowledge this truth.

Recently in a conversation with a white male lawyer at his home where I was a guest, he informed me that someone had commented to him that children are learning very little history these days in school, that the attempt to be all-inclusive, to talk about Native Americans, blacks, women, etc. has led to a fragmented focus on particular representative individuals with no larger historical framework. I responded to this comment by suggesting that it has been easier for white people to practice this inclusion rather than change the larger framework; that it is easier to change the focus from Christopher Columbus, the important white man who "discovered" America, to Sitting Bull or Harriet Tubman, than it is to cease telling a distorted version of U.S. history which upholds white supremacy. Really teaching history in a new way would require abandoning the old myths informed by white supremacy like the notion that Columbus discovered America. It would mean talking about imperialism, colonization, about the Africans who came here before Columbus (see Ivan Van Sertima's *They Came Before Columbus*). It would mean talking about genocide, about the white colonizers' exploitation and betrayal of Native American Indians; about ways the legal and governmental structures of this society from the Constitution on supported and upheld slavery, apartheid (see Derrick Bell's *And We Are Not Saved*). This history can be taught only when the perspectives of teachers are no longer shaped by white supremacy. Our conversation is one of many examples that reveal the way black people and white people can socialize in a friendly manner, be racially integrated, while deeply ingrained notions of white supremacy remain intact. Incidents like this make it necessary for concerned folks, for righteous white people, to begin to fully explore the way white supremacy determines how they see the world, even as their actions are not informed by the type of racial prejudice that promotes overt discrimination and separation.

Significantly, assimilation was a term that began to be more commonly used after the revolts against white supremacy in the late 1960s and early 1970s. The intense, passionate rebellion against racism and white supremacy of this period was crucial because it created a context for politicization, for education for critical consciousness, one in which black people could begin to confront the extent of our complicity, our internalization of white supremacy and begin the process of self-recovery and collective renewal. Describing this effort in his work. *The Search for a Common Ground,* black theologian Howard Thurman commented:

> "Black is Beautiful" became not merely a phrase—it was a stance, a total attitude, a metaphysics. In very positive and exciting terms it began undermining the idea that had developed over so many years into a central aspect of white mythology: that black is ugly, black is evil, black is demonic. In so doing it fundamentally attacked the front line of the defense of the myth of white supremacy and superiority.

Clearly, assimilation as a social policy upholding white supremacy was strategically an important counter-defense, one that would serve to deflect the call for radical transformation of black consciousness. Suddenly the terms for success (that is getting a job, acquiring the means to provide materially for oneself and one's family) were redefined. It was not enough for black people to enter institutions of higher education and acquire the necessary skills to effectively compete for jobs previously occupied solely by whites; the demand was that blacks become "honorary whites," that black people assimilate to succeed.

The force that gave the social policy of assimilation power to influence and change the direction of black liberation struggle was economic. Economic distress created a climate wherein militancy—overt resistance to white supremacy and racism (which included the presentation of self in a manner that suggests black pride)—was no longer deemed a viable survival strategy. Natural hair styles, African dress, etc. were discarded as signs of militancy that might keep one from getting ahead. A similar regressive, reactionary move was taking place among young white radicals, many of whom had been fiercely engaged in left politics, who suddenly began to seek reincorporation into the liberal and conservative mainstream. Again the force behind their re-entry into the system was economic. On a very basic level, changes in the cost of housing (as in the great apartment one had in 1965 for $100 a month cost $400 by 1975) had a frightening impact on college-educated young people of all ethnicities who thought they were committed to transforming society, but who were unable to face living without choice, without the means to escape, who feared living in poverty. Coupled with economic forces exerting pressure, many radicals despaired of the possibility that this white-supremacist, capitalist patriarchy could really be changed.

Tragically, many radical whites who had been allies in the black liberation struggle began to question whether the struggle to end racism was really that significant, or to suggest that the struggle was over, as they moved into their new liberal positions. Radical white youth who had worked in civil rights struggles, protested the war in Vietnam, and even denounced U.S. imperialism could not reconstruct their ties to prevailing systems of domination without creating a new layer of false consciousness—the assertion that racism was no longer pervasive, that race was no longer an important issue. Similarly, critiques of capitalism, especially those that urged individuals to try and live differently within the framework of capitalism, were also relegated to the back burner as people "discovered" that it was important to have class privilege so that one could better help the exploited.

It is no wonder that black radicals met these betrayals with despair and hopelessness. What had all the contemporary struggle to resist racism really achieved? What did it mean to have this period of radical questioning of white supremacy, of black is beautiful, only to witness a few years later the successful mass production by white corporations of hair care products to straighten black hair? What did it mean to witness the assault on black culture by capitalist forces which stress the production on all fronts of an image, a cultural product that can "cross over"—that is, that can speak more directly to the concerns, to the popular imagination of white consumers, while still attracting the dollars of black consumers. And what does it mean in 1987 when television viewers watch a morning talk show on black beauty, where black women suggest that these trends are only related to personal preferences and have no relation to racism; when viewers witness a privileged white male, Phil Donahue, shaking his head and trying to persuade the audience to acknowledge the reality of racism and its impact on black people? Or what does it mean when many black people say that what they like most about the Bill Cosby show is that there is little emphasis on blackness, that they are "just people"? And again to hear reported on national news that little black children prefer playing with white dolls rather than black dolls? All these popular narratives remind us that "we are not yet saved," that white supremacy prevails, that the racist oppression and exploitation which daily assaults the bodies and spirits of black people in South Africa, assaults black people here.

Years ago when I was a high school student experiencing racial desegregation, there was a current of resistance and militancy that was so fierce. It swept over and through our bodies as we—black students—stood, pressed against the red brick walls, watching the national guard with their guns, waiting for those moments when we would enter, when we would break through racism, waiting for the moments of change—of victory. And now even within myself I find that spirit of militancy growing faint; all too often it is assaulted by feelings of despair and powerlessness. I find that I must work to nourish it, to keep it strong. Feelings of despair and powerlessness are intensified by all the images of black self-hate that indicate that those militant 1960s did not have sustained radical impact—that the politicization and transformation of black consciousness did not become an ongoing revolutionary practice in black life. This causes such frustration and despair because it means that we must return to this basic agenda, that we must renew efforts at politicization, that we must go over old ground. Perhaps what is more disheartening is the fear that the seeds, though planted again, will never survive, will never grow strong. Right now it is anger and rage (see Audre Lorde's "The Uses of Anger" in *Sister Outsider*) at the continued racial genocide that rekindles within me that spirit of militancy.

Like so many radical black folks who work in university settings, I often feel very isolated. Often we work in environments predominately peopled by white folks (some of whom are well-meaning and concerned) who are not committed to working to end white supremacy, or who are unsure about what that commitment means. Certainly feminist movement has been one of the places where there has been renewed interest in challenging and resisting racism. There too it has been easier for white women to confront racism as overt exploitation and domination, or as personal prejudice, than to confront the encompassing and profound reality of white supremacy.

In talking about race and gender recently, the question most often asked by white women has to do with white women's response to black women or women of color insisting that they are not willing to teach them about their racism—to show the way. They want to know: What should a white person do who is attempting to resist racism? It is problematic to assert that black people and other people of color who are sincerely committed to struggling against white supremacy should be unwilling to help or teach white people. Challenging black folks in the 19th century, Frederick Douglass made the crucial point that "power accedes nothing without demand." For the racially oppressed to demand of white people, of black people, of all people that we eradicate white supremacy, that those who benefit materially by exercising white-supremacist power, either actively or passively, willingly give up that privilege in response to that demand, and then to refuse to show the way is to undermine our own cause. We must show the way. There must exist a paradigm, a practical model for social change that includes an understanding of ways to transform consciousness that are linked to efforts to transform structures.

Fundamentally, it is our collective responsibility as radical black people and people of color, and as white people to construct models for social change. To abdicate that responsibility, to suggest that change is just something an individual can do on his or her own or in isolation with other racist white people is utterly misleading. If as a black person I say to a white person who shows a willingness to commit herself or himself to the struggle to end white supremacy that I refuse to affirm, or help in that endeavor is a gesture that undermines my commitment to that struggle. Many black people have essentially responded in this way because we do not want to do the work for white people, and most importantly we cannot do the work, yet this often seems to be what is asked of us. Rejecting the work does not mean that we cannot and do not show the way by our actions, by the information we share. Those white people who want to continue the dominate/subordinate relationship so endemic to racist exploitation by insisting that we "serve" them—that we do the work of challenging and changing their consciousness—are acting in bad faith. In his work, *Pedagogy in Progress: The Letters to Guinea-Bissau*, Paulo Freire reminds us:

> Authentic help means that all who are involved help each other mutually, growing together in the common effort to understand the reality which they seek to transform.

It is our collective responsibility as people of color and as white people who are committed to ending white supremacy to help one another. It is our collective responsibility to educate for critical consciousness. If I commit myself politically to the black liberation struggle, to the struggle to end white supremacy, I am not making a commitment to working only for and with black people, I must engage in the struggle with all willing comrades to strengthen our awareness and our resistance. (See *The Autobiography of Malcolm X* and *The Last Year of Malcolm X—The Evolution of a Revolutionary* by George Breitman.) Malcolm X is an important role model for those of us who wish to transform our consciousness for he was engaged in ongoing critical self-reflection, in changing both his words and his deeds. In thinking about black response to white people, about what they can do to end racism, I am reminded of that memorable example when Malcolm X expressed regret about an incident with a white female college student who asked him what she could do and he told her: "nothing." He later saw that there was much that she could have done. For each of us, it is work to educate ourselves to understand the nature of white supremacy with a critical consciousness. Black people are not born into this world with innate understanding of racism and white supremacy. (See John Hodge, ed., *Cultural Bases of Racism and Group Oppression*.)

In recent years, particularly among women active in feminist movement, much effort to confront racism has focussed on individual prejudice. While it is important that individuals work to transform their consciousness, striving to be anti-racist, it is important for us to remember that the struggle to end white supremacy is a struggle to change a system, a structure. Hodge emphasizes in his book "the problem of racism is not prejudice but domination." For our efforts to end white supremacy to be truly effective, individual struggle to change consciousness must be fundamentally linked to collective effort to transform those structures that reinforce and perpetuate white supremacy.

Questions

1. Why does bell hooks use the category "white supremacy"?
2. What is "internalized racism"?
3. Why does bell hooks criticize the social policy of assimilation? Do you agree with this critique? Explain.
4. bell hooks doesn't mention the social policy of "integration." What is this policy? Would bell hooks criticize it? Explain.
5. What is the "apartheid structure of Jim Crow"?
6. Did Christopher Columbus discover America? Explain.
7. What would be involved in building a "collective effort to transform those structures that reinforce and perpetuate white supremacy"?

Multicultural Education, Social Positionality, and Whiteness

Christine Sleeter

Recently in one of my Multicultural Education preservice courses, eighteen students (fifteen white, two Latina, and one African American) completed the "why" paper assignment. . . . I had their finished papers duplicated and bound as a text for the last few weeks of class. Having experienced earlier the excitement of students learning to investigate issues from someone else's perspective, this time I also experienced frustration as students filtered new insights through their still taken-for-granted perspectives.

Five of the students' "why" papers addressed school and community problems: dropping out, low-achievement, inadequate parent involvement, gangs, and black-on-black crime. Questions included: "Why do many Hispanic youth drop out of high school?" and "Why do low-income students achieve less well in school than middle-income students?" Ten papers addressed various issues related to curriculum and instruction: culture and communication style, culture and language, and inclusion of people of color and women in textbooks. One paper addressed Title IX, one addressed disability, and one paper (by a white student) addressed racial segregation of local schools, briefly exploring racial politics in the community. Students were encouraged to probe for constructive solutions as well as examinations of why problems exist and I helped students make sure they were obtaining perspectives of members of the groups to whom the questions pertained.

Class discussion of the first five "problem" papers illustrates how whites often process information about issues of oppression. The sources students obtained information from collectively discussed multi-leveled causes of the problems, including poverty and lack of jobs, lack of teacher support, lack of school support, family characteristics, the drug culture, the peer culture, families' attitudes about education, family's socioeconomic status, poor work habits, lack of role models, etc. Exclusion from jobs and from challenging and supportive education were common themes.

In the conclusions of their papers, most students tended to ignore systemic causes they had uncovered in their research and offered solutions that focused largely on constructive, but fairly mild, forms of help. The solutions they suggested for educators included attempting to work with parents (e.g., holding parent-teacher conferences during hours when parents can come), maintaining high expectations for children, reducing tracking, teaching non-violent ways to address problems, matching students with tutors, and offering programs for parents. These are all helpful suggestions. However, they sidestep the larger context of oppression within which problems arise, specifically economic exclusion and systemic racism.

As the class discussed the papers, I tried to push them to consider why jobs are leaving inner cities, how the race of people relates to where they live and to where most jobs are located, actions teachers can take as community citizens, why students of color in low-income communities that are losing employment opportunities might distrust schools, and how teachers could address realities children perceive. The most insightful contributions to the discussion came from one of the Latina students (who discussed vividly the limited future many children of color see for themselves based on the experiences their parents are having currently) and the African American student (who described ways educators demonstrate to children that schools are primarily interested in white children rather than African American children). Most of the white students seemed to have difficulty going beyond a focus on how "we" can help "them," and difficulty thinking of collective political solutions to poverty and racism. Only two white students and two students of color sustained discussions in class about systemic racism. While the rest of the class did not exhibit hostility to discussions about racism (white racism had been a main topic of study in at least one previous class), they were either silent or changed the subject. As one white student commented, she didn't feel she had much to contribute because, "I'm not used to thinking about things from 'downs' perspectives" (referring to an article by Terry, 1993).

Racism and Multicultural Education

. . . multicultural education grew out of the civil rights movement of the 1960s. As Banks (1992) pointed out, educators with roots in African American studies have been among the most active conceptualizers of multicultural education, viewing it as a discourse community that would advance power-sharing and uplifting communities of color. Having its roots in minority discourses about oppression, multicultural education was part of a larger quest for redistribution of power and economic resources. As such, the field should be advancing strategies to address white racism: white control over most of the wealth, land,

and power in the nation. Building on analyses of race, social class, and gender that have been advanced over the past two decades, multicultural education should also direct our attention to concentrations of power and wealth in the hands of a small elite and to manifestations of that concentration in contemporary culture and social institutions. Multicultural education might, for example, help us analyze how schools are situated within a capitalistic structure that continues to transfer wealth to a white elite, while deflecting attention away from itself through various forms of media. Such critique would suggest teaching young people to engage in critical media analysis, to examine the distribution of wealth, to examine social movements that historically have successfully advanced the interests of marginalized groups, and to use political action skills. Such teaching does, in fact, sometimes take place within the field of multicultural education.

However, often multicultural education as a discourse mutes attention to white racism (and usually ignores patriarchy and the class hierarchy), focusing mainly on cultural difference. Culture and cultural difference is certainly important and ought to be a central construct. However, white racism and racial oppression, as well as capitalist and patriarchal oppression, should also be central constructs. Generally they are not, or they disappear from consideration in the minds of white educators. The example of my students is illustrative: although their research suggested unemployment and blocked access to resources as significant underlying causes of problems such as dropping out of school, neither the papers nor class discussions focused much attention on systemic problems—white racism or political responses to economic exclusion.

That multicultural education often skirts around white racism results from white people's reluctance to address it more so than people of color's disregard for it. Those of us who are white usually experience a social reality that does not lead us to critique white racism; rather, we have a vested interest not to "see" it. We are a part of the "norms and models set by white elites" (West, 1993, p. 20) and are accustomed to extending acceptance and approval to educators of color who frame their work within the parameters of our reality and rejection to the ideas of those who do not. The present white understanding of race and ethnicity "emerged into prominence during a period when the civil rights movement was most active and racial minorities were challenging in basic respects the fairness of the American system" (Alba, 1990, p. 317). White society felt threatened and attempted to reframe ethnicity and race within our own worldview and experience. "The thrust of European-American identity is to defend the individualistic view of the American system, because it portrays the system as open to those who are willing to work hard and pull themselves over barriers of poverty and discrimination" (Alba, p. 317).

In what follows, I will examine insights that people who occupy dominant social positions find it very difficult to internalize. Everybody interprets the world from their location in a stratified society. As the work of theorists such as Sandra Harding (1991) and Renato Rosaldo (1989) argue, this means that our understandings are always partial; we always interpret and filter the world through our own life histories and the ideological frameworks we have learned to use.

> Like form and feeling, culture and power are inextricably intertwined. In discussing actors, one must consider their social positions. What are the complexities of the speaker's social identity? What life experiences have shaped it? Does the person speak from a position of relative dominance or relative subordination? (Rosaldo, 1989, p. 167)

This is a broader and deeper issue than charging teachers with "prejudice," which is how audiences sometimes interpret the main idea of this chapter. Usually when one speaks of teacher prejudice, one is speaking of the tendency to prejudge individuals on the basis of stereotypes, before coming to know them as individuals. When one attempts to reduce prejudice, one is attempting to help people view others on their own merits and treat them accordingly. When I speak of worldview, however, I am referring not just to how one interprets and feels about individuals, but also how one frames the contemporary and historic patterns of relationships among sociocultural groups, how one situates humans within a larger cosmology, and how one conceives of human nature itself.

Dominant Viewpoints Rooted in Euro-American Experiences

Four interconnected concepts are discussed that white preservice students find very difficult to grasp, partly because they do not fit white people's daily experience or understanding of our own Euro-American history. Although these concepts have been separated for discussion here, it is important to recognize that they are interconnected and must be addressed as such. Prospective teachers of color probably also need to address issues and concepts discussed below (Montecinos, 1995), but usually in my experience grasp the concepts below much more readily than white prospective teachers because these concepts mesh with their life experiences.

Historic Roots of Racist Opportunity Structures

Euro-Americans often describe the U.S. as a nation of immigrants, but describing it in this way minimizes very important distinctions in groups' historic experiences with opportunity. Ogbu (1991) argues that how a group became a part of the United States defines the trajectory for the group's subsequent experiences and perspectives. European ethnic groups, as well as some Asian and Latino groups, voluntarily, for the most part, immigrated to North America in search of better opportunities, expecting to endure some hardships and discrimination initially. African Americans, indigenous Native people, Puerto Ricans, and Mexican Americans, on the other hand, whom he refers to as "involuntary minorities ... were brought into their present society through slavery, conquest or colonization" (p. 9). Rather than seeking voluntarily to affiliate with the dominant society to gain opportunities, they were forced to become part of it and in the process lost vast amounts of freedom, land, and economic resources. European groups developed an opportunity structure that allowed for individual upward mobility for whites (a process that did involve considerable conflict among European groups), but until 1954 legally barred groups of color from participating in that structure. These very different histories generated present life conditions and perspectives that diverge to a much greater degree than most white people grasp.

White people in general find it very difficult to appreciate the impact of colonization and slavery on both oppressed groups as well as whites; we tend to prefer to regard everyone as descendants of immigrants. I believe whites retreat from confronting the profound impact of conquest and slavery because doing so calls into question the legitimacy of the very foundation of much of white peoples' lives. The economic legacy of conquest is that whites are indebted to Indian, Mexican, Puerto Rican, and Hawaiian people for the land we inhabit, as well as gold and other resources our ancestors extracted from the land to build industries (Weatherford, 1988). The economic legacy of slavery is that whites owe African Americans about three hundred years of back-wages, money that whites used instead to build profits and profit-generating industries. Economic disparities today are legacies of that history (Roediger, 1991).

However, the view of the United States as a nation of voluntary immigrants is consistent with the family histories of Euro-Americans and affirms the desire of whites to believe that our ancestors earned fairly what we have inherited and that what we control is rightly ours. Generally when acknowledging conquest and slavery, Euro-Americans bracket these off as historic incidents that have little bearing on today. Typical white responses to this history are: "I didn't do it, why punish me?" "My family worked for what they got, we didn't have anything to do with slavery," and "That was a long time ago, can't we just forget all that?" Also, typically white preservice students have only a sketchy idea of the histories of Americans of color and do not situate current issues in a historic context (Lauderdale & Deaton, 1993). Learning history can help to develop a sense of how different the historical experiences have been for voluntary immigrants versus non-voluntary minorities. Yet, white people seem more willing to disconnect history from the present than do many people of color because for whites the present system is fair.

The Nature and Impact of Discrimination

Oppressed groups experience discrimination daily in relationship to individuals and in interaction with institutions; the impact of discrimination is psychological as well as material. This is true of voluntary non-white immigrants (such as Korean Americans) as well as involuntary minority groups, poor whites, women, and gays and lesbians. While immigrants often attribute discrimination they experience to their foreign ways (Ogbu, 1991), involuntary minority group members, particularly African Americans, see systematic racial discrimination as a deep and ongoing problem (Kluegel & Smith, 1986).

Most white teachers greatly minimize the extent and impact of racial (as well as other forms of) discrimination, viewing it as isolated expressions of prejudice that hurt a person's feelings. Americans in general attribute differences in wealth, income, and lifestyle to individual effort on a playing field we assume to be even, particularly with passage of civil rights legislation (Kluegel & Smith, 1986). In fact, many white university students regard legislation such as affirmative action as giving groups of color an unfair advantage, racial discrimination itself having been largely eliminated.

The view that discrimination has minimal impact was illustrated to me in how one of my white students interpreted an exercise. For an assignment, she spent an hour at the mall with an African American friend, then with a white friend, in order to compare the treatment they received. She reported that when she was with the African American friend, two sales clerks seemed more rude than sales clerks normally are to her; aside from these two, she saw no difference in treatment. Her initial conclusion was that discrimination does not happen very often, although when it does, it makes African American people feel bad. I suggested to her that a different interpretation is that her African American friend probably faces some negative treatment everytime he goes to the mall, as well as other places, which may limit where he goes; she had not considered it that way and had some difficulty doing so.

Further, discrimination restricts opportunities, an impact that extends far beyond hurt feelings. For example, racial housing patterns result partially from housing discrimination, which still occurs on a very wide scale despite open housing laws. Where people live affects access to jobs and schools, which in turn affects access to income; exclusionary barriers are, thus, interconnected and have a huge impact on living conditions. But the impact of systematic and persistent discrimination is a very difficult concept for most whites to grasp since we do not experience racial discrimination ourselves. In spite of having spent over an hour of classtime on housing discrimination, for example, the following semester a white student selected as her topic for investigation: Why do many African Americans live in the inner city?

Recently a white former student asked for my help in constructing lessons about discrimination. As we talked, I noticed that she conceptualized discrimination largely as stereotyping and biased interpersonal treatment. When I probed for her understanding of institutional discrimination, she at first drew a blank, then slowly gave a rather vague definition. As we talked, I realized that although she had learned what I taught while in class, when the semester was over she filed much of it away in the recesses of her mind. She did not normally think in terms of systemic racism and had reduced racism to interpersonal tensions and stereotypes.

. . . [w]omen experience sex discrimination, and seem more likely to acknowledge the presence of other forms of discrimination than men. However, most have not engaged in a systematic study of patriarchy and often resist examining how their own lives have been shaped by it. Many white female students view sex discrimination as no more than an annoying patronizing attitude that some males display and that women need to ignore. If this is what discrimination is, they reason, then why can't people of color simply ignore it?

Because they conceptualize discrimination as consisting of isolated acts by prejudiced individuals, most teachers do not explain inequality in terms of systemic discrimination. Mark Ginsburg (1988) interviewed 75 preservice students (75% female, 85% White) to find out how they interpret inequalities in achievement (in both schools and the larger society) and what implications their interpretations had for teaching. A small minority "emphasized the school's role in reproducing inequalities," contextualizing children within a stratified and unjust social structure (p. 167). A much larger second group viewed individuals as freely choosing their own destinies and degree of social mobility; they believed schools neutrally facilitate mobility for everyone. A third group also viewed individuals as freely choosing their own destinies, but believed that people are hindered by individual attitudes and prejudice.

If discrimination consists largely of one-on-one acts by overtly prejudiced people, then the solution must be to be open-minded and accept everyone. If I as a teacher adopt an open attitude, I am not part of a problem. This line of thinking denies a need to learn much that people of color are saying, but it is a common view.

The Significance of Group Membership

The dominant ideology of the U.S. is strongly individualistic, a perspective that teachers commonly share. Americans commonly learn that the United States is a nation in which affiliations are voluntary and people participate in the public arena as individuals. For example, Alan Bloom (1989) wrote that in the American political system, "Class, race, religion, national origin or culture all disappear or become dim when bathed in the light of natural rights, which give men common interests and make them truly brothers" (p. 27). The purpose of schooling is to cultivate reason so that citizens can rise above their own particular circumstances and participate as individuals in a common culture. Similarly, Arthur Schlesinger (1992) described the United States as a nation in which people "escape from origins" (p. 15) and go about "casting off the foreign skin" (p. 112) in order to rise or fall on their own merit and effort as individuals, rather than as members of ascribed groups. This ideology suggests that Americans should not identify themselves with any ascribed group for purposes of public participation and that it is possible and valuable to ignore ascribed group memberships of other people, thus treating them as individuals.

Historically for whites, the significance of ethnic membership has indeed diminished; the ideology above fits family histories. When Europeans immigrated to the United States, ethnicity structured many aspects of their lives such as choice of spouse, job, and location of residence. Today, however, with a few exceptions, European ethnicity is unrelated to life chances and choices (Alba, 1990). The problem is that, while European ethnic group membership no longer structures opportunity to a significant degree, continent of origin does, as do gender and wealth. Insisting on the individual as the main unit of analysis deflects attention away from examination of social responses to visible differences.

As a part of our adherence to the idea that ethnicity does not matter, most whites profess to be colorblind. But in doing so, we cover over the meanings we attach to race, rather than actually dissociating race from meaning. If one conceives of the United States as a nation of voluntary immigrants and the rules of society as essentially fair (with some isolated instances of discrimination still occurring), then why do some groups fare better than others? Typically, most Americans explain group differences in terms of characteristics and desires of group members themselves: for example, women choose low-paying jobs, Mexicans don't want to learn English, low-income people lack the desire to work or keep up their homes. If one asks a white audience to jot down all the negatives they have heard associated with another racial group, then all the positives, the list of negatives is usually much longer. For teachers, trying to be colorblind, therefore, means trying to suppress the application of those negative associations to individual children one is teaching.

Trying to be colorblind also means denying the existence of racial boundaries whites see and usually do not cross. If one asks a white audience how many of them have ever chosen to live in a neighborhood or attend a school or church in which the majority of the people are not white, few hands go up. Whites do see and adhere to racial boundaries, and most feel very uncomfortable crossing them. But whites with at least modest income have many choices (such as where to live, who to associate with) within white dominated terrain, and use the range of such choices to deny that race is a factor in their decisions.

Ironically, this failure to think seriously about meanings of race is a part of western culture which Goldberg (1993) argues solidifies racism. Race, socially constructed historically for purposes of colonization, has become a normalized category that most people today accept as fact.

> This deep disjunction between moral idealization and actual racial appeal, between color blindness and racial consciousness, must imply either that morality is irrelevant, that in the case of race it has no force or that liberalism's relative silence concerning racial considerations masks a much more complex set of ideas and experiences than commonly acknowledged. (p. 6)

Most white people assume race, but also assume that open acknowledgement of race violates the ideal of colorblindness. Paradoxically, this refusal to examine race openly strengthens racialized behavior patterns. To dismantle racism and race as a category, we must first confront race.

Since ethnic and racial identities and cultures are difficult concepts to deal with for most white teachers, they tend to reduce multicultural education to a question of individual differences (Goodwin, 1994). This, in conjunction with denying institutional racism and its profound consequences, often leads white teachers to frame multicultural education as a depoliticized discourse of differences, in which differences can be reduced to individual variation that have minimal social consequences. We can learn to acknowledge and examine markers of collectives to which we do adhere. The more we critically attend to our behavior, the more guilty many white people feel because we realize the degree to which we adhere to racial boundaries, as well as boundaries of social class, language, and so forth. One could begin to replace guilt with different actions, but this requires some change in how we live, so many of us retreat into the more comfortable position of denying the significance of group membership.

Nature of Culture

Multicultural education is very often reduced to folksongs and folktales, food fairs, holiday celebrations, and information about famous people. Even when teachers are shown more substantive examples of multicultural practice, many still revert to superficial renditions of cultural differences and teach culture as habits and customs frozen in the past, passed on as if they were "genetic inheritance" (Garvey, 1993, p. 21). The popular term "cultural heritage" conveys this image well.

How white teachers often conceptualize culture is rooted in European immigrant backgrounds. In his study of European ethnic identity, Richard Alba (1990) found that the most salient expression of ethnic "culture" among Euro-Americans is eating ethnic foods; Euro-Americans also experience "culture" by using words or phrases of an ancestral language, attending ethnic festivals, and practicing "Old World" holiday customs. Ethnic culture defined in this way consists of remnants of Old World practices that are celebrated and often shared across ethnic groups, at particular times. Alba's description of Euro-Americans' expressions of ethnicity correspond very well to multicultural education as white teachers commonly construct it.

Rosaldo (1989) connects the myth of immigration with what he terms "cultural stripping," in which Euro-Americans believe that immigrants brought culture, but lost it as they assimilated. "Social analysts sat at the 'postcultural' top of a stratified world and looked down the 'cultural' rungs to its 'precultural' bottom" (p. 209). In this conception, "primitive" people lack culture; immigrants brought culture from another country and era, culture consisting of folkways from the past; and mainstream Americans have surpassed the need for culture through technological development.

Culture viewed as folkways becomes romanticized, but culture can also be viewed as pathological. Most white people do not know very much about the daily lives of non-white people, and find it difficult to conceptualize poor white homes and neighborhoods, as well as those of color, in terms of cultural strengths or sensible behavior. Since most of us grow up in race and social class segregated neighborhoods, our firsthand contact with the homes and communities of other groups is very limited. For example, it is difficult to conceptualize how an extended family structure may be highly functional if one has limited contact with close extended families. As a result, if we assume that the context in which people live is fair and neutral, we draw on media images, hearsay, stereotypes, and suppositions to explain differences that we see in who has what. These explanations take the form of group characteristics. Generally we regard these characteristics as descriptions of fact rather than as stereotypes. The degree to which they focus on presumed capabilities or deficiencies is in proportion to the group's status in the broader society. Thus, Anglos will romanticize piñatas and Mexican hat dances, and at the same time argue that characteristics of Mexican culture keep Mexican people from advancing (such as large families, adherence to Spanish language, external locus of control, lack of ambition—mañana, etc.).

This is a very different notion of culture from that advocated in multicultural education. By "culture," I mean the totality of a people's experience: its history, literature, language, philosophy, religion, and so forth. The term "culture" was probably adopted by multicultural education advocates in response to the myth of "cultural deprivation" that was popularized during the early 1960s. All of us grow up in a culture and participate in constructing as well as living culture, everyday.

While my teacher education students can usually grasp the idea intellectually that "culture" refers to the totality of a group's socially-constructed way of carrying on life, most have very little knowledge of the culture of any group other than that into which they were born. And schools have been inducting them since kindergarten into that culture—which they regard not as culture but as given. Without some depth of knowledge of at least one other cultural group and of how another group views one's own taken-for-granted culture, teachers will probably continue to greatly oversimplify the meaning of "culture."

The four concepts discussed above were evident in most of the fifteen white students' viewpoints. Partly as a result of our teaching throughout the teacher education program, they turned more readily to forms of discrimination than to presumed cultural deficiencies to explain differences in groups' attainments. Further, most students developed a degree of facility in thinking about sociocultural groups and identifying themselves as members of groups (e.g., as white). However, their analyses of discrimination usually focused on interpersonal interactions rather than on systems of oppression. Their proposed solutions therefore tended to be simplistic and to appeal to educators and community workers to do the right thing, with little or no reference to the history of white collective behavior or to the desire of a capitalist elite to retain and expand control.

As I listened to my students, I heard silences that became very loud as they persisted. White silence about white racism is a silence that roars, not only from white preservice students but also from white people in general.

❧

White Solidarity and White Silence about Racism

White people talk very little about white racism (Scheurich, 1993). Even those of us involved in multicultural education spend far less energy examining and critiquing how white racism works than we ought. Most whites who read this book are probably aware that racism is an important issue to multicultural education and probably do talk about it from time to time. However, I would suggest that our talk does not delve into racism in very much depth. For example, I can write much more fluently about multicultural curricula or multicultural teacher education than I can about white racism. My own discussions of racism rarely move beyond the introductory level I use with my white students. Other white academics sometimes try to close off discussions of white racism by describing such discussions as "navel gazing," as whites who have "seen the light" bashing other whites, as too politically correct, or as insufficiently post-structural in their essentializing of whiteness.

I first noticed white silence on racism about twenty years ago, although I was not able at the time to name it as such. I recall realizing one day, after having shared many meals with African American friends while teaching in Seattle, that racism and race-related issues were fairly common topics of dinner-table conversation, which African Americans talked about quite openly. It struck me that I could not think of a single instance in which racism had been a topic of dinner-table conversation in white contexts. Race-related issues sometimes came up, but not *racism*. For example, I could remember short discussions about what one would do if a black family moved next door, or about a very bigoted relative, or about policies such as desegregation or immigration. In these discussions, what was viewed as problematic was people of color themselves, changes in policies that relate to race, or outspoken bigots.

White people have developed various strategies that enable us to talk about racial issues while avoiding white supremacy and our own participation in it. One of these strategies, described above, is to equate racism with individual prejudice, thus allowing us to assume that every group is racist and to avoid acknowledging the power differential between whites and groups of color. Another strategy is to focus on cultural difference. Cultural differences do exist, of course; however, whites transmute many issues that are rooted in racism into depoliticized questions of difference, which often take on a "tourist" frame of thinking. For example, a line of action whites could take vis-à-vis Indians, Mexicans, Puerto Ricans, or Hawaiians is to return good land and control over that land. But few of us take such action seriously. Instead, we show interest in such groups by learning about certain cultural artifacts and practices (and then sometimes appropriating them) and paying homage to Indian, Latino, and Hawaiian heroes and contributions to white culture.

Equating ethnicity with race is a related strategy for evading racism. At a women's studies conference I attended, participants were divided into racially homogeneous groups to compile a list of the main concerns facing their group. I was in the European-American group, and it floundered. Participants discussed mainly family history and ethnic immigrant background. By focusing on our ethnic differences, the group tried to place itself on a parallel status with the other racial groups, defining our problems as comparable to theirs. Our whiteness seemed to be invisible to us—we could discuss our religious, ethnic, and social class differences, but not our common whiteness (see Dyer, 1988).

We semantically evade our own role in perpetuating white racism by constructing sentences that allow us to talk about racism while removing ourselves from discussion. One such semantic evasion is to personify racism, making it (rather than ourselves) the subject of sentences. This allows us to say, for example, "Racism forced urban housing to deteriorate." Constructing a sentence in this way hides *who* was responsible for the deterioration of urban housing. We also evade our role semantically by avoiding use of a subject altogether; passive sentence constructions allow us to talk about racism without ever naming our own complicity. For example, consider the following sentence: "Africans were brought to the colonies and forced to labor a lifetime for no wages" (McKissack & McKissack, 1990, p. 16). *Who* brought them and forced them? The sentence does not say.

Whites exert pressure on each other to adhere to common definitions of racial issues. In contexts in which these definitions are contested, one can observe active processes by which whites attempt to maintain racial solidarity. This observation struck me recently, when I watched white teacher education students respond to an issue. The dean had been working with a committee of faculty, school administrators, teachers, and the dean of another institution to create an alternative certification program for prospective teachers of color. When word of this program reached white students in the regular program (actually, a few white students were on the planning committee, but had not regarded the program as a problem needing discussion), a large segment of the white student population mobilized overnight to affirm a common definition of the program: It was racially biased and wrong. When I tried to direct the few students who talked with me about it toward sources of more information about the program and reasons for its need, I realized that these students did not want information; they wanted my validation of their perception of it. In a meeting between the students and the faculty, white students vented openly a degree of racism that caught us off guard, and no white student rose to defend the program (although a few did silently support it). Although part of the students' anger was frustration over the length of the regular teacher education program, part of it was racial.

I began to ask myself: Given the coursework and field experiences the students had . . . , why did the white students coalesce so strongly and quickly into a common condemnation of the alternative program? How did they know their peers would support thinly-veiled as well as overt expressions of racial hostility? Why did the supporters of the program decide to keep quiet?

These questions led me to examine "white racial bonding" processes white people engage in everyday, which is one of the processes by which whites attempt to maintain racial solidarity. By "racial bonding," I mean simply interactions in which whites engage that have the purpose of affirming a common stance on race-related issues, legitimating particular interpretations of groups of color, and drawing conspiratorial we–they boundaries. These interaction patterns take such forms as inserts into conversations, race-related "asides" in conversations, strategic eye contact, jokes, and code words. Often they are so short and subtle that they may seem relatively harmless, and we don't remember specific exchanges for very long. I used to regard such utterances as annoying expressions of prejudice or ignorance, but that seems to underestimate their power to demarcate racial lines and communicate solidarity.

Inserts into conversations may go like this. Two white people are talking casually about various things. One comments, "This community is starting to change. A lot of Mexicans have been moving in." This comment serves as an invitation to white bonding, in which the other person is being asked to agree with the implication that Mexicans create problems and do not belong here, although this has not been said directly. The other person could respond very simply, "Yeah, that's a bummer," affirming the first person's viewpoint; this could be the end of a successful exchange. Or, the other person could complain about Mexicans, the ensuing conversation taking the form of Mexican-bashing. In either case, both parties will have communicated agreement that there is a linkage between "Mexicans" and "problems" and will have defined themselves as "insiders" in a network of people who view it as acceptable to articulate a negative valuation of Mexicans. Further, they will have communicated the acceptability of viewing favorably policies limiting Mexican access to the community. Even silence can serve as tacit acquiescence for the purpose of winning approval. Patricia Williams (1991, pp. 126–8) described in exquisite detail such an exchange in which she participated passively.

How do I know this kind of exchange serves the purpose of racial bonding? I know because if I do not give the desired response, the other person very often presses the issue much more explicitly; I also may never hear from the other person again (including relatives). For example, if I change the subject, it usually reappears but more forcefully ("Mexicans bring gang problems, you know; I'm really concerned about the future of this community."). Sometimes I give a response I know the other person is not looking for, such as, "Yes, I'm really pleased to see this community becoming more multicultural, I've been working on my Spanish." More often than not, the other person responds with a lecture on problems associated with Mexican American people, and the misguidedness of my judgment. I am usually uncomfortable when people who do not know me well ask what I teach; quite often responses such as "multicultural education" or "urban education" provoke uninvited lectures on race relations or on their own beliefs as a white liberal (hoping that either I will agree or be persuaded to accept their viewpoint).

These kinds of interactions seem to serve the purpose of defining racial lines and inviting individuals to either declare their solidarity or mark themselves as deviant. Depending on degree of deviance, one runs the risk of losing the other individual's approval, friendship, and company. (This usually occurs in the form of feeling "uncomfortable" around the deviant white person.) Many whites who do not support racist beliefs, actions, or policies, but who also do not want to risk social bonds with other whites, simply remain silent. We tacitly agree not to talk about racism.

No white person is exempt from pressures from other white people to "fit in," with the price of conformity to a racial norm very often being approval and friendship. While active anti-racist whites may not be affected by such processes, I would hypothesize that it does affect white educators who are less certain about their own racial beliefs and loyalties. Janet Helms (1990), for example, posited a stage of Reintegration in white racial identity development in which the white person, following coursework and/or experiences that challenged one's previous beliefs about race, returns to those prior, more comfortable and socially acceptable (in white circles) beliefs. We all need affective bonds with people. Given the segregation of our society, the strongest bonds are usually with members of our own race. In a predominantly white teaching profession, white teachers make sure that their peers are "one of us." "Us" may be compassionate, child-oriented, and open-minded, but "us" also defines racial issues from a white vantage point.

Whiteness and the Teaching Profession

As the teaching profession becomes increasingly white and as white educators become increasingly involved in multicultural education, it is likely that what teachers do with multicultural education increasingly will reflect a white worldview. The eighteen students I mentioned at the beginning of this chapter learned to engage with many concepts of multicultural education, and most shaped those concepts to fit their own reality. That reality is one in which social change is not a priority and multicultural education rarely means social reconstruction (Goodwin, 1994). White definitions of multicultural education may become self-perpetuating in schools to the degree that there are few other professionals within the school who bring and articulate alternative perspectives and to the degree that teachers regard themselves as knowing more than the students and parents who might challenge their viewpoints.

Multicultural education ought to be a collaborative process involving dialog and bonding across racial and ethnic boundaries for the purpose of forging greater equality and social justice. This does not mean that white people should be absent from the process, but rather, that we should not dominate or control it.

What is to be done? I can speak most appropriately to what whites should be doing. First, white educators should be engaging in regular dialog and collaborative work with people of color in our own communities, but that dialog and work needs to include regular and continued self-analysis. Dialog is most productive when we are aware of our own biases, limitations, and vested interests that keep us from hearing. Rosaldo (1989) illustrated with his own encounter with Ilongot headhunters:

> This encounter suggests that we ethnographers should be open to asking not only how our descriptions of others would read if applied to ourselves but how we can learn from other people's descriptions of ourselves. In this case I was repositioned through an Ilongot account of one of my culture's central institutions [warfare]. I could no longer speak

about headhunting as one of the clean addressing the dirty. My loss of innocence enabled me and the Ilongots to face each other on more nearly equal ground, as members of flawed societies. (p. 64)

Through his experience with Ilongot people, Rosaldo learned at least as much about himself and his own culture as he did about the "Other." As whites learn to hear how Americans of color experience white racism in general and our own actions in particular and as we learn to examine our own worldview in order to identify its boundaries and limitations, we can learn to engage in more productive dialog and action.

Those of us who are white should be spending as much time working on ourselves as attempting to draw in other whites. There is a tendency for white educators, especially those who are new to multicultural education, to proselytize: to attempt to "convert" our friends and colleagues. My students often talk about doing this, while I see them as needing to focus on their own growth. Cornel West (1993) reminds us that, "it is naive to think that being comfortably nested within this very same system [of oppression] . . . does not affect one's work, one's outlook, and most important, one's soul" (p. 21). Multicultural education partly means studying ourselves critically in order to listen more openly. This is not easy, and it takes time and work. My eighteen students had begun the process—they had learned to ask questions that elicited information about racism and exclusion.

Second, the field of multicultural education needs to develop vocabulary and action strategies for addressing white racism and other forms of oppression. When my eighteen students attempted to discuss why jobs are leaving inner-city areas, for example, their limited ability to visualize collective political actions was probably a part of the problem. Educators in general don't usually think in terms of collective political action to make changes; rather, educators tend to conceptualize change strategies in terms of individually persuading other individuals to "do the right thing" (Sleeter, 1992). As a result, many whites don't see what we could be doing differently, and many educators of color become too focused on trying to persuade whites to change when collective pressure politics may be more fruitful. John Garvey (1993) argued that,

Our most enduring problems will be most satisfactorily addressed by the emergence and growth of a resurgent movement. No one can will that movement into being. But we might assist in its development by establishing situations, within and without formal school settings, for individuals to expand their own political capacities. (p. 85).

History contains numerous examples of white people who have worked collaboratively with oppressed racial groups to combat racist policies and practices (Aptheker, 1992). We are not starting from scratch; we have a history to guide us.

Third, those of us who work to develop teachers' understanding of various forms of oppression must connect teachers with other people who are engaged in active work to dismantle white supremacy and other forms of social injustice. It is naive to believe that one or two university courses will reconstruct an individual's worldview and personal affiliations. My own history attests to the slowness of change and the importance of developing bonds with people who work to challenge racism. Perhaps one form of action we can take is to mentor individuals who have ventured into an unstable stage of racial (or gender or social class) identity development, who are hovering somewhere between tacit acceptance of the status quo and active partnership in struggle. As mentors, we can offer the support and personal care that is needed to help people such as the students discussed here, to stick with the issues and not to turn back.

References

Alba, R. D. 1990. *Ethnic identity.* New Haven: Yale University Press.

Aptheker, H. 1992. *Anti-racism in U.S. history.* New York: Greenwood Press.

Banks, J. A. 1992. African American scholarship and the evolution of multicultural education. *Journal of Negro Education* 61 (3), 273–286.

Bloom, A. C. 1989. *The closing of the American mind.* New York: Simon & Schuster.

Dyer, R. 1988. White. *Screen* 29, 44–64.

Garvey, J. 1993. Reading, 'riting, and race. *Race Traitor* 1 (Winter), 73–87.

Ginsburg, M. B. 1988. *Contradictions in teacher education and society: A critical analysis.* London: The Falmer Press.

Goldberg, D. T. 1993. *Racist culture: Philosophy and the politics of meaning.* Oxford, UK: Blackwell.

Goodwin, A. L. 1994. Making the transition from self to other: What do preservice teachers really think about multicultural education? *Journal of Teacher Education* 45 (2), 119–131.

Harding, S. 1991. *Whose science? Whose knowledge? Thinking from women's lives.* Ithaca, NY: Cornell University Press.

Helms, J. E., ed. 1990. *Black and white racial identity: Theory, research, and practice.* Westport, CT: Greenwood Press.

Kluegel, J. R. & Smith, E. R. 1986. *Beliefs about inequality: Americans' views of what is and what ought to be.* New York: Aldine de Gruyter.

Lauderdale, W. B. & Deaton, W. L. 1993. Future teachers react to past racism. *The Educational Forum* 57 (3), 266–276.

McKissack, P. & McKissack, F. 1990. *Taking a stand against racism and racial discrimination.* New York: Franklin Watts.

Montecinos, C. 1995. Culture as an on-going dialog: Implications for multicultural teacher education. In *Multicultural education, critical pedagogy, and the politics of difference,* eds. C. E. Sleeter & P. McLaren, pp. 96–108. Albany: SUNY Press.

Ogbu, J. U. 1991. Immigrant and involuntary minorities in comparative perspective. In *Minority status and schooling,* eds. M. A. Gibson & J. U. Ogbu, pp. 3–33. New York: Garland.

Roediger, D. R. 1991. *The wages of whiteness.* London: Verso.

Rosaldo, R. 1989. *Culture and truth: The remaking of social analysis.* Boston: Beacon Press.

Scheurich, J. 1993. Toward a white discourse on white racism. *Educational Researcher* 22 (8), 5–10.

Schlesinger, A. M., Jr. 1992. *The disuniting of America.* New York: Norton.

Sleeter, C. E. 1992. *Keepers of the American dream.* London: The Falmer Press.

Terry, B. 1993. A parable: The ups and downs. In *Oppression and social justice: Critical frameworks,* 3rd edition, ed. J. Andrzejewski, pp. 61–63. Needham Heights, MA: Ginn Press.

Weatherford, J. 1988. *Indian givers.* New York: Fawcett Columbine.

West, C. 1993. The new cultural politics of difference. In *Race, identity, and representation in education,* eds. C. McCarthy & W. Crichlow, pp. 11–23. New York: Routledge.

Williams, P. 1991. *The alchemy of race and rights.* Cambridge: Harvard University Press.

Questions

1. Why did most of Sleeter's students tend to ignore systemic causes for the "problems" they researched?
2. What is a social problem? Explain by identifying an example and its systemic causes.
3. Why is Sleeter critical of multicultural education? Do you agree or disagree with this criticism? Explain.
4. What are "racist opportunity structures"? What are the historic origins of these?
5. What is the difference between "discrimination" and "prejudice"?
6. What is the difference between voluntary and involuntary immigration?
7. What are some of the different ways of defining the term "culture"?
8. How would you describe your culture?
9. What is the "white solidarity and silence about racism"?
10. Do you agree with Sleeter's point about "racial bonding"? Why or why not? Explain.
11. What do you think about the solutions Sleeter offers in her conclusion?
12. In her conclusion Sleeter writes "History contains numerous examples of white people who have worked collaboratively with oppressed racial groups to combat racist policies and practices." Identify five of these examples.

Multicultural or Antiracist Education? The Need to Choose

Robin Grinter

Multicultural and antiracist education are incompatible philosophies between which a choice has to be made to ensure effective education against racism in British society. They work from different philosophical bases and towards different purposes. They cannot be run in harness—although this is often the case in practice—because they pull against one another. Nor can they be combined in one 'antiracist multicultural' package, because, despite shared elements in teaching content and methodology, and theoretical moves in this direction (Grinter, 1985; Lynch, 1987), the differences between the two strategies make this concept a contradiction in terms.

It is the argument of this chapter that these differences cannot be reconciled. Multicultural education is based on the belief that racism is founded on misunderstanding and ignorance that leave individuals open to racist misrepresentation of non-White ways of life and value systems. The philosophy attempts to promote a more positive understanding and appreciation of Black cultures, and thereby begin to undermine racism. Antiracist education on the other hand believes that racism as an ideology is based on learnt attitudes of White superiority to human groups that Europe and North America have historically exploited. These attitudes have helped to ensure that an unequal distribution of power and resources between racial groups is accepted as natural, and that structural factors that maintain this inequality are not questioned. 'Positive images' of Black peoples (Jeffcoate, 1978) are therefore unlikely to have any effect beyond covering inequalities and deprivation of human rights with a veneer of good feelings, and therefore rendering racism in the social, economic and political systems more acceptable to its victims.

As a result, antiracist education as a philosophy maintains that education based on individual cultural understanding will not eradicate racism, because racism is not rooted in cultural misunderstanding and negative images of Black cultures. The impact of positive cultural images is under constant erosion from the effects of social and economic competition for limited resources and opportunities. Negative images are seen as important contributory elements to racism, but essentially as symbols rather than causes. British thinking on this issue is, from the antiracist perspective, stuck at the point of negative images, rather than examining the processes that have produced significant, though unevenly distributed, elements of achievement and prosperity in Black communities.

Antiracist education maintains that multicultural education has been relatively ineffective. In terms of educational thinking and practice, multicultural education has been the more widely influential approach. It was created by White teachers in the 1960s to meet perceived problems of Black youth, and adopted in a half-hearted manner by the state in the 1970s. However, two decades of multicultural education and race relations work in Britain have not significantly reduced the racist behaviour and discrimination which have been so evident in Britain since large-scale Black immigration began in the 1950s. The denial of human rights on racial grounds was, if anything, increasing at the end of the 1980s. The same has been true in Europe generally, where policy has been an 'intercultural' variant of multicultural education. Even where multicultural education has been regarded as successful, and in Canada elevated to national policy, this is arguably because, until recently, racism as understood in Britain in terms of Black-White relations has not been part of the national experience: instead the country has had to deal with cultural and religious differences and antagonisms more amenable to a multicultural treatment.

It was this relative ineffectiveness of multicultural education that led at the end of the 1970s to the emergence of antiracist education as an initiative led by Black communities and scholars, and of an increasingly bitter debate between the two philosophies. It is the argument of this chapter that, in theoretical terms, antiracist education has won the argument. Its theory incorporates a fuller range of factors contributing to racism, particularly its historical roots, class contexts and the denial of political, social and economic rights by group discrimination for the benefit of the existing holders of power. Antiracist educational practice relates to that full context, and thus to the living experience of those experiencing discrimination. In contrast, multicultural education, as practised in the United Kingdom at least, has the fundamental shortcoming that it cannot incorporate and respond to this context and these experiences, without abandoning its philosophical base of cultural causation of conflict, and, in fact, becoming antiracist education.

Therefore, antiracist education is not an addition to multicultural education which its advocates can hope for multicultural educators to 'take on board'. The antiracist perspective transforms the whole approach, and demands a fundamental rethinking of all teaching, including multicultural teaching, and of the nature of educational structures. This is why it has been resisted, and why a smooth transition from the multicultural to an antiracist position is a utopian hope, and an 'antiracist multiculturalism' an impossibility.

The conflict between the two strategies is now proving counterproductive. This was particularly true in Britain in the 1980s, when the philosophy of government, although paying lip-service to equality and cultural diversity, disliked and opposed both. Government policies have created a context of social, economic and political polarization. One aspect of these policies has been support for gradualist multicultural education in order to blunt a more direct education against racism, using a classic stratagem of divide and rule. The 'approved' multicultural philosophy has been associated with the British political tradition of pragmatic evolutionary reform based on a consensual view of society. Government policy has characterized the opposing antiracist philosophy as part of a more theoretical and 'socialist' tradition of thoroughgoing reform based on a recognition of conflict in society. There is a great deal of truth in these characterizations, but the political conflict between the two philosophies has made government policies only too easy to implement.

It is now urgent to move beyond this debate, while recognizing its validity and its creative value in the immediate past. British society needs a new and more comprehensive vision towards which to aim once the unrepresentative orthodoxy of the 1980s is abandoned. This vision must refer to a society in which all people, whatever their differences of 'race', culture, gender, physical or intellectual abilities, are valued equally, have the opportunity to make contributions which are equally valued and rewarded appropriately. To achieve this vision, both multicultural and antiracist education will have to be incorporated in a movement that is greater than both, and in which their present bitter dispute can become part of a wider and still more positive debate, assisted perhaps by the adoption of a new terminology.

Historical Context: The 1960s and 1970s

It is important to place the debate between these two forms of education in its historical context. As James Banks has pointed out, multicultural education (in which, writing from an American viewpoint analyzed below, he includes antiracist education) was part of the reform movements of the 1960s in both Europe and America (Banks and Banks, 1989). It was a pragmatic movement, dedicated in the UK to removing such obstacles to Black students operating effectively in the education system as lack of language facility and an ethnocentric curriculum. It was closely related to a child-centred philosophy of education, relating educational provision and strategies to students' needs and experiences. It was regarded by many as left-wing and 'trendy', but in many ways was associated with the existing national policy of 'assimilating' immigrants into national life with as little disturbance as possible to the existing system. It was inevitably problem-centred, and soon to be criticized as an attempt to compensate for presumed deficiencies of Black students and their communities.

This view was supported by a government-defined objective for 'The Education of Immigrants' to 'safeguard against any lowering of standards, due to the presence of large numbers of non-English speaking children which might adversely affect the progress of other children' (DES, 1971).

This ad hoc approach to multicultural education was continued through the 1970s with a wide range of initiatives, some superficial and others more radical according to teachers' situations and personal philosophies. Practice was far from homogeneous: some teachers attempted to tackle racism by attacking stereotypes and ethnocentric images in the curriculum (Jeffcoate, 1978), while others remained satisfied with the celebration of festivals associated with 'other' cultures. These celebrations were designed to increase the self-esteem of Black students by giving value to their cultures, and thereby increase their identification with school, their motivation and their academic achievement. Equally important was the hope to nurture esteem for these cultures among indigenous pupils, which would then transfer to the Black students whose way of life had been 'experienced'. Accurate information would replace the ignorance and half-truths which had nourished negative stereotypes and racist opinions. Unfortunately, the presentations of Black cultures often took a very traditional form, and celebrations were not followed up with analysis. A 'tokenist' treatment often confirmed the stereotypes that teachers had sought to eradicate.

Moreover, all initiatives took place in a local context, whether that of individual teachers, schools or local education authorities. This has meant that 'the overall objectives and philosophy of multicultural education have been insufficiently thought out' (Swann, 1985, p. 222). The variation in practice has been reflected in the variety of terminologies that developed in an attempt to create a theoretical framework, including 'multiracial', 'multiethnic', 'culturally pluralist' and 'intercultural' education. There was no one definition of multicultural education, which, as the Swann Report concluded, 'has permitted not only the widest theoretical interpretations and broadest policy objectives, but also a considerable mismatch between these and educational practices' (*ibid.*, p. 198).

However, an important step forward in the theory and practice of multicultural education had been taken, from compensation for 'cultural inferiority' as part of what the Home Secretary Roy Jenkins in 1968 described as 'a flattening process of assimilation', to a celebration of 'cultural pluralism'. Developed first in the USA (Glazer, 1977), this is the present-day orthodoxy. It is the 'major foundation' of the Swann Report, *Education for All*, which has been described as a multicultural manifesto (Brandt, 1986). Under the term 'ethnic diversity' it has been adopted as the frame of reference in the emerging National Curriculum (DES, 1989). Central to the concept of pluralism is that all cultures in British society are recognized as equal in status and validity. The pluralist policy is, therefore, one 'allowing and where necessary assisting the ethnic minority communities in maintaining their distinct ethnic identities. . . . Moreover, it enables, expects and encourages members of all ethnic groups, both minority and majority, to participate fully in shaping the society as a whole within a framework of commonly accepted values, practices and procedures' (Swann, 1985, p. 5).

Of central importance was the Report's insistence that this education should be provided for *all* students, to reduce racial prejudice and educate all citizens into the value of cultural pluralism for social cohesion and consensus. Cultural pluralism provided the theoretical basis for policies of cultural celebration and affirmation to promote understanding through cultural exchange, adding a new emphasis on common elements rather than exotic differences. Cultural pluralism is an important reinforcement to the consensual view of society. As a concept it allowed for further developments in the multicultural philosophy which will be examined below, but it also set a limit to these by excluding antiracism. It thus set multicultural education even more firmly on a collision course in the 1980s with the antiracist education movement that had emerged at the end of the previous decade, as a powerful critique of multicultural education's earlier theory and practice.

This critique was particularly effective, since multicultural education during the 1970s was working through exploratory stages that left it open to criticism from antiracist education for failing to understand and address the real issues involved in racism. In this respect the most important characteristic of the existing multicultural approaches was that they relied on transmission and sharing of a wide range of 'positive' educational experiences in the classroom, and hoped that the resulting insights would transfer to and transform personal and social behaviour. Antiracist education denied this as a possibility. It demanded a more overt, direct and analytical approach to the living experiences of racism for pupils and their communities, both inside and outside school, and for assistance in combatting these experiences. It thus began as a more coherent movement than multicultural education at that time, and one that was highly divergent from it. The only possibility for convergence between the two movements was through changes in the theory and practice of multicultural education.

The Historical Context: 1980s

The changes in multicultural education during the 1980s need to be set in the distinctive political context of that decade, particularly the government's sustained attack on socialist values and policies, and its wholesale transformation of the educational system by the legislation of 1986–1988 (Education Reform Acts 1 and 11, 1986, National Curriculum, 1988, etc.).

Several established features of state policy were maintained. There has been no systematic attempt to eradicate racism in society, despite growing evidence of the damage racism does to life chances through the way social structures operate and are reinforced in education (Wright, 1985; Commission for Racial Equality, 1988). Nor has there been a coherent overall strategy for education against racism, since policy-making and implementation have been both delegated and limited. Policy-making has been delegated to research bodies like the National Federation for Educational Research, curriculum development bodies like the Schools Council (before its restructuring in 1983 to curb its innovative tendencies) and Committees of Enquiry, whose Reports (Rampton, 1981; Swann, 1985) could be selectively commended and then largely ignored. In fact, the major response to the Swann Report was to write out its references to antiracist education, and then in 1986 downgrade multicultural education from a recently acquired 'national priority' status. All these bodies lacked power of enforcement.

Policy-making and implementation in practice have been delegated to local education authorities (LEAs), who thus have the immediate responsibility to counter Black protest and absorb Black anger against inadequate policies. Moreover, the initially considerable, and in several cases well used, powers of LEAs to initiate policies of multicultural and antiracist education have been severely reduced as part of a general reduction of LEA independence in policy-making. The Inner London Education Authority, which made and supported the most significant policy initiatives against racism in education, was abolished in 1990.

This policy of delegation and control has been completed by the restructuring of educational policy-making in the Education Reform Act (II), 1986. Essentially, it places the major responsibility for each school's policies and curriculum in the hands of its Governing Body, where LEA representatives will be only one of many voices, quite possibly outvoted on issues of principle by parents, community and teacher representatives. Ironically, it was the Swann Committee, pursuing the implementation of a coherent strategy for all children, who suggested that the matter could not be left to separate LEA initiatives, and thus helped unwittingly to legitimize a process which has emasculated the hitherto most effective agents for both multicultural and antiracist education.

The Education Reform Acts of 1986 are the institutional expression in education of the government's overall philosophy of privatization and promotion of the market economy. Intervention on behalf of interest groups is disapproved, and its agents rendered impotent on their clients' behalf. The reality of conflict in society in protest against unjust and uneven distribution of resources and opportunities is ignored, in favour of a consensual view of British society. This view does include cultural diversity, as will be shown in analysis of the National Curriculum Guidelines, but the governing philosophy opposes group identities in favour of a single 'British' identity, which it sees as the major focus for each citizen's loyalty. Undoubtedly, the race riots of 1981 and 1985 have contributed to this strategy of disempowering those social groups who were attempting to empower themselves. Struggles for justice are now regarded as matters of private concern and endeavour.

Schooling therefore becomes a matter for private choice in the educational market, and each school tailors its product to meet demand. Ideological preferences have been legitimized as criteria for choice in education, since racist or class-conscious parents will be able to insulate their children from educational experiences or philosophies of which they disapprove (Grinter, 1989). One form of multicultural education, yet to be defined in detail in the National Curriculum, and even then to be applied according to each school's perceptions and situation, is required for all. Antiracist education, to whatever extent it can be included in the prescribed National Curriculum, will however be a matter for local choice. There is little doubt that it is inner-city schools that will opt for an antiracist approach, and 'all-White' suburban and country area schools that will in all probability exclude it.

This system can legitimately be seen as one of containing antiracist education within geographical areas, and pacification by response to local needs, within a national framework of culturally plural 'education for all'. Some might call it a form of educational apartheid. It is the outcome of a policy of divide and rule, implemented through private choice in an unequal, stratified society where racism is active in many people's thinking and institutionalized to significant degrees in many areas of national life.

The strategy has also included selective incorporation of 'approved' policies and the exclusion of those that are disapproved. It is instructive to note that government policy took up and legitimized cultural pluralism as a basis for 'Education for All' from the Swann Report, and excluded its many and often forceful recommendations for antiracist education from its guidelines for the National Curriculum. This is quite consistent with its response to the work of the Committee of Enquiry at all stages. Its interim report on *West Indian Children in Our Schools*, published in 1981 under the chairmanship of Anthony Rampton, treated racism in schools and society at large as a significant cause of Black underachievement in education. No action was taken. When the final Report, *Education for All*, was published in 1985, under the chairmanship of Lord Swann, it contained much information on the damaging effects of racism in education, and a number of radical proposals for antiracist education under the heading 'political education', that are considered in detail in a later section. Lord Swann then wrote a summary of the lengthy Report, which made hardly any references to racism and concentrated on cultural pluralism. It was on these terms that the Report was incorporated into public policy. The Committee had, in fact, been prevented from attempting to incorporate antiracist education into multicultural education. The government had quite clearly made its choice between what it saw as two incompatible philosophies in what has become a campaign against antiracist education. There has been no opportunity for convergence in practice between the two philosophies.

This political context is the source of the continued and bitter debate in the UK between the two philosophies. Government policy has taken on board multicultural education in its cultural pluralism form, as part of a policy that will in all probability exclude effective antiracist education from the largely White areas where it is most needed. This has been done in a context of policies designed to emasculate the struggle of Black communities for justice. Moreover, inadequate and damaging forms of multicultural education have been legitimized along with more effective education against racist stereotyping. It is not surprising that there is deep distrust by antiracists of any multicultural theorizing that attempts to operate within the education system on the terms that have been imposed.

The Extent of Divergence

The nature of antiracist education and its conflict with multicultural education are more fully seen by development of the points of divergence that have already been established.

First, multicultural education believes in the perfectibility of the existing social structure, and assimilation of its component cultures into a social consensus with shared values. The hope is that, given an adequate start through the motivation and self-esteem created by positive images of all cultures, all groups can prosper and progress. Underachievement is seen in terms of cultural interference.

In contrast, antiracist education believes in the reality and significance of conflict in a social system that concentrates power in White, middle-class and male hands, and which discriminates against other groups on grounds of their 'inadequacy' or 'incompetence'. Society is not seen as a neutral area for sharing values, but an arena in which dominant values impose themselves on cultures that are not equal in power or value. Powerful forces operate against prosperity and progress for minority groups, and reduce the impact of any increase in educational qualifications, that may result from increased self-esteem. Ethnic identity is seen as strong (Stone, 1981), and underachievement as much more the outcome of the damaging effects on motivation from limited employment and promotion opportunities in society. Equally important contributions to underachievement are institutional factors such as the low numbers and status of Black teachers, and the low expectations of underachieving groups that are held by teachers, and reflected in streaming and assessment procedures that place Black students disproportionately in low academic classes (Wright, 1985), or categorize them disproportionately as in special educational need. The focus on identity by multicultural education is seen as essentially a focus on the problems of the victims, made to divert attention from the real, institutional sources of underachievement. Education is only of value if it can affect these procedures. The two philosophies reflect significantly different political philosophies, split at their root between acceptance and rejection of the existing socio-economic system and its power relationships.

Second, multicultural education believes in long-term educational policies that persuade individuals to change their attitudes towards other people and their culture. Racism is seen as an unfortunate personal aberration (Brandt, 1986), based on ignorance and misunderstanding which can be countered by accurate information. This approach, it is hoped, will lead to greater appreciation of cultural pluralism, and thus prevent fragmentation of society into separate and conflicting cultural groups. For multicultural education, 'race' is seen in cultural terms and 'depoliticized'. This is deliberate policy, since one of the main charges made by multicultural education against antiracism is that its political emphasis deliberately creates social fragmentation. The multicultural philosophy therefore consciously attempts to be 'non-political'. This accounts for its popularity with teachers who have a social conscience, but who would not consider themselves activists in a political sense.

Antiracist education, in contrast, sees racism as an organizing principle of the social and political structure, closely linked to a system of class and other forms of discrimination that deny human rights—'an artificial construct designed to facilitate and perpetuate inequalities' (Garrison, 1984). Cultures themselves are oppressed as part of this system, and multiculturalism has not tackled the discrimination that cultural minorities suffer. The 'fossilized views' of traditional cultures used in some versions of multicultural education are regarded as part of this process, and a means of dividing the Black struggle on cultural grounds (Murray, 1985). The system of discrimination can only be confronted by examining the unequal power networks in society that reduce some groups to powerlessness, and the power of the racist stereotypes that reinforce them. Given that power, cultural information on its own is likely only to produce better informed racists. An improvement in life chances is the aim, not an improvement in understanding lifestyles, and the belief that the latter can lead to the former is considered to be utopian (Hatcher and Shallice, 1983).

Third, these differences in emphasis on cultural or political factors distinguish the aims of the two philosophies. It is sometimes argued from the multicultural perspective that both philosophies are concerned to achieve greater social justice. But the philosophies have different conceptions of social justice: multicultural education looks for justice in cultural terms of equal valuation, while antiracist education demands equivalent opportunities and equivalent progress for members of all racial groups. In the antiracist view, multicultural education, by reducing racial issues to cultural ones, has avoided the key issue of empowerment against racist practices.

Certainly the respective emphases on educational and political purposes are chiefly responsible for the bitterness in the conflict between the two philosophies. It is clear that antiracist education sees the multicultural approach as indirectly strengthening the hold of racism by reducing some of its more extreme symptoms in schools. Multicultural education is analyzed as a 'cooling-out' process (Stone, 1981), as an attempt to pre-empt or diffuse Black anger (Mullard, 1980) or 'palliate ethnic rage' (Banks, 1984b). The policy has been reduced by one commentator to that of negotiating classroom peace by pacification (Carby, 1982). For antiracist education, even if the damage done by racism is reduced by multicultural teaching, the potential for damage remains because the system has not been changed. If the structure is made more acceptable, it is strengthened and perpetuated. Indeed, some commentators regard multicultural education as a policy of containment, that operates by coopting Black people into the social and educational system. For its part, multicultural education characterizes antiracism as a policy that brings political confrontation into education. Antiracist education is accused of using techniques of political indoctrination that alienate colleagues, and damage multicultural policies for improving the life chances of minority children through conventionally approved educational processes.

The experience of the 1980s has confirmed the conflict. Multicultural education has been incorporated into the education system because it relates to existing educational practice, contributes to forming a social consensus, is 'non-political' and does not challenge the existing status quo. Even if, as we shall see, it widens its range to demand changes outside the curriculum, it can be accommodated to the benefit of the existing structure. Antiracist education cannot be part of that process. It is oppositional to the existing structure by its very nature, and cannot be incorporated into its existing processes.

Antiracist education aims, through learning processes that question the social structure and its basic assumptions, to produce activists against social injustice. Part of antiracist education is to involve students in analysis of the whole school ethos and power structure, and in work to identify and remove racism from their educational institution. Its emphasis is far less on the cultural content of the curriculum than on learning processes that will develop students' powers of analysis and action. As Brandt points out, these processes are collaborative rather than child-centred. Antiracist education must challenge racism. Its theorists argue that thereby it develops learning skills as effective as any other version of 'good education'. Brandt summarizes the skills as those that can enable students to recognize and dismantle stereotypes, deconstruct the ethnocentric view of the world, and reconstruct a more just vision of society (Brandt, 1986).

Antiracist education claims to relate to the real world that most children of all minority communities know only too well. Either as individuals or as members of their communities, they know conflict and resistance as real experiences. Antiracist education is consistently seen by its theorists and practitioners as support for the struggle of minority communities for justice, as an education in liberation that will change the consensus in partnership with social and political movements outside the school. This is the very reverse of assimilation. The White consensus is the problem, and it is this that needs analysis by Mullard's 'Three O's': Observation of the processes of racism, a new Orientation towards White society and adoption of a strategy of Opposition to the system of racial discrimination (Mullard, 1984).

Since antiracist education is oppositional to the existing system of class and race-based inequality, and to educational practices that reflect and reinforce that structure, it is not surprising that antiracist education policies have almost always to date been linked to local education authorities in large urban areas, administered by Councils responsive to the needs of minorities. In the national context of Britain in the 1980s antiracist policies have therefore almost always been oppositional within the system, and an object of political attack. It is quite logical that the area of operation for antiracist education is likely to be severely restricted through the working of the Education Reform Act outlined earlier.

This oppositional characteristic of antiracist education is the conclusive demonstration that it cannot be reconciled with a multicultural education constructed on a basis of consensus in a culturally pluralist society. Unlike that policy, it cannot be taken on board by the established system. Its task has been and will remain that of designing an effective and subversive role within the established system.

Convergence or Takeover?

Major initiatives for convergence in this debate have recently been made from the multicultural education perspective. Radical and progressive theorists, active in the area from the 1970s, have recognized the shortcomings in their policies and the implications of cultural pluralism in a spirit consistent with the pragmatic tradition. They have attempted to establish a 'more broadly conceived multicultural education' (Lynch, 1987, p. 9) by incorporating elements of antiracist education.

As James Banks points out, some moves forward have been made in response to 'right-wing' criticism. The 'strong' cultural pluralism of the Swann Report, set within a common framework of shared values, has been developed by attempts to define a 'common core' of basic democratic principles (Lynch, 1987), and the concept of 'intercultural competence' of equal citizens (Banks and Banks, 1989), as a response to the criticism that cultural support meant cultural fragmentation. Further developments that recognize and legitimize elements of fundamental value conflict will be necessary in response to the Muslim community's protests against the publication of *The Satanic Verses* (Rushdie, 1988). The academic benefits of drawing on all students' life experiences, and the need to use a blend of learning strategies that responds to individual (and, in pluralist terms, 'cultural') learning styles have been stressed, in response to accusations of sacrificing children's life chances in a watered-down educational menu of 'steel bands, samosas and saris' (Stone, 1981). Multicultural education has also been extended by far-sighted teachers to include collaborative learning for a global perspective (Fisher and Hicks, 1985) and recognition of the achievements of indigenous as well as Black minority cultures.

It is important to note that antiracist education damages its credibility with teachers if it does not recognize that these initiatives have a valid contribution to make to all children's education. Multicultural education is recognizably 'good education' in British terms, building up children's confidence and beginning indirectly to modify ethnocentric attitudes which are undoubtedly part of racism. The appropriate point of criticism is that, like much 'good education', this is not antiracist, because it does not address British racism in structural terms.

The major attempts to broaden multicultural education to incorporate antiracism began with the Swann Report. In its second chapter it identified White racism as the key obstacle to successful cultural pluralism, and demanded education to combat it. It termed ethnocentric education a 'fundamental *miseducation*', encouraged a critical analysis of British society in a global context, and a 'fundamental reconsideration' of attitudes found in teaching materials. Under the heading 'Political Education', it allied cultural pluralism with education in the skills of rational argument to combat prejudice, and proclaimed a commitment to equality and justice. The Report argued for 'providing ethnic minority youth with the skills necessary to participate in political activities . . . opening their minds to the possibility that existing practices may and sometimes should be amended or replaced' (Swann, 1985, p. 339). In terms that are very relevant to the National Curriculum, it advocated that if this cannot be done directly, the political dimension of existing subject areas should be explicitly developed.

However, this is still not antiracist education. There is a clear emphasis on 'positive rather than negative forms of expression' within the political framework, and the stated aim of 'countering the sense of alienation' of Black youth speaks the language of containment (*ibid.*, p. 339). This sets a limit to the empowerment of Black youth, which may often run beyond existing practices to create new processes. Antiracist education argues that these activities need to be assisted on their own terms and legitimized, whatever their implications for the 'system'.

The multicultural philosophy has been taken further to become a policy for 'prejudice reduction' in schools to undermine discrimination by the majority community that 'usurps human rights' and 'denies equality of opportunity or status' to minority groups (Lynch, 1987, p. 24). Rational analysis of indoctrination by ethnocentric images is now claimed to be central to multicultural education: moreover, this must include analysis of the social context and the impact of discriminatory stereotypes on all students from all cultures.

In common with many other educators, and with recent publications by British teacher unions (AMMA, 1987; NUT, 1989), Lynch places great emphasis on the need for a whole school, holistic approach to cultural pluralism. This must include full discussion of the norms and values of the schools, teacher expectations of their pupils, and the adoption of collaborative and open learning activities. He also argues for changes in the institutional structure, such as assessment and grouping procedures, and the ethnic composition of its staff, and for policies to respond effectively to racist incidents. It is at this point, if not before, that the attempts to incorporate antiracist education change the policy to one of antiracist education.

From the American perspective, James Banks also argues for a 'total school response' as a fourth 'level' in a comprehensive package that includes antiracist education (Banks and Banks, 1989). His first three 'levels' are 'Ethnic contributions' in terms of heroes and festivals, 'Ethnic additions' in terms of separate units and courses, and 'Transformation', where the perspectives of all cultures involved in topics of study are given equal validity and significance. All these are recognizably multicultural education, although the latter opens up important and in the UK not yet fully explored antiracist curriculum possibilities. His fourth 'level' is 'Social action', where students become 'reflective social critics' and 'agents of social change to close the gap between ideals and reality'. This again marks the point where multicultural education becomes antiracist and changes the basis for action. But, very much as the author of this chapter in an earlier article (Grinter, 1985), Banks regards the move to his fourth 'level' as a smooth and natural one, and argues for a 'mix and blend' approach. He argues that 'one approach can be used as a vehicle to move to another and more intellectually challenging approach', and that 'the move from the first to the higher levels of ethnic content is likely to be gradual and culmulative' (Banks and Banks, 1989, p. 202).

It is interesting that in the American context Banks sees no conflict between multicultural and antiracist education. As he himself points out, antiracism, and indeed equal opportunities for both genders, has been a major concern of American educators since the 1960s. The national experience of massive immigration during the last century had already moved social policy on from assimilation into a national 'melting pot', and even beyond the 'cultural mosaic' version of pluralism, before multicultural education emerged as a philosophy. This development in the 1960s happened at a time of major movements for Constitutional civil rights for Black citizens, who had been first enslaved and then exploited throughout American history. Multicultural education in the USA had education against racism as its basis, and has never been the object of severe criticism from the left wing.

The British experience has been historically very different. Large numbers of Black immigrants and 'overt' racism arrived together in the 1950s and 1960s. The problems that emerged were treated by a multicultural approach which, as described earlier, worked through assimilationist and cultural pluralist stages within two decades, but did not seriously address racism. The reasons for this may be related to a left-wing and basically Marxist analysis of racism, with which a teaching profession brought up to individualist, 'non-political' and anti-Marxist thinking did not easily identify. Moreover the importance of the political context already analyzed reappears. Whereas the American political system incorporates as many interest groups as possible, the British tradition of conflict between parties representing class interests marginalizes and labels concern about racism as left-wing. The historical, political and educational contexts are central to understanding the relationships between the two educational philosophies, and the debate in these two chapters may well be one between the appropriateness of different strategies for different national and political contexts.

In the UK context of conflict between the two philosophies, antiracist education is clearly, from recent developments, 'winning the debate'. Multicultural education is becoming increasingly 'antiracist', by emphasizing its role in the struggle against racism, and incorporating 'conative' behavioural elements as well as cognitive and affective ones (Lynch, 1987). The problem for antiracist education is that protagonists for broadened multicultural education are moving to take over and incorporate their philosophy.

> None of the educational strategies proposed by anti-racist writers are per se incompatible with a more broadly conceived multicultural education. Most of them are indeed already on the agenda. . . . But it is essential that not only the educational but also the broader social critique

is taken seriously and scrutinised for its educational content and implications. In this way the antiracist critique can contribute to the development of a more effective multicultural education, not least because it has focussed on the way in which discrimination, prejudice and their correlates inhibit and destroy that very intercommunication and interlinking which are so necessary to a pluralist society, and to the negotiation of the common core values essential to its survival. (Lynch, 1987, p. 10)

But antiracist education can and will resist this pressure to absorb its emphasis on class and political factors into an emphasis on intercultural communication. The crucial factor is the multicultural move towards taking up political action. This is a move that cannot be made convincingly, because multicultural education is a school-based philosophy that believes that, as schools reflect the social structure, they therefore have a limited power to change society (Lynch, 1987). It works through schools rather than by confrontation with them. Moreover, if schools are racist, it is difficult, if not futile, as Banks points out, to try to promote change within them (Banks, 1984a). There must, therefore, be pressure from outside, and this can operate since schools are places of conflict where, as in society, many ideals are compromised in practice (Green, 1982). These conflicts can be identified and strategies can be devised to question them in conjunction with community movements. This is a political exercise, and, as teachers instinctively recognize, a point at which antiracist education as an oppositional philosophy must separate from multicultural education.

Multicultural education can, using children's life experiences, promote the understanding of inequality, commitment to social change and some of the intellectual skills to employ in the process. This is a grey area between the two philosophies which many teachers would unhesitatingly label 'antiracist'. But even if multicultural education is against racism and cultural oppression on these terms, it cannot be overtly 'political'. This proposes a new function for educators where they will, at least in existing terms, have forsaken their professional function (Banks, 1984b). This demands a new definition of 'professional' in education, based on antiracist education's oppositional role, in effective conjunction with community groups. This is essential while the state remains uncommitted to social justice and racism remains so powerful. Antiracist education must remain a separate philosophy, to operate on behalf of powerless or underempowered groups and communities. It must resist attempts at incorporation, because, if this occurs, it will no longer be oppositional or credible with communities, since it will be compromised with the traditional elements still powerful within multicultural education. If theory allows itself to be compromised, so will the freedom and rights for which it campaigns be compromised, and the theory become just another element in the policy of containment which is still being pursued. The 'interminable debate' must go on (Mogdil *et al.*, 1986).

Some elements in the debate have been counterproductive, because important elements in the situation of minorities are excluded on both sides. Multicultural education excludes 'class oppression', and antiracist education excludes 'cultural oppression'. Some aspects of the debate, for example the political rhetoric which has alienated many teachers, have allowed the state to divide and rule in this aspect of education and therefore assisted that strategy in relation to society at large. Changes are needed, and perhaps more subtle strategies by antiracist education at this time of challenge by multicultural education. The new context created by the now evolving National Curriculum offers the opportunity for new strategies in which both multicultural and antiracist education operate to reduce racism, but from quite separate philosophical positions.

The Context of the National Curriculum

The National Curriculum, emerging in the UK since 1988 for all state-maintained schools, will establish a new context for education against racism. It will standardize approved good practice in prescribed 'Programmes of Study' in ten academic disciplines, with attainment targets for students in each discipline, to be assessed four times during a school career.

The National Curriculum is fully consistent with the analysis of government policy made in this chapter. It is an exercise in control and containment, intended to exclude unsatisfactory or undesirable classroom practice. There is little doubt that antiracist education curriculum packages for direct study of racism are seen in this second category and will be excluded. There is no reference in any of the official documents to antiracist education, nor to concepts like equality or justice. There are strong statements against political indoctrination, and little reference to any elements of conflict in national life. Moreover, this emphasis on the curriculum in education reduces concern with institutional structures which are the more important determinants of life chances for minority students. Antiracist education is therefore confirmed in its oppositional stance through exclusion. Its freedom for action is also severely reduced, and its role is now quite evidently a subversive one from outside the system.

In contrast, emphasis on the curriculum is very appropriate for multicultural education, which is quite clearly included in the new structure. Programmes of Study must 'take into account the ethnic and cultural diversity of British society . . . and multicultural issues across the curriculum' (DES, 1989). Moreover, these programmes are for all students, as Swann recommended, and conceived in a spirit of cultural pluralism. Multicultural education is thus enabled to work through the curriculum structure to promote cultural understanding and to work against stereotyping. But the National Curriculum is emerging in most subject areas in very traditional forms. It is clearly a major reinforcement for the consensual view of British society, and the creation of a single national identity as a focus for loyalty. This focus is very likely to remain ethnocentric, since the Secretary of State's response to the Interim Report on History's proposal for more global history was to require that at every stage at least half the time is devoted to teaching national history.

It is hard to predict how the relationship between multicultural and antiracist education will be affected by the National Curriculum. At first sight the new context will confirm the divergence between the two philosophies, since it places them in very different positions in relationship to the new structure. Multicultural education will concentrate on developing its curriculum role with official support, permeating the work of each subject area—a policy that has been already criticized as a 'road to nowhere', since it is at the mercy of existing teacher attitudes (ARTEN, 1987). Antiracist education will have to make use of non-National Curriculum areas like personal and social education, and the opportunity for 'political-education' offered by Sections 44 and 45 of the Education Reform Act, 1986. This insists on a 'balanced presentation of opposite views', but at least allows discussion of 'politically controversial issues', to 'encourage pupils to form their own opinions on the basis of evidence and discussion'. There is still a role for work with teachers to influence their attitudes and expectations in the new assessment procedures, with some opportunity to influence institutional thinking and organization, and thereby the whole school structure. Efforts for antiracist education will concentrate on influencing teachers to use the freedom they have in delivery of the National Curriculum to employ learning processes that draw on students' life experiences and develop life skills that assist young Black people to operate successfully in antiracist campaigns, as well as meeting attainment targets. 'Equity and Justice do not eliminate commitment to academic excellence' (Lynch, 1987). This subversive role will be particularly relevant in multiracial areas where school Governing Bodies will endorse such efforts.

But there are forces for convergence between the two philosophies created by the National Curriculum structure. Antiracist education cannot allow a national ethnocentric curriculum monopolized by cultural pluralism to dictate the images and messages conveyed to students. It may have to develop a more coherent curriculum policy, using the same programmes of study and attainment targets as multicultural education. An antiracist perspective must be developed in line with the best academic teaching to 'deconstruct and reconstruct' the knowledge in the prescribed curriculum. For example, history teachers may be able to use opportunities provided by local studies and the global context in programmes of study, and the understanding of bias in attainment targets to combat racism. At Key Stages 1–3 (ages 5–14) there should be good opportunities still for all teachers to develop cross-curriculum work that can explore human relationships from a variety of perspectives. But this shared context will mean that multicultural and antiracist education are working perforce in combination, though for very different purposes.

A New Vision

This chapter ends with an attempt to look ahead in the UK context. The governing philosophy and spirit which dominated the 1980s and have been so powerful an influence on the debate between these two educational philosophies, will change. The new educational structure will remain, although there may well be more room for change within it than is intended. The important issue for this debate is whether two divergent philosophies can operate effectively in the new structure on their own terms without continuing to damage by their conflict the campaign against racism in education.

A new view of teacher professionalism will be part of any positive outcome. In a sense all good teachers are at present involved in an oppositional stance to the new structure, to preserve good practice and also the right to choose the most appropriate education for their students. 'Broader' multicultural and antiracist education are both involved in this campaign through their association with learning activities such as collaborative learning, role play and assertiveness training based on valuing all students' life experiences. On a wider perspective, the National Curriculum embodies a particular view of society, and antiracist education needs to work for the professional legitimacy of education for a different form of society, in association with social groups whose interests are damaged by the existing one.

Both philosophies need to strengthen their credibility in the profession. Antiracist education must overcome the association with political indoctrination. There needs to be a non-Marxist, 'Western democratic' version of antiracism that is as powerful as the Marxist version, against all indoctrination based on class, cultural, ethnocentric or gender stereotypes. Multicultural education is beginning to recognize its political implications, and to oppose racist attacks on 'positive images'. In a recent publication, a teachers' organization not noted for its 'radicalism' has stressed the importance of antiracist education to clear away racist stereotypes that devalue cultures before multicultural education can build—or defend—more positive images (AMMA, 1987). But antiracist education cannot and will not allow itself to be combined with multicultural education to play a role as a short-term strategy to allow cultural pluralism to operate through long-term attitude change. For antiracist education, that process is too long and uncertain to eradicate an immediate and pressing evil.

A wider vision is required. Both philosophies are part of a struggle for a more democratic society against a system where many social groups face covert, if not open, discrimination. A system of exclusion from full power operates against minority groups, including women as a gender, Black communities, unemployed or low-paid working-class families and disabled people, for the benefit of an identifiable group of largely White, male, middle-class holders of social status and political power. The system discriminates on a similar basis for all minority groups, categorizing their members and applying stereotypes based on 'innate characteristics' that determine behaviour, make inferior status 'natural' and change impossible. This is a denial of full human rights, which makes conflict inevitable and creates a political dimension for all social and political activity. The vision needed for all who work against racism, sexism, cultural or class oppression is of a society that empowers members of all its component groups to make their full contribution. It is a vision based on inclusion rather than exclusion, through liberation from discrimination by undemocratic practices, so that all now devalued have equal opportunities to achieve positions where they can exercise power to influence and change decision-making. The outcome will be a new and better consensus.

But many campaigners for greater social justice do not recognize the link between these manifestations of inequality, and the debate—multicultural against antiracist, feminists against both over gender inequalities in cultural practices, Black feminists against White feminists, working-class activists against Black activists—throw campaigns against one another and lessen their credibility. In the USA these movements have been able to unite more effectively, and this must be the model for the UK.

A loose confederation of forces for empowerment is probably the best that can be expected, because debate and disagreement are the lifeblood of campaigns. But this must not obscure the common goal. The emphasis on recovering human rights for all powerless or underempowered groups will assist the credibility of each campaign. It will, for example, go a long way to overcoming the reluctance to accept multicultural and antiracist education in 'all-White' areas if this is linked with work in schools to empower women and unemployed or low-paid white families. A long-term view is needed by all, accepting conflict but working to eradicate the need for it in the long term. A lot of people will have cause for bitter complaint if present conflicts between discrete philosophies prevent this greater empowerment that is essential to a just democratic society.

References

AMMA (Assistant Masters and Mistresses Association (1987) *Multi-Cultural and Anti-racist Education Today*, London, AMMA.

ARTEN (AntiRacist Teacher Education Network) (1987) *Permeation: A Road to Nowhere* (Occasional Paper 6), Jordanhill College Publications.

Banks, J.A. (1984a) *Teaching Strategies for Ethnic Studies*, Boston, Mass., Allyn and Bacon.

Banks, J.A. (1984b) 'Multicultural Education and Its Critics: Britain and the USA', *New Era*, 65, 3, World Education Fellowship, Bembridge, Isle of Wight, pp. 28–35.

Banks, J.A. and Banks, C.A.M. (Eds) (1989) *Multicultural Education: Issues and Principles*, Boston, Mass., Allyn and Bacon.

Brandt, G. (1986) *The Realisation of Antiracist Teaching*, Lewes, Falmer.

Carby, H. (1982) 'Schooling in Babylon', in *The Empire Strikes Back*, Centre for Contemporary Cultural Studies, Birmingham University; London, Hutchinson.

Commission for Racial Equality (1988) *Living in Terror*, London, CRE.

Department of Education and Science (1971) *The Education of Immigrants*, London, HMSO.

Department of Education and Science (1989) *The National Curriculum: from Policy to Practice*, London, DES.

Fisher, S. and Hicks, D. (1985) *World Studies 8–13: A Teachers Handbook*, Edinburgh, Oliver and Boyd.

Garrison, L. (1984) in Occasional Paper for Afro-Caribbean Education Resource Centre, London.

Glazer, N. (1977) 'Cultural Pluralism: The Social Impact', in Tumin, M.M. and Plotch, W. (Eds) *Pluralism in a Democratic Society*, Westport, Conn., Praeger.

Green, A. (1982) 'In Defence of Antiracist Teaching', *Multiracial Education*, 10, 2, pp. 19–36, National Association for Multi-Racial Education.

Grinter, R. (1985) 'Bridging the Gulf: The Need for an Antiracist Multiculturalism', *Multicultural Teaching*, 3, 2, pp. 7–11, Stoke on Trent, Trentham Books.

Grinter, R. (1989) 'Developing an Antiracist National Curriculum', *Multicultural Teaching*, 7, 3, pp. 32–37, Stoke on Trent, Trentham Books.

Hatcher, R. and Shallice, J. (1983) 'The Politics of Antiracist Education', *Multiracial Education*, 12, 1, pp. 3–21, National Association for Multiracial Education.

Jeffcoate, R. (1978) *Positive Image: Towards a Multiracial Curriculum*, London, Writer and Leader Publishing Cooperative.

Lynch, J. (1986) *Multicultural Education: Principles and Practice*, London, Routledge.

Lynch, J. (1987) *Prejudice Reduction and the Schools*, London, Cassell.

Mogdil, S., Verma, G., Mallick, K. and Mogdil, C. (1986) *Multicultural Education: The Interminable Debate*, Lewes, Falmer.

Mullard, C. (1980) *Racism in Society and Schools: History, Policy and Practice* (Occasional Paper), University of London, Institute of Education.

Mullard, C. (1984) *Antiracist Education: The 3 'O's* (Occasional Paper), Derby, National Association for Multicultural Education.

Murray, N. (1985) 'The Multicultural Mask', *New Internationalist*, 145, March, pp. 24–25.

NUT (National Union of Teachers) (1989) *Antiracism in Education: Towards a Whole-School Policy*, London, NUT.

Rampton, A. (1981) *West Indian Children in Our Schools*, London, HMSO.

Rushdie, S. (1988) *The Satanic Verses*, London, Viking.

Stone, M. (1981) *The Education of the Black Child in Britain: The Myth of Multicultural Education*, London, Fontana.

Swann, M. (1985) *Education for All*, London, HMSO.

Wright, C. (1985) 'Who Succeeds at School—and Who Decides?' and 'Learning Environment or Battleground?' *Multicultural Teaching*, 4, 1, pp. 11–23, Stoke-on-Trent, Trentham Books.

Questions

1. Why does Grinter claim that multicultural and antiracist education are incompatible?

2. Describe the evolution of the antiracist movement in the United Kingdom in the 1960's and 1970's.

3. What is a state or national curriculum? Can this type of curriculum accommodate the multicultural condition or the demands of a pluralistic society? Why or why not?

4. What is "educational apartheid"?

5. What are three points of divergence between antiracist and multicultural education? Identify and explain.

6. What is the ethos and power structure of your learning organization?

7. Why hasn't the United States produced a debate between antiracism and multicultural education?

Retain, Relinquish or Revise: The Future for Multicultural Education

Geoffrey Short

Abstract   The recently revived debate between proponents of multicultural and antiracist education provides the starting point for this paper. Whilst not advocating an exclusively multicultural focus, the paper nonetheless seeks to defend multiculturalism against its antiracist critics. It does so in two ways. The first is by showing that the criticisms of its central tenets are either trivial, misguided or equally applicable to antiracist education. The second is by offering a previously unarticulated justification in terms of confronting the 'new racism' and removing the psychological barriers to an effective antiracist education. It is urged that multiculturalism be retained but in a revised form. In particular, stress is placed on the importance of teachers identifying and challenging their pupils' misconceptions of other cultures.

Introduction

The introduction to Troyna's (1993) latest book *Racism and Education* revives what some might regard as the rather hackneyed debate between proponents of multicultural and antiracist education, for it reiterates the author's previously voiced conviction (Troyna, 1987) that these two conceptions of educational reform are irreconcilable. Further on in the volume Troyna notes that 'some theorists and practitioners have remained stubbornly committed to [multiculturalism]' (p. 30). He clearly sees this as a regrettable state of affairs, referring to multicultural education (MCE) as 'a discredited ideological and policy stance'. My own view of MCE is diametrically opposed to Troyna's. I believe it to be entirely compatible with antiracist education and insist, along with others (e.g. Grinter, 1985; Leicester, 1986; Massey, 1991), that both forms of education must be present if initiatives to promote racial justice are to succeed. In this paper, I intend to show that an antiracist intervention shorn of multiculturalism will fail in its objectives. To achieve this aim it will be necessary, in the first instance, to rebut Troyna's core accusation that multiculturalism rests on dubious theoretical and empirical foundations. Before attempting such a rebuttal, however, I want briefly to consider one or two of the more peripheral criticisms that have been directed at multiculturalism. The criticisms are peripheral in the sense that they relate to the practice of MCE rather than to its justification. For example, Troyna and Hatcher (1992) state that:

> both black and white children have reservations about the promotion of ethnic life styles and cultures in the curriculum. Black children feel embarrassed, even stigmatised, in such lessons and other research studies have highlighted their resentment towards the fossilised, sometimes racist presentations of their cultures in school curricula (Mac an Ghaill, 1988). White children, on the other hand, resent the school's apparent privileging of ethnic minority cultures and, as a corollary, the devaluation of their own. (Troyna & Hatcher, 1992: 200)

Sarap (1991: 30) has levelled a peripheral criticism of a different kind. He maintains that MCE presents 'black cultures as homogeneous, static and conflict-free.'

Troyna and Hatcher do not provide any evidence of black children's alleged embarrassment and the only evidence given for white children's resentment is a reference to the events, seven years ago, at Burnage High school in Manchester (Macdonald *et al.*, 1989)—an institution not widely recognised as exemplary of MCE. Nor are we told whether all children react as described, or whether the reaction is a function of one or more factors such as the children's age and the ethnic composition of the school. No one would dispute that ethnic minority cultures *can* be presented in ways that cause embarrassment, but this is a point equally applicable to antiracist education. (Do we know how black children feel when learning about slavery and colonialism or about contemporary manifestations of racism?) Likewise, there is no doubt that an insensitive approach to MCE *could* lead to resentment on the part of white children. But these undesirable consequences are not inherent in MCE; nor is the presentation of black culture as 'homogeneous, static and conflict-free'. The critics have merely identified bad practice.

More fundamental, and thus of more concern, is Troyna's attack on the allegedly 'dubious foundations' of MCE. Although he adumbrates his reservations in *Racism and Education*, I will focus and draw heavily on his 1987 paper where he outlines essentially the same objections, but in considerably more detail. The most basic argument in favour of MCE that Troyna sees as spurious is the claim that because Britain is multicultural, the curriculum should be as well. Other claims he believes to be ill-founded are that learning about different cultures will benefit all students and that cultural relativism is not just a tenable position but one that ought to be actively embraced.

I will argue that Troyna's criticisms of these 'central tenets' are either trivial, misguided or just as pertinent to his preferred strategy of antiracist education. However, I also intend to put forward two arguments in support of a multicultural curriculum that have thus far been overlooked by those committed to it. The first is the role that such a curriculum can play in helping to combat the 'new racism' (Barker, 1981). The second is the need for MCE as a prerequisite of an effective antiracist education.

Troyna's Critique of Multicultural Education

Troyna (1987) begins his critique be referring to Bullivant's (1986) observation that Britain's non-white population largely originates from three parts of the world (Africa, Asia and the Caribbean) and thus Britain, in Bullivant's view, is more accurately described as a tricultural than as a multicultural society. Troyna goes on to say that he is not especially interested in 'the validity' or otherwise of this argument (p. 313). The point he wishes to stress 'is that it is a plausible corrective to the taken-for-granted and most basic premise of (multicultural education)' (p. 313). But if the argument is not valid, it cannot function as a corrective. It is, in fact, difficult to discern the significance of Bullivant's observation, for even if one accepts its validity, the curricular and pedagogic implications would be much the same regardless of whether Britain is deemed to be multicultural or tricultural. The criticism is trivial.

Troyna proceeds to challenge the view [expressed, for example, in the DES (1977) Green Paper, *Education in Schools*] that the curriculum should reflect the fact that Britain is no longer (if it ever was) a monocultural society. He grounds his criticism in Hume's naturalistic fallacy, that is, in the illegitimacy of deriving an 'ought' from an 'is'. Troyna insists that the case for a multicultural curriculum 'needs to be argued cogently rather than asserted' (p. 313). He is, of course, quite right and this particular criticism provides the rationale for those sections of the paper below dealing with the 'new racism' and the implementation of antiracist initiatives.

Moving on to the third foundation, or central tenet, Troyna maintains that two assertions underpin the claim that learning about other cultures will further the interests of all students. The first is that 'black students will benefit academically from learning about their own ethnic and cultural life styles' (p. 313). Specifically, he takes issue with the Rampton Report's (DES, 1981) assumption that learning about their own culture will raise the attainment levels of black students, thereby enabling them to compete more effectively in the labour market. The charge levelled at the Rampton Report is essentially one of naiveté in that if conflates 'the presentation of lifestyles with the enhancement of life chances and, in the process, obscures the determining impact of racism on the school and post-school experiences and opportunities of black students'

(p. 313). Now whilst it is quite possible that a multicultural curriculum will fail to improve the academic attainment of black pupils (not least because their self-concept is perfectly adequate for the purpose (Stone, 1981)) it is manifestly absurd to argue that those who favour such a curriculum ignore or play down the malign influence of racism in the search for employment. The Rampton Report, in fact, states explicit (p. 52) 'that the *overriding* disadvantage which young West Indians face in the jobs market is racial discrimination at all levels' (emphasis added). All that is being claimed is that, other things being equal, black school leavers will find it easier to obtain a job—certainly a job that requires a spell in higher education—the better their academic qualifications. The Swann Report (DES, 1985) had no doubt about the validity of this assumption when lamenting the paucity of ethnic minority teachers:

> The major obstacle to seeking ethnic minority teachers, especially of West Indian origin, . . . is . . . that as long as such pupils continue to underachieve in academic terms . . . they will lack the necessary qualifications for entry to teacher training . . . (Swann Report, 1985: 610)

The supplementary schools that have proliferated since the 1960s suggest that Afro-Caribbean parents are also in no doubt about the value of academic qualifications, despite having to live in a racist society.

The second assertion supporting the claim that MCE will benefit all students relates to its alleged effects in helping to eradicate white children's prejudice. In my view, this is the most important claim made on behalf of MCE and, whilst in need of considerable qualification, has much to commend it. The importance of the claim requires a detailed consideration and, for this reason, I will come back to it after looking briefly at Troyna's final objection to MCE. It concerns the assumption that cultural relativism is a desirable and tenable position. Surprisingly, he makes this criticism despite appearing to recognise that relativism is tenable only if a weak form is espoused (Zec, 1980). The latter is roughly equivalent to objectivity plus empathy. Troyna, though, objects even to a weak relativism on the grounds that it is of no help to teachers wishing to discuss with their pupils some controversial aspect of a minority culture. The illustrative example he provides involves the status of women in Islam. Now insofar as there is a problem here, it is hard to see why it applies only to advocates of multicultural education. What is it about the issue that renders it unproblematic for antiracist educators? Would they ignore it or deal with it differently? Troyna does not tell us. I believe that raising such matters does pose a dilemma for both multicultural *and* antiracist educators and I have recently discussed ways of confronting it in the context of a study exploring 10- and 11-year olds learning about Islam:

> The dilemma relates to the fact that practices such as the ritual slaughter of meat by Muslims, even if properly understood, may cause offence to members of other cultural groups. Teachers are faced with a stark choice: if they choose to keep their pupils in the dark about such prac-

tices this is tantamount to indoctrination. On the other hand, to take up Lynch's (1983) position and to argue that 'not all cultural values are of equal worth' and that some, therefore, ought to be proscribed, could play into the hands of assimilationists on the New Right. For such a stance might be construed as lending support to populist images of Muslims in Britain as not only different but 'alien' . . . In the event, we did not have to deal with the dilemma as time did not permit us to examine this particular controversial issue, but had circumstances been otherwise, we would not have considered it right to censor such discussion. Our way out of the dilemma would have been to stress to the children that while they may well find some aspects of Muslim culture unacceptable and feel the need to argue for their proscription, it is wholly wrong to go further than this and discriminate in any way against other aspects of Islam. (Carrington & Short, 1993: 172)

Troyna (1987: 311) correctly points out that 'multicultural . . . and antiracist education are diffuse conceptions of educational reform and it would . . . be misleading to depict either formulation as embracing a single trajectory or motivating force'. However, it seems to be universally agreed that whatever differences there may be among proponents of multicultural education, there is a consensus that its chief defining characteristic is the need to acquaint children with other cultures. As stated above, multiculturalists believe that, amongst other things, such acquaintance will assist in the battle against prejudice. Troyna finds this premise no less questionable than others. I turn now to consider the basis of his scepticism.

Multiculturalism as a Means of Undermining Prejudice

Before examining the claim that MCE can help to lessen prejudice it may be useful to consider the ways in which educationalists have conceptualised the source of prejudice. According to Troyna (1987), multiculturalists see it as stemming from ignorance. Antiracists, on the other hand, are said to locate its roots in the social and political structure. Now unless one is committed to the irreconcilability of antiracist and multicultural education, there is no need to opt for one explanation in preference to the other. It is perfectly possible for prejudice to stem from more than one source and Troyna, in fact, gives us no reason to think otherwise.

Insofar as MCE can contribute to diminishing prejudice, it will succeed only where the prejudice arises from cultural ignorance. Even so, advocates of MCE will have to concede that, for some children, nothing that is done in the classroom to challenge their ignorance will have the desired effect.

Allport (1954) pointed out nearly forty years ago that prejudice takes many forms, a critical point that some enthusiasts for MCE seem to have disregarded. With Adorno *et al.*'s (1950) classic study of *the Authoritarian Personality* in mind,

Allport noted that some people have an ontological stake in racial or ethnic prejudice and are consequently impervious to reason. In their case:

> realism is low: [they neither know nor care] what the facts are concerning minority groups . . . the functional significance of these attitudes lies deep, and nothing short of an upheaval in the character structure will change them. (Allport, 1954: 505)

At the same time as he drew attention to a section of the population that was psychologically incapable of benefiting from teaching about prejudice, Allport observed that:

> the ethnic attitudes of many individuals lack internal integration. They are shifting and amorphous and for the most part are linked to the immediate situation. The person himself may be said to be ambivalent— more accurately, multivalent, for, lacking a firm attitude structure, he bends with every pressure. *It is with this group that pro-tolerance appeals may be effective . . . This type is susceptible to education* . . . [emphasis added]. (Allport, 1954: 505)

In the light of Allport's analysis, it would seem that advocates of MCE will need to temper some of the grander claims made on its behalf. Clearly, it will not have a favourable impact on *all* children. Those like Troyna, however, who wish to see MCE replaced by antiracist education appear less than convinced that learning about other cultures will have beneficial effects on the racial attitudes of *any* children. He asks:

> what impact might learning about other cultures have on the perceptions and attitudes of white students? . . . (The) conventional wisdom would lead us to believe that 'prejudice reduction' would be a logical and inevitable outcome. However, Amir's (1969) review of the literature on the theme of 'contact hypothesis in ethnic relations' demonstrates the wishful thinking nature of this proposition. (Troyna, 1987: 313)

I have dealt with Troyna's objection to the contact hypothesis elsewhere (Short, 1993). Basically I contend that if the contact conforms to a specified set of conditions (initially laid down and subsequently extended by Cook, 1978) prejudice can be reduced, at least among the participants. If, in addition, the contact is accompanied by measures targeted directly at the cognitive basis of prejudice, it may help diminish children's tendency to indulge in unsupported generalisations. But more important than the baseless criticism Troyna levels at the contact hypothesis is the fact that he apparently chooses to equate 'learning about other cultures' with mixing with members of other cultural groups.

Admittedly, the essence of multicultural education is acquiring knowledge about other cultures, but such knowledge can come about in other (and perhaps better) ways than mixing in groups. Apart from anything else, the latter is just not feasible in many ('all-white') areas of the country where supporters of MCE would nonetheless proclaim its value.

In the remainder of this paper I want to justify the need to learn about different cultures on grounds which have not previously been articulated. They are the need to combat the 'new racism' and the importance of establishing the psychological conditions necessary for children to benefit from an antiracist education.

The New Racism

More than ten years ago, Barker (1981) drew attention to a form of hostility towards Britain's Black and South Asian population that he referred to as 'the new racism'. He coined the phrase to highlight the fact that this form of xenophobia has no truck with notions of inferiority (either biological or cultural) and no need for negative stereotypes. Such things are two of the defining properties of what he would presumably think of as the old racism. The new racism, moreover, does not see hostility towards outgroups as in some degree the product of ignorance (as advocates of multicultural education allegedly maintain) or as a legacy of colonialism (as argued by many adherents of antiracist education). The basis of the new racism is rather the instinctive need of the nation to protect itself against any perceived threat to its continued existence. With its philosophical roots in the writings of David Hume and its 'scientific' roots in sociobiology, the new racism contends that it is human nature to create bounded social groups (nation states) and for such groups to separate themselves from those they perceive to be different. The differences are defined culturally, taking the form of different ways of life. National culture is viewed not only as the source of individual identity, but as the guarantor of social and political cohesion. Thus, anything that endangers the national way of life, anything that disrupts what Enoch Powell in 1977 referred to as the homogeneous 'we' (such as a relatively large immigrant community with an alien culture), will be disorientating and resented. It will inevitably give rise to genuinely held fears. As Barker puts it:

> You do not need to think of yourself as superior—you do not even need to dislike or blame those who are so different from you—in order to say that the presence of these aliens constitutes a threat to our way of life. (Barker, 1981: 18)

The new racism is distinguished not just by its lack of interest in notions of racial or cultural superiority but also by its failure to blame 'immigrants' for any of the economic or social problems currently facing the country. As has been noted, its emphasis is on the allegedly destabilising impact on national cohesion of an alien culture.

Prior to the dissemination of Barker's views on the new racism any disparaging reference to alien cultures would have been dismissed as no more than a gloss on the old racism—a translation to accommodate the demands of polite discourse. Milner (1983) exemplifies this point of view:

> To be sure, cultural differences . . . provided available rationalizations for inter-group hostility. But this is a more superficial and secondary reason for hostility. They may well be the 'reasons' for hostility that people will admit to, for there are no other admissible reasons for racism. However, we would maintain that the reality is one of racial hostility rationalised by cultural differences, rather than hostility engendered by the cultural distinctiveness of peoples who, coincidentally, happen to be black. (Milner, 1983: 226)

In the light of Barker's analysis, one can see straight away the inadequacy of antiracist prescriptions in education. For example, as one of the ways forward for this strategy, Troyna (1987) proposes intervention 'constructed around forms of political education.' In relation to the widespread tendency to blame 'immigrants' for problems such as unemployment and drug-taking he argues:

> If these conceptions of reality are to be challenged effectively then it is essential to provide superior and more plausible explanations of these phenomena. This cannot be done if the issues of 'race' and ethnic relations are considered in isolation; rather they need to be seen and considered as pertinent aspects of the social structure along with, say, class and gender . . . the aim is to ensure that students not only recognise the specific nature of racial inequality but the nature of the inequalities they themselves experience and share with black people as girls, students, young people or as members of the working class. (Troyna, 1987: 316)

Now whilst some commentators (e.g. Cohen, 1988) might have doubts about the rationalist basis of this proposal, no one concerned to advance social justice would wish to challenge the ethical imperative it embodies. Clearly, teachers ought not to allow children to subscribe to racist myths. But from the standpoint of the new racism, the proposal offers only a partial antidote because it fails to engage with the perceived *cultural* threat.

Barker makes his case by quoting from House of Commons' debates of the 1970s and from newspaper articles written around the same time. It should not be thought, however, that the phenomenon of the new racism is historically circumscribed. Its most recent articulation has come from the M.P. Winston Churchill. When addressing a private meeting in May 1993, he said:

> A halt must be called [to immigration] if the British way of life is to be preserved. The population of many of our northern cities is well over 50% immigrant, and Muslims claim there are now more than two million of their co-religionists in Britain. Mr. Major seeks to reassure us with the old refrain 'There'll always be an England'. He promises us that 50

years on from now, spinsters will be cycling to Communion on Sunday mornings—more like the muezzin will be calling Allah's faithful to the high street mosque. (*The Times*, 29 May 1993: 1)

He reiterated these views a couple of months later:

We must not ignore or sweep under the carpet the impact on our society and the British way of life of the arrival in our midst . . . of three to four million immigrants from Africa, Asia and the Caribbean. (*The Times*, 20 July 1993: 2)

Consequences of Neglecting the New Racism

There have been many texts on antiracist education since the early 1980s, including some written recently (e.g. Troyna & Carrington, 1990; Epstein, 1992) that refer to the new racism. They tend to treat it though very much as an *obiter dictum*. It is mentioned in passing rather than discussed, and its educational implications are never considered. The consequences of neglecting the new racism are as serious as they are self-evident. For if a critical dimension of racist thought is not addressed and challenged in schools, the chances are that it will not be addressed and challenged anywhere. There is thus a real risk that some children will leave school effectively offering themselves as electoral fodder to any politician peddling new racist ideology. The need to tackle the ideology in schools is not simply a matter of countering its inevitable consequences (i.e. repatriation) but a recognition of the strength of its appeal beyond the confines of the school. It does not suffer from the Nazi connotations of parties on the lunatic fringe of British politics. On the contrary, it appears as a pre-eminently reasonable ideology based on commonsense rather than bigotry. And it is precisely because it eschews crude and overtly insulting racist stereotypes that it can be embraced, more or less with impunity, by establishment figures such as Members of Parliament. Associations of this kind can only enhance its attractiveness to sections of the white community.

Clearly the new racism has to be combated. Antiracist education (as defined by those who see it as necessarily distinct from MCE) cannot serve this purpose, as its concerns—institutional racism and the unequal distribution of power—do not, in any way, connect with those of the new racism. As I have shown, the latter essentially revolves around a fear that the nation is imperilled by the intrusion of an alien culture. And it is the centrality accorded to culture within new racist ideology that indicates a critical role for MCE. Specifically, the latter needs to show that what appears to be alien and menacing, may, in reality, give little or no cause for concern and may indeed be seen as enriching. To achieve these ends it will be necessary to operate on a number of fronts simultaneously. In the first place there ought to be a continuation of what many regard as the essence of MCE, namely, teaching about different faiths and encouraging children to participate in a range of culturally diverse activities. The value of this recommendation is suggested by a body of research (admittedly carried out in contexts unrelated to 'race' or ethnicity) claiming that familiarity promotes liking (e.g. Zajonc, 1968). However, for the learning to be maximally effective, it will be essential to confront directly any misconceptions that children may harbour about minority cultures. For it is misconceptions, rather than unadorned ignorance, that have the power to transform the unfamiliar into the threatening. Ignorance and misconceptions, of course, can affect any ethnic minority. I illustrate below some of the ways in which they manifest themselves in regard to Jews. The decision to focus on the Jewish dimension reflects my concern at the dearth of data on children's knowledge of this minority group at a time of rising anti-Semitism across Europe (Institute for Jewish Affairs, 1991; Wistrich, 1992).

Over the past two to three years I have been investigating the development of children's knowledge and understanding of Jewish culture (Short, 1991a; Short, in press; Short & Carrington, 1992). The research was conducted with a group of 8- to 13-year-olds who came overwhelmingly from Christian (or nominally Christian) backgrounds and who lived in close proximity to a substantial Jewish community. The children attending primary schools had not engaged in any sustained study of Judaism. Those attending secondary school had done so as part of their RE curriculum. Even then, many of them revealed what Dearden (1968) describes as rucksack knowledge (i.e. information without understanding). Superficial knowledge of this kind is a matter for concern, not just because of the doubt it casts on the quality of the teaching, but because of the opportunity it affords the creative imagination to substitute invention for understanding. The effect is to drive a wedge between cultures, rendering Judaism (in this case) potentially alien. I cite below some examples of this 'knowledge':

They have Passover.
(GS): Do you know what the Passover celebration is all about?
No.

They have special food like crackers and apple and honey.
(GS): When do they have the apple and honey?
Don't know.

Do they celebrate something on Friday night?
(GS): Yes. Do you know what it is?
No.

Among the more common misconceptions were those relating to the nature of the deity within Judaism. A significant proportion of the children, regardless of age, had no idea of the sense in which Jews and Christians can be said to worship the same god. Some did not know who or what Jews worship while others were under the impression that Jews prayed to a number of gods.

Discussion of the Passover among a group of 12- and 13-year-olds revealed another area in which misconceptions were rife.

> When they used to live, wherever it was, every so often something flew over and killed all the oldest sons in the house, so they used to kill a lamb then paint a door with its blood and then they used to have a celebration or something.

> We know about the Passover . . . that they have to put blood on their doors otherwise the oldest child of the family—the Jewish family—will die.

> They have to put those things outside their door.
> (**GS**): What's that?
> They put blood.

Had the research been conducted in areas where children had no opportunity to mix with Jews it is possible that the misunderstanding encapsulated in these comments would have been even further divorced from reality. For under such circumstances the most accessible means of testing ill-founded beliefs is unavailable. A small-scale study by Denoon (1973) supports this contention. He worked at a school in Inverness where the Jewish population for 1973 was too small to warrant inclusion in the Jewish Year Book for that year. He reported the following incident involving a group of low-ability fourth-formers (aged 14 and 15) who were discussing an anthology of poems called *Discrimination*:

> . . . a question directed at the class elicited the reply from one boy that all Jews were dirty and slimy.
> **Denoon:** Have you ever met a Jew?
> Yes.
> Where?
> One asked me the way to the station.
> How did you know he was a Jew? Was he wearing a badge or something.
> Yes. He had the mark on his forehead.

There can be little doubt that had Denoon or I questioned our respective samples on their knowledge of Islam, Hinduism or any other non-Christian faith, the level of ignorance would have been much the same. There is thus good reason for teachers to check on their pupils' misconceptions about other faiths, not just at the beginning of a study block, but also at the end for, as has been suggested, misconceptions might arise as an unintended by-product of the teaching itself.

On the assumption that we are attracted to those who are like us in significant respects (Byrne, 1971), teachers should also make a point of stressing similarities between cultures. In making this recommendation, there is, of course, no suggestion that teachers should shy away from discussing with their pupils those elements within non-indigenous cultures that, in the opinion of some, stretch the limits of tolerance to the breaking point. As was pointed out earlier, MCE does not advocate an untenable relativism in which 'anything goes'. Children should be enabled and encouraged to argue rationally for the retention *or proscription* of any cultural practice.

Finally, children need to focus directly on the central thesis of the new racism and to this end it would seem useful for them to examine the nature and history of cultural diversity within the indigenous population. They should be made aware of the cultural impact of previous waves of immigration and should know that the social fabric of the United Kingdom has long been able to withstand the cultural variations stemming from different religious affiliations not to mention those relating to social class, region and age.

MCE as a Prerequisite of Antiracist Education

I come now to the critical role of MCE in helping to realise the goals of antiracism. Troyna (1987: 312) points out that in order to fulfil the aims of antiracist education it will be necessary to forge 'alliances between groups both within and beyond the school gates . . .' He argues that 'informed collective action constitutes the most effective challenge to racism' (p. 316) and goes on to identify the importance of pedagogy in the promotion of antiracism. He notes, in particular, the need for 'forms of co-operative learning within a non-competitive environment' (p. 317).

In this section of the paper I want to suggest that Troyna's hostility to MCE indicates that he has not fully thought through the implications of these various recommendations. For it seems to me that he has completely ignored the psychological factors that may inhibit the forming of alliances and the willingness to work co-operatively. I am referring here to children's prejudices based on their misconceptions of other cultures. In order to get children (or anyone else) to form an alliance, it is essential to recognise the sub-tasks involved. One is the need to demonstrate to those concerned the benefits of working together; the other is the need to remove any impediment to the potential collaboration. In his various writings Troyna seems only to acknowledge the former.

As was pointed out above, Troyna stresses the importance of providing pupils with 'superior and more plausible explanations' (p. 316) than those supplied by racists for phenomena such as unemployment and drug-taking. However, he seems not to appreciate the futility of offering 'superior explanations' to children whose minds are closed to such explanations because of their resentment of ethnic minority cultures. I have argued elsewhere that:

Prejudice serves to distort information with which it conflicts as well as to discredit the source of such information. Consequently no form of teaching is likely to achieve its aims if it fails to take cognizance of those beliefs held by children that contradict the teaching. (Short, 1991b: 6)

In his recent study of Frogmore Community College in the south of England, Massey recounted the following comment from a fifth-year pupil.

I hate the Pakis because they are so dirty and they work all the hours that God sends and send all the bloody money back home to Grandma in the mud huts back in India. (Massey, 1991: 78)

What chances are there of white teenagers who think in this way forming any sort of alliance with 'Pakis'? If antiracists ignore misconceptions of this kind about minority life styles, their message will inevitably fall on deaf ears.

In view of the inveterate anti-Semitism of far-right political parties, the antiracist neglect of Judaism is equally worrying. In a recent court case, the dowager Lady Birdwood was charged with distributing anti-Semitic literature repeating the medieval slander that Jews murder Christian children in order to use their blood for ritual purposes (*Jewish Chronicle*, 11 October 1991). Now, to the extent that children absorb this message they are effectively inoculated against any attempt by antiracists to give the lie to Jews as the cause of economic crisis, moral degeneracy or any other cancer for which Jews have traditionally been blamed.

It is ironic to note that precisely the same form of argument as I have employed in support of MCE has been adopted by Gaine (1987) to illustrate its irrelevance. He writes:

Teaching about cultures . . . does not necessarily do anything to racist attitudes, since many pupils simply do not want to know or are applying (perhaps unconscious) filtering mechanisms. They do not listen to the distinctions between Sikhs and Muslims, Gujeratis and Bengalis, West Indians and Indians, because they are not interested; they do not want to know because the most important thing to them is that these people . . . are responsible for all the unemployment, bad housing etc. . . . Because many people believe they *are* responsible, this has to be tackled first. (Original emphasis) (Gaine, 1987: 86)

Gaine's argument is basically a sound one and is, in effect, the mirror image of my own. He is saying that to attack one set of prejudices (cultural) whilst leaving the other (socio-economic) untouched, is bound to prove unsuccessful because the untouched prejudices effectively shield the others from attack. Clearly, a twin-track approach is required; that is, one combining multicultural and antiracist elements.

If MCE is to function in such a way as to enable children to derive maximum benefit from antiracist education, its form will have to change. Merely telling children about other cultures may have benefits in terms of promoting familiarity, but it is not sufficient. As has been pointed out, an effective MCE must focus on children's misconceptions. This, in turn, will require questioning them on their existing ideas and beliefs in order to be able to identify and then grapple with their misconceptions. The need for such an approach was confirmed by the comments, previously cited, on the Passover and on the nature of the deity within Judaism. Multifaith RE as currently practised is not a panacea, for merely imparting information has the power to confuse as well as to clarify. If not carefully planned and monitored, teaching about different faiths may actually *foster* misconceptions.

On the assumption that we learn most effectively that which we find most interesting, it may be valuable to structure the teaching, at least to some extent, around facets of other cultures that pupils themselves wish to know more about (see, for example, Carrington & Short, 1993). MCE should also look broadly at life styles rather than narrowly at religions. A restricted focus is manifestly inadequate for dealing with views such as those expressed (above) by the pupil at Frogmore. Moreover, a concern with life styles has the added benefit of offering teachers more scope to emphasise the similarities between different ethnic groups.

Conclusion

It seems to be universally agreed that one of the major impulses behind MCE was concern at the alleged academic failure of Afro-Caribbean children. This, in turn, was seen by multiculturalists as partly due to a poor self-image which, to some degree, could be overcome by the children having their own culture represented in the curriculum and around the school. Whilst not wishing to endorse what he refers to as 'pure multiculturalism', Milner nonetheless thought it:

> intuitively obvious that the school and the teacher who have set up within their practice resonances with the child's home and culture are more likely to encourage a general involvement in learning than alienation from it. (Milner, 1983: 223)

The Swann Report (1985) noted that in recent years the gap between the academic performance of Afro-Caribbean and other groups had narrowed and hoped that this may have been due, in part, to the increased sensitivity of teachers. But it is difficult to know for certain whether MCE has, in fact, contributed anything to the improvement. Nor can we be sure whether MCE, as commonly practised, has helped to reduce prejudice. Thus, it would seem that the original justification for MCE rests on imprecise foundations. It would be a *non sequitur*, however, to conclude on the basis of this analysis that MCE has no value. For it has been my purpose to establish that MCE can be justified if it is modified along the lines outlined above, and if the justification is couched in terms of combating the new racism and helping to realise the goals of antiracism. The latter involves a willingness to accept alternative explanations of socio-economic problems and a preparedness to form alliances with other groups.

Although I have written in support of MCE I do not wish to be seen as hostile to antiracist education. For whilst I regard these conceptions of educational change as having somewhat different functions, I have no doubt about their compatibility. MCE is principally concerned to diminish prejudice against other cultures. It has nothing *directly* to do with promoting equality. This is the province of antiracist education. However, I have argued that MCE, by tackling cultural misconceptions, lays the essential foundation for an effective antiracist education. MCE has to be retained, but revision is necessary both in its justification and in its practice.

References

Adorno, T. W., Frenkel-Brunswik, E., Levinson, D. J. and Sanford, R. N. (1950) *The Authoritarian Personality.* New York: Harper & Row.

Allport, G. (1954) *The Nature of Prejudice.* Cambridge, MA: Addison-Wesley.

Amir, Y. (1969) Contact hypothesis in ethnic relations. *Psychological Bulletin* 71, 319–42.

Barker, M. (1981) *The New Racism.* London: Junction Books.

Bullivant, B. (1986) Towards radical multiculturalism: Resolving tensions in curriculum and educational planning. In S. Modgil, G. K. Verma, K. Mallick and C. Modgil (eds) *Multicultural Education: The Interminable Debate.* Lewes: Falmer.

Byrne, D. (1971) *The Attraction Paradigm.* New York: Academic Press.

Carrington, B. and Short, G. (1993) Probing children's prejudice: A consideration of the ethical and methodological issues raised by research and curriculum development. *Educational Studies* 19, 163–79.

Cohen, P. (1988) The perversions of inheritance: Studies in the making of multi-racist Britain. In P. Cohen and H. S. Bains (eds) *Multi-racist Britain.* London: Macmillan.

Cook, S. W. (1978) Interpersonal and attitudinal outcomes in cooperating interracial groups. *Journal of Research and Development in Education* 12, 97–113.

Dearden, R. (1968) *The Philosophy of Primary Education: An Introduction.* London: Routledge and Kegan Paul.

Denoon, B. (1973) Racial prejudice. *The Times Educational Supplement,* 31st August.

Department of Education and Science (DES) (1977) *Education in Schools: A Consultative Document.* London: HMSO.

——— (1981) *West Indian Children in our Schools* (The Rampton Report) London: HMSO.

——— (1985) *Education for All* (The Swann Report) London: HMSO.

Epstein, D. (1992) *Changing Classroom Cultures: Anti-racism, Politics and Schools.* Stoke-on-Trent: Trentham Books.

Gaine, C. (1987) *No Problem Here: A Practical Approach to Education and 'Race' in White Schools.* London: Hutchinson.

Grinter, R. (1985) Bridging the gulf: The need for antiracist multicultural education. *Multicultural Teaching* 3, 8–11.

Institute for Jewish Affairs (1991) Anti-Semitism in the 1990s: A symposium. *Patterns of Prejudice* 25, 4–85.

Leicester, M. (1986) Multicultural curriculum or antiracist education: Denying the gulf. *Multicultural Teaching* 4, 4–7.

Lynch, J. (1983) *The Multicultural Curriculum.* London: Batsford.

Mac an Ghaill, M. (1988) *Young, Gifted and Black.* Milton Keynes: Open University Press.

Macdonald, I., Bhavnani, T., Khan, L. and John, G. (1989) *Murder in the Playground: The Report of the Macdonald Inquiry into Racism and Racial Violence in Manchester Schools.* London: Longsight Press.

Massey, I. (1991) *More than Skin Deep.* London: Hodder and Stoughton.

Milner, D. (1983) *Children and Race: Ten Years On.* London: Ward Lock Educational.

Sarap, M. (1991) *Education and the Ideologies of Racism.* Stoke-on-Trent: Trentharn Books.

Short, G. (1991a) Teaching the holocaust: Some reflections on a problematic area. *British Journal of Religious Education* 14, 28–34.

—— (1991b) Prejudice, power and racism: Some reflections on the antiracist critique of multicultural education. *Journal of Philosophy of Education,* 25, 5–15.

—— (1993) Prejudice reduction in schools: The value of inter-racial contact. *British Journal of Sociology of Education* 14, 31–40.

—— (In Press) Teaching the holocaust: The relevance of children's perceptions of Jewish culture and identity. *British Educational Research Journal* 20.

Short, G. and Carrington, B. (1992) The development of children's understanding of Jewish identity and culture. *School Psychology International* 13, 73–89.

Stone, M. (1981) *The Education of the Black Child in Britain: The Myth of Multi-racial Education.* London: Fontana.

Troyna, B. (1987) Beyond multiculturalism: Towards the enactment of anti-racist education in policy, provision and pedagogy. *Oxford Review of Education* 13, 307–20.

—— (1993) *Racism and Education.* Buckingham: Open University Press.

Troyna, B. and Carrington B. (1990) *Education, Racism and Reform.* London: Routledge.

Troyna, B. and Hatcher, R. (1992) *Racism in Children's Lives: A Study of 'Mainly-White' Primary Schools.* London: Routledge in association with the National Children's Bureau.

Wistrich, R. S. (1992) 'Once again, anti-Semitism without Jews'. *Commentary,* August, 45–9.

Zajonc, R. B. (1968) Attitudinal effects of mere exposure. *Journal of Personality and Social Psychology* 9, 1–29.

Zec, P. (1980) Multicultural education: What kind of relativism is possible? *Journal of Philosophy of Education* 14, 77–86.

Questions

1. Why does Short claim that multicultural and antiracist education are compatible?

2. What is Troyna's critique of multicultural education.

3. What, according to Short, are some the different sources for prejudice?

4. Short identifies the phenomenon of "new racism" in the United Kingdom. Do you think this phenomenon exists in the United States?

5. Why, according to Short, are the philosophical roots of the new racism in the philosophy of David Hume? Have other philosophers contributed (directly, or indirectly) to racism? Explain.

6. What is "sociobiology," and why, according to Short, are the "scientific" roots of the new racism located in this discipline?

7. What are the consequences for neglecting the new racism?

8. Would Short's program to reduce "cultural ignorance" be more conducive to elementary education than the antiracism education advocated by Sleeter or Grinter? Explain.

Section Two: Suggestions for Further Reading

Freire, Paulo (1994). *Pedagogy of the Oppressed.* New York: Continuum.

hooks, bell (1989). *Talking Back: Thinking Feminist, Thinking Black.* Boston: South End Press.

———— (1994). *Teaching to Transgress: Education as the Practice of Freedom.* New York: Routledge.

Lynch, James (1986). *Multicultural Education: Principles and Practices.* London: Routledge.

Lynch, James, Modgil, Cecil and Modgil, Sohan (1992). *Cultural Diversity and the Schools volume one: Education for Cultural Diversity: Convergence and Divergence.* Washington: Falmer.

McCarthy, Cameron and Crichlow, Warren (Eds.) (1993). *Race, Identity, and Representation in Education.* New York: Routledge.

Sleeter, Christine (1996). *Multicultural Education as Social Activism.* Albany: State University of New York.

Sleeter, Christine (Ed.) (1991). *Empowerment through Multicultural Education.* Albany: State University of New York.

Troyna, Barry (1993). *Racism and Education.* Buckingham: Open University Press.

Troyna, Barry and Williams, Jenny (1986). *Racism, Education and the State.* London: Croom Helm.

West, Cornel (1993). *Race Matters.* New York: Vintage Books.

Section Three

Critical Multiculturalism

As noted in our introduction, multiculturalists are identified in large measure by their rejection of, and resistance to, assimilationism. For critical multiculturalism, the rejection of assimilation compels one to identify the potentially undemocratic nature of schools with respect to cultural diversity. Like antiracist pedagogy, critical multiculturalism argues that monocultural hegemony within schools undermines the democratic commitment to the creation of learning environments in which *all* students are provided the resources and liberties needed for the practice of freedom. And like proponents of ethnic studies, critical multiculturalists argue that students of color are rarely offered opportunities to attend schools that are organized around a specific commitment to promoting an understanding and appreciation of cultural diversity. The failure of most schools to infuse the educational experience with the practice of cultural inclusivity is the result of a complex set of political and economic practices which, historically, have not been attuned to ideals of social justice nor the already existing cultural pluralism. For critical multiculturalists, this discordance has pervaded life in schools and produced learning organizations that have been dismissive or repressive of the pluralism emergent within the multicultural condition.

Critical multiculturalists are dedicated to exposing the specific administrative, curricular, and instructional practices, as well as the organizational policies within schools that produce cultural alienation for students of color. *Cultural alienation*—the experience of feeling one's culture unwelcome, one's ethnicity unacknowledged, and one's tradition unimportant—occurs within school settings which are inhospitable to cultural diversity. Critical Multiculturalists are intent on identifying and explaining the multiple and often overlapping sources for those policies and practices which produce monoculturalism and institutional racism within U.S. public schools.

Mapping the causes and outcomes of cultural exclusion, and likewise identifying ways for intervening within schools so as to identify alternative strategies for the establishment of cultural democracy, is a demanding assignment for any change agent working within schools. The critical educator who takes this on must be equipped with a multifaceted theoretic vocabulary, one which is capable of producing historical, linguistic, philosophical, political, and sociological analysis. In essence, the critical multicultural educator must model the diversity and democracy of voices she/he desires to see within the life of schools. The results are intriguing theoretic hybrids, as demonstrated by the three selections in this chapter.

Each of the following selections in this chapter emphasizes, in various ways, critical multiculturalism's attempt to incorporate postmodern and poststructural analysis into a critique which focuses on the challenges of schooling within democratic and pluralistic societies; societies, critical multiculturalists point out, where public institutions are increasingly dominated by a corporate "bottom-line" thinking which emphasizes top down policymaking and management of schools from district and state levels.

In their article "Multicultural Education and Postmodernism: Movement Toward a Dialogue," Carl A. Grant and Judyth M. Sachs demonstrate how and why "postmodern theory can contribute to understanding the complexities of education for a multicultural society." Grant and Sachs argue that the type of multicultural educational theories and practices that currently dominate schools are those grounded within a three f's approach: foods, fairs, and festivals. While this approach to cultural diversity is certainly a progressive first step for many schools, Grant and Sachs argue that so-called celebratory initiatives can actually reinforce the dominant assimilationist thinking which defines non-European cultural traditions as exotic, alien, and foreign—*Others*. In turn, the three f's approach can, in effect, marginalize those cultures or traditions that are "celebrated" during a designated week or month.

According to Grant and Sachs, the language of postmodern and poststructural critique allows teachers to guide their students in the deconstruction of the socially constructed "meanings" of words which dominate our understanding of ourselves. Michel Foucault's (1980) category of *discourse* is particularly relevant to Grant and Sachs. They write, "With an understanding of discourse, students of color and other marginalized groups will not only learn about their own histories, they also will be provided with the opportunity to examine how discourses emerge to suit the interests of particular groups and deny other groups." Grant and Sachs argue that understanding the relationship between power and knowledge offers them the opportunity to unveil and criticize those discourses that present obstacles to members of subaltern groups. Postmodern and poststructural critique, they explain, enable critical multiculturalists to identify how dominant discourses within the educational sphere incorporate values, priorities, experiences and ideas that propagate and "make natural inequalities of outcomes and opportunity." Sachs and Grant argue that multicultural education that is guided by Foucauldian critique will ensure that all students have a knowledge of the formal and informal structures that reduce the scope and depth of democracy in schools and thereby cause cultural alienation and exclusion.

Postmodernism and poststructuralism, Grant and Sachs argue, allow educators to develop a *critical conception of culture;* that is, one which enables the African American, Asian American, Latina/o, Native American, and "Others" to displace the Euro-American tradition as the primary reference point for the learning organization. This critical approach aims to deconstruct the administrative and pedagogical practices within schools so as to unveil how ideas such as "achievement," "failure," and "learning" are actually defined within the narrow parameters of the Euro-American cultural vocabulary. In turn, rather than objectifying the diverse traditions represented in the school and society as an "Other" to be "appreciated," critical multicultural approaches allow students, teachers and administrators to step back and ask "Other to whom or what?"; and thereby to interrogate the hidden yet omnipresent force of the "white" American tradition. This critical approach to culture is one example, according to Grant and Sachs, of how the postmodern and poststructural attention to power infuses multicultural education with an oppositional stance.

Like Grant and Sachs, contributor Henry Giroux expresses concern with multicultural education that simply aims to "promote" pluralism by asking members of a learning organization to "appreciate" diversity. While it is obvious that one would not describe three f's approach as "transgressive," it is not self-evident that this approach is consistently silent and unappreciative about a particular cultural tradition. Indeed, the three f's approach seems committed to being sensitive and appreciative of any and all groups represented in the United States. Yet, as Giroux indicates in his article "Insurgent Multiculturalism," when celebratory approaches to multicultural education are implemented questions concerning "white racism" and the category of "whiteness" itself are muted. For Giroux, this silence must be shattered. Indeed, multiculturalism, he insists, "is about making whiteness visible; that is, it point to the necessity of providing white students with the cultural memories that enable them to recognize the historically- and socially-constructed nature of their own identities."

According to Giroux, when critical educators take up the discourse of multiculturalism, they immediately identify the question of diversity with the social injustices of racism and economic inequity. They develop an insurgent multiculturalism which tries to identify the sources of this injustice and inequity. The analysis, Giroux explains, ultimately arrives at the conclusion that the problem of misrecognition and cultural alienation cannot be understood without looking at the privilege that is awarded to being "white" as opposed to being "brown," "black," "red," or "yellow." For Giroux, the concern of multicultural education is not the celebration and appreciation of diversity, but the "unlearning racial privilege." Thus, like Grant and Sachs, Giroux identifies critical multiculturalism as the "critical referent for interrogating the racist representations and practices of the dominant culture." This critical interrogation, Giroux hopes, will create the conditions for what he calls cultural democracy.

In his contribution, "White Terror and Oppositional Agency: Towards a Critical Multiculturalism," Peter McLaren follows Grant and Sachs by defining critical multiculturalism in opposition to multicultural approaches that "celebrate" diversity, but remain silent about the dynamics of racism and exclusion that are embedded within the fabric of schooling. And like Henry Giroux, McLaren offers an extended critique of "conservative" reactions to multicultural education. McLaren echoes Giroux's explanation of the conservative tactic of labelling "anti-American" those multiculturalists who dare to question the legitimacy of assimilationism. McLaren insists that conservatives support three f's approach and thereby "use the term 'diversity' to cover up the ideology of assimilation that undergirds [this] position. In this view, ethnic groups are reduced to 'add-ons' to the dominant culture."

McLaren's *resistance multiculturalism* represents another example of a critical theory which attends to the complex and multifarious nature of culture and cultural identity. McLaren is particularly attentive to the fact that this complexity has been compounded by the hyperdissemination of cultural symbols that has become "normal" within our cyber-information world. For McLaren, this context demands an analysis that emphasizes "the role that language and representation play in the construction of meaning and identity. The poststructuralist insight I am relying on," McLaren writes, "is located within the larger context of postmodern theory . . . and asserts that signs and significations are essentially unstable and shifting and can only be temporarily fixed." McLaren's use of postmodernism (cf. Derrida, 1982; Lyotard, 1984) allows him to argue for a multicultural education that does not objectify cultural traditions as something "out-there" to be studied or appreciated. On the contrary, McLaren's argues that critical multiculturalism enables students to participate in the construction of their cultural identity. Because it understands culture and cultural identity as a dynamic unfolding process with a past, present, and unknown future, McLaren's critical multiculturalism aims to provide students with a context of self-creation, or the ability to construct what he calls *border identities*. In a classic McLarenesque explanation, he writes "Border identities are intersubjective spaces of cultural translation—linguistically multivalenced spaces of intercultural dialogue." One would be hard pressed to find a food, festival, or fair that would facilitate the border identity experience.

Finally, it should be noted that all three selections in this chapter call attention to the desire of critical multiculturalism to combine critical interrogation with utopian visions. All three are concerned, in distinct ways, with providing educators with the analytic tools to enlarge the scope of democracy, or as Giroux writes, create "new cultural spaces that deepen and extend the possibility of democratic public life." For McLaren, this means that critical or "resistance multiculturalism does not see diversity itself as a goal but rather argues that diversity must be affirmed within a politics of cultural criticism and a commitment to social justice." And this commitment to social justice, Grant and Sachs insist, increases the "possibility of emancipatory teaching for students from a variety of ethnic and cultural backgrounds."

Guiding Questions for Section Three

- What are the primary concerns and aims of Critical Multiculturalism?
- What are Critical Multiculturalism's criticisms against mainstream and conservative approaches to multiculturalism?
- What does Critical Multiculturalism borrow from postmodern and/or poststructural theory?

Multicultural Education and Postmodernism: Movement Toward a Dialogue

Carl A. Grant and Judyth M. Sachs

Introduction

Multicultural education developed in the United States, the United Kingdom, Canada, and Australia during the 1970s as an educational concept and process to help galvanize and articulate the competing social and political interests of diverse ethnic and cultural groups (e.g., blacks, women). Issues such as equality of opportunity, gender equity, ethnic identity and cultural diversity, and cultural pluralism provided the theoretical and conceptual platform on which multicultural education rested, and was developed to be implemented into educational institutions. Its implementation in schools as policy and pedagogic practice has taken a variety of forms in the above contexts. Similarly, its impetus in the above countries has been motivated by different initiatives. Given the different historical, material, and ideological conditions and motivating initiatives existing in the United States, the United Kingdom, and Australia, it is not surprising that the conceptualization and practice of multicultural education differs significantly in its emphasis (Lynch, 1986; Sleeter, 1989).

In this chapter we argue that postmodern theory can contribute to understanding the complexities of education for a multicultural society (i.e., multicultural education). In order to do this, we will review recent theoretical literature concerning multicultural education. We assert that much of this literature is concerned with "a normative politics of cultural difference" in the form of practical concerns for teachers and administrators. Such an orientation renders silent or ignores the development of the critical perspective of multicultural education.

Drawing on current debates within postmodernist and poststructuralist theory, we propose a discussion on multicultural education that will help to illuminate the changes taking place in contemporary culture. As Featherstone (1988, p. 208) suggests, these can be understood in terms of changes in the everyday practices and experiences of different groups "who may be using regimes of signification in different ways and developing new means of orientation and identity structures." In this chapter our intent is twofold: First, we are concerned with identifying the nature and scope of current multicultural education practice. Second, given the silences and omissions evident in much of the mainstream literature, we propose a discussion of multicultural education and postmodernism that may serve to open up lines of communication between proponents of these two paradigms and their concerns about issues of metanarratives regarding race, gender, class, and other areas of oppression. Liberal rhetoric, we maintain, is often concerned with focusing on specific interventions, such as educational programs for culturally different groups, while not being concerned with structural inequities as they exist in society that help reinforce social and economic disadvantage. Such perspectives omit two theoretically important concepts—discourse and culture. In this chapter these concepts provide the basis for our discussion of postmodernism and multicultural education.

Postmodernism: A Useful Lens for Educators of Multicultural Education?

The postmodernist debate poses in a dramatic way the issue of competing paradigms for social theory and the need to choose paradigms that are most theoretically and practicably applicable to social conditions in the present era (Kellner, 1988, p. 267). West (1987, p. 27) tells us that "the postmodernism debate is principally a battle over how we conceive of culture and, most importantly, how we interpret the current crisis in our society and muster resources to alleviate it." Its project is to move beyond all totalizing discourses and to be incredulous of what Lyotard (1984) called metanarratives. For Lyotard the postmodern condition is one in which "grand narratives of legitimation" are no longer credible. Postmodernism recognizes that canons are socially constructed and always will need to be reconstructed through dialogues among and between various communities. The strength of postmodernism is that it simultaneously holds out possibilities for the revival and widening of a cultural politics and for its neutralization (Connor, 1989, p. 224). Postmodernism is concerned with rethinking culture and the power relations embodied not only in cultural representations but also material practices. For multicultural education this is particularly important. First, because it offers another lens through which to analyze and interrogate the literature on school practice and the distribution of culture and power in society. Second, the treatment of difference and Otherness is central to any investigation or understanding of the dynamics of social change, and postmodernism can contribute to how multicultural educators engage in this discussion. For example, "difference theory" versus "deficit theory" has for decades been a part of the multicultural debate. How teachers perceive their students greatly determines how they work with them. Nieto (1992, p. 79), an advocate of multicultural education, recently posited:

> If students are perceived as to be "deficient," the educational environment will reflect a no-nonsense, back-to-basics, drill orientation. However, if they are perceived as intelligent and motivated young people with an interest in the world around them, the educational environment will tend to reflect an intellectually stimulating and academically challenging orientation.

Postmodernism and its "suspiciousness ... [of the] ways in which we subordinate, exclude, and marginalize" (Giroux, 1988, p. 24) can serve to illuminate and reinforce the argument that multicultural educators make to mainstream educators regarding their hard-to-release doubts about the academic ability of students of color, especially African American and Hispanic students.

We share Hebdige's (1988) qualified view that the term "postmodernism," while characterized by much abstract theoretical debate and to some extent a degree of incoherence, is so wide-ranging that it must describe something. We maintain that for multicultural educators, postmodernism provides another lens through which to examine everyday experiences and the role common sense has in the constitution of ethnic, racial, socioeconomic, and gender difference as a focus of power in society. It also can lead to a more comprehensive study of the various subject positions that individuals inhabit, since "one is not just one thing" (Spivak, 1990, p. 60).

Central to postmodernism and poststructuralism is the investigation of power and how power relations are played out among various groups, whether they be gender, ethnic, cultural, or sexual identities. Theoretically it helps us to analyze mechanisms of power locally, focusing on contextualizing notions of power-in-use, and, as Lather (1991, p. 156) states, "to explore the meanings of difference and the possibilities for struggling against multiple oppressive formations simultaneously."

An implication of postmodernism is to redefine the strategies of critique and to challenge the criterion of critique that has been used to legitimate the policies and practices of Western society. Giroux (1991, p. 23) argues:

> As a form of cultural criticism, postmodernism has challenged a number of assumptions central to the discourse of modernism. These include modernism's reliance on metaphysical notions of the subject, its advo-

cacy of science, technology, and rationality are the foundation for equating change with progress, its ethnocentric equation of history with the triumphs of European civilization, and its globalizing view that the industrialized Western countries constitute [quoting Richard, 1987/1988, p. 6] "a legitimate center—a unique and superior position from which to establish control and to determine hierarchies."

An additional implication of postmodernism, Popkewitz (1992) explains, is how language constructs "self" and "other" and can marginalize and/or colonialize.

Detractors of postmodern and poststructural theory have been critical of its subjectivism and relativism, which often border on nihilism. We are concerned with "a critical theory which is committed to emancipation from all forms of oppression, as well as to freedom, happiness and a rational ordering of society" (Kellner, 1990, p. 12).

In practice the role of the postmodern critic is to contest hegemonic discourses. This requires a detailed, scholarly comprehension of one's own location within the field of discourse and cultural practice (Bove, 1986). Accordingly there is a need to

> pay full attention to the social and institutional context of textuality in order to address the power relations of everyday life. Social meanings are produced within social institutions and practices in which individuals, who are shaped by these institutions, are agents of change, rather than its authors, change which may either serve hegemonic interests or challenge existing power relations. (Weedon, 1987, p. 25)

This practice is important and in agreement with many multicultural educationists for it forecasts the need for educators to reposition themselves as "critical intellectuals [who] must understand the historical specificity of the cultural practices of their own period with an eye to bringing their own practice and discourse in line with other oppositional forces in a society struggling against hegemonic manipulation" (Bove, 1986, p. 7). The specificities of this and strategies for teachers will be presented later in this chapter.

Multicultural Education

Earlier we argued that much of the multicultural education literature is concerned with the implementation of practical solutions derived from a liberal tradition to provide solutions for specific social and educational problems. Grant, Sleeter, and Anderson (1986) after a review and analysis of sixty-nine books written on multicultural education from four countries—Australia, 3; Canada, 3; England, 9; and the United States, 54—reported that most of this multicultural literature was written for classroom teachers. Importantly, teachers were seen as the primary agent of change. Grant and Sleeter's (1985) review and analysis of 200 journal articles on multicultural education from seven countries (Australia, Canada, England, Indonesia, Scotland, Sweden, and the United States) produced similar results. In particular the results showed that most of these articles were very short (about five pages), with little if any discussion of power, and the majority of them advocated an assimilationist approach. Also these reviews and another by Sleeter and Grant (1987) revealed that the multicultural education literature does not show a tight correspondence between ideas and practice, nor does it provide a thorough discussion of the theoretical framework in relationship to proposed approaches or goals. Furthermore, while there are suggested multicultural education goals for several educational areas, including curricula, instruction, and school policy, most school practices are often limited to curricula. The curricula, as Gay (1979, 1988) and Hernandez (1989) among others have argued, are not ethnically pluralistic and culturally relevant, especially for students of color.

Additionally, in the literature and in everyday discourse (similar to postmodernism) the term "multicultural education" takes on numerous meanings, leading to conceptual confusion and ambiguity (Gibson, 1976; Banks, 1977; Grant, 1977; Gay, 1983; Gollnick and Chinn, 1983; Pratte, 1983). For example, Gibson (1976) identified four meanings or approaches educators took to multicultural education: (1) education of the culturally different, or benevolent multiculturalism, which seeks to incorporate culturally different students more effectively into mainstream culture and society; (2) education about cultural difference, which teaches all students about cultural differences in an effort to promote better cross-cultural understanding; (3) education for cultural pluralism, which seeks to preserve ethnic cultures and increase the power of ethnic minority groups; and (4) bicultural education, which seeks to prepare students to operate successfully in two different cultures.

Important to this discussion of multicultural education and postmodernism is to note that an increasing number of multicultural educators (Banks, 1991; Ladson-Billings, 1991; Gay, 1988; Gollnick and Chinn, 1993; Grant and Sleeter, 1985; Nieto, 1992) are arguing that multicultural education should prepare students to deal with race, class, and gender oppression in society, and to take charge of their life circumstances. For example, Sleeter and Grant (1988, p. 176) argue:

> Education that is Multicultural and Social Reconstructionist deals . . . with oppression and social structural inequality based on race, social class, gender, and disability. It prepares future citizens (students) to reconstruct society so that it better serves the interests of all groups and especially those who are of color, poor, female, and/or disabled.

Having provided a synopsis of the multicultural educational literature, our task as cultural critics is to examine the ideas identified earlier as the conceptual touchstones of postmodernism and apply them to the area of multicultural education. The first of these concepts is "discourse."

Discourse

Drawing on the work of Foucault (1978), the concept of discourse can be used to discuss multicultural education. Discourse provides the basis for understanding what people say, think, and do, but also, as Ball (1990) argues, who can speak, when, and with what authority. This concept helps us to understand and interrogate the relationship between power and knowledge. Knowledge and power are inseparable to the extent that forms of power are situated, constituted, and distributed within knowledge. For multicultural education this is significant because it provides the opportunity to further examine which discourses deny access to institutional structures that the dominant groups take for granted.

These discourses may well be imbedded within both overt and hidden curricula, the structure of language required in schools, or the commonsense knowledge that people use in their everyday interactions inside and outside of schools. In all contexts "any discourse concerns itself with certain objects and puts forward certain concepts at the expense of others" (Macdonell, 1986, p. 3). Having recognized that discourses provide for certain possibilities of thought, the project of multicultural education then becomes one of identifying which discourses are constituted as legitimate and which are excluded. In practice, Foucault argues that we must make allowances for the discourses that can be instruments and effects of power, but also hindrances, stumbling blocks, points of resistances and starting points for opposing strategies (Foucault, 1978). The oppositional strategy for multicultural education means giving both teachers and students a legitimate voice to contest and critique educational policy and practice. It requires that teachers and students develop the confidence and competence to speak what has previously been unspoken, to identify sources of individual and collective oppression, and to work to eliminate them. In policy and practice the focus of multicultural education would be on developing a discourse that illuminates a greater understanding of the self and the multiple ascribed characteristics (ethnicity, gender, socioeconomic status) that are used to define oneself, both by others and by oneself, understanding how institutions work, their histories of exploitation and repression. It further means, as Shapiro (1991, p. 114) argues, "the classroom becomes the site not merely of an individual's apprehension of his or her own experience, but a place where there is a collective reinterpretation of our lived world. There is, in other words, the making of a communal culture that opposes that which is hegemonic." The use of the postmodern lens would help to validate the urgency and need that proponents of multicultural education have to point out how language structures who people are (e.g., at-risk, disadvantaged, dominated group, culturally deprived). Also, the postmodern lens would support the need and be of assistance in the search by proponents of multicultural education for a language that critiques, facilitates the discussion of and between the diverse groups in the country, articulates a vocabulary of empowerment, and makes clearer discussion of educational programs and practices. For example, teachers because of personal and organizational constraints often find it expedient to adopt the language (e.g., latchkey kid, single-parent home, Head Start, bussed-in students, color-blind teaching) and the implicit meanings that it carries, that is given to them by social scientists and administrators, with very little means and structure for critique. Without this language of critique, teachers become less able to participate in the deconstruction of these socially constructed "meanings" and thereby become marginalized and deskilled in the education of their students. Other issues relating to cleavages in the distribution of power that dominant groups take for granted and that some oppressed people may not consider to serve as a barrier to oneself would also constitute areas of study.

With an understanding of discourse, students of color and other marginalized groups will not only learn about their own histories, they also will be provided with the opportunity to examine how discourses emerge to suit the interests of particular groups and deny other groups. Welch (1985 [quoted in Shapiro, 1991, p. 121]) declares: "It is oppressive to free people if their own history and culture do not serve as the primary source of the definitions of their freedom." Discourses and meanings arise out of struggle "in which what is at stake is ultimately quite a lot more than either words or discourses" (Macdonell, 1986, p. 51). At stake are not only the life chances and lives of nondominant groups, but also the rights and privileges that accompany equal and equitable participation. Additionally, some discourses may be seen not only to deny, or provide access, or say who can or cannot speak, or say when or where one may speak, and with what authority, but rather they may be seen as "neutral." This idea of neutral discourses must also be examined. For many unassuming teachers, especially preservice teachers, discourse as it is presented in textbooks and other curricular material is thought to be neutral and the teachers' teaching position is also thought to be neutral. For example, two questions asked by one of the authors to the students in an Introduction to Education class—"Is K–12 education neutral?" and "To what extent do you believe that your K–12 teachers took a neutral position while teaching?"—present interesting results and give emphasis to our discussion. For more than fifteen years, most preservice teachers in that class (twenty students out of an average class size of twenty-six) have reported that K–12 education is neutral, and that for the most part their K–12 teachers took a neutral position while teaching. Most of these students had not developed their own awareness of the persuasiveness of schooling, nor were they familiar with the thesis of Bourdieu and Passeron (1979 [1964]), who argued that schools are not socially neutral institutions but reflect the experience of the dominant class. A postmodern lens would enrich this discussion by raising questions about neutral as even a position that a teacher could take. In other words, when a teacher takes a neutral position or offers a neutral discourse, he or she is merely presenting a perspective. And all discourses (including a so-called neutral one) are merely perspectives (Poster, 1984, in Shapiro, 1991, p. 117).

Finally, a postmodern lens will help proponents of multicultural education to better understand how educational words are changed, manipulated, and deployed and come to be what Popkewitz (1991) describes as the language of regulation as a "means of control." Popkewitz (p. 199) points out how language use in educational reform standards can seem to represent and convey socially accepted interests, which upon a closer critique are misleading. He explains that the language of reform standards is cast as the rhetoric of schooling, which addresses learning competencies, and measurement:

> The universal language [of schooling] homogenizes social distinctions and conflicts by casting them as procedural categories. Policy is articulated through an instrumental language that makes the problems seem administrative in focus and universal in application. The rationality of reform pays no attention to new goals but takes for granted the goals of the existing institutional relations. Human ends are no longer conceived as ends in themselves or as subjects of philosophic discourse . . . This provides significance to what is specified, but at the same time, creates silence about the social arrangements implicit in the organization of schooling. The assumption is that there is a common school for all and equity is only a matter of equalizing the effectiveness of "delivery systems."

Multicultural education supported by a postmodern perspective would increase the number of critics, sharpen the critique, and better inform teachers that the discourse of multicultural education that they choose to espouse in their classrooms will bring with it a particular ideology regarding classroom policy and practice, power and knowledge, and view of the world.

The dominant discourses of schooling incorporate values, priorities, experiences, and ideas that play out and make natural inequalities of outcome and opportunity. For example, "at-risk" has become a part of the education vocabulary in practically every part of the school culture (e.g., policy, practice, informal conversation). Administrators, teachers, parents, community members, and even students use "at-risk" as a synonym to refer to students in Chapter I programs, students who live at or below the poverty level, students of color, especially Hispanic and African Americans. Recently, a school where one of the authors regularly visits requested volunteers to work with middle school at-risk students, who were below grade level in reading achievement. A potential female volunteer was asked during the screening interview to become a tutor: "What credentials, skills or knowledge do you have that qualify you to work with underachievers in reading?" The potential volunteer responded, without being informed who the students were, "Black children live next door to me and we get along very well."

Knowledge and discourses become the sites for struggle between dominant and subordinate groups. In theoretical terms this is a significant point, for
as Ball (1990, p. 18) reminds us: "Meanings thus are not from language but
from institutional practices, from power relations, from social position. Words
and concepts change their meaning and their effects as they are deployed
within different discourses." As illustrated earlier, we noted that "multicultural
education" lacks conceptual clarity. This has enabled critics and dissenters of
multicultural education (who have social and political positions of power to
use their influence to gain access to the popular and professional media and to
selectively choose the definition of multicultural education they want to criticize and to structure the nature of the discourse regarding its meaning) to have
political and social value and importance. For example, Diane Ravitch (1990, p.
A44), at present the assistant to the secretary of Education, recently wrote: "The
real issue on campus and in the classroom is not whether there will be multiculturalism, but what kind of multiculturalism will there be." Ravitch is
against "particularism"—that is, multicultural education that is defined as
Afrocentric or Hispanocentric. Similarly, Arthur Schlesinger, Jr. (1991, p. 2) in
The Disuniting of America: Reflections on a Multicultural Society posits:

> Instead of a transformative nation with an identity all its own, America
> increasingly sees itself as preservative of old identities. Instead of a na-
> tion composed of individuals making their own free choices, America
> increasingly sees itself as composed of groups more or less indelible in
> their ethnic character. The national ideal had once been *e pluribus unum.*
> Are we now to belittle *unum* and glorify *pluribus?* Will the center hold?
> or will the melting pot yield to the Tower of Babel?

is this white? as well.

The project then of multicultural education is to ensure that all students
have a knowledge of the apparatus, formal and informal, structures and discourses that oppress them. Accordingly, they need to have access to knowledge
of more than one discourse and the recognition that meaning is plural allows
for a measure of choice on the part of the individual and even where choice is
not available, resistance is possible (Weedon 1987, p. 106). Furthermore, it requires a rethinking and re-examination of the form and content of curriculum.
Questions such as whose knowledge is taught, whose cultures and languages
and so on become a legitimate part of educational praxis. This means that students' "habitus" (Bourdieu, 1977) as well as their experience outside of schools
is seen as a legitimate form of knowledge and as such has a place within the
formal school curriculum. With regard to "habitus" an analysis and examination can be made of those who occupy similar positions in social and historical
space, and who tend to possess a certain sense of place, including categories of
perception that provide a commonsense understanding of the world, especially, what is natural or even imaginable. (Bottomley, 1992, p. 211)

Discourse, knowledge, and power are complementary concepts that enable
us to understand and interpret the complexities and dynamics of contempo-

rary life. A further dimension needs to be added to our understanding of the symbolic aspects of everyday life—the dimension of culture. This concept is important for the purposes of this chapter for as Pettman (1992, p. 126) argues, "Culture isn't just a disguise or a mobilizing or containing strategy. Cultural expectations do inform our ways of being, knowing and understanding." As previously suggested, access to dominant cultural capital is crucial to getting on in either America or Australia.

Culture

"Culture," a powerful analytic concept in the social sciences, is often one of the most neglected concepts in multicultural education (Sachs, 1986). For the purposes of our argument here, "culture is highly political in its representation and reinforcement of structures of power" (Pettman, 1992, p. 119). Nevertheless, despite this important political point, much educational literature has downplayed the concept to incorporate normative characteristics of behavior, group and individual lifestyles, or essentialized and reified it as "the total way of life of any group." It reflects as well our vested disciplinary interests in characterizing "exotic otherness" (Keesing, 1990). It is worth quoting Keesing at length regarding the consequences of this:

> In pervading popular thought, anthropology's concept of culture has been applied to complex, contemporary ways of life—"Greek culture," "Chinese culture"—as well as exotic "primitive" ones in the TV documentaries. Ironically, with our all-inclusive conception of "culture," as it has passed into popular discourse have gone our habits of talk that reify, personify and essentialize. (p. 48)

The essentializing (e.g., the primacy of the Western canon) and popularizing of culture fails to apprehend that culture varies in status from society to society and group to group, and that there are variations in its invocation and its very meaning. The work of Bourdieu and Passeron (1979 [1964]) addressed the point of culture status and variation. They analyzed the impact of culture on the class system and on the relationship between action and social structure. Specifically, and important to our position on multicultural education, we point out that students from the dominant class and possessing high culture begin school with key social and cultural cues, which students from working-class backgrounds do not have and must learn in order to have a successful school experience. E. T. Hall (1976, pp. 1–2) speaks of the variations of culture across societies when he claims that

> culture has always been an issue, not only between Europe and Russia, but among the European states as well. The Germans, the French, the

Italians, the Spanish, Portuguese, and English, as well as the Scandinavian and Balkan cultures, all have their own identity, language, system of nonverbal communication, material culture, history, and ways of doing things.

The essentializing and popularizing of culture fails to acknowledge that the social distribution of culture is skewed, and that its meaning favors the interests of the dominant groups. Bourdieu and Passeron (1979 [1964]) and other social scientists refer to this as the dominant group having "cultural capital." They conclude that students from the dominant class enter schools with key cultural and social cues and experiences that correspond to the way school practices are conducted, while working-class and minority students have to learn these cues and have middle-class experiences in order to have school success.[1] Legitimacy is given to particular notions of participation, progress, and social identity in a way that transforms cultural struggles to coincide with rules of existing institutional arrangements (Popkewitz, 1988, p. 82).

By using a depoliticized or apolitical concept of culture, the experiences of people of color are effectively silenced insofar as they do not fit in what counts as true, real, and important. What counts as important, and thus worthy of study, is the culture and knowledge of hegemonic groups.

Moving beyond essentialist notions of culture means that we must examine how knowledge and ideas are produced and distributed within groups. For multicultural education this is particularly significant, for as numerous studies on the hidden curriculum have pointed out, knowledge is differentially distributed among different cultural and ethnic groups. S. Hall (1988, p. 44) makes the important point that "The circle of dominant ideas does accumulate the symbolic power to map or classify the world for others; its classifications do acquire not only the constraining power dominance over other modes of thought. . . . It becomes the horizon of the taken-for-granted: what the world is and how it works."

Postmodernism has helped to raise new questions about the terrain of culture as a field of domination and contestation. The historical situatedness, production, and hegemonic force of cultural meanings, in terms of internal structures and cleavages in society, are the focus of study (Keesing, 1990). However, as Giroux (1988) correctly points out, the postmodern problematic of culture and Otherness is not without its ambiguities and problems. There is the danger of affirming difference, simply as an end in itself without acknowledging how difference is formed, erased, and resuscitated within and despite asymmetrical relations in power. Lost here is any understanding of how difference is forged in both domination and opposition (Giroux, 1988, p. 18).

Ways Forward for Teachers

The challenge for multicultural education then is to identify the symbolic aspects of everyday life as well as the various cultures that constitute contemporary social relations. Giroux (1988, p. 13) gives us some idea of what this means: "We need to understand how the field of the everyday is being reconstituted not simply as a commodity sphere but as a site of contestation that offers new possibilities for engaging the memories, histories and stories of those who offer not simply otherness but an oppositional resistance to various forms of domination." To achieve this, first, we need to provide students with the knowledge and skills to enable them to give a definitive account of how "culture" is acquired, transmitted and distributed, as well as its meaning and the part it plays in the formation of commonsense knowledge and assumptions that are so important for the maintenance of hegemonic forms of power in our society. Furthermore, students must realize that the acquisition or non-acquisition of certain cultural beliefs, values and experiences can lead to their exclusion or inclusion from certain jobs, resources and high status groups (Lamont and Lareau, 1988).

An important benefit that postmodernism provides for multicultural education is to be found by analyzing the discourses of education and schooling. Such an approach provides students with opportunities to "ask questions about what we have not thought to think, about what is most densely invested in our discourses/practices, about what has been muted, repressed, unheard in our liberatory efforts" (Lather, 1991, p. 156). There has been a tendency for teachers to teach about culture in practical and essentialist ways (Sachs, 1989). Much of the literature and day-to-day discussion on multicultural education informs preservice and inservice education of teachers as well as their students that culture should be represented through the three "f's": foods, fairs, festivals; while culture in single-sex schools and in schools for people of color is mainly defined by the celebration of special days or weeks, recognition of certain ethnic heroes and heroines, eliminating biases, and developing acceptance of human difference. In many classrooms culture is presented as something possessed by individuals, learned and ideological insofar as ideologies define the world in terms of idealized subject positions. Culture thus presented is marginalized and the possibility of emancipatory teaching for students from a variety of ethnic and cultural backgrounds is reduced.

Second, Keesing (1990) makes a useful suggestion about how we might proceed by advocating a critical conception of culture. Such a conception would take the production and reproduction of cultural forms as problematic: that is,

> it would examine the way symbolic production is linked to power and interest (in terms of class, hierarchy, gender, etc.) . . . a critical conception of the cultural would begin with the assumption that in any "community" or "society" there will be multiple, subdominant and partially submerged cultural traditions (again, in relation to power, rank, class, gender, age, etc.), as well as the dominant tradition. (p. 57)

Using this perspective the type of multicultural education we have presented would not only be concerned with the identification of the multiple sources of cultural knowledge and how these are used by various groups, but also how such knowledge is distributed within various communities and institutions. Having done this it is possible for both teachers and students to examine the nature and effects of hegemony, especially as it relates to the educational experience of various cultural groups, whether these be based on race, gender, religion, sexuality, or whatever.

By focusing on the everyday and how this is experienced by various sectorial interests, the multicultural education we envisage, informed by postmodern perspectives on concepts such as discourse and culture, provides powerful ways for students to rethink their own personal and group experiences and strategies for dealing with these. One outcome may well be that ideas such as equity and social justice become the stuff of education, not just abstract peripheral rhetoric favored by bureaucrats and politicians. In such a situation multicultural education may well be a postmodern solution!

Conclusion

The title of this chapter suggests that proponents of multicultural education and proponents of postmodernism should enter a discussion, because many of their interests are similar, and they could possibly be of help to one another. For us, preparing for this chapter has shed a new light on old problems. We did not find agreement with all that we read on postmodernism, but we did discover points of agreement and, perhaps more importantly, we found points that beg for a collective discussion. We have tried to offer encouragement for that discussion to take place. By pointing out how the lens of postmodernism could assist multicultural education, we believe if proponents of postmodernism would review the literature on multicultural education they may reach a similar conclusion.

We have noted that an increasing number of proponents of multicultural education are dealing with both theories and practices that promote or sustain race, class, gender, and disability oppression. We further noted that an increasing number of proponents of multicultural education advocate the importance of teaching students how to take charge of their life circumstances. Implicit in the multicultural literature is praising diversity and advocating the affirmation of all groups of color, women (white and of color), people who have disabilities, and people who are poor or live on the margin of the economy. It is from our knowledge and respect for this multicultural population, the problems, issues, and challenges they face, and contributions they make, that we believe proponents of multicultural education can contribute to this discussion. Cornel West (1987) in an article, "Postmodernism and Black America," offers some important words that we can relate to this discussion. He says that distinctive issues of the postmodern debate surface: the relation of high and popular culture, the effectiveness of opposition in politics and culture, the possibilities of a post-European world. These issues involve the culture and political agency of peoples of color owing to the centrality of race in the U.S. and the decolonization process in the Third World. . . . It is not just racial parochialism that circumscribes postmodernism debate, but the larger political and cultural contexts which permit the parochialism to flourish . . . (p. 27)

Perhaps, even more poignantly, bell hooks' (1990) reflections on postmodernism further address the reason why multiculturalists and postmodernists should begin a dialogue.[2] We quote her at length:

Radical postmodernist practice, most powerfully conceptualized as a "politics of differences," should incorporate the voices of displaced, marginalized, exploited and oppressed black people. It is sadly ironic that the contemporary discourse which talks the most about heterogeneity, the decentered subjects, declaring breakthroughs that allow recognition of Otherness, still directs its critical voice primarily to a specialized audience that shares a common language rooted in the very master narratives it claims to challenge. If radical postmodernist thinking is to have a transformative impact, then a critical break with the notion of "authority" as "mastery over" must not simply be a rhetorical device. It must be reflective in habits of being, including styles of writing as well as chosen subject matter. (p. 25)

We have taken Shapiro's (1991, p. 112) comment seriously: "It is surprising that those concerned with education, with some few exceptions, have failed to join the debate on the meaning and implications of a postmodern culture, philosophy and politics." Similarly, we suggest Sleeter's (1989, p. 69) advice be taken seriously: "Multicultural education in the United States has many insights and theorists needed to strengthen and lead radical challenges to racism through education. Rather than ignoring or dismissing the field, educators on the left should be working with it." Proponents of multicultural education, we believe, would contribute much to the discussion of postmodernism.

Notes

The authors are very appreciative of the suggestions and encouragement received from several colleagues, especially Ann D. De Vaney, Gloria Ladson-Billings, Thomas S. Popkewitz, and William F. Tate.

1. Although we find Bourdieu's work useful, we disagree with his belief that people of color do not have a "culture" that has value in the marketplace.
2. bell hooks and Cornel West's illuminating comments are posited directly toward African Americans. We believe for the most part that their comments are applicable to other peoples of color, low-income people, and women, and we have used them within that context.

References

Ball, S. (1990). *Politics and Policy Making in Education.* London: Routledge.

Banks, J. (1977). "The Implication of Multicultural Education for Teacher Education." In F. H. Klassen and D. M. Gollnick (eds.), *Pluralism and the American Teacher* (pp. 1–34). Washington, DC: AACTE.

———. (1991). "A Curriculum for Empowerment, Action, and Change." In C. E. Sleeter (ed.), *Empowerment Through Multicultural Education* (pp. 125–142). Albany: State University of New York Press.

Bottomley, G. (1992). "Culture, Ethnicity and the Politics/Poetics of Representation." *Australian and New Zealand Journal of Sociology,* 28(2).

Bourdieu, P. (1977). *Outline of a Theory of Practice.* Cambridge: Cambridge University Press.

Bourdieu, P. and Passeron, J. C. (1979[1964]). *The Inheritors: French Students and Their Relation to Culture.* Chicago: University of Chicago Press.

Bove, P. (1986). "The Ineluctability of Difference: Scientific Pluralism and the Critical Intelligence." In J. Arac (ed.), *Postmodernism and Politics.* Minneapolis: University of Minnesota Press.

Connor, S. (1989). *Postmodernist Culture: An Introduction to Theories of the Contemporary.* Oxford: Basil Blackwell.

Featherstone, M. (1988). "In Pursuit of the Post Modern: An Introduction." *Theory, Culture and Society,* 5(2–3): 195–215.

Foucault, M. (1978). "Politics and the Study of Discourse." *Ideology and the Study of Discourse,* 3: 7–26.

Gay, G. (1979). "On Behalf of Children: A Curriculum Design for Multicultural Education in the Elementary School." *Journal of Negro Education,* 48 (3): 324–340.

———. (1983). "Multiethnic Education: Historical Developments and Future Prospects." *Phi Delta Kappan,* 64(8): 560–563.

———. (1988). "Designing Relevant Curricula for Diverse Learners." *Education and Urban Society,* 20 (4): 327–340.

Gibson, M. A. (1976). "Approaches to Multicultural Education in the United States: Some Concepts and Assumptions." *Anthropology and Education Quarterly,* 7: 7–18.

Giroux, H. (1988). "Postmodernism and the Discourse of Educational Criticism." *Journal of Education,* 170(3): 5–30.

Gollnick, D. and Chinn, P. (1983). *Multicultural Education in a Pluralistic Society.* St. Louis: C. V. Mosby.

Grant, C. (1977). "Education That Is Multicultural—Isn't That What We Mean?" *Journal of Teacher Education,* 29 (5): 45–48.

Grant, C. and Sleeter, C. (1985). "The Literature on Multicultural Education: Review and Analysis." *Educational Review,* 37(2): 97–118.

Grant, C., Sleeter, C., and Anderson, J. (1986). "The Literature on Multicultural Education: Review and Analysis II. *Educational Studies,* 12(1): 47–72.

Hall, E. T. (1976). *Beyond Culture.* New York: Doubleday.

Hall, S. (1988). "The Toad in the Garden: Thatcherism among the Theorists." In C. Nelson and L. Grossberg (eds.), *Marxism and the Interpretation of Culture.* Urbana: University of Illinois Press.

Hebdige, D. (1988). *Hiding in the Light: On Images and Things.* London: Comedia.

Hernandez, H. (1989). *Multicultural Education.* Columbus, OH: Merrill.

hooks, b. (1990). *Yearning: Race, Gender, and Cultural Politics.* Boston: South End Press.

Keesing, R. (1990). "Theories of Culture Revisited." *Canberra Anthropology,* 13(2): 46–60.

Kellner, D. (1988). "Postmodernism as Social Theory: Some Challenges and Problems." *Theory, Culture and Society,* 5(2–3): 239–269.

———. (1990). "Critical Theory and the Crisis of Social Theory." *Sociological Perspectives,* 33(1): 11–33.

Ladson-Billings, G. (1991). "Beyond Multicultural Illiteracy." *Journal of Negro Education,* 60(2): 147–157.

Lamont, M. and Lareau, A. (1988). "Cultural Capital: Allusions, Gaps and Glissandos in Recent Theoretical Development." *Sociological Theory,* 6(Fall): 153–168.

Lather, P. (1991). *Getting Smart: Feminist Research and Pedagogy with/in the Post-modern.* London: Routledge.

Lynch, J. (1986). "Multicultural Education in Western Europe." In James Banks and James Lynch (eds.), *Multicultural Education in Western Societies* (pp. 125–152). New York: Praeger.

Lyotard, J. F. (1984). *The Postmodern Condition: A Report on Knowledge,* trans. G. Bennington and B. Massumi. Manchester: Manchester University Press.

Macdonell, D. (1986). *Theories of Discourse,* Oxford: Blackwell.

Nieto S. (1992). *Affirming Diversity.* New York: Longman.

Pettman, J. (1992). *Living in the Margins: Racism, Sexism and Feminism in Australia.* Sydney: Allen and Unwin.

Popkewitz, T. (1988). "Culture, Pedagogy and Power: Issues in the Production of Values and Colonialization." *Boston University Journal of Education,* 170(2): 77–90.

———. (1991). *A Political Sociology of Educational Reform.* New York: Teachers College Press.

———. (1992). personal communication.

Pratte, R. (1983). "Multicultural Education: Four Normative Arguments." *Educational Theory,* 33: 21–32.

Ravitch, D. (1990). "Multiculturalism, Yes, Particularism, No." *The Chronicle of Higher Education,* October 24: A44.

Sachs, J. (1986). "Putting Culture Back into Multicultural Education." *New Community,* 13(2).

———. (1989). "Match or Mismatch: Multicultural Education Policy and Teachers' Conceptions of Culture." *Australian Journal of Education,* 33(1).

Schlesinger, A. Jr., (1991). *The Disuniting of America: Reflections on a Multicultural Society.* Knoxville, TN: Whittle Direct Books.

Shapiro, S. (1991). "The End of Radical Hope? Postmodernism and the Challenge to Critical Pedagogy." *Education and Society,* 9(2): 112–122.

Sleeter, C. E. (1989) "Multicultural Education as a Form of Resistance to Oppression." *Journal of Education,* 171(3). 51–71.

Sleeter C. and Grant, C. (1987). "An Analysis of Multicultural Education in the United States." *Harvard Educational Review,* 57(4): 421–444.

Sleeter, C. E. and Grant, C. A. (1988). *Making Choices for Multicultural Education.* New York: Merrill.

Spivak, G. (1990). *The Postcolonial Critic.* London: Routledge.

Weedon, C. (1987). *Feminist Practice and Post-Structuralist Theory.* Oxford: Basil Blackwell.

West, C. (1987). "Postmodernism and Black America." *Zeta Magazine,* 1(6): 27–29.

Questions

1. According to Grant and Sachs, what is "culture"?

2. According to Grant and Sachs, what is "postmodernism"?

3. What are some of the differences between "postmodernism" and "poststructuralism"? When exploring your response identify some of the major theorists associated with each of these movements.

4. Do you agree with Grant and Sachs' claim that postmodernism is a useful lens for multiculturalism? Explain.

5. What is the meaning of the term *discourse.?*

6. What is the relation of "discourse" to multicultural education?

7. Consider the claim made by Grant and Sachs that most teacher education programs offer a three *F*'s approach to multicultural education. Why do you think this approach predominates?

Insurgent Multiculturalism and the Promise of Pedagogy

Henry A. Giroux

Introduction

Multiculturalism has become a central discourse in the struggle over issues regarding national identity, the construction of historical memory, the purpose of schooling, and the meaning of democracy. While most of these battles have been waged in the university around curriculum changes and in polemic exchanges in the public media, today's crucial culture wars increasingly are being fought on two fronts. First, multiculturalism has become a "tug of war over who gets to create public culture."[1] Second, the contested terrain of multiculturalism is heating up between educational institutions that do not meet the needs of a massively shifting student population and students and their families for whom schools increasingly are perceived as merely one more instrument of repression.

In the first instance, the struggle over public culture is deeply tied to a historical legacy that affirms American character and national identity in terms that are deeply exclusionary, nativist, and racist. Echoes of this racism can be heard in the voices of public intellectuals such as George Will, Arthur Schlesinger Jr, and George Gilder. Institutional support for such racism can be found in neoconservative establishments such as the Olin Foundation and the National Association of Scholars.

In the second instance, academic culture has become a contested space primarily because groups that have been traditionally excluded from the public school curriculum and from the ranks of higher education are now becoming more politicized and are attending higher education institutions in increasing numbers. One consequence of this developing politics of difference has been a series of struggles by subordinate groups over access to educational resources,

gender and racial equity, curriculum content, and the disciplinary-based organization of academic departments.

While it has become commonplace to acknowledge the conflicting meanings of multiculturalism, it is important to acknowledge that in its conservative
and liberal forms multiculturalism has placed the related problems of white
racism, social justice, and power off limits, especially as these might be addressed as part of a broader set of political and pedagogical concerns. In what
follows, I want to reassert the importance of making the pedagogical more political. That is, I want to analyze how a broader definition of pedagogy can be
used to address how the production of knowledge, social identities, and social
relations might challenge the racist assumptions and practices that inform a variety of cultural sites, including but not limited to the public and private
spheres of schooling. Central to this approach is an attempt to define the pedagogical meaning of what I will call an insurgent multiculturalism. This is not a
multiculturalism that is limited to a fascination with the construction of identities, communicative competence, and the celebration of tolerance. Instead, I
want to shift the discussion of multiculturalism to a pedagogical terrain in
which relations of power and racialized identities become paramount as part of
a language of critique and possibility.

In part, this suggests constructing "an educational politics that would reveal the structures of power relations at work in the racialization of our social
order" while simultaneously encouraging students to "think about the invention of the category of whiteness as well as that of blackness and, consequently,
to make visible what is rendered invisible when viewed as the normative state
of existence: the (white) point in space from which we tend to identify difference."[2] As part of a language of critique, a central concern of an insurgent multiculturalism is to strip white supremacy of its legitimacy and authority. As
part of a project of possibility, an insurgent multiculturalism is about developing a notion of radical democracy around differences that are not exclusionary
and fixed, but that designate sites of struggle that are open, fluid, and that will
provide the conditions for expanding the heterogeneity of public spaces and
the possibility for "critical dialogues across different political communities and
constituencies."[3]

Multiculturalism and White Racism

If . . . one managed to change the curriculum in all the schools so that [Afro-
Americans] learned more about themselves and their real contributions to this
culture, you would be liberating not only [Afro-Americans], you'd be liberating white people who know nothing about their own history. And the reason is
that if you are compelled to lie about one aspect of anybody's history, you must
lie about it all. If you have to lie about my real role here, if you have to pretend
that I hoed all that cotton just because I loved you, then you have done something to yourself. You are mad.[4]

What James Baldwin, the renowned Afro-American novelist, is suggesting in the most immediate sense is that issues concerning multiculturalism are fundamentally about questions of race and identity. A more penetrating analysis reveals that multiculturalism is not only about the discourse of racialized identities, but is also fundamentally about the issue of whiteness as a mark of racial and gender privilege. For example, Baldwin argues that multiculturalism cannot be reduced to an exclusive otherness that references Afro-Americans, Hispanics, Latinos, or other suppressed "minorities," as either a problem to be resolved through the call for benevolent assimilation or as a threat to be policed and eliminated. For Baldwin, multiculturalism is primarily about whiteness and its claims to a self-definition that excludes the messy relations of race, ethnicity, power, and identity. Baldwin highlights how differences in power and privilege authorize who speaks, how fully, under what conditions, against what issues, for whom, and with what degree of consistent, institutionalized support. In this sense multiculturalism raises the question of whether people are speaking within or outside a privileged space, and whether such spaces provide the conditions for different groups to listen to each other differently to address how the racial economies of privilege and power work in American society.

I want to argue that educators need to rethink the politics of multiculturalism as part of a broader attempt to engage the world of public and global politics. This suggests challenging the narratives of national identity, culture, and ethnicity as part of a pedagogical effort to provide dominant groups with the knowledge and histories to examine, acknowledge, and unlearn their own privilege. But more is needed in this view of multiculturalism than deconstructing the centers of colonial power and undoing the master narratives of racism. A viable multicultural pedagogy and politics must also affirm cultural differences while simultaneously refusing to essentialize and grant immunity to those groups that speak from subordinate positions of power. As Graff and Robbins point out, the most progressive aspect of multiculturalism "has been not to exalt group 'particularism' but to challenge it, to challenge the belief that blackness, femaleness, or Africanness are essential, unchanging qualities."[5]

Within the current historical conjuncture, the struggles over national identity, race, and what it means to be an "American" have taken place largely within discussions that focus on questions of self- and social representation. While a politics of representation is indispensable in creating a multicultural and multiracial society, educators must also address the systemic, structural changes that are needed to produce such a social order. In part, this demands an approach to multiculturalism that addresses "the context of massive black unemployment, overcrowded schools, a lack of recreational facilities, dilapidated housing and racist policing."[6] Cornel West builds upon this position by arguing that white America needs to address the nihilism that permeates black communities in the United States. He defines such nihilism as "the lived experience of coping with a life of horrifying meaninglessness, hopelessness, and (most important) lovelessness."[7] In this scenario, the black community is depicted as a culture that has lost the moral strength, hope, and resistance once provided by the institutions of black civil society: "black families, neighbor-hoods, schools, churches, mosques."[8]

I want to extend West's argument and suggest that if the depiction of black nihilism is not to reproduce the culture of poverty thesis made popular among conservatives, then educators must attempt to understand how white institu-tions, ethnicity, and public life is structured through a nihilism that represents another type of moral disorder, impoverishment of the spirit, and decline of public life. In this analysis, cultural criticism moves from a limited emphasis on the effects of racism and the workings of black nihilism to the origins of racism in the political, social, and cultural dynamics of white "supremacy." More specifically, a critical multiculturalism must shift attention away from an exclu-sive focus on subordinate groups, especially since such an approach tends to highlight their deficits, to one that examines how racism in its various forms is produced historically, semiotically, and institutionally at various levels of soci-ety. This is not meant to suggest that blacks and other subordinate groups do not face problems that need to be addressed in the discourse of multicultural-ism. On the contrary, it means that a critical analysis of race must move beyond the discourse of blaming the victim in which whites view multiculturalism as a code word for black lawlessness and other "problems" blacks create for white America. Viewing black people in this manner reveals not only white su-premacy as the discursive and institutional face of racism, but it also presents us with the challenge of addressing racial issues not as a dilemma of black peo-ple but as a problem endemic to the legacy colonialism rooted in "historical in-equalities and longstanding cultural stereotypes."[9]

In opposition to a quaint liberalism, a critical multiculturalism means more than simply acknowledging differences and analyzing stereotypes; more fun-damentally, it means understanding, engaging, and transforming the diverse histories, cultural narratives, representations, and institutions that produce racism and other forms of discrimination. As bell hooks points out, for too long white people have imagined that they are invisible to black people. Not only does whiteness in this formulation cease to mark the locations of its own privi-leges, it reinforces relations in which blacks become invisible in terms of how they name, see, experience, and bear the pain and terror of whiteness. hooks puts it succinctly:

> In white supremacist society, white people can "safely" imagine that they are invisible to black people since the power they have historically asserted, and even now collectively assert over black people, accorded them the right to control the black gaze.... [And yet] to name that whiteness in the black imagination is often a representation of terror. One must face written histories that erase and deny, that reinvent the past to make the present vision of racial harmony and pluralism more plausible. To bear the burden of memory one must willingly journey to places long uninhabited, searching the debris of history for traces of the unforgettable, all knowledge of which has been suppressed.[10]

It is worth noting that many educational commentators who address the issue of multiculturalism have ruled out any discussion of the relationship between race and class and how they are manifested within networks of hierarchy and subordination in and out of the schools. This particular silence, coupled with the popular perception bolstered by the media that recent racial disturbances and uprisings such as the rape of the female jogger in Central Park, the murder of Michael Jordan's father, and the LA uprising can be explained by pointing to those involved as simply thugs, looters, and criminals, makes it clear why the multicultural peril is often seen as a black threat; it suggests what such a belief shares with the dominant ideological view of the "other" as a disruptive outsider. In this scenario, multiculturalism is seen as an impediment rather than an essential condition for the survival of democratic public life.

To understand fully the conservative response to multiculturalism, it is crucial to situate the debates around the politics of cultural difference within the broader assault on democracy that has taken place in the last decade. But before I address. this issue, I want to suggest that public schooling and higher education are crucial sites in which the relationship between multiculturalism and democracy should be acknowledged and incorporated into the curriculum. A democratic or insurgent multiculturalism is one that offers a new language for students and others to move between disciplinary borders and to travel within zones of cultural difference. This is a language that challenges the boundaries of cultural and racial difference as sites of exclusion and discrimination while simultaneously rewriting the script of cultural difference as part of a broader attempt to expand and deepen the imperatives of a multicultural and multiracial democracy.

An insurgent multiculturalism takes as its starting point the question of what it means for educators and cultural workers to treat schools and other public sites as border institutions in which teachers, students, and others engage in daily acts of cultural translation and negotiation. For it is within such institutions that students and teachers are offered the opportunity to become border crossers, to recognize that schooling is really an introduction to how culture is organized, a demonstration of who is authorized to speak about particular forms of culture, what culture is considered worthy of valorization, and what forms of culture are considered invalid and unworthy of public esteem. Drawing upon Homi Bhabha, I want to contend that schools, in part, need to be understood as sites engaged in the "strategic activity of 'authorizing' agency," of exercising authority "to articulate and regulate incommensurable meanings and identities."[11] Within this perspective, pedagogy is removed from its exclusive emphasis on management and is defined as a form of political leadership and ethical address. The pedagogical imperative here is to weigh cultural differences against the implications they have for practices that disclose rather than mystify, democratize culture rather than close it off, and provide the conditions for people to believe that they can take risks and change existing power relations. Translated into a critical pedagogical practice, multiculturalism pluralizes the spaces for exchange, understanding, and identity formation among a variety of dominant and subordinate groups. It is precisely because of the possibility of rewriting dominant cultural narratives and social relations that multiculturalism appears so threatening to conservatives and liberals. One of the most frank expressions of this position came from the 1975 Trilateral Commission report *The Crisis of Democracy* which boldly alleged that a substantive democracy represents an unwarranted challenge to government authority and existing configurations of power. Viewed in this context, the current assault on multiculturalism must be understood as a part of a broader assault on democracy itself.

Multiculturalism and the Perils of Democracy

Within the last decade, cultural authority and legislative policy have combined to extend massively the influence of domination to increasing numbers of subordinate groups in America. In the face of escalating poverty, increasing racism, growing unemployment among "minorities," and the failure of an expanding number of Americans to receive adequate health care and education, the Reagan/Bush administrations invoked a wooden morality coupled with a disdain for public life by blaming the nation's ills on the legislation of the Great Society, TV sitcom characters such as Murphy Brown, and the alleged breakdown of family values. Within this scenario, poverty is caused by the poverty of values, racism is seen as a "black" problem (lawlessness), and social decay is rectified by shoring up the nuclear family and social relations of the alleged free market.

Abandoning its responsibility for political and moral leadership, the federal government, during the last decade, reduced its intervention in public life to waging war against Iraq, using taxpayers' money to bail out corrupt bankers, and slashing legislation that would benefit the poor, the homeless, and the disadvantaged. There is a tragic irony at work when a government can raise 500 billion dollars to bail out corrupt bankers and 50 billion to fight a war in Iraq (put in perspective, the combined costs of these adventures exceeds the cost of World War II, including veterans benefits) while at the same time that same government cuts back food stamp and school lunch programs in a country in which nearly one out of every four children under six live in poverty. But there is more at stake here than simply the failure of moral and political leadership. The breadth and depth of democratic relations are being rolled back at all levels of national and daily life. For example, this is seen in the growing disparity between the rich and poor, the ongoing attacks by the government and courts on civil rights and the welfare system, and the proliferating incidents of racist harassment and violence on college and public school sites.

The retreat from democracy is evident also in the absence of serious talk about how as a nation, we might educate existing and future generations of students in the language and practice of moral compassion, critical agency, and public service. The discourse of leadership appears trapped in a terminology in which the estimate of a good society is expressed in indices that measure profit margins and the Dow Jones Average. Missing in this vocabulary is a way of nourishing and sustaining a popular perception of democracy as something that needs to be constantly struggled for in public arenas such as the schools, churches, and other sites which embody the promise of a multiracial and multicultural democracy.

This current assault on democratic public life has taken a new turn in the last few years. At one level, American conservatives have initiated a long-term project of discrediting and dismantling those institutions, ideologies, and practices that are judged incompatible with the basic ideology of the market place with its unswerving commitment to the principles of individualism, choice, and the competitive ethic. Accompanying this attempt has been a parallel effort to reprivatize and deregulate schools, health care, the welfare system, and other public services and institutions.

Part of the attempt to rewrite the terms of a discourse of democratic public life can be seen in the emergence of a new breed of intellectuals, largely backed by conservative think tanks such as the Madison Group, the Hoover Institute, Heritage Foundation, and a host of other conservative foundations. With access to enormous cultural resources infused by massive financial backing from the Olin, Scaife, and Smith Richardson foundations, right-wing think tanks have begun to mount mammoth public campaigns to promote their cultural revolution. Many of the major right-wing intellectuals who have helped to shape popular discourse about educational reform in the last decade have received extensive aid from the conservative foundations. These include intellectuals such as Diane Ravitch, Chester Finn Jr., Dinish D'Souza, and Thomas Sowell; all of whom have targeted public schools and higher education as two principal spheres of struggle over issues of curricula reform, privatization, choice, and difference. To understand the model of leadership these intellectuals provide, it is important to examine how some of their underlying ideological concerns relate to the broader issues of democracy, race, and public accountability.

For many conservatives, the utopian possibility of cultural democracy has become dangerous at the current historical conjuncture for a number of reasons. Most important, cultural democracy encourages a language of critique for understanding and transforming those relations that trap people in networks of hierarchy and exploitation. That is, it provides normative referents for recognizing and assessing competing political vocabularies, the visions of the future they presuppose, and the social identities and practices they produce and legitimate. Clearly, such a position poses a challenge to right-wing educators whose celebration of choice and the logic of the market place often abstracts freedom from equality and the imperatives of citizenship from its historical grounding in the public institutions of modern society.

In fact, many conservatives have been quite aggressive in rewriting the discourse of citizenship *not* as the practice of social responsibility but as a privatized act of altruism, self-help, or philanthropy. It is crucial to recognize that within this language of privatization, the disquieting, disrupting, interrupting difficulties of sexism, crime, youth unemployment, AIDS, and other social problems, and how they bear down on schools and subordinated groups, are either ignored or summarily dismissed as individual problems caused, in part, by the people who are victimized by them. This position accentuates individual character flaws and behavioral impediments to economic and social mobility to elide the political and economic conditions that produces the context of victimization and the systemic pressures and limits that must be addressed to overcome it. By focusing on the privatized language of individual character, conservatives erase the moral and political obligation of individuals, groups, and institutions to recognize their complicity in creating the racial problems that multicultural critics have addressed. In this scenario, we end up with a vision of leadership in which individuals act in comparative isolation and without any sense of public accountability. This is why many right-wing educators praise the virtues of the competition and choice but rarely talk about how money and power, when unevenly distributed, influence "whether people have the means or the capacity" to make or act on choices that inform their daily lives.[12]

Choice in this case serves to rewrite the discourse of freedom within a limited conception of individual needs and desires. What disappears from this view of leadership is the willingness to recognize that the fundamental issues of citizenship, democracy, and public life can neither be understood nor addressed solely within the restricted language of the marketplace or choice. Choice and the market are not the sole conditions of freedom, nor are they adequate to constituting political subjects within the broader discourses of justice, equality, and community. In fact, no understanding of community, citizenship, or public culture is possible without a shared conception of social justice, yet it is precisely the notion of social justice that is missing in mainstream discussions of multiculturalism and school reform.

Conservatives not only view multiculturalism as a threat to national identity, they have actively attempted to remove it from the language of community and social justice. Rather than asserting the primacy of the ethical in responding to the suffering of subordinated groups in America's schools and other social institutions, conservatives have developed educational and public policies that expand cost-benefit analyses and market relations at the expense of addressing major social problems such as racism, poverty, crime, and unemployment. For example, it is worth noting that 45 per cent of all "minority" children live in poverty while the dropout rate among "minority" students has attained truly alarming proportions, reaching as high as 70 per cent in some major urban areas. These problems are compounded by an unemployment rate among black youth that is currently 38.4 per cent. In the face of these problems, conservatives are aggressively attempting to enact choice legislation that would divert funds away from the public schools to private schools. Against these efforts, it is worth noting, as Peter Drier, points out that:

> since 1980 the federal government has slashed successful urban pro-
> grams—public works, economic development, health and nutrition,
> schools, housing, and job training—by more than 70 per cent. . . . In
> 1980, federal dollars accounted for 14.3 per cent of city budgets; today,

the federal share is less then five per cent. . . . To avert fiscal collapse, many cities have been closing schools, hospitals, police and fire stations; laying off of essential employees; reducing such basic services as maintenance of parks and roads; neglecting housing and health codes, and postponing or canceling capital improvements.[13]

The claim by conservatives that these problems can be solved by raising test scores, promoting choice, developing a national curriculum, and creating a uniform standard of national literacy is cruel and mean-spirited. But, of course, this is where the discourse of critical democracy becomes subversive; it makes visible the political and normative considerations that frame such reforms. It also offers a referent for analyzing how the language of excessive individualism and competitiveness serves to make social inequality invisible, promoting an indifference to human misery, exploitation, and suffering. Moreover, it suggests that the language of excellence and individualism when abstracted from considerations of equality and social justice serves to restrict rather than animate the possibilities of democratic public life. Increasingly, conservatives also have used the language of individual rights; that is, the right of individuals to think and act as they please, to attack any discourse or program that questions the existence of social inequalities. As Joan Scott points out, there is more at stake here than what the conservatives call the existence of dangerous orthodoxies in the university.

> We are experiencing another phase of the ongoing Reagan-Bush revolution which, having packed the courts and privatized the economy, now seeks to neutralize the space of ideological and cultural nonconformity by discrediting it. This is the context within which debates about political correctness and multiculturalism have taken shape.[14]

Rather than engage the growing insistence on the part of more and more groups in this country to define themselves around the specificity of class, gender, race, ethnicity, or sexual orientation, conservatives have committed themselves simply to resisting and subverting these developments. While conservatives rightly recognize that struggles over the public school curriculum and the canon in higher education are fueled, in part, over anxiety about the issue of national identity, they engage this issue from a largely defensive posture and in doing so appear to lack any understanding of how the curriculum itself is implicated in producing relations of inequality, domination, and oppression. For example, even moderate liberals who adopt a conservative stance on multicultural issues resort to rhetorical swipes that share ideological ground with nativist writing against Catholics and immigrants in the 1920s. For example, Schlesinger refers to the multiculturalists in the United States as part of an "ethnic upsurge" that threatens to become a full-fledged counterrevolution against the alleged common culture and the "American ideal of assimilation."[15] Schlesinger is quite clear, as are many of his conservative allies, that as soon as public schools refuse to serve as vehicles for cultural assimilation, they have betrayed their most important historically-sanctioned role. Unfortunately, Schlesinger does not see anything wrong with the schools producing social identities in which cultural differences are seen as a deficit rather than a strength. That the assimilation model of schooling maintains its hegemony through the racist, class-specific dynamics of tracking and cultural discrimination appears to Schlesinger to be unworthy of critical attention. When critical multiculturalists criticize how the curriculum through a process of exclusion and inclusion privileges some groups over others, such critics are summarily dismissed as being political, partisan, and radically anti-American by critics such as Schlesinger.

It is difficult to imagine what is either unpatriotic or threatening about subordinate groups attempting to raise questions such as: "Whose experiences, histories, knowledge, and arts are represented in our educational and cultural institutions? How fully, on whose terms, and with what degree of ongoing, institutionalized participation and power?"[16] Nor in a democratic society should subordinate groups attempting to fashion a pedagogy and politics of inclusion and cultural democracy be derisively labeled as particularistic because they have raised serious questions regarding how the canon and public school curriculum work to secure specific forms of cultural authority or how the dynamics of cultural power works to silence and marginalize specific groups of students. Responding to these concerns, academic conservatives such as William Kerrigan simply recycle their own beliefs about the superiority of the established canon without revealing the slightest element of self criticism. Kerrigan argues that "an undergraduate education that *saddles* (my emphasis) students with 'cultural diversity' requirements encourages them to flit incoherently from this concentration to that major."[17] That the knowledge that constitutes the academic disciplines is neither universal nor the highest expression of scholarship given its exclusion of women and "minorities" does not seem to bother Kerrigan. In this case, the claims that subordinate groups make upon the shaping of cultural memory and the promise of democratic pluralism are dismissed by Kerrigan through the arrogant, self-serving assertion that "educators have become pathologically sensitive to complaints of ethnocentrism. Rather than elevating the minds of students from historically oppressed groups, the whole educational system is sinking."[18] This emerging critique of schools and other cultural institutions is based on the elitist and racist assumptions that the enemy of democracy is not intolerance, structured inequality, and social injustice, but cultural differences.

In treating cultural narrative and national history in fixed and narrow terms, conservatives relinquish one of the most important defining principles of any democracy; that is, they ignore the necessity of a democratic society to rejuvenate itself by constantly reexamining the strengths and limits of its traditions. In the absence of a critical encounter with the past and a recognition of the importance of cultural diversity, multiculturalism becomes acceptable only if it is reduced to a pedagogy of reverence and transmission rather than a pedagogical practice that puts people in dialogue with each other as part of a broader attempt to fashion a renewed interest in cultural democracy and the creation of engaged and critical citizens. Bhikhu Parekh rightly argues that such an uncritical stance defines what he calls demagogic multiculturalism. For Parekh, the traditionalists' refusal of cultural hybridity and differences and the fixity of identity and culture promotes a dangerous type of fundamentalism. He writes:

> When a group feels besieged and afraid of losing its past in exchange for a nebulous future, it lacks the courage to critically reinterpret its fundamental principles, lest it opens the door to "excessive" reinterpretation. It then turns its fundamentals into fundamentalism, it declares them inviolate and reduces them to a neat and easily enforceable package of beliefs and rituals.[19]

Parekh's fear of demagogic multiculturalism represents a pedagogical problem as much as it does a political one. The political issue is exemplified in the conservative view that critical multiculturalism with its assertion of multiple identities and diverse cultural traditions represents a threat to democracy. As I have mentioned previously, the fatal political transgression committed here lies in the suggestion that social criticism itself is fundamentally at odds with democratic life. Indeed, this is more than mere rhetoric, it is a challenge to the very basic principles that inform a democratic society. Pedagogically, demagogic multiculturalism renders any debate about the relationship between democracy and cultural difference moot. By operating out of a suffocating binarism that pits "us" against "them" conservatives annul the possibility for dialogue, education, understanding, and negotiation. In other words, such a position offers no language for contending with cultures whose boundaries cross over into diverse spheres that are fluid and saturated with power. How this type of fundamentalism will specifically impact the schools can be seen in the increased calls for censorship as well as in the bleaching of the curriculum to exclude or underrepresent the voices and histories of various subordinate groups.

Instead of responding to the increasing diversity of histories, ethnicities, and cultures complexly layered over time, dominant institutions and discourses appear increasingly indifferent to the alarming poverty, shameful school dropout rate, escalating unemployment and a host of other problems that accentuate the alienation, inequality, and racial segregation that fuel the sense of desperation, hopelessness, and disempowerment felt by many "minorities" in the United States. It appears morally careless and politically irresponsible to define multiculturalism as exclusively disruptive and antithetical to the most fundamental aspects of American democracy. Such a position fails to explore the potential that multiculturalism has as a critical referent for linking diversity and cultural democracy while simultaneously serving to ignore the social, economic, and political conditions that have spurned the current insurgency among "minorities" and others around the issue of multiculturalism.

ᴄ∕ᴑ

Toward an Insurgent Multiculturalism

> To make a claim for multiculturalism is not . . . to suggest a juxtaposition
> of several cultures whose frontiers remain intact, nor is it to subscribe to
> a bland "melting-pot" type of attitude that would level all differences. It
> lies instead, in the intercultural acceptance of risks, unexpected detours,
> and complexities of relation between break and closure.[20]

Multiculturalism like another broadly signifying term is multiaccentual
and must be adamantly challenged when defined as part of the discourse of
domination or essentialism. The challenge the term presents is daunting given
the way in which it has been appropriated by various mainstream and orthodox positions. For example, when defined in corporate terms it generally is reduced to a message without critical content. Liberals have used multiculturalism to denote a pluralism devoid of historical contextualization and the
specificities of relations of power or they have depicted a view of cultural
struggle in which the most fundamental contradictions "implicating race, class,
and gender can be harmonized within the prevailing structure of power relation."[21] For many conservatives, multiculturalism has come to signify a disruptive, unsettling, and dangerous force in American society. For some critics, it
has been taken up as a slogan for promoting an essentializing identity politics
and various forms of nationalism. In short, multiculturalism can be defined
through a variety of ideological constructs, and signifies a terrain of struggle
around the reformation of historical memory, national identity, self- and social
representation, and the politics of difference.

Multiculturalism is too important as a political discourse to be exclusively
appropriated by liberals and conservatives. This suggests that if the concept of
multiculturalism is to become useful as a pedagogical concept, educators need
to appropriate it as more than a tool for critical understanding and the pluraliz-
ing of differences; it must also be used as an ethical and political referent which
allows teachers and students to understand how power works in the interest of
dominant social relations, and how such relations can be challenged and transformed. In other words, an insurgent multiculturalism should promote pedagogical practices that offer the possibility for schools to become places where
students and teachers can become border crossers engaged in critical and ethical reflection about what it means to bring a wider variety of cultures into dialogue with each other, to theorize about cultures in the plural, within rather
than outside "antagonistic relations of domination and subordination."[22]

In opposition to the liberal emphasis on individual diversity, an insurgent
multiculturalism also must address issues regarding group differences and
how power relations function to structure racial and ethnic identities. Furthermore, cultural differences cannot be merely affirmed to be assimilated into a
common culture or policed through economic, political, and social spheres that
restrict full citizenship to dominant groups. If multiculturalism is to be linked

to renewed interests in expanding the principles of democracy to wider spheres of application, it must be defined in pedagogical and political terms that embrace it as a referent and practice for civic courage, critical citizenship, and democratic struggle. Bhikhu Parekh provides a definition that appears to avoid a superficial pluralism and a notion of multiculturalism that is structured in dominance. He writes:

> Multiculturalism doesn't simply mean numerical plurality of different cultures, but rather a community which is creating, guaranteeing, encouraging spaces within which different communities are able to grow at their own pace. At the same time it means creating a public space in which these communities are able to interact, enrich the existing culture and create a new consensual culture in which they recognize reflections of their own identity.[23]

In this view, multiculturalism becomes more than a critical referent for interrogating the racist representations and practices of the dominant culture, it also provides a space in which the criticism of cultural practices is inextricably linked to the production of cultural spaces marked by the formation of new identities and pedagogical practices that offers a powerful challenge to the racist, patriarchal, and sexist principles embedded in American society and schooling. Within this discourse, curriculum is viewed as a hierarchical and representational system that selectively produces knowledge, identities, desires, and values. The notion that curriculum represents knowledge that is objective, value free, and beneficial to all students is challenged forcefully as it becomes clear that those who benefit from public schooling and higher education are generally white, middle-class students whose histories, experiences, language, and knowledge largely conform to dominant cultural codes and practices. Moreover, an insurgent multiculturalism performs a theoretical service by addressing curriculum as a form of cultural politics which demands linking the production and legitimation of classroom knowledge, social identities, and values to the institutional environments in which they are produced.

As part of a project of possibility, I want to suggest some general elements that might inform an insurgent multicultural curriculum. First, a multicultural curriculum must be informed by a new language in which cultural differences are taken up not as something to be tolerated but as essential to expanding the discourse and practice of democratic life. It is important to note that multiculturalism is not merely an ideological construct, it also refers to the fact that by the year 2010, people of color will be the numerical majority in the United States. This suggests that educators need to develop a language, vision, and curriculum in which multiculturalism and democracy become mutually reinforcing categories. At issue here is the task of reworking democracy as a pedagogical and cultural practice that contributes to what John Dewey once called the creation of an articulate public. Manning Marable defines some of the essential parameters of this task.

Multicultural political democracy means that this country was not built by and for only one group—Western Europeans; that our country does not have only one language—English; or only one religion—Christianity; or only one economic philosophy—corporate capitalism. Multicultural democracy means that the leadership within our society should reflect the richness, colors and diversity expressed in the lives of all of our people. Multicultural democracy demands new types of power sharing and the reallocation of resources necessary to great economic and social development for those who have been systematically excluded and denied.[24]

Imperative to such a task is a reworking of the relationship between culture and power to avoid what Homi Bhabha has called "the subsumption or sublation of social antagonism . . . the repression of social divisions . . . and a representation of the social that naturalizes cultural difference and turns it into a 'second'-nature argument."[25]

Second, as part of an attempt to develop a multicultural and multiracial society consistent with the principles of a democratic society, educators must account for the fact that men and women of color are disproportionately underrepresented in the cultural and public institutions of this country. Pedagogically this suggests that a multicultural curriculum must provide students with the skills to analyze how various audio, visual, and print texts fashion social identities over time, and how these representations serve to reinforce, challenge, or rewrite dominant moral and political vocabularies that promote stereotypes that degrade people by depriving them of their history, culture, and identity.

This should not suggest that such a pedagogy should solely concentrate on how meanings produce particular stereotypes and the uses to which they are put. Nor should a multicultural politics of representation focus exclusively on producing positive images of subordinated groups by recovering and reconstituting elements of their suppressed histories. While such approaches can be pedagogically useful, it is crucial for critical educators to reject any approach to multiculturalism that affirms cultural differences in the name of an essentialized and separatist identity politics. Rather than recovering differences that sustain their self-representation through exclusions, educators need to demonstrate how differences collide, cross over, mutate, and transgress in their negotiations and struggles. Differences in this sense must be understood not through the fixity of place or the romanticization of an essentialized notion of history and experience but through the tropes of indeterminacy, flows, and translations. In this instance, multiculturalism can begin to formulate a politics of representation in which questions of access and cultural production are linked to what people do with the signifying regimes they use within historically-specific public spaces.

While such approaches are essential to giving up the quest for a pure historical tradition, it is imperative that a multicultural curriculum also focus on dominant, white institutions and histories to interrogate them in terms of their injustices and their contributions for "humanity." This means, as Cornel West points out that

> to engage in a serious discussion of race in America, we must begin not with the problems of black people but with the flaws of American society—flaws rooted in historical inequalities and longstanding cultural stereotypes. . . . How we set up the terms for discussing racial issues shapes our perception and response to these issues. As long as black people are viewed as "them," the burden falls on blacks to do all the "cultural" and "moral" work necessary for healthy race relations. The implication is that only certain Americans can define what it means to be American—and the rest must simply "fit in."[26]

In this sense, multiculturalism is about making whiteness visible as a racial category; that is, it points to the necessity of providing white students with the cultural memories that enable them to recognize the historically- and socially-constructed nature of their own identities. Multiculturalism as a radical, cultural politics should attempt to provide white students (and others) with the self-definitions upon which they can recognize their own complicity with or resistance to how power works within and across differences to legitimate some voices and dismantle others. Of course, more is at stake here than having whites reflect critically on the construction of their own racial formation and their complicity in promoting racism. Equally important is the issue of making all students responsible for their practices, particularly as these serve either to undermine or expand the possibility for democratic public life.

Third, a multicultural curriculum must address how to articulate a relationship between unity and difference that moves beyond simplistic binarisms. That is, rather than defining multiculturalism against unity or simply for difference, it is crucial for educators to develop a unity-in-difference position in which new, hybrid forms of democratic representation, participation, and citizenship provide a forum for creating unity without denying the particular, multiple, and the specific. In this instance, the interrelationship of different cultures and identities become borderlands, sites of crossing, negotiation, translation, and dialogue. At issue is the production of a border pedagogy in which the intersection of culture and identity produces self-definitions that enables teachers and students to authorize a sense of critical agency. Border pedagogy points to a self/other relationship in which identity is fixed as neither Other nor the same; instead, it is both and, hence, defined within multiple literacies that become a referent, critique, and practice of cultural translation, a recognition of no possibility of fixed, final, or monologically authoritative meaning that exists outside of history, power, and ideology.

Within such a pedagogical cartography, teachers must be given the opportunity to cross ideological and political borders as a way of clarifying their own moral vision, as a way of enabling counterdiscourses, and, as Roger Simon points out, as a way of getting students "beyond the world they already know in order to challenge and provoke their inquiry and challenge of their existing views of the way things are and should be."[27]

Underlying this notion of border pedagogy is neither the logic of assimilation (the melting pot) nor the imperative to create cultural hierarchies, but the attempt to expand the possibilities for different groups to enter into dialogue to understand further the richness of their differences and the value of what they share in common.

Fourth, an insurgent multiculturalism must challenge the task of merely re-presenting cultural differences in the curriculum; it must also educate students of the necessity for linking a justice of multiplicity to struggles over real material conditions that structure everyday life. In part, this means understanding how structural imbalances in power produce real limits on the capacity of subordinate groups to exercise a sense of agency and struggle. It also means analyzing specific class, race, gender, and other issues as social problems rooted in real material and institutional factors that produce specific forms of inequality and oppression. This would necessitate a multicultural curriculum that produces a language that deals with social problems in historical and relational terms, and uncovers how the dynamics of power work to promote domination within the school and the wider society. In part, this means multiculturalism as a curricula discourse and pedagogical practice must function in its dual capacity as collective memory and alternative reconstruction. History, in this sense, is not merely resurrected but interrogated and tempered by "a sense of its liability, its contingency, its constructedness."[28] Memory does not become the repository of registering suppressed histories, albeit critically, but of reconstructing the moral frameworks of historical discourse to interrogate the present as living history.

Finally, a multicultural curriculum must develop, in public schools and institutions of higher education, contexts that serve to refigure relations between the school, teachers, students, and the wider community. For instance, public schools must be willing to develop a critical dialogue between the school and those public cultures within the community dedicated to producing students who address the discourse and obligations of power as part of a larger attempt at civic renewal and the reconstruction of democratic life. At best, parents, social activists, and other socially-concerned community members should be allowed to play a formative role in crucial decisions about what is taught, who is hired, and how the school can become a laboratory for learning that nurtures critical citizenship and civic courage. Of course, the relationship between the school and the larger community should be made in the interest of expanding "the social and political task of transformation, resistance, and radical democratization."[29] In both spheres of education, the curriculum needs to be decentralized to allow students to have some input into what is taught and under what conditions. Moreover, teachers need to be educated to be border crossers, to explore zones of cultural difference by moving in and out of the resources, histories, and narratives that provide different students with a sense of identity, place, and possibility. This does not suggest that educators become tourists traveling to exotic lands; on the contrary, it points to the need for them to enter into negotiation and dialogue around issues of nationality, difference, and identity so as to be able to fashion a more ethical and democratic set of pedagogical relations between themselves and their students while simultaneously allowing students to speak, listen, and learn differently within pedagogical spaces that are safe, affirming, questioning, and enabling.

In this instance, a curriculum for a multicultural and multiracial society provides the conditions for students to imagine beyond the given and to embrace their identities critically as a source of agency and possibility. In addition, an insurgent multiculturalism should serve to redefine existing debates about national identity while simultaneously expanding its theoretical concerns to more global and international matters. Developing a respect for cultures in the plural demands a reformulation of what it means to be educated in the United States and what such an education implies for the creation of new cultural spaces that deepen and extend the possibility of democratic public life. Multiculturalism insists upon challenging old orthodoxies and reformulating new projects of possibility. It is a challenge that all critical educators need to address.

Notes

1. Alice Kessler-Harris, "Cultural Locations: Positioning American Studies in the Great Debate," *American Quarterly*, 44, 3 (1992), p. 310.
2. Hazel Carby, "The Multicultural Wars," in *Black Popular Culture*, ed. Gina Dent (Seattle: Bay Press, 1992), pp. 193–4.
3. Kobena Mercer, "Back to my Routes: A Postscript on the 80s," *Ten. 8*, 2, 3 (1992), p. 33.
4. James Baldwin, "A Talk to Teachers," in *Multicultural Literacy: Opening the American Mind*, eds. Rick Simonson and Scott Waler (Saint Paul, MN: Graywolf Press, 1988), p. 8.
5. Gerald Graff and Bruce Robbins, "Cultural Criticism," in *Redrawing the Boundaries*, eds. Stephen Greenblat and Giles Gunn (New York: MLA, 1992), p. 435.
6. Alan O'Connor, "Just Plain Home Cookin'," *Borderlines*, 20/21 (Winter 1991), p. 58.
7. Cornel West, *Race Matters* (Boston: Beacon Press, 1993), p. 14.
8. Ibid., p. 16.
9. Cornel West "Learning to Talk of Race," *The New York Times Magazine*, 6 (August 2, 1992), p. 24.
10. bell hooks, *Black Looks: Race and Representation* (Boston: South End Press, 1992), p. 168.
11. Homi K. Bhabha, "The Postcolonial Critic—Homi Bhabha interviewed by David Bennett and Terry Collits," *Arena*, 96 (1991), pp. 50–1.
12. Stuart Hall and David Held, "Citizens and Citizenship," in *New Times: The Changing Face of Politics in the 1990s*, eds. Stuart Hall and Martin Jacques (London: Verso, 1989), p. 178.
13. Peter Drier, "Bush to the Cities: Drop Dead," *The Progressive* (July 1992), p. 22.
14. Joan Scott, "Multiculturalism and the Politics of Identity," *October*, 61 (Summer 1992), p. 13.
15. Arthur Schlesinger Jr, *The Disuniting of America* (Knoxville, TN: Whittle District Books, 1992), pp. 21, 78.
16. James Clifford, "Museums in the Borderlands," in *Different Voices*, ed. Association of Art Museum Directors (New York: Association of Art Museum Directors, 1992), p. 119.
17. William Kerrigan, "The Falls of Academe," in *Wild Orchids and Trotsky*, ed. Mark Edmundson (New York: Penguin Books, 1993), p. 166.
18. Ibid., p. 167
19. Homi K. Bhabha and Bhikhu Parekh, "Identities on Parade: A Conversation," *Marxism Today* (June 1989), p. 3

20. Trinh T. Minh-Ha, *Woman, Native, Other: Writing Postcoloniality and Feminism* (Bloomington: Indiana University Press, 1989), p. 232.
21. E. San Juan Jr, *Racial Formations/Critical Transformations: Articulations of Power in Ethnic and Racial Studies in the United States* (Atlantic Highlands, NJ: Humanities Press, 1992), p. 101.
22. Hazel Carby, "Multi-Culture," *Screen Education, 34* (Spring 1980), p. 65.
23. Bhabha and Parekh, "Identities on Parade: A Conversation," p. 4.
24. Manning Marable, *Black America: Multicultural Democracy* (Westfield, NJ: Open Media, 1992), p. 13.
25. Homi K. Bhabha, "A Good Judge of Character: Men, Metaphors, and the Common Culture" in *Race-ing Justice, Engendering Power: Essays on Anita Hill, Clarence Thomas, and the Construction of Social Reality*, ed. Toni Morrison (New York: Pantheon, 1992), p. 242.
26. Cornel West, "Learning to Talk of Race," p. 24.
27. Roger I. Simon, *Teaching Against the Grain* (New York: Bergin and Garvey Press, 1992), p. 17.
28. Henry Louis Gates Jr., "The Black Man's Burden," *Black Popular Culture*, ed. Gina Dent (Seattle: Bay Press, 1992), p. 76.
29. Judith Butler, "Contingent Foundations: Feminism and the Question of 'Postmodernism'," in *Feminists Theorize the Political*, eds. Judith Butler and Joan Scott (New York: Routledge, 1992), p. 13.

Questions

1. What are the general features of "insurgent multiculturalism"?
2. Why does Giroux's use the term "whiteness"? Explain this term and explore its relation to insurgent multiculturalism.
3. Evaluate Giroux's claim that critical multiculturalism ought to "shift attention from an exclusive focus on subordinate groups . . . ." What does such a shift imply?
4. Why does Giroux's claim that "cultural democracy" is threatening or seen by some as dangerous? Do you agree with this claim? Explain.
5. What is Giroux's critique of the conservative reaction to multiculturalism?
6. Why, according to Giroux, is curriculum an example of "cultural politics"? Apply Giroux's hypothesis to a school where you are or could be working.
7. Explain Giroux's claim that insurgent multiculturalism is a "project of possibility"?
8. What does Giroux mean by "border pedagogy"?
9. Explore and evaluate Giroux's claim that insurgent multiculturalism is dialogic, and, therefore, capable of deepening and extending democratic public life.

White Terror
and Oppositional Agency:
Towards a Critical
Multiculturalism*

Peter McLaren

Nothing can be denounced if the denouncing is done within the system
that belongs to the thing denounced.

Julio Cortázar, *Hopscotch*

As we approach the year 2000, we are increasingly living simulated identities that help us adjust our dreams and desires according to the terms of our imprisonment as schizo-subjects in an artificially generated world. These facsimile or imitative identities are negotiated for us by financial planners, corporate sponsors, and marketing strategists through the initiatives of transnational corporations, enabling a privileged elite of white Euro-Americans to control the information banks and terrorize the majority of the population into a state of intellectual and material impoverishment. With few, if any, ethically convincing prospects for transformation—or even survival—we have become cyber-nomads whose temporary homes become whatever electronic circuitry (if any) is available to us. In our hyper-fragmented and postmodern culture, democracy is secured through the power to control consciousness and semioticize and zombify bodies by mapping and manipulating sounds, images, and information and by forcing identity to take refuge in forms of subjectivity increasingly experienced as isolated and separate from larger social contexts. The idea of democratic citizenship has now become synonymous with the private, consuming citizen and the increasing subalternization of the "other." The representation of reality through corporate sponsorship and promotional culture has impeded the struggle to establish democratic public spheres and furthered the dissolution of historical solidarities and forms of community, accelerating the experience of circular narrative time (cultural implosion) and the postindustrial disintegration of public space. The proliferation and phantasmagoria of the image has hastened the death of modernist identity structures and has interpellated individuals and groups into a world of cyborg citizenry in which "other" individuals are reconstituted through market imperatives as a collective assemblage of "them" read against our "us."

c✷ɔ

The Debate Over Multiculturalism

It is no secret, especially after the Los Angeles uprising—or what Mike Davis calls the "L.A. Intifada" (Katz and Smith 1992)—that the white-controlled media (often backed by victim-blaming white social scientists) have ignored the economic and social conditions responsible for bringing about in African American communities what Cornel West has called a "*walking nihilism* of pervasive drug addiction, pervasive alcoholism, pervasive homicide, and an exponential rise in suicide" (cited in Stephanson 1988, p. 276). They have additionally ignored or sensationalized social conditions in Latin and Asian communities, polemicizing against their value systems and representing them as teleologically poised to explode into a swelter of rioting and destruction. Such communities have been described as full of individuals who lash out at the dominant culture in an anarcho-voluntaristic frenzy in a country where there are more legalized gun dealers than gas stations. In this view, agency seems to operate outside of forces and structures of oppression, policing discourses of domination, and social relations of exploitation. Subalternized individuals appear politically constituted outside of discursive formations and are essentialized as the products of their pathological "nature" as drug or alcohol users and as gleeful participants in crime.

Furthermore, the white media has generated the racially pornographic term "wilding" to account for recent acts of violence in urban centers by groups of young African Americans (Cooper 1989). Apparently the term *wilding*, first reported by New York City newspapers in relation to the Central Park rapists, was relevant only to violence committed by black male youth since the term was conspicuously absent in press reports of the attack by white male youths on Yusef Hawkins in Bensonhurst (Wallace 1991). Thus, the postmodern image which many white people now entertain in relation to the African American underclass is one constructed upon violence and grotesquerie. They picture a population spawning mutant youths who, in the throes of bloodlust, roam the perimeter of the urban landscape high on angel dust, and with steel pipes in hand, randomly hunt whites. In addition to helping to justify police "attitude adjustments" inflicted upon black people in places such as L.A., Detroit, and Hemphill in Sabine County, Texas, this image of minorities has engendered hostility to their efforts to articulate their own understanding of race relations and to advance a conception of democracy in a way that is compatible with a critical multiculturalism.

Forms of Multiculturalism

This paper attempts to advance a conception of critical multiculturalism by exploring various positions held within the debate over multiculturalism which I have termed conservative or corporate multiculturalism, liberal multiculturalism, and left-liberal multiculturalism. These are, to be sure, ideal-typical labels meant to serve only as a heuristic device. In reality the characteristics of each position tend to blend into each other within the general horizon of our social lifeworld. As with all typologies and criteriologies, one must risk monolithically projecting them onto all spheres of cultural production and instantiating an overly abstract totality that dangerously reduces the complexity of the issues at stake. My effort should be understood only as an initial attempt at transcoding and mapping the cultural field of race and ethnicity so as to formulate a tentative theoretical grid that can help discern the multiple ways in which difference is both constructed and engaged. This chapter is to be read as an *essai*, an exploration.

Conservative Multiculturalism

Conservative multiculturalism can be traced to colonial views of African Americans as slaves, servants, and entertainers, views which were embedded in the self-serving, congratulatory, and profoundly imperialist attitude of Europe and North America. Such an attitude depicted Africa as a savage and barbaric continent populated by the most lowly of creatures who were deprived of the saving graces of Western civilization.[1] It can also be located in evolutionary theories which supported U.S. Manifest Destiny, imperial largesse, and Christian imperialism. It can further be seen as a direct result of the legacy of doctrines of white supremacy which biologized Africans as creatures by equating them with the earliest stages of human development. Africans were likened by whites to savage beasts or merry-hearted singing and dancing children. The former stereotype led a ten-year-old black boy—Josef Moller—to be exhibited at the Antwerp Zoo at the turn of the century. Closer to home and less remote in time is the case of Ota Benga, a Pygmy boy exhibited in 1906 at the Monkey House in the Bronx Zoo as an "African momunculus" and as the "missing link" and encouraged by zoo keepers to charge the bars of his cage with his mouth open and teeth bared (Bradford and Blume 1992). In less sensational guise, this attitude continues right up to the present time. For instance, in 1992, the Secretary of Health and Human Services in the Bush Administration appointed Frederick A. Goodwin, a research psychiatrist and career federal scientist, as Director of the National Institute for Mental Health. Goodwin used animal research findings to compare youth gangs to groups of "hyperaggressive" and "hypersexual" monkeys and commented that "maybe it isn't just the careless use of the word when people call certain areas of certain cities, 'jungles'" (*Observer* 1992 p. 20).

Whether conceived as the return of the repressed of Victorian puritanism, a leftover from Aristotelian hierarchical discourse or colonial and imperialist ideology, it remains the terrible truth of history that Africans have been forcibly placed at the foot of the human ladder of civilization (Pieterse 1992). As Jan Nederveen Pieterse notes, America historically has been the "white man's country," in which "institutional and ideological patterns of the supremacy of white over black, and of men over women, supplemented and reinforced one another" (Ibid., p. 220).

While I do not wish to lapse into either an essentialized nativism which sees non-Western indigenous cultures as homogeneous or a view of the West that sees it as all of one piece—a monolithic block—unaffected by its colonized subjects, or solely as an engine of imperialism, I need to affirm the fact that many conservative multiculturalists have scarcely removed themselves from the colonialist legacy of white supremacy. Although they would like to officially distance themselves from racist ideologies, conservative multiculturalists pay only lipservice to the cognitive equality of all races and charge unsuccessful minorities with having "culturally deprived backgrounds" and a "lack of strong family-oriented values." This "environmentalist" position still accepts black cognitive inferiority to whites as a general premise and provides conservative multiculturalists with a means of rationalizing why some minority groups are successful while other groups are not (Mensh and Mensh 1991). This also gives the white cultural elite the excuse they need for unreflectively and disproportionately occupying positions of power. They are not unlike the inscripti of the right-wing Roman Catholic organization, Opus Dei, who attempt to intellectually and culturally sequester or barricade their members from the tools for a critical analyses of social life in order to shore up their own power to manipulate and propagandize. Or the Heritage Foundation that creates a climate of legitimacy for books like *The Bell Curve*.

One particularly invidious project of conservative or corporate multiculturalism is to construct a common culture—a seamless web of textuality—a project bent on annulling the concept of border cultures through the delegitimization of foreign languages and regional and ethnic dialects, a persistent attack on nonstandard English, and the undermining of bi-lingual education (Macedo, 1995). Gramsci's understanding of this process is instructive, and is cogently articulated by Michael Gardiner (1992):

> For Gramsci, the political character of language was most apparent in the attempt by the dominant class to create a common cultural "climate" and to "transform the popular mentality" through the imposition of a national language. Therefore, he felt that linguistic hegemony involved the articulation of signs and symbols which tended to codify and reinforce the dominant viewpoint. Thus, Gramsci argued that there existed a close relationship between linguistic stratification and social hierarchization, in that the various dialects and accents found within a given

society are always rank-ordered as to their perceived legitimacy, appropriateness, and so on. Accordingly, concrete language usage reflects underlying, asymmetrical power relations, and it registers profound changes which occur in the cultural, moral, and political worlds. Such changes were primarily expressed through what Gramsci termed "normative grammar"; roughly, the system of norms whereby particular utterances could be evaluated and mutually understood . . . which was an important aspect of the state's attempt to establish linguistic conformity. Gramsci also felt that the maintenance of regional dialects helped peasants and workers partially to resist the forces of political and cultural hegemony. (p. 186)

In addition to its position on common culture and bilingual education, there are further reasons why corporate multiculturalism needs to be rejected. First, conservative or corporate multiculturalism refuses to treat whiteness as a form of ethnicity and in doing so posits whiteness as an invisible norm by which other ethnicities are judged. Second, conservative multiculturalism—as in the positions taken by Diane Ravitch, Arthur Schlesinger, Jr., Lynne V. B. Cheney, Newt Gingrich, and others—uses the term "diversity" to cover up the ideology of assimilation that undergirds its position. In this view, ethnic groups are reduced to "add-ons" to the dominant culture. Before you can be added on to the dominant U.S. culture, you must first adopt a consensual view of culture and learn to accept the essentially Euro-American patriarchal norms of the "host" country. Third, as I mentioned earlier, conservative multiculturalism is essentially monolingual and adopts the position that English should be the only official U.S. language. It is often virulently opposed to bi-lingual education programs. Fourth, conservative multiculturalists posit standards of achievement for all youth that are premised on the cultural capital of the Anglo middle-class. Fifth, conservative multiculturalism fails to interrogate the high status knowledge—knowledge that is deemed of most value in the white, middle-class U.S.—to which the educational system is geared. That is, it fails to question the interests that such knowledge serves. It fails, in other words, to interrogate dominant regimes of discourse and social and cultural practices that are implicated in global dominance and are inscribed in racist, classist, sexist, and homophobic assumptions. Conservative multiculturalism wants to assimilate students to an unjust social order by arguing that every member of every ethnic group can reap the economic benefits of neocolonialist ideologies and corresponding social and economic practices. But a prerequisite to "joining the club" is to become denuded, deracinated, and culturally stripped.

Recent popular conservative texts set firmly against liberal, left-liberal, and critical strands of multiculturalism include Richard Brookhiser's *The Way of the Wasp: How it Made America, and How it Can Save it, So to Speak,* Arthur Schlesinger, Jr.'s *The Disuniting of America: Reflections on a Multicultural Society,* and Laurence Auster's *The Path to National Suicide: An Essay on Immigration and Multiculturalism.* According to Stanley Fish (1992), these texts, which appeal to national unity and a harmonious citizenry, can readily be traced to earlier currents of Christianity (which proclaimed that it was God's wish that the future of civilization be secured in the United States) and social Darwinism (U.S., Anglo-Saxon stock is used to confirm the theory of natural selection). Reflecting and enforcing the assumptions made by the authors (whom Fish describes as racist not in the sense that they actively seek the subjugation of groups but who perpetuate racial stereotypes and the institutions that promote them) is the SAT test used in high school for college admission. Fish notes that one of the authors of this test, Carl Campbell Brigham, championed in his *A Study of American Intelligence* a classification of races which identified the Nordic as the superior race and, in descending order, located the less superior races as Alpine, Mediterranean, Eastern, New Eastern, and Negro. This hierarchy was first expounded by Madison Grant in *The Passing of the Great Race* (Fish 1992) and reflected in earlier European works such as *Essai sur l'inégalité des races humaines,* a four-volume testament to the racial superiority of the Germanic race by Joseph Arthur (Comte de Govineau), and Edward Gibbon's *Decline and Fall of the Roman Empire,* a work which blamed miscegenation for the decline of civilization (Pieterse 1992). Not surprisingly, this hierarchy is confirmed in Brigham's later comparative analysis of intelligence. The library at the Educational Testing Service compound still bears Brigham's name (Fish 1992). Also problematic, as Mike Dyson (1993) points out, are theories linking white racism to biological determinism, such as recent discussions of "melanin theory" in which black researchers view whiteness as a genetic deficiency state that leads whites to act violently against Blacks because of white feelings of color inferiority.

When we contrast Brookhiser's key WASP virtues with non-WASP virtues (those of the Asians, African Americans, or Latinos), we see the Western virtues of the former—conscience, antisensuality, industry, use, success, and civic mindedness—being distinguished as more American than the lesser virtues of the latter—self, creativity, ambition, diffidence, gratification, and group mindedness. This also reflects a privileging of Western languages (English, French, German, and ancient Greek) over non-Western languages (see Fish 1992). Supposedly, Western European languages are the only ones sophisticated enough to grasp truth as an "essence." The search for the "truth" of the Western canon of "Great Works" is actually based on an epistemological error that presumes there exists a language of primordial Being and Truth. This error is linked to the phenomenalist reduction of linguistic meaning which endows language (through analogy) with sense perceptions and thereby reduces the act of interpretation to uncovering the "true understanding" that reciprocally binds the truth of the text to the preunderstanding, tacit knowledge, or foreknowledge of the reader (Norris 1990). From this view of the mimetic transparency of language, aesthetic judgments are seen as linked directly to ethics or politics through a type of direct correspondence (Ibid.). Language, therefore, becomes elevated to a "truth-telling status" which remains exempt from its ethico-political situatedness or embeddedness. It is this epistemological error that permits conservatives to denounce totalitarianism in the name of its own truth and serves as a ruse for expanding present forms of domination. It is not hard to see how racism can become a precondition for this form of conservative multiculturalism in so far as Western virtues (which can be traced back as far as Aristotle's Great Chain of Being) become the national-aestheticist ground for the conservative multiculturalist's view of civilization and citizenship. The power of conservative multiculturalism lays claim to its constituents by conferring a space for the reception of its discourses that is safe and sovereignly secure. It does this by sanctioning empiricism as the fulcrum for weighing the "truth" of culture. What discursively thrives in this perspective is an epistemology which privileges the logic of cause and effect narrative construction (see Norris 1990). In this case, "bell curve" quotients and test scores become the primary repository of authoritative exegeses in interpretations of successful school citizenship. Fortunately, as Foucault points out, subjectivity is not simply constituted through the discourses and social practices of subjugation. Liberal, left-liberal, and critical forms of multiculturalism envisage a different "practice of the self" and new forms of self-fashioning and subjectivity based on more progressive conceptions of freedom and justice.

Liberal Multiculturalism

Liberal multiculturalism argues that a natural equality exists among whites, African Americans, Latinos, Asians and other racial populations. This perspective is based on the intellectual "sameness" among the races, that is, on their cognitive equivalence or the rationality imminent in all races that permits them to compete equally in a capitalist society. However, from the point of view of liberal multiculturalism, equality is absent in U.S. society not because of black or Latino cultural deprivation but because social and educational opportunities do not exist that permit everyone to compete equally in the capitalist marketplace. Unlike their critical counterparts, they believe that existing cultural social and economic constraints can be modified or "reformed" in order for relative equality to be realized. This view often collapses into an ethnocentric and oppressively universalistic humanism in which the norms which govern the substance of citizenship are identified most strongly with Anglo-American, cultural-political communities.

Left-Liberal Multiculturalism

Left-liberal multiculturalism emphasizes cultural differences and suggests that the stress on the equality of races smothers those important cultural differences between races that are responsible for different behaviors, values, attitudes, cognitive styles, and social practices. Left-liberal multiculturalists feel that mainstream approaches to multiculturalism occlude characteristics and differences related to race, class, gender, and sexuality. Those who work within this perspective have a tendency to essentialize cultural differences, however, and ignore the historical and cultural "situatedness" of difference. Difference is understood as a form of signification removed from social and historical constraints. That is, there is a tendency to ignore difference as a social and historical construction that is constitutive of the power to represent meanings. It is often assumed that there exists an authentic "Female" or "African American" or "Latino" experience or way of being-in-the-world. Left-liberal multicultural-ism treats difference as an "essence" that exists independently of history, cul-ture, and power. Often one is asked to show one's identity papers before dia-logue can begin.

This perspective often locates meaning through the conduit of "authentic" experience in what I feel to be the mistaken belief that one's own politics of lo-cation somehow guarantees one's "political correctness" in advance. Either a person's physical proximity to the oppressed or their own location as an op-pressed person is supposed to offer a special authority from which to speak. What often happens is that a populist elitism gets constructed as inner city teachers or trade unionists or those engaged in activist politics establish a pedi-gree of voice based on personal history, class, race, gender, and experience. Here, the political is often reduced only to the personal where theory is dis-missed in favor of one's own personal and cultural identity. Of course, one's lived experience, race, class, gender, and history is important in the formation of one's political identity, but one must be willing to examine personal experi-ence and one's speaking voice in terms of the ideological and discursive com-plexity of its formation.

Admittedly, when a person speaks, it is always from somewhere (Hall 1991), but this process of meaning production needs to be interrogated in order to understand how one's identity is constantly being produced through a play of difference linked to and reflected by shifting and conflicting discursive and ideological relations, formations, and articulations (see Giroux 1992; Scott 1992). Experience needs to be recognized as a site of ideological production and the mobilization of affect and can be examined largely through its imbrication in our universal and local knowledges and modes of intelligibility and its rela-tionship to language, desire, and the body (an issue that I have explored else-where in McLaren 1990). As Joan Scott (1992) notes, "experience is a subject's history. Language is the site of history's enactment" (p. 34). Of course, I am not arguing against the importance of experience in the formation of political iden-tity but rather pointing out that it has become the *new imprimatur* for legitimat-ing the political currency and uncontestable validity of one's arguments. This has often resulted in a reverse form of academic elitism. Not only is the author-ity of the academic under assault (and rightly so, in many cases), but it has been replaced by a populist elitism based on one's own identity papers.

Critical and Resistance Multiculturalism

Multiculturalism without a transformative political agenda can just be another form of accommodation to the larger social order. I believe that because they are immersed in the discourse of "reform," liberal and left-liberal positions on multiculturalism do not go nearly far enough in advancing a project of social transformation. With this concern in mind, I am developing the idea of critical multiculturalism from the perspective of both a neo-Marxist and poststruc-turalist approach to meaning and emphasizing the role that language and rep-resentation play in the construction of meaning and identity. The poststructuralist insight that I am relying on is located within the larger context of post-modern theory—that disciplinary archipelago that is scattered through the sea of social theory—and asserts that signs and significations are essentially unstable and shifting and can only be temporarily fixed, depending on how they are articulated within particular discursive and historical struggles. From the perspective of what I am calling "critical multiculturalism," representations of race, class, and gender are understood as the result of larger social struggles over signs and meanings and in this way emphasize not simply textual play or metaphorical displacement as a form of resistance (as in the case of left-liberal multiculturalism) but stress the central task of transforming the social, cultural, and institutional relations in which meanings are generated.

From the perspective of critical multiculturalism, the conservative and liberal stress on sameness and the left-liberal emphasis on difference is really a false opposition. Both identity based on sameness and identity based on difference are forms of essentialist logic: in both, individual identities are presumed to be autonomous, self-contained and self-directed. Resistance multiculturalism also refuses to see culture as non-conflictual, harmonious and consensual. Democracy is understood from this perspective as busy—it is not seamless, smooth, or always a harmonious political and cultural state of affairs (Giroux and McLaren 1991; 1991a; 1991b). Resistance multiculturalism does not see diversity itself as a goal but rather argues that diversity must be affirmed within a politics of cultural criticism and a commitment to social justice. It must be attentive to the notion of difference. Difference is always a product of history, culture, power, and ideology. Differences occur between and among groups and must be understood in terms of the specificity of their production. Critical multiculturalism interrogates the construction of difference and identity in relation to a radical politics. It is positioned against the neoimperial romance with monoglot ethnicity grounded in a shared or "common" experience of America that is associated with conservative and liberal strands of multiculturalism. Difference is intimately related to capitalist exploitation.

Viewed from the perspective of a critical multiculturalism, conservative attacks on multiculturalism as separatist and ethnocentric carry with them the erroneous assumption by white, Anglo constituencies that North American society fundamentally constitutes social relations of uninterrupted accord. The liberal view is seen to underscore the idea that North American society is largely a forum of consensus with different minority viewpoints simply accretively added on. We are faced here with a politics of pluralism which largely ignores the workings of power and privilege. More specifically, the liberal perspective "involves a very insidious exclusion as far as any structural politics of change is concerned: it excludes and occludes global or structural relations of power as 'ideological' and 'totalizing'" (Ebert in press). In addition, it presupposes harmony and agreement—an undisturbed space in which differences can coexist. Within such a space, individuals are invited to shed their positive characteristics in order to become disembodied and transparent American citizens (Copjec 1991; Rosaldo 1989), a cultural practice that creates what David Lloyd (1991) calls a "subject without properties" (p. 70). In this instance, citizens are able to occupy a place of "pure exchangeability." This accords the universalized white male, heterosexual, and Christian subject a privileged status. Yet such a proposition is dangerously problematic. Chandra Mohanty (1989/90) notes that difference cannot be formulated as negotiation among culturally diverse groups against a backdrop of benign variation or presumed cultural homogeneity. Difference is the recognition that knowledges are forged in histories that are riven with differentially constituted relations of power; that is, knowledges, subjectivities, and social practices are forged within "asymmetrical and incommensurate cultural spheres" (p. 181).

Homi K. Bhabha (1992) makes the lucid observation that in attributing the racism and sexism of the common culture solely to "the underlying logic of late capitalism and its patriarchal overlay," leftists are actually providing an alibi for the common culture argument. The common culture is transformed in this instance into a form of ethical critique of the political system that supposedly fosters unity within a system of differences. The concept of cultural otherness is taken up superficially to celebrate a "range of 'nation-centered' cultural discourses (on a wide axis from right to left)" (p. 235). It is worth quoting at length Bhabha's notion of common culture as the regulation and normalization of difference:

> Like all myths of the nation's "unity," the common culture is a profoundly conflicted ideological strategy. It is a declaration of democratic faith in a plural, diverse society and, at the same time, a defense against the real, subversive demands that the articulation of cultural difference—the empowering of minorities—makes upon democratic pluralism. Simply saying that the "nation's cement" is inherently sexist or racist—because of the underlying logic of late capitalism and its patriarchal overlay—ironically provides the "common culture" argument with the alibi it needs. The vision of a common culture is perceived to be an ethical mission whose value lies in revealing, prophylactically, the imperfections and exclusions of the political system as it exists. The healing grace of a culture of commonality is supposedly the coevality it establishes between social differences—ethnicities, ideologies, sexualities—"an intimation of simultaneity across homogeneous empty time" that welds these different voices into a "unisonance" that is expressive of the "contemporaneous community of the national culture." (pp. 234–235).

Too often liberal and conservative positions on diversity constitute an attempt to view culture as a soothing balm—the aftermath of historical disagreement—some mythical present where the irrationalities of historical conflict have been smoothed out (McLaren in press). This is not only a disingenuous view of culture; it is profoundly dishonest. It overlooks the importance of engaging on some occasions in dissensus in order to contest hegemonic forms of domination and to affirm differences. The liberal and conservative position on culture also assumes that justice already exists and needs only to be evenly apportioned. However, both teachers and students need to realize that justice does not already exist simply because laws exist. Justice needs to be continually created and constantly struggled for (Darder 1992; McLaren and Hammer 1992). The question that I want to pose to teachers is this: Do teachers and cultural workers have access to a language that allows them to sufficiently critique and transform existing social and cultural practices that are defended by liberals and conservatives as unifyingly democratic?

Critical Multiculturalism and the Politics of Signification

Since all experience is the experience of meaning, we need to recognize the role that language plays in the production of experience (McLaren in press a; Giroux and McLaren 1992). You do not have an experience and then search for a word to describe that experience. Rather, language helps to constitute experience by providing a structure of intelligibility or a mediating device through which experiences can be understood. Rather than talking about experience, it is more accurate to talk about "experience effects" (Zavarzadeh and Morton 1990).

Western language and thought are constructed as a system of differences organized *de facto* and *de jure* as binary oppositions—white/black, good/bad, normal/deviant, etc.—with the primary term being privileged and designated as the defining term or the norm of cultural meaning, creating a dependent hierarchy. Yet the secondary term does not really exist outside the first, but, in effect, exists inside of it, even though the phallocentric logic of white supremacist ideology makes you think it exists outside and in opposition to the first term. The critical multiculturalist critique argues that the relationship between signifier and signified is insecure and unstable. Signs are part of an ideological struggle that attempts to create a particular regime of representation that serves to legitimate a certain cultural reality. For instance, we have witnessed a struggle in our society over the meaning of terms such as "negro," "black," and "African American."

According to Teresa Ebert (1991a), our current ways of seeing and acting are being disciplined for us through forms of signification, that is, through modes of intelligibility and ideological frames of sense making. Rejecting the Saussurian semiotics of signifying practices (and its continuing use in contemporary poststructuralism) as "historical operations of language and tropes," Ebert characterizes signifying practices as "an ensemble of material operations involved in economic and political relations" (p. 117). She maintains, rightly in my view, that socioeconomic relations of power require distinctions to be made among groups through forms of signification in order to organize subjects according to the unequal distribution of privilege and power.

To illustrate the politics of signification at work in the construction and formation of racist subjects, Ebert offers the example of the way in which the terms *negro* and *black* have been employed within the racial politics of the United States. Just as the term *negro* became an immutable mark of difference and naturalized the political arrangements of racism in the 1960s, so too is the term *black* being refigured in the white dominant culture to mean criminality, violence, and social degeneracy. This was made clear in the Willie Horton campaign ads of George Bush and in the Bush and David Duke position on hiring quotas. In my view this was also evident in the verdict of the Rodney King case in Los Angeles. It is also evident in some of the media coverage of the O. J. Simpson trial and in the Gingrich demonization of the poor and powerless.

Carlos Muñoz, Jr. (1989) has revealed how the term *Hispanic* in the mid-1970s became a "politics of white ethnic identity" that deemphasized and in some cases rejected the Mexican cultural base of Mexican Americans. Muñoz writes that the term *Hispanic* is derived from *Hispania* which was the name the Romans gave to the Iberian peninsula, most of which became Spain, and "implicitly emphasizes the white European culture of Spain at the expense of the nonwhite cultures that have profoundly shaped the experiences of all Latin Americans" (p. 11). Not only is this term blind to the multiracial reality of Mexican-Americans through its refusal to acknowledge "the nonwhite indigenous cultures of the Americas, Africa, and Asia, which historically have produced multicultural and multiracial peoples in Latin America and the United States" (Ibid.), but also it is a term that ignores the complexities within these various cultural groups. Here is another example of the melting pot theory of assimilation fostered through a politics of signification. We might ask ourselves what signifieds (meanings) will be attached to certain terms such as "welfare mothers"? Most of us know what government officials mean when they refer derisively to "welfare mothers." They mean black and Latino mothers.

Kobena Mercer (1992) has recently described what he calls "black struggles over the sign" (p. 428). Mercer, following Volosinov, argues that every sign has a "social multi-accentuality," and it is this polyvocal character that can rearticulate the sign through the inscription of different connotations surrounding it. The dominant ideology always tries to stabilize certain meanings of the term. Mercer writes that for over four centuries of Western civilization, the sign "black" was "structured by the closure of an absolute symbolic division of what was white and what was non-white" (Ibid.) through the "morphological equation" of racial superiority. This equation accorded whiteness with civility and rationality and blackness with savagery and irrationality. Subaltern subjects themselves brought about a reappropriation and rearticulation of the "proper name"—Negro, Colored, Black, Afro-American—in which a collective subjectivity was renamed. Mercer notes that in the sixties and seventies, the term "ethnic minorities" connoted the black subject "as a minor, an abject childlike figure necessary for the legitimation of paternalistic ideologies of assimilation and integration that underpinned the strategy of multiculturalism" (Ibid., p. 429). The term "black community" arose out of a reappropriation of the term "community relations." The state had tried to colonize a definition of social democratic consensus designed to "manage" race relations through the use of "community relations."

The examples discussed above underscore the central theorectical position of critical multiculturalism: differences are produced according to the ideological production and reception of cultural signs. As Mas'ud Zavarzadeh and Donald Morton (1990) point out, "Signs are neither eternally predetermined nor pan-historically undecidable: they are rather 'decided' or rendered as 'undecidable' in the moment of social conflicts" (p. 156). Difference is not "cultural obviousness" such as black versus white or Latino versus European or Anglo-American; rather, differences are historical and cultural constructions (Ebert 1991a).

Just as we can see the politics of signification at work in instances of police brutality or in the way Blacks and Latinos are portrayed as drug pushers, gang members, or the minority sidekick to the white cop in movies and television, we can see it at work in special education placement where a greater proportion of black and Latino students are considered for "behavioral" placements whereas white, middle-class students are provided, for the most part, with the more comforting and comfortable label of "learning disabled" (McLaren 1989). Here, a critical multiculturalist curriculum can help teachers explore the ways in which students are differentially subjected to ideological inscriptions and multiply-organized discourses of desire through a politics of signification.

A critical multiculturalism suggests that teachers and cultural workers need to take up the issue of difference in ways that do not replay the monocultural essentialism of the "centrisms"—Anglocentrism, Eurocentrism, phallocentrism, Afrocentrism, androcentrism, and the like. They need to build a politics of alliance building, of dreaming together, of solidarity that moves beyond the condescension of, say, "race awareness week" that actually serves to keep forms of institutionalized racism in tact. A solidarity has to be struggled for that is not centered around market imperatives but develops out of the imperatives of freedom, liberation, democracy, and critical citizenship.

The notion of the citizen has been pluralized and hybridized, as Kobena Mercer (1990) notes, by the presence of a diversity of social subjects. Mercer is instructive in pointing out that "solidarity does not mean that everyone thinks the same way, it begins when people have the confidence to disagree over issues because they 'care' about constructing a common ground" (p. 68). Solidarity is not impermeably solid but depends, to a certain degree, on antagonism and uncertainty. Timothy Maliqualim Simone (1989) calls this type of multiracial solidarity "geared to maximizing points of interaction rather than harmonizing, balancing, or equilibrating the distribution of bodies, resources, and territories" (p. 191).

Whereas left-liberal multiculturalism equates resistance with destabilizing dominant systems of representation, critical multiculturalism goes one step further by asserting that all representations are the result of social struggles over signifiers and their signifieds. This assertion suggests that resistance must take into account an intervention into social struggle in order "to provide equal access to social resources and to transform the dominant power relations which limit this access according to class privilege, race, and gender" (Ebert 1991, p. 294). Differences within culture must be defined as political difference and not just formal, textual, or linguistic difference. Global or structural relations of power must not be ignored. The concept of totality must not be abandoned but rather seen as an overdetermined structure of difference. Differences are always differences in relation, they are never simply free-floating. Differences are not seen as absolute, irreducible or intractable, but rather as undecidable and socially and culturally relational (see Ebert 1991a).

The theorists of resistance or critical multiculturalism do not agree with those left-liberal multiculturalists who argue that difference needs only to be interrogated as a form of rhetoric, thereby reducing politics to signifying structures and history to textuality (Ebert 1991a). We need to go beyond desta-bilizing meaning by transforming the social and historical conditions in which meaning-making occurs. Rather than remaining satisfied with erasing the privilege of oppressive ideologies that have been naturalized within the dom-inant culture or with restating dangerous memories that have been repressed within the political unconscious of the state, critical multiculturalist praxis at-tempts to revise existing hegemonic arrangements. A critical multiculturalist praxis does not simply reject the bourgeois decorum that has consigned the imperialized other to the realm of the grotesque but effectively attempts to remap desire by fighting for a linguistically multivalenced culture and new structures of experience in which individuals refuse the role of the omniscient narrator and conceive of identity as a polyvalent assemblage of (contradictory and overdetermined) subject positions. Existing systems of difference which organize social life into patterns of domination and subordination must be re-constructed. We need to do more than unflaggingly problematize difference as a condition of rhetoric, or unceasingly interrogate the status of all knowledge as discursive inscription, because, as Ebert notes, this annuls the grounds of both reactionary and revolutionary politics. Rather, we need a rewriting of dif-ference as *difference-in-relation* followed by attempts to dramatically change the material conditions that allow relations of exploitation to prevail over rela-tions of equality and social justice. This is a different cultural politics than one of simply reestablishing an inverse hierarchical order of Blacks over whites or Latinos over whites. Rather it is an attempt to transform the very value of hi-erarchy itself, followed by a challenge to the material structures that are re-sponsible for the overdetermination of structures of difference in the direction of oppression, injustice, and human suffering. However, this is not to claim that individuals are oppressed in the same ways since groups are oppressed non-synchronously in conjunction with systems such as class, race, gender, age, ethnicity, sexuality, etc. (McCarthy 1988). People can be situated very dif-ferently in the same totalizing structures of oppression. We need to analyze and challenge both the specific enunciations of microdifferences within differ-ence and the macrostructure of difference-in-relation (Ebert 1991a). We need to refocus on structural oppression in the forms of patriarchy, capitalism, and white supremacy—structures that tend to get ignored by liberal multicultural-ists and their veneration of difference as identity. As educators and cultural workers, we must critically intervene in those power relations that organize difference.

Whiteness: The Invisible Culture of Terror

Educators need to critically examine the development of pedagogical discourses and practices that demonize others who are different (through transforming them into absence or deviance). Critical multiculturalism calls serious
attention to the dominant meaning systems readily available to students and
teachers, most of which are ideologically stitched into the fabric of Western imperialism and patriarchy. It challenges meaning systems that impose attributes
on the "other" under the direction of sovereign signifiers and tropes. This
means not directing all our efforts at understanding ethnicity as "other than
white," but interrogating the culture of whiteness itself. This is crucial because
unless we do this—unless we give white students a sense of their own identity
as an emergent ethnicity—we naturalize whiteness as a cultural marker against
which otherness is defined. Coco Fusco warns that "To ignore white ethnicity is
to redouble its hegemony by naturalizing it. Without specifically addressing
white ethnicity there can be no critical evaluation of the construction of the
other" (cited in Wallace 1991, p. 7). White groups need to examine their own
ethnic histories so that they are less likely to judge their own cultural norms as
neutral and universal. The supposed neutrality of white culture enables it to
commodify blackness to its own advantage and ends. It allows it to manipulate
the other but not see this otherness as a white tool of exploitation. Whiteness
does not exist outside of culture but constitutes the prevailing social texts in
which social norms are made and remade. As part of a politics of signification
that passes unobserved into the rhythms of daily life, and a "politically constructed category parasitic on 'Blackness'" (West 1990, p. 29), whiteness has become the invisible norm for how the dominant culture measures its own worth
and civility.

Using an ethnosemiotic approach as a means of interrogating the culture
of whiteness and understanding ethnicity as a rhetorical form, Dean MacCannell (1992), in his new book, *Empty Meeting Grounds,* raises the question: "In
their interactions with others, how can groups in power manage to convey the
impression that they are less ethnic than those over whom they exercise their
power; in other words, how can they foster the impression that their own
traits and qualities are correct, while the corresponding qualities of others are
'ethnic'?" (p. 121–122). Furthermore, asks MacCannell, how does the consensus that is achieved in this matter structure our institutions? His answer leads
us to explore the secret of power in discourse—that simply because language
is essentially rhetorical (i.e., free of all bias because it is pure bias) we cannot
escape the fact that rhetoric and grammar always intersect in particular ideological formations which makes language unavoidably a social relation. And
every social relation is a structurally located one that can never be situated
outside of relations of power. MacCannell locates this power in the ability of
the speaking subject to move into the position of "he" without seeming to
leave the position of "I" or "you" (which are empty or "floating" signifiers
that have no referent outside the immediate situation). The personal pronoun

"he" refers to an objective situation outside of the immediate subjectively apprehended situation. MacCannell asserts that whites have mastered interactional forms that permit them to operate as interactants while seeming to be detached from the situation, to be both an "I" or a "you" and a "he" at the same time—both to operate within the situation *and* to judge it. Dominant groups will always want to occupy the grammatical power position: that is, assume the external objective and judgmental role of the "he" by suggesting that their use of language is free of bias. White culture, according to MacCannell, is an enormous totalization that arrogates to itself the right to represent all other ethnic groups. For instance, binary oppositions such as "white as opposed to nonwhite" always occupy the grammatical position of "him", never "I" nor "you," and we know that in white culture, "whiteness" will prevail and continue to be parasitic on the meaning of "blackness" (p. 131).

Cornel West (1990, p. 29) remarks that "'Whiteness' is a politically constructed category parasitic on 'blackness.'" He further asserts that "One cannot deconstruct the binary oppositional logic of images of Blackness without extending it to the contrary condition of Blackness/Whiteness itself." According to Jonathan Rutherford (1990):

> Binarism operates in the same way as splitting and projection: the centre expels it anxieties, contradictions and irrationalities onto the subordinate term, filling it with the antithesis of its own identity: the Other, in its very alienness, simply mirrors and represents what is deeply familiar to the centre, but projected outside of itself. It is in these very processes and representations of marginality that the violence, antagonisms and aversions which are at the core of the dominant discourses and identities become manifest-racism, homophobia, misogyny and class contempt are the products of this frontier (p. 22).

Of course, when binarisms become racially and culturally marked, *white* occupies the grammatical position of *him,* never *I* nor *you* and, notes MacCannell (1992), "always operates as *if* not dependent on rhetoric to maintain its position" (p. 131). Rhetoric is aligned with *non-truth,* and whiteness is perceived as neutral and devoid of interest. Of course, "whiteness" projects onto the term "blackness" an array of specific qualities and characteristics such as wild, exotic, uncontrolled, deviant, and savage. Whiteness is founded on the principle of depersonalization of all human relationships and the idealization of objective judgment and duty. MacCannell is worth quoting at length on this issue:

> To say that white culture is impersonal is not the same thing as saying that it does not function like a subject or subjectivity. But it is the kind that is cold, the kind that laughs at feelings while demanding that all surplus libido, energy and capital be handed over to it. . . . White culture begins with the pretense that it, above all, does not express itself rhetorically. Rather, the form of its expression is always represented as only incidental to the truth. And its totalizing power radiates from this pretense

which is maintained by interpreting all ethnic expression as "representative," and therefore, *merely* rhetorical. (Ibid., p. 130)

When people of color attack white ground rules for handling disputes, or bureaucratic procedures, or specific policies of institutionalized racism, these are necessary oppositional acts but insufficient for bringing about structural change because, as MacCannell notes, this work is "framed by the assumption of the dominance of white culture" (Ibid., p. 131). This is because white culture is predicated upon the universalization of the concept of "exchange values"—systems of equivalences, the transcribability of all languages, the translatability of any language into any other language, and the division of the earth into real estate holdings in which it is possible to precisely calculate and calibrate the worth of every person. MacCannell is quite clear on this. Within such a totalization brought about by white culture, indigenous groups can only belong as an "ethnicity." As long as white culture, as the defining cultural frame for white-ethnic transactions, sets the limits on all thought about human relations, there can be no prospect for human equality.

Richard Dyer (1988) has made some useful observations about the culture of whiteness, claiming that its property of being both "everything" and "nothing" is the source of its representational power in the sense that white culture possesses the power to colonize the definition of the normal with respect to class, gender, heterosexuality, and nationality. Perhaps white culture's most formidable attribute is its ability to mask itself as a category. Whites will often think of their Scottishness, Irishness, or Jewishness, and so on, before they think of their whiteness. Michael Goldfield (1992) argues that white supremacy has been responsible for holding back working-class struggle in the United States, as labor groups tragically failed to grasp the strategic importance for labor in fighting the system of white supremacy, missing an opportunity—especially during Reconstruction—for changing the face of U.S. politics.

In her recent book, *Black Looks*, bell hooks (1992) notes that white people are often shocked when black people "critically assess white people from a standpoint where 'whiteness' is the privileged signifier" (p. 167). She remarks that

Their [white people's] amazement that black people match white people with a critical "ethnographic" gaze, is itself an expression of racism. Often their rage erupts because they believe that all ways of looking that highlight difference subvert the liberal belief in a universal subjectivity (we are all just people) that they think will make racism disappear. They have a deep emotional investment in the myth of "sameness," even as their actions reflect the primacy of whiteness as a sign informing who they are and how they think. Many of them are shocked that black people think critically about whiteness because racist thinking perpetuates the fantasy that the Other who is subjugated, who is subhuman, lacks the ability to comprehend, to understand, to see the working of the powerful. Even though the majority of those students politically consider themselves liberals and anti-racist, they too unwittingly invest in the sense of whiteness as mystery. (pp. 167–168).

Hooks discusses the representation of whiteness as a form of terror within black communities and is careful not simply to invert the stereotypical racist association of whiteness as goodness and blackness as evil. The depiction of whiteness as "terrorizing" emerges in hooks' discussion not as a reaction to stereotypes but, as she puts it, "as a response to the traumatic pain and anguish that remains a consequence of white racist domination, a psychic state that informs and shapes the way black folks 'see' whiteness" (Ibid., p. 169).

Are You an American or a Liberal?

Critical pedagogy needs to hold a nonreductionist view of the social order; that is, society needs to be seen as an irreducible indeterminacy. The social field is always open, and we must explore its fissures, fault-lines, gaps and silences. Power relations may not always have a conscious design, but they have unintended consequences which define deep structural aspects of oppression even though every ideological totalization of the social is designed to fail. This is not to affirm Schopenhauer's unwilled patterns of history but rather to assert that while domination has a logic without design in its sign systems and social practices, it does operate through overdetermined structures of race, class, and gender difference. Resistance to such domination means deconstructing the social by means of a reflexive intersubjective consciousness—what Freire terms "conscientizaçao." With this comes a recognition that ideology is more than an epistemological concern about the status of certain facts. It is also the way in which discourse and discursive systems generate particular social relations as well as reflect them. A reflexive intersubjective consciousness is the beginning—but only the beginning—of revolutionary praxis.

We also need to create new narratives—new "border narratives"—in order to reauthor the discourses of oppression in politically subversive ways as well as to create sites of possibility and enablement. For instance, we need to ask: How are our identities bound up with historical forms of discursive practices? It is one thing to argue against attacks on polyvocal and unassimilable difference and on narrative closure or to stress the heterogeneity of contemporary culture. However, in doing so we must remember that dominant discourses are sites of struggle and their meanings are linked to social antagonisms and labor/economic relations and then naturalized in particular textual/linguistic referents. Consequently, self-reflection alone—even if it is inimicably opposed to all forms of domination and oppression—is only a necessary but not nearly sufficient condition for emancipation. This process must go hand-in-hand with changes in material and social conditions through counter-hegemonic action (Hammer and McLaren 1991; 1992). The sociohistorical dynamics of race, clan, and gender domination must never be left out of the equation of social struggle or take a back seat to the sociology seminar room. We need a language of criticism as an antidote to the atheoretical use of "personal experience" in advancing claims for emancipatory action. Commonsense consciousness is not enough. However, this needs to be followed by the development of truly counterhegemonic public spheres. We need more than rhetorical displacements of oppression but rather strategic and coordinated resistance to racist, patriarchal capitalism and gender-divided labor relations. According to Teresa Ebert (in press), what is needed is an intervention into the system of patriarchal oppression at both the macropolitical level of the structural organization of domination (a transformative politics of labor relations) and the micropolitical level of different and contradictory manifestations of oppression (cultural politics).

Those of us working in the area of curriculum reform need to move beyond the tabloid reportage surrounding the political correctness debate, take the issue of difference seriously, and challenge the dimissive undercutting of difference by the conservative multiculturalists. First, we need to move beyond admitting one or two Latin American or African American books into the canon of great works. Rather, we need to legitimize multiple traditions of knowledge. By focusing merely on diversity we are actually reinforcing the power of the discourses from the Western traditions that occupy the contexts of social privilege. Second, curriculum reform requires teachers to interrogate the discursive presuppositions that inform their curriculum practices with respect to race, class, gender, and sexual orientation. In addition, curricularists need to unsettle their complacency with respect to Eurocentrism. Third, what is perceived as the inherent superiority of whiteness and Western rationality needs to be displaced. The very notion of the "West" is something that critical educators find highly problematic. Why is Toni Morrison, for instance, denounced as non-Western simply because she is African American? (This scenario is complicated by the fact that conservative multiculturalists often retort with the insinuation that any attack on Western culture is an attack against being American.) Fourth, curriculum reform means recognizing that groups are differentially situated in the production of Western, high-status knowledge. How are certain groups represented in the official knowledge that makes up the curriculum? Are they stigmatized because they are associated with the Third World? Are we, as teachers, complicitous with the oppression of these people when we refuse to interrogate popular films and TV shows that reinforce their subaltern status? Educators would do well to follow hooks (1992) in dehegemonizing racist discourses such that "progressive white people who are anti-racist might be able to understand the way in which their cultural practice reinscribes white supremacy without promoting paralyzing guilt or denial" (p. 177). In addition, curriculum reform means affirming the voices of the oppressed teachers need to give the marginalized and the powerless a preferential option. Similarly, students must be encouraged to produce their own oppositional readings of curriculum content. Lastly, curriculum reform must recognize the importance of encouraging spaces for the multiplicity of voices in our classrooms and of creating a dialogical pedagogy in which subjects see others as subjects and not as objects. When this happens, students are more likely to participate in history rather than become its victims.

In taking seriously the irreducible social materiality of discourse and the fact that the very semantics of discourse is always organized and interested, critical pedagogy has revealed how student identities are differentially constructed through social relations of schooling that promote and sustain asymmetrical relations of power and privilege between the oppressors and the oppressed. It has shown that this construction follows a normative profile of citizenship and an epistemology that attempts to reconcile the discourse of ideals with the discourse of needs. Discourses have been revealed to possess the power to nominate others as deviant or normal. Dominant discourses of schooling are not laws. Rather, they are strategies—disciplined mobilizations for normative performances of citizenship. Ian Hunter (1992) has shown that the concept of citizenry taught in schools has less to do with ethical ideals than with disciplinary practices and techniques of reading and writing and with the way students are distributed into political and aesthetic spaces. We are being aesthetically and morally reconciled with the governing norms of a civic unconscious. The "unconscious" is not a semiotic puzzle to be opened through the discovery of some universal grammar but is rather an ethical technology designed to "complete" students as citizens. Pedagogically, this process is deceptive because it uses liberal humanism and progressive education to complete the circuit of hegemony. The liberal position on pedagogy is to use it to open social texts to a plurality of readings. Because we live in an age of cynical reason, this pedagogy provides a "knowing wink" to students which effectively says: "We know there are multiple ways to make sense of the world and we know that you know, too. So let's knowingly enter this world of multiple interpretations together and take pleasure in rejecting the dominant codes." Consequently, teachers and students engage in a tropological displacement and unsettling of normative discourses and revel in the semantic excess that prevents any meaning from becoming transcendentally fixed. The result of this practice of turning knowledge into floating signifiers circulating in an avant-garde text (whose discursive trajectory is everywhere and nowhere and whose meaning is ultimately undecidable) is simply a recontainment of the political. By positing undecidability in advance, identity is reduced to a form of self-indexing or academic "vogue-ing." Liberation becomes transformed into a form of discursive "cleverness," of postmodern transgressive-chic grounded in playfully high vogue decodings of always already constructed texts, of fashionable language gaming by academic apostates.

I would also like to argue, in conclusion, that students need to be provided with opportunities to construct border identities. Border identities are intersubjective spaces of cultural translation—linguistically multivalanced spaces of intercultural dialogue. It is a space where one can find an overlay of codes, a multiplicity of culturally inscribed subject positions, a displacement of normative reference codes, and a polyvalert assemblage of new cultural meanings (see Giroux 1992; McLaren in press; in press a).

Border identities are produced in sites of "occult instability" and result in *un laberinto de significados*. Here, knowledge is produced by a transrepresentational access to the real—through reflexive, relational understanding amidst the connotative matrixes of numerous cultural codes. It is a world where identity and critical subjectivity depend upon the process of translating a profusion of intersecting cultural meanings (Hicks 1991; Giroux 1992). We need to remember that we live in a repressive regime in which identities are teleologically inscribed towards a standard end—the informed, employed citizen. There is a tension between this narrative which schools have attempted to install in students through normative pedagogical practices and the nonlinear narratives that they "play out" in the world outside of the school. However, students and even their often well-intentioned teachers are frequently incapable of intervening (McLaren 1986).

Especially in inner-city schools, students can be seen inhabiting what I call *border cultures*. These are cultures in which a repetition of certain normative structures and codes often "collide" with other codes and structures whose referential status is often unknown or only partially known. In Los Angeles, for instance, it is possible that an inner-city neighborhood will contain Latino cultures, Asian cultures, and Anglo cultures. Students live interculturally as they cross the borderlines of linguistic, cultural, and conceptual realities. Students, in other words, have the opportunity to live multidimensionally. Living in border cultures is an anti-centering experience as time and space experienced at school is constantly displaced. Often a carnivalesque liminal space emerges as bourgeois linear time is displaced. Because the dominant model of multiculturalism in mainstream pedagogy is of the corporate or conservative variety, the notion of sameness is enforced and cultural differences that challenge white, Anglo cultures are considered deviant and in need of enforced homogenization into the dominant referential codes and structures of Euro-American discourse.

I am in agreement with critics who assert that border identity cannot be subsumed under either dialectical or analytic logic (Hicks 1991). It is, rather, an experience of deterritorialization of signification (Larsen 1991) in a postnationalist cultural space—that is, in a postcolonial, postnational space. Border identity is an identity structure that occurs in a postimperial space of cultural possibility. The postcolonial subject that arises out of the construction of border identity is nonidentical with itself. It acquires a new form of agency outside of Euro-American, Cartesian discourses. It is not simply an inverted Eurocentrism but one that salvages the modernist referent of liberation from oppression for all suffering peoples. I am here stressing the universality of human rights but at the same time criticizing essentialist universality as a site of transcendental meaning. In other words, I am emphasizing the universality or rights as historically produced. Social justice is a goal that needs to be situated historically, contextually, and contingently as the product of material struggles over modes of intelligibility as well as institutional and social practices. I need to be clear about what I mean by a referent for social justice and human freedom. I mean that the project underlying multicultural education needs to be situated from the standpoint not only of the *concrete other* but also of the *generalized other*. All universal rights in this view must recognize the specific needs and desires of the concrete other without sacrificing the standpoint of a generalized other, without which it is impossible to speak of a radical ethics at all. Selya Benhabib distinguishes between this perspective—what she refers to as an "interactive universalism"—and a "substitutionalist universalism"; "Substitutionalist universalism dismisses the concrete other behind the facade of a definitional identity of all as rational beings, while interactive universalism acknowledges that every generalized other is also a concrete other" (1992, p. 165). This position speaks neither exclusively to a liberal, humanist ethics of empathy and benevolence nor to a ludic, postmodernist ethics of local narratives or *les petits recits*, but to one based on engagement, confrontation and dialogue, and collective moral argumentation between and across borders. It takes into account both macro and micro theory (Best and Keller 1991) and some degree of normative justification and ajudication of choices. As Best and Kellner note (1991), "one needs new critical theories to conceptualize, describe, and interpret macro social processes, just as one needs political theories able to articulate common or general interests that cut across divisions of sex, race, and class" (p. 301). In this sense I take issue with ludic voices of postmodernism that proclaim an end both to self-reflective agenthood and to the importance of engaging historical narratives and that proclaim the impossibility of legitimizing institutions outside of "practices and traditions other than through the immanent appeal to the self-legitimation of 'small narratives'" (Benhabib 1992, p. 220). Rather, a critical multiculturalism must take into account the "methodological assumptions guiding one's choice of narratives, and a clarification of those principles in the name of which one speaks" (p. 226).

A border identity is not simply an identity that is anticapitalist and counterhegemonic but is also critically utopian. It is an identity that transforms the burden of knowledge into a scandal of hope. The destructive extremes of Eurocentrism and national-cultural identities (as in the current crisis in what was formerly Yugoslavia) must be avoided. We need to occupy locations between our political unconscious and everyday praxis and struggle but at the same time be guided by a universalist emancipatory world view in the form of a provisional utopia or contingent foundationalism (See Butler 1991). A provisional utopia is not a categorical blueprint for social change (as in fascism) but a contingent utopia where we anticipate the future through practices of solidarity and community. Such a utopian vision demands that we gain control of the production of meaning but in a postnationalist sense. We can achieve this goal by negotiating with the borders of our identity—those unstable constellations of discursive structures—in our search for a radical otherness that can empower us to reach beyond them.

Border identities constitute a bold infringement on normalcy, a violation of the canons of bourgeois decorum, a space where we can cannibalize the traces of our narrative repression or engage them critically through the practice of cultural translation—a translation of one level of reality into another, creating a multidimensional reality that I call the *cultural imaginary,* a space of cultural articulation that results from the collision of multiple strands of referential codes and sign systems. Such collisions can create hybrid significations through a hemorrhage of signifiers whose meanings endlessly bleed into each other or else take on the force of historical agency as a new *mestizaje* consciousness. Mestizaje consciousness (Anzaldúa 1987) is not simply a doctrine of identity based on cultural bricolage or a form of bric-a-brac subjectivity but a critical practice of cultural negotiation and translation that attempts to transcend the contradictions of Western dualistic thinking. As Chandra Talpade Mohanty (1991) remarks:

> A mestiza consciousness is a consciousness of the borderlands, a consciousness born of the historical collusion of Anglo and Mexican cultures and frames of reference. It is a plural consciousness in that it requires understanding multiple, often opposing ideas and knowledges, and negotiating these knowledges, not just taking a simple counterstance. (p. 36).

Anzaldúa speaks of a notion of agency that moves beyond the postmodernist concept of "split subject" by situating agency in its historical and geopolitical specificity (p. 37). Borders cannot simply be evoked in an abstract, transcendental sense but need to be identified specifically. Borders can be linguistic, spacial, ideological, and geographical. They not only demarcate otherness but also stipulate the manner in which otherness is maintained and reproduced. A mestizaje consciousness is linked, therefore, to the specificity of historical struggles (Ibid., p. 38).

A critical multiculturalism needs to testify not only to the pain, suffering, and "walking nihilism" of oppressed peoples but also to the intermittent, epiphanic ruptures and moments of *jouissance* that occur when solidarity is established around struggles for liberation. As I have tried to argue, with others, elsewhere (McLaren and Hammer 1989; McLaren, 1995), we need to abandon our pedagogies of protest (which, as Houston Baker (1985) reminds us, simply reinforces the dualism of "self" and "other," reinstates the basis of dominant racist evaluations, and preserves the "always already" arrangements of white male hegemony [see Baker 1985]) in favor of a politics of transformation. Those of us who are white need also to avoid the "white male confessional" that Baker (1985) describes as the "confessional *manqué* of the colonial subject" (p. 388).

White male confessionals simply "induce shame" rather than convince people to change their axiology, yet still employ the language and "shrewd methods of the overseers." It is the type of confessional that proclaims that oppressed people of color are "as good as" white people. It simply asserts that subaltern voices measure up to dominant voices and that African Americans are merely "different" and not deviant. In contrast, Baker calls for a form of *"supraliteracy"* or "guerrilla action" carried out *within* linguistic territories. This constitutes an invasion of the dominant linguistic terrain of the traditional academic disciplines—an invasion that he describes as a "deformation of mastery." From this perspective, critical pedagogy needs to be more attentive to the dimension of the vernacular—"to sound racial poetry in the courts of the civilized" (Ibid., p. 395). Teachers need to include nonliterary cultural forms into our classrooms—such as video, film, popular fiction, and radio—and a critical means of understanding their role in the production of subjectivity and agency.

Concentrating on the reflexive modalities of the intellect or returning to some pretheoretical empirical experience are both bad strategies for challenging the politics of the white confessional. The former is advocated mostly by academics while the latter is exercised by educational activists suspicious of the new languages of deconstruction and the fashionable apostasy of the poststructuralists whose intellectual home is in the margins. Academic theorists tend to textualize and displace experience to the abstract equivalence of the signified while activists view "commonsense" experience as essentially devoid of ideology or interest. We need to avoid approaches that disconnect us from the lives of real people who suffer and from issues of power and justice that directly affect the oppressed.

Critical social theory as a form of multicultural resistance must be wary of locating liberatory praxis in the realm of diachrony—as something to be resolved dialectically in some higher unity outside of the historical struggle and pain and suffering to which we must serve as pedagogical witnesses and agents of radical hope. Yet at the same time, critical pedagogy needs to be wary of forms of populist elitism that privilege only the reform efforts of those who have direct experience with the oppressed. After all, no single unsurpassable and "authentic" reality can be reached through "experience" since no experience is preontologically available outside of a politics of representation.

As multicultural educators informed by critical and feminist pedagogies, we need to keep students connected to the power of the unacceptable and comfortable with the unthinkable by producing critical forms of policy analysis and pedagogy. In tandem with this, we must actively help students to challenge sites of discursive hierarchy rather than delocalizing and dehistoricizing them, and to contest the ways that their desires and pleasures are being policed in relationship to them. It is important that as critical educators, we do not manipulate students simply to accept our intellectual positions nor presume at the same time to speak for them. Nor should our critical theorizing be simply a service to the culture of domination by extending student insights into the present system without at the same time challenging the very assumptions of the system. We cannot afford to just temporarily disengage students from the *doxa*—the language of common sense. If we want to recruit students to a transformative praxis, students must not only be encouraged to choose a language of analysis that is undergirded by a project of liberation but must affectively invest in such a project.

If we are to be redeemed from our finitude as passive supplicants of history, we must, as students and teachers, adopt more directly oppositional and politically combatative social and cultural practices. The destructive fanaticism of present day xenophobia is only exacerbated by the current ethical motionlessness among many left constituencies. Insurgent intellectuals and theorists are called to steer a course between the monumentalization of judgment and taste and riding the postmodern currents of despair in a free-fall exhilaration of political impotence.

The present historical moment is populated by memories that are surfacing at the margins of our culture, along the fault lines of our logocentric consciousness. Decolonized spaces are forming in the borderlands—linguistic, epistemological, and intersubjective—and these will affect the classrooms of the future. Here saints and Iwa walk together and the Orishas speak to us through the rhythms of the earth and the pulse of the body. The sounds produced in the borderlands are quite different from the convulsive monotones voiced in "waspano" or "gringoñol" that echo from the schizophrenic boundaries of Weber's iron cage. Here it is in the hybrid polyrhythms of the drum that the new pulse of freedom can be felt. Within such borderlands our pedagogies of liberation can be invested once again with the passion of mystery and the reason of commitment. This is neither a Dionysian rejection of rationality nor a blind, prerational plunge into myth but rather an attempt to embrace and reclaim the memories of those pulsating, sinewed bodies that have been forgotten in our modernist assault on difference and uncertainty. An attempt to begin an *asiento*.

Notes

* Slightly altered versions of this paper [are published] in Peter McLaren, Rhonda Hammer, David Sholle, and Susan Reilly, *Rethinking Media Literacy*. New York: Peter Lang Publishers and Peter McLaren, *Critical Pedagogy and Predatory Culture*. London and New York: Routledge, in press. Some sections of this paper have appeared in Peter McLaren, "Multiculturalism and the Postmodern Critique: Towards a Pedagogy oú Resistance and Transformation." *Cultural Studies* 7(1), 1993, pp. 118–146 and Peter McLaren, "Critical Pedagogy, Multiculturalism, and the Politics of Risk and Resistance: Response to Kelly and Portelli," 1991. *Journal of Education* 173(3): 29–59. This paper was originally published in *Strategies*, no. 7, 1994, pp. 98–131, and *Multiculturalism: A Critical Reader*, edited by David Theo Goldberg. Oxford: Blackwell, pp. 45–74. See also Peter McLaren, "Critical Multiculturalism, Media Literacy, and the Politics of Representation. In Jean Frederickson (Ed.) *Reclaiming Our Voices: Bilingual Education, Critical Pedagogy and Praxis*. Ontario, California: California Association for Bilingual Education, 1995, pp. 99–138, for an earlier version of this article.

1. Africa is still demonized as a land uncivilized, corrupt, and savage and as a continent divided into countries that are viewed as not evolved enough to govern themselves without Western guidance and stewardship. We shamefully ignore Africa's victims of war and famine in comparison, for instance, to the "white" victims of Bosnia. When the U.S. media does decide to report on Africa, many of the images it reinforces are of a land of jungle, wildlife, famine, poachers, and fierce fighting among rival tribal factions (Naureckas 1993). The white supremacist and colonialist discourses surrounding the recent intervention in Somalia by heroic U.S. troops and relief workers (referred to by General Colin Powell as sending in the "cavalry") is captured in comments made by Alan Pizzey of CBS when he described the intervention in "humanitarian" terms as "just a few good men trying to help

another nation in need, another treacherous country where all the members of all the murderous factions look alike" (cited in Jim Naureckas, *Extra*, March 1993, p. 12). Described as a land populated by helpless and historyless victims and drug-crazed thugs high on khat (a mild stimulant) who ride around in vehicles out of a Mad Max movie, an implicit parallel is made between Somali youth and the cocaine-dealing gangs of toughs who participated in the L.A. rioting (Ibid.). This "othering" of Africa encouraged a preferred reading of Somalia's problems as indigenous and camouflaged the broader context surrounding the famine in Somalia and its subsequent "rescue" by U.S. marines. Occluded was the fact that the U.S. had previously obstructed U.N. peacekeeping efforts in Somalia, Angola, Namibia, and Mozambique because it was too costly (the U.S. still owes $415 million to the U.N., including $120 million for peacekeeping efforts)—a factor absent in nearly all the media coverage (Ibid.). From a U.S. foreign policy perspective, Somalia still plays an important role geopolitically, not simply because of its potential interest to Israel and the Arab nations but because of its rich mineral deposits and potential oil reserves. As Naureckas notes, Amoco, Chevron and Sunoco are engaged in oil exploration there (Ibid.).

The media have rarely reported on other factors surrounding the famine in Somalia. For instance, they have virtually ignored the U.S. support (to the sum of $200 million in military aid and half a billion in economic aid) to the Siad Barre regime (1969–1991). The U.S. ignored its corruption and human rights abuses because the dictatorship kept Soviet-allied Ethiopia embroiled in a war. Naureckas also points out that until the 1970s, Somalia was self-sufficient in grain and its agricultural land productive enough to withstand famine. However, U.S. and international agencies like the IMF pressured Somalia to shift agricultural from local subsistence to export crops (Ibid.).

References

Anzaldúa, Gloria. 1987. *Borderlands/La Frontera*. San Francisco: Spinsters/Aunt Lute.

Auster, Laurence. 1990. *The path to national suicide: An essay on immigration and multiculturalism*. American Immigration Control Foundation.

Baker, Houston A. 1985. "Caliban's triple play." In *"Race," writing, and difference*, ed. Henry Louis Gates, Jr., p. 381–395. Chicago, Illinois, University of Chicago Press.

Benhabib, Seyla. 1992. *Situating the self: Gender, community, and postmodernism in contemporary ethics*. London and New York: Routledge.

Best, Steven, and Kellner, Douglas. 1991. *Postmodern theory: Critical interrogations*. New York: The Guilford Press.

Bhabha, Homi K. 1992. A good judge of character: Men, metaphors, and the common culture. In *Race-ing justice, engendering power*, Ed. Tony Morrison, pp. 232–249. New York: Pantheon Books.

Bradford, Phillips Verner, and Blume, Harvey. 1992. *Ota Benga: The pygmy in the zoo*. New York: St. Martin's Press.

Brookhiser, Richard. 1991. *The Way of the WASP: How it made America, and how it can save it, so to speak*. New York: Free Press.

Butler, Judith. 1991. Contingent foundations: Feminism and the question of "postmodernism." *Praxis International* 11(2): 150–165.

Cooper, B. M. 1989. Cruel and the gang: Esposing the Schomburg Posse. *Village Voice* 34(19): 27–36.

Copjec, Joan. 1991. The unvermögender other: Hysteria and democracy in America. *New Formations* 14(Summer): 27–41.

Cortázar, Julio. 1963. *Hopscotch*. Trans. Gregory Rabassa. New York: Random House.

Darder, Antonia. 1992. *Culture and power in the classroom*. South Hadley, MA: Bergin and Garvey.

Dyer, Richard. 1988. White. *Screen* 29(4): 44–64.

Dyson, M. E. 1993. *Reflecting Black: African-American cultural criticism*. Minneapolis and London: University of Minnesota Press.

Ebert, Teresa. 1991a. Writing in the political: Resistance (post)-modernism. *Legal Studies Forum* 14(4): 291–303.

————. 1991b. Political semiosis in/of American cultural studies. *The American Journal of Semiotics* 8(1/2): 113–135.

————. In press. Ludic feminism, the body, performance and labor: Bringing materialism back into feminist cultural studies. *Cultural Critique.*

Estrada, Kelly, and McLaren, Peter. In press. A dialogue on multiculturalism and democracy. *Educational Researcher.*

Fish, Stanley. 1992. Bad company. *Transition* 56: 60–67.

Gardiner, Michael. 1992. *The dialogics of critique: M. M. Bakhtin and the theory of ideology.* London and New York: Routledge.

Giroux, Henry. 1992. *Border crossings.* London and New York: Routledge.

Giroux, Henry, and McLaren, Peter. 1991a. Media hegemony. Introduction to *Media Knowledge* by James Schwoch, Mimi White, and Susan Reilly. Albany, NY: State University of New York Press, pp. xv–xxxiv.

————. 1991b. Leon Golub's radical pessimism: Toward a pedagogy of representation. *Exposure* 28(12): 18–33.

————. 1991. Radical pedagogy as cultural politics: Beyond the discourse of critique and anti-utopianism. In *Theory/Pedagogy/Politics,* ec. D. Morton and M. Zavarzadeh, pp. 152–186. Chicago: University of Illinois Press.

————. 1992. Writing from the margins: Geographies of identity, pedagogy, and power. *Journal of Education* 174(1): 7–30.

————. In press. Paulo Freire, postmodernism, and the utopian imagination: A Blochian reading. In *Bloch in our time,* ed. Jamie Owen Daniel and Tom Moylan. London and New York: Verso.

Goldfield, Michael. 1992. The color of politics in the United States: White supremacy as the main explanation for the pecularities of American politics from colonial times to the present. In *The bounds of race,* ed. Dominick LaCapra, pp. 104–133. Ithaca and London: Cornell University Press.

Hall, Stuart. 1991. Ethnicity: Identity and difference. *Radical America* 23(4): 9–20.

Hammer, Rhonda and McLaren, Peter. 1992. Spectacularizing subjectivity: Media knowledges and the new world order. *Polygraph,* No. 5, 46–66.

Hammer, Rhonda, and McLaren, Peter. 1991. Rethinking the dialectic. *Educational Theory* 41(1): 23–46.

Hicks, D. Emily. 1991. *Border writing.* Minneapolis: University of Minnesota Press.

hooks, bell. 1992. *Black looks.* Boston: South End Press.

Hunter, Ian. 1992. *Culture and government: The emergence of literary education.* Houndmills, Basingstoke, Hampshire and London: MacMillan Press.

Katz, Cindi, and Smith, Neil. 1992. L.A. intifada: Interview with Mike Davis. *Social Text* 33: 19–33.

Larsen, Neil. 1991. Foreword to *Border writing* by Emily Hicks, pp. xi–xxi. Minneapolis: University of Minnesota Press.

Lloyd, David. 1991. Race under representation. *Oxford Literary Review* 13(1–2): 62–94.

MacCannell, Dean. 1992. *Empty meeting grounds: The tourist papers.* London and New York: Routledge.

Macedo, Donaldo. 1995. *Literacies of Power.* Boulder, Colorado: Westview Press.

McCarthy, Cameron. 1988. Rethinking liberal and radical perspectives on racial inequality in schooling: Making the case for nonsynchrony. *Harvard Educational Review* 58(3): 265–279.

McLaren, Peter, and Hammer, Rhonda. 1989. Critical pedagogy and the postmodern challenge: Towards a critical postmodernist pedagogy of liberation. *Educational Foundations* 3(3): 29–62.

————. 1992. Media knowledges, warrior citizenry, and postmodern literacies. *Journal of Urban and Cultural Studies* 2(2): 41–77.

McLaren, Peter. 1985. Contemporary ritual studies: A post-Turnerism perspective. *Semiotic Inquiry* 5(1): 78–85.

————. 1986. *Schooling as a ritual performance: Towards a political economy of educational symbols and gestures.* London and New York: Routledge (Revised edition in press).

————. 1988. Culture or canon? Critical pedagogy and the politics of literacy. *The Harvard Educational Review* 58(2): 213–234.

————. 1989. *Life in schools.* White Plains, NY: Longman.

————. 1990. Schooling the postmodern body. In *Postmodernism, feminism, and cultural politics*, ed. Henry A. Giroux, pp. 144–173. Albany, NY: State University of New York Press.

————. In press a. Collisions with otherness: Multi-culturalism, the politics of difference, and the ethnographer as nomad. *American Journal of Semiotics*.

————. In press b. Border disputes: Multicultural narrative, critical pedagogy and identity formation in postmodern America. In *Naming silenced lives*, ed. J. McLaughlin and William Tierney. New York and London: Routledge.

————. 1995. *Critical Pedagogy and Predatory Culture*. London and New York: Routledge.

Mensh, E. and Mensh, H. 1991. *The IQ mythology: class, race, gender*. Carbondale, Illinois: Southern Illinois University Press.

Mercer, Kobena. 1990. Welcome to the jungle: Identity and diversity in postmodern politics. In *Identity: Community, culture, difference*, ed. Jonathan Rutherford, pp. 43–71. London: Lawrence and Wishart.

Mercer, Kobena. 1992. 1968: Periodizing politics and identity. In *Cultural studies*, ed. Lawrence Grossberg, Cary Nelson and Paula Treichler, pp. 424–449. London and New York: Routledge.

Mohanty, Chandra Talpade. 1989/90. On race and voice: Challenges for liberal education in the 1990s. *Cultural Critique* (Winter): 179–208.

————. 1991. Introduction: Cartographies of struggle: Third world women and the politics of feminism. In *Third world women and the politics of feminism*, ed. Chandra Talpade Mohanty, Ann Russo, and Lourdes Torres, pp. 1–47. Bloomington: Indiana University Press.

Muñoz, Carlos. 1989. *Youth, identity, power*. London and New York: Verso.

Murray, C. and Hernstein, R. 1994. *The bell curve: Intelligence and class structure in American life*. New York: Free Press.

Naureckas, Jim. 1993. The Somalia intervention: Tragedy made simple. *Extra* 6(2): 10–13.

Nieto, Sonia. 1992. *Affirming diversity: The sociopolitical context of multicultural education*. White Plains, NY: Longman Publishers.

Norris, Christopher. 1990. *What's wrong with postmodernism?* Baltimore, Maryland: The Johns Hopkins University Press.

Observer 5(2), (March 1992).

Pieterse, Jan Nederveen. 1992. *White on black: Images of Africa and blacks in western popular culture*. New Haven and London: Yale University Press.

Rosaldo, Renato. 1989. *Culture and truth: The remaking of social analysis*. Boston: Beacon.

Rutherford, Jim. 1990. A place called home: Identity and the cultural politics of difference. In *Identity: Community, culture, difference*, ed. J. Rutherford, pp. 9–27. London: Lawrence and Wishart.

Schlesinger, Jr., Arthur M. 1991. *The disuniting of America: Reflections on a multicultural society*. Knoxville: Whittle Direct Books.

Scott, Joan W. 1992. Experience. In *Feminists theorize the political*, ed. Judith Butler and Joan W. Scott, pp. 22–40. New York and London: Routledge.

Simone, Timothy Maliqualim. 1989. *About face: Race in postmodern America*. Brooklyn, New York: Autonomedia.

Sleeter, Christine E. 1991. *Empowerment through multicultural education*. Albany, NY: State University of New York Press.

Stephanson, Anders. 1988. Interview with Cornel West. In *Universal abandon? The politics of postmodernism*, ed. Andrew Ross, pp. 269–286. Minneapolis: University of Minnesota Press.

Wallace, Michele. 1991. Multiculturalism and oppositionality. *Afterimage* (October): 6–9.

West, Cornel. 1990. The new cultural politics of difference. In *Out there: Marginalization and contemporary cultures*, ed. Russell Ferguson, et al., pp. 19–36. Cambridge, MA: MIT Press; New York: New Museum of Contemporary Art.

Questions

1. Explore McLaren's claim that "the idea of the democratic citizenship has now become synonymous with the private, consuming citizen and the increasing subalternization of the 'other.'"

2. According to McLaren, what is "conservative multiculturalism"?

3. What are the infamous events surrounding Ota Benga?

4. What is McLaren's critique of "liberal multiculturalism"? (Consider this critique as you read the selections in Section 4, Liberal Democratic Multiculturalism.)

5. According to McLaren, what is "left-liberal multiculturalism"?

6. According to McLaren, what is "critical multiculturalism"?

7. What is the "politics of signification"? How is it related to critical multiculturalism?

8. Why do critical multiculturalists like McLaren believe teachers and cultural worker need to build a politics of solidarity?

9. How does McLaren use the term "whiteness"? Compare this term to the "politics of signification."

10. What does McLaren mean by "border narratives," "border identity," and "border cultures"? Compare this to Giroux's category of "border pedagogy."

Section Three: Suggestions for Further Reading

Aronowitz, Stanley and Giroux, Henry A. (1991). *Postmodern Education: Politics, Culture and Social Criticism*. Minneapolis: University of Minnesota Press.

Cherryholmes, Cleo H. (1988). *Power and Criticism: Poststructural Investigations in Education*. New York: Teachers College Press.

Derrida, Jacques (1982). *Margins of Philosophy*. Chicago: University of Chicago Press.

Duarte, Eduardo Manuel (1998). "Expanding the Borders of Liberal Democracy: Multicultural Education and the Struggle for Cultural Identity." *Educational Foundations*. Volume 12, number 2 (Spring), 5–30.

Foucault, Michel (1980). *Power/Knowledge: Selected Interviews and Other Writings 1972–1977*. Colin Gordon (ed.) New York: Pantheon.

Giroux, Henry A., and McLaren, Peter (Eds.) (1994). *Between Borders: Pedagogy and the Politics of Cultural Studies*. New York: Routledge.

Kanpol, Barry and McLaren, Peter (Eds.) (1995). *Critical Multiculturalism: Uncommon Voices in a Common Struggle*. Westport: Bergin and Garvey.

Leistyna, Pepi, Woodrum, Arlie and Sherblom, Stephen A. (Eds.) (1996) *Breaking Free: The Transformative Power of Critical Pedagogy*. Cambridge: Harvard Education Review.

Lyotard, Jean François (1984). *The Postmodern Condition: A Report on Knowledge*. Minneapolis: University of Minnesota Press.

McLaren, Peter (1997). *Revolutionary Multiculturalism: Pedagogies of Dissent for the New Millennium*. Boulder: Westview.

Rorty, Richard (1989). *Contingency, Irony and Solidarity*. Cambridge: Cambridge University Press.

Ross, Andrew (Ed.) (1988). *Universal Abandon? The Politics of Postmodernism*. Minneapolis: University of Minnesota Press.

Section Four

Liberal Democratic Multiculturalism

As we explained in the introduction, Liberal Democratic Multiculturalism is concerned with identifying political values and institutions that can be commonly shared by the diverse citizenry of a multicultural society. This tradition is comprised primarily of political theorists who struggle with questions about how cultural pluralism can be reconciled with the individual rights and collective agreements valued by liberal democratic societies. The distinct conceptual strands within this orientation strike this balance in unique ways. Some theorists tend to emphasize the liberal principles of universal, individual rights; others insist that democratic processes of engaging in political action and reaching collective agreements are primary. This section includes writings that reflect, and sometimes combine, these various positions.

In the first selection, Burbules and Rice set the stage for comparing critical with liberal democratic approaches to multiculturalism by critiquing specific aspects of critical education theory and calling for a reappropriation of modernist political ideals. In their article, "Dialogue Across Difference: Continuing the Conversation," Nicholas Burbules and Suzanne Rice fault "critical educational studies," which is a launching point for much of Critical Multiculturalism, for certain postmodernist tendencies. The authors distinguish between "capital P" versus "small p" postmodernisms. "Capital P" Postmodernism includes two strands: antimodernism and "small p" postmodernism. Burbules and Rice are particularly troubled by what they perceive to be antimodernists' wholesale rejection of modernist values—such as liberty, equality, and freedom—and the absence of a "positive" agenda to replace these values. They also fault "small p" postmodernists for attempting to appropriate and expand modernist principles without offering adequate arguments for why one would endorse their views.

In an effort to both reconceptualize and defend modernist principles, Burbules and Rice outline three prospective benefits of "dialogue across differences": (1) construction of identity along lines that are flexible without becoming arbitrary; (2) broadening understanding of others; (3) fostering more reasonable and sustainable communicative practices. They emphasize that dialogue across differences is especially important in the educational arena due to "important aims of personal development and moral conduct." In conclusion, they urge educators "to help foster the disposition to work toward understanding across differences, and the communicative virtues and skills that make this possible."

In the next selection, "Culture, Subculture, Multiculturalism: Educational Options," Anthony Appiah turns our attention from what educators *should do* to what public schools in particular *should not do* in culturally plural liberal democracies. Appiah is concerned with approaches to multicultural education that endorse separatism among groups or that want students to be taught the particular traditions of groups that they belong to. In response to what he calls "separatist rationales" Appiah invokes a public/private distinction that is common to modern liberal theory. According to this public/private distinction, institutions of the state, or "public" institutions such as public schools, remain neutral toward different cultural groups. As Appiah explains, his view emphasizes ". . . the division between public and private spheres in the education of children: on such a view, ethnicity and religion are not to be transmitted by the organs of the state. Both, rather, are created and preserved outside the state by families, and by wider communities, including religious ones."

In keeping with this public/private distinction surrounding educational tasks, Appiah goes on to argue that although "the public schools . . . should not teach particular traditions and religions; . . . of course, they should teach *about* them." In this way, children who attend public schools will gain knowledge of other cultures and traditions. And such knowledge should encourage respect for different groups within the state. But, in the final analysis, Appiah concludes that all that is necessary for political cohesion amidst cultural pluralism is a shared commitment across groups to the institutions and organization of the state.

Canadian philosopher Charles Taylor disagrees with Appiah's endorsement of state neutrality toward cultural groups. In his essay, "The Politics of Recognition," Taylor distinguishes between two different forms of liberalism. The first form calls for state neutrality toward various groups and traditions in public institutions and political life. The second form of liberalism does not require state neutrality. Instead, as philosophers Michael Walzer and Amy Gutmann both explain, this form allows public institutions to support particular cultural values if: (a) basic rights are protected; (b) no one is manipulated into acceptance of the cultural values promoted by public institutions; (c) public officials and institutions making cultural choices are democratically accountable.

Whereas Appiah's argument reflects the first form of liberalism, Taylor endorses the second approach. He advocates a "model of liberal society that does not always claim complete cultural neutrality and is willing to weigh uniform treatment against cultural survival and sometimes opt for the latter." Essentially, Taylor is claiming that cultural groups, not just individuals, have rights and that one of these rights is a right to survival. Such rights are not guaranteed, but need to be balanced within the democratic processes of public institutions and against the basic rights of individuals.

After addressing the issue of whether cultural groups can legitimately claim rights of cultural survival, Taylor turns to the question of cultural worth. Here Taylor examines how determinations should be made regarding the equal value or equal worth of various cultures. First, he urges a "presumption of equal worth" between cultures. Then, he argues that the actual assessment which follows such a good faith presumption can best be made based upon shared standards of evaluation. He ends by suggesting that shared standards might be derived across cultural groups from what German philosopher Hans Gadamer called a "fusion of horizons."

In the final selection, "Challenges of Multiculturalism in Democratic Education," Amy Gutmann takes issue with Taylor's claim that cultural groups have rights to ensure future survival. In her view, "[c]ultures do not have rights to survival." According to Gutmann, individual rights, combined with democratic principles such as tolerance and mutual respect, protect the cultural differences of individual citizens. But within public institutions, and especially public schools, a shared civic commitment to "basic liberty, opportunity, and a commitment to deliberate about politically relevant issues" trumps the particularistic values and claims of cultural groups. Gutmann does not defend her position from under the umbrella of liberal neutrality, but instead as a non-neutral position whereby liberal democratic values supersede conflicting cultural values. Her argument recalls Appiah's emphasis on a shared political culture as well as Burbules and Rice's insistence on the importance of dialogue, which she refers to as *deliberation.*

A couple of themes persist throughout these four selections. The first is a recurring tension between liberal and democratic principles and cultural pluralism. In a distinctive fashion, each of these authors attempts to achieve a fragile balance between universal citizenship, political equality, and cultural pluralism. Appiah leans toward liberal emphases on individual rights and state neutrality. Taylor also turns to liberalism, but outlines a rationale for granting rights to cultural groups. Gutmann rejects this argument and instead defends democratic principles of mutual respect and the importance of deliberative processes. Her attention to deliberation closely reflects the treatment given by Burbules and Rice to the importance of "dialogue across differences."

A second theme revolves around this attention to deliberation or dialogue. An emphasis on dialogue appears in all four selections, whether theorizing the function of dialogue in forming individual identity or its public role in facilitating understanding and agreement across diverse perspectives. In terms of these themes, each of these selections raises, and leaves largely unanswered, questions about the specific implications of cultural pluralism for the arena of public education. As you read each selection, the following questions encourage you to reflect upon how institutions of public education within liberal democratic societies can best face the challenges posed by cultural pluralism.

Guiding Questions for Section Four

- In multicultural, liberal democratic societies what should constitute a common political culture?
- In such societies, what is the role of public education in creating and sustaining a common political culture?
- How should public educational institutions balance particular cultural values against common political values?

Dialogue Across Differences: Continuing the Conversation

Nicholas C. Burbules and Suzanne Rice*

In this article, Nicholas Burbules and Suzanne Rice engage several of the central claims made by postmodern authors about the possibilities and limits of education. Specifically, they focus on postmodern conceptions of difference, and on the question of whether dialogue across differences, particularly differences in social power, is possible and worthwhile. In order to answer this question, Burbules and Rice distinguish two trends within postmodern thought: one extends and redefines modernist principles such as democracy, reason, and equality; the other deconstructs and rejects these principles. They argue that it is the redefinition of modernist principles, not their wholesale rejection, that offers educators the most hopeful and useful conception of dialogue across differences.

Postmodernism has had a growing influence on critical educational studies. Leftist theoretical approaches that argue for a specific method of analysis and assume the explanatory primacy of some particular social factor—including Marxism and some versions of feminism—are being challenged by an outlook that stresses the constructed and essentially arbitrary character of any explanatory framework. By situating all claims of knowledge and value within a web of discursive and nondiscursive practices, Postmodernism[1] seeks to disclose the partiality and contentiousness of any purportedly universal social theory:

> The study of language itself and of the way it is used in discursive practices to constitute the social structure answered many of the problems created by earlier models. Individuals were no longer lost in the overpowering, controlling social structure—they were, rather, constituting those social structures through the discursive practices in which they were engaged. Class and gender were no longer imposed unitary

structures but shifting sets of possibilities, of subject positionings made available in the texts, the narrative structures, the discursive practices in which each person participates.[2]

For these authors, the active processes by which we construct and interpret systems of belief or value are infinitely variable and highly contingent. This contingency is thought to undercut any purely intellectual, internal justification for epistemic, moral, or political claims. Any such justification is rejected as simply the special pleading of a particular group seeking to promote a discursive order that legitimates their own advantages and privileges by promoting a specific basis of justification as the best one; any ultimate claim to "rightness" is a ploy to discourage further investigation or to allow investigation only on one's terms, and thus is seen as restrictive. Postmodernism regards itself as a challenge to these restrictions, often by directly and purposely flouting them:

> [Postmodern writers] want to "interrupt" academic norms by writing inside of another logic, a logic that displaces expectations of linearity, clear authorial voice, and closure. . . . The deconstructive text is a point of interrogation where binary notions of "clarity" are displaced as the speaking voice uses its authority to displace authority.[3]

On such a view, the only possible non-hierarchical, non-dominating, non-monolithic discursive approach is one that decenters all claims to transcendental justification (even its own). The very aims of developing general theories or universalizable moral claims are dismissed as anachronistic, and frequently totalitarian, like the styles of epic architecture. Hence one frequently encounters terms in Postmodern writing such as "fracturing," "breaking," and—of course—"deconstruction." This outlook embraces incommensurability across worldviews, not as an unfortunate failure to establish common meanings and values, but as a desired state:

> Postmodernism . . . is completely indifferent to the questions of consistency and continuity. It self-consciously slices genres, attitudes, styles. It relishes the blurring or juxtaposition of forms . . . stances . . . moods . . . cultural levels. . . . It neither embraces nor criticizes, but beholds the world blankly, with a knowingness that dissolves feeling and commitment into irony. It pulls the rug out from under itself, displaying an acute self-consciousness about the work's constructed nature. It takes pleasure in the play of surfaces, and derides the search for depth as mere nostalgia.[4]

Accordingly, we should encourage the multiplicity of as many voices and perspectives as possible, without seeking to reconcile them or combine them into a single, consistent, unified account: Bakhtin terms this a state of "heteroglossia."[5] In the context of social and political theories, this outlook has often been expressed as a celebration of "difference." While particular Postmodern theorists might implicitly favor a factor such as race, gender, class, ethnic identity, or sexual preference as a primary theoretical/political category, they undercut this claim by arguing at the same time that all these factors (and others as well) must also be accommodated within a broader theoretical/political analysis. This theoretical pluralism is not justified by any particular value placed on complexity or comprehensiveness; rather, Postmodernists argue that, from the standpoint of the subjective construction of identity, such factors cannot be regarded separately: a person is, for example, Black, and female, and poor. Any external attempt to isolate or prioritize such factors is simply another dimension of an "essentialism" that is dominating.[6]

These ideas have made rapid headway into critical studies of education. One reason for their popularity has been the widespread rejection of the "economism," "determinism," or "pessimism" of Marxian analyses of education, such as that of Samuel Bowles and Herbert Gintis's *Schooling in Capitalist America*.[7] The language of Postmodernism has served well in articulating the limits of such accounts, by stressing the ideological, cultural, and discursive elements that they fail to illuminate. In this, Postmodernism seeks to broaden the terrain of struggle available to pedagogues at a time when the traditional Left struggles over work, resources, and political access seem sharply limited.[8]

In this article, we focus on the Postmodern elevation of *difference* as a value that is in opposition to such traditional values as consensus and intersubjectivity, and examine whether a sympathetic response to the Postmodern critique can be made consistent with positive educational goals—in this case, the pedagogical value of *dialogue*. We will consider whether dialogue can be maintained across differences, whether it is desirable to try, and what conditions might make it possible.

Postmodernism, By and Large

Because the term *Postmodernism* has been used to refer to so many different views, it is difficult to attribute essential themes to the Postmodern trend.[9] But at least three ideas recur in the literature generally, and specifically in Postmodern work in educational studies.

First is the rejection of absolutes. Postmodernists usually insist that there can be no single rationality, no single morality, and no ruling theoretical framework for the analysis of social and political events. The conventional language here, deriving from Jean-François Lyotard, is that there are no "metanarratives" that are not themselves the partial expressions of a particular point of view.[10] As Zygmunt Bauman puts it:

> The philosophers' search for the ultimate system, for the complete order, for the extirpation of everything unknown and unruly, stems from the dream of having a firm soil and a secure home, and leads to closing

down the obstinately infinite human potential. Such search for the universal cannot but degenerate into a ruthless clamp-down on human possibilities.[11]

Second is the perceived saturation of all social and political discourses with power or dominance.[12] Any metanarrative is taken to be synonymous with the hegemony of a social and political order:

> To learn to see not only what we do but also what structures what we do, to deconstruct how ideological and institutional power play in our own practices, to recognize the partiality and open-endedness of our own efforts, all of this is to examine the discourses within which we are caught up. Imploding canons and foregrounding the power/knowledge nexus by deconstructing "natural" hierarchies demonstrate that what had seemed transparent and unquestionable is neither. All of this is to participate in the radical unsettling that is postmodernism in ways that have profound implications for pedagogy and curriculum. . . . In this context of ferment, educational inquiry is increasingly viewed as no more outside the power/knowledge nexus than any other human enterprise.[13]

If, as many Postmodernists argue, there are no sustainable norms of rationality and value, then all educational discourse is political discourse; it exists, in this view, only for the purpose of enfranchising certain group interests over others. If this is true, then the burden of responsibility is placed on any progressive educator to consider the political consequences of the vocabulary, structures of argument, and substantive conclusions of his or her teaching and writing. While teachers and scholars are inclined to see themselves as answerable only to their disciplinary standards of truth, evidence, accuracy, and so on, this critique challenges them to consider also the way in which their statements and actions exist within a system of power and privilege, and to reflect critically on their practices in light of the effects their speaking and writing are likely to have.

For example, this critical vantage point enjoins teachers to consider when classroom relations, even the most apparently benign, might instantiate and help perpetuate broader patterns of social and political dominance. The Postmodern critique argues that teacher authority, even if it is adopted with beneficial intent, takes significance against a pervasive background of relations of domination; some authors argue that the only alternative is to abandon all relations of classroom authority and disinterested claims to knowledge.[14] Obviously, such a criticism poses a direct challenge to our standard models of teaching.

A third idea that recurs in the Postmodern literature is the celebration of "difference." Rather than attempting to judge or prioritize the explanatory or political significance of given elements in a social situation, the Postmodern trend is to argue that, because all signifiers are mere constructions, there is no clear reason to grant any one special significance or value over others:

> What the inherently polysemous and controversial idea of *postmodernity* most often refers to . . . is first and foremost an acceptance of the inerad-icable plurality of the world—not a temporary state on the road to the not-yet-attained perfection, sooner or later to be left behind, but the con-stitutive quality of existence. By the same token, postmodernity means a resolute emancipation from the characteristically modern urge to over-come difference and promote sameness. . . . In the plural and pluralistic world of postmodernity, every form of life is *permitted on principle;* or, rather, no agreed principles are evident which may render any form of life impermissible.[15]

Thus, previous theoretical efforts, even from the Left, have been blamed with neglecting, or even suppressing, the perspectives and experiences of marginal-ized groups:

> We and you do not talk the same language. When we talk to you we use your language: the language of your experience and your theories. We try to use it to communicate our world of experience. But since your lan-guage and theories are inadequate in expressing our experiences, we only succeed in communicating our experience of exclusion. We cannot talk to you in our language because you do not understand it. So the brute facts that we understand your language and that the place where most theorizing . . . is taking place is your place, both combine to require us either to distort our experience not just in the speaking of it, but in the living of it, or that we remain silent.[16]

An increased sensitivity to such difference clearly urges a more inclusive approach to pedagogy. It is crucial to recognize that for the Postmodernist, this responsibility goes beyond mere "pluralism," or an invitation for all to partici-pate. It is not enough merely to create the conditions of a forum in which all parties present have the right to speak. In a society structured by power, not all differences reside at the same level. Therefore, further questions must be posed: Who may feel unable to speak without explicit or implicit retribution? Who may want to speak, but feel so demoralized, or intimidated, by the cir-cumstances that they are effectively "silenced"? What tacit rules of communi-cation may be operating in schools and classrooms that rule certain areas of concern or modes of speech out of bounds by the very procedures that the dis-cussion takes for granted? All of these constitute forms of exclusion. In each of these cases, the Postmodernist will argue, the promulgation of many voices and the representation of the concerns of different groups extend beyond mere tolerance or the creation of an "open forum" that may be less open than it ap-pears, when judged from the perspective of marginalized persons or groups.

☙

Two Varieties of Postmodernism

Postmodernism provides a set of critical categories that pose a serious challenge, not only to conventional educational activities, but to many previous efforts by Leftist scholars to develop a progressive educational theory and practice. However, because the Postmodern tradition avoids committing itself to a political/moral metanarrative of its own, it often discloses and rejects the shortcomings of other views without positing clear alternatives to them. Instead, it relies on an implicitly normative vocabulary of liberation, empowerment, and issue-specific critique that is much clearer in specifying what it is against than what it is for and why.[17]

Part of the difficulty in identifying and justifying positive aims in the Postmodern tradition is that there seem to be two distinct trends within Postmodernism, which adopt fundamentally different positions relative to modernism itself. We call these two trends postmodernism and antimodernism, the first of which we see as fundamentally continuous with the modernist tradition, although it seeks to challenge and redefine it, the second of which regards itself as making a complete break from modernism.[18] These are not, however, discrete or self-contained schools of thought; we will show how postmodern and antimodern elements co-exist in numerous authors, although some clearly tend toward one position rather than the other. Complicating this analysis further is the tendency of certain authors to slide back and forth between these positions—authors for whom rejection and reformulation are not clearly distinguished.

First, then, is what we have called *postmodernism* per se. The "post" implies a moving beyond, of course, but also a continuity; any tradition identifying itself as post-something is also accepting the basic significance of the tradition it proposes to go beyond—if it did not accept this, there would be no reason to define itself in relation to that earlier tradition. In this sense, postmodernism is not entirely alien to modernism; it frequently invokes modernist categories, such as reason or equality, but seeks to reappropriate, redefine, and reground them. In this, postmodernism does identify a potential basis for defining a positive social and political agenda, although it faces a difficulty in defending this agenda, since it has foresworn the modernist "metanarratives" that had previously underlaid it.

Within the educational literature, this approach is best exemplified by the work of Henry Giroux and Peter McLaren.[19] Their arguments often take the form of invoking modernist categories, which they seek to reappropriate and expand in significance. For example:

> Postmodernism must extend and broaden the most democratic claims of modernism. . . . [It must be] linked with the modernist language of public life . . . as part of a public philosophy that broadens and deepens individual liberties and rights. . . . [Postmodern pedagogy] is informed by a political project that links the creation of citizens to the development of

a critical democracy; that is, a political project that links education to the struggle for public life in which discourse, vision, and compassion are attentive to the rights and conditions that organize public life as a democratic social form.[20]

Here we see a clear attempt to reappropriate and expand modernist concepts such as democracy, liberty, rights, citizenship, and so forth. Giroux and McLaren explicitly and repeatedly challenge other views that fail to offer a positive educational and political agenda.[21] We believe they are quite justified in this criticism. Yet, we also see reflected in their work the difficulty postmodernism encounters in providing principled arguments to support positive positions; in place of such arguments we often find a highly charged rhetorical style that *asserts* the primacy of certain values or *condemns* their suppression without articulating why anyone not already sympathetic with their position ought to be so. This endeavor is made even more difficult when postmodern skepticism about modernist values and metanarratives blurs into an antimodern rejection of them.

This *antimodernist* position is characterized by a strong antipathy to the language, issues, and values of modernism, and seeks to formulate an entirely different problematic. It defines itself in opposition to modernism, not as a position growing out of and moving beyond modernist concerns. Hence it is not concerned with recapturing and reformulating modern values, such as reason or equality, but with deconstructing them and rejecting them. Not surprisingly, this tradition in particular has been more convincing in pointing out the limitations and contradictions of modernism than in reformulating positive alternatives. Having deconstructed all metanarratives and radically relativized all possible values, antimodernism is left with no clear way of justifying *any* alternatives. For example, a strong critic of Giroux and McLaren, Elizabeth Ellsworth, writes:

> By prescribing moral deliberation, engagement in the full range of views present, and critical reflection, the literature on critical pedagogy implies that students and teachers can and should engage each other in the classroom as fully rational subjects. . . . In schools, rational deliberation, reflection, and consideration of all viewpoints has become a vehicle for regulating conflict and the power to speak. . . . In a racist society and its institutions, such debate has not and cannot be "public" or "democratic" in the sense of including the views of all affected parties and affording them equal weight and legitimacy.[22]

It is one thing to note society's failure in practice to fulfill such values as "public" or "democratic" debate and the consideration of all viewpoints, and to disclose the ways in which rhetorical aspirations to such values have frequently masked practices that actually undermine them. But it is very difficult to see what could follow, educationally, from their wholesale rejection.

We do not question for a moment the relations of dominance, or histories of conflict and hostility, or gulfs of non-understanding or misunderstanding across differences, that undercut conventional educational aims and practices. Indeed, identifying and criticizing these is the necessary starting point for any new thinking on the problems of education. But unless one conceives freedom only negatively (as the mere avoidance or removal of such impediments), it is not clear what follows from this critique for educational or political practice. Antimodernism lacks a clear conception of a "positive freedom" that identifies social conditions in which freer thought and action are possible; lacking this, antimodernism has not been able to articulate a clear and defensible educational theory.

As we have noted, many writers exhibit both postmodern and antimodern tendencies, and their positions tend to slide back and forth between the two views. The argument that traditional modernist principles are inadequate or ineffective, and so need to be reformulated and regrounded on less absolutistic premises, is frequently conflated with the position that these principles are inherently illegitimate and ought to be abandoned entirely. We will further develop this point later.

These two critical vantage points pose strong challenges to educational thought and practice: the deconstruction of conventional claims to knowledge and authority; the analysis and critique of the power relations underlying traditional educational aims and practices; and the insistence that we abandon presumptions of homogeneity and acknowledge the real and possibly unbridgeable gulfs of diversity among people. The view we have termed postmodernism has sought to turn these critiques toward an alternative conception of education based partly on the reformulation of selected modernist principles such as democracy or self-determination, but without sharing modernist assumptions, such as a belief in progress or the rational rule of law. The view we have termed antimodernism has, on the other hand, been largely content with emphasizing points of critique. The educational practices that are generated from the antimodern perspective seem largely dependent upon the preferences of those who advance them. This is not necessarily to denigrate such practices, but merely to stress, again, that antimodernism cannot justify them by reference to generalizable values. As a result, value assumptions that actually do underlie these practices are frequently left implicit and unexamined.

As noted, one concern shared by both postmodern and antimodern writers has been the question of *difference*. The rejection of metanarratives has often been taken to imply what Bauman calls an "ineradicable plurality" of languages and worldviews, a conclusion especially prominent in antimodern arguments. At this point we want to turn to a detailed discussion of "difference" and dialogue. In the process, we hope to show how certain postmodern conceptions of difference yield more fruitful educational implications than do antimodern conceptions.

Difference and *Différance*

The notion of "difference" appealed to in this literature derives primarily from Jacques Derrida, although originating in Saussurian linguistics. For Ferdinand de Saussure, it was the *difference* between two signifiers that allowed them to serve as such; this difference is, typically, arbitrary and meaningless in and of itself—but there must be some difference between signifiers for them to work. To pick a very simple instance, O and Q are quite similar shapes, distinguished only by a small mark that is present in one, absent in the other; yet they are distinct letters (in English). But precisely the same mark added, say, as a flourish at the end of a word written in cursive, may not constitute a significant difference. Which differences mean something is entirely a consequence of how those differences exist in the context of a system of differences; a point of difference only *makes* a difference under specific circumstances. While often intrinsically arbitrary, the overall significance of a mark of difference, for Saussure, can be analyzed objectively.

Derrida coined the term *différance* to identify a different sort of difference. For Derrida, what constitutes a significant difference (*différance*) is a changing determination; a differentiating factor is not merely an arbitrary and "passive" element in a sign system, but also an "active," context-sensitive variant:

> [*Différance*] is a structure and a movement no longer conceivable on the basis of the opposition presence/absence. *Différance* is the systematic play of difference, of the traces of difference, of the *spacing* by means of which elements are related to each other. This spacing is the simultaneously active and passive . . . production of the intervals without which the "full" terms would not signify, would not function.[23]

Derrida's analysis constitutes a rejection of formalism, and an assertion of the dynamic character of all signification. In place of Saussure's abstract analysis of relational structures, Derrida and other poststructuralists insist that the *relations* that bind and the *spaces* that distinguish cultural elements are themselves in constant interaction, so that—as for Werner Karl Heisenberg's measures of motion and position for subatomic particles—each changes as one attempts to fix the other. For Derrida, this simultaneity of passive and active elements in signification is tied to a larger rejection of the Saussurian dichotomy of *langue* (formal language) and *parole* (discourse, or practical speech).[24] Formal analysis is insufficient to describe the practical elements of interpretation and judgment that give language its meaning in use; furthermore, any particular formalization is for Derrida nothing more than the momentary crystallization and institutionalization of one particular set of rules and norms—others are always possible.

Extended now into the domain of social or political theories, this concept of *différance* denies the purely external and formal assignment of persons to membership in a sociological category or position in the social structure by virtue of some characteristic they possess; it pertains as well to the active, subjective process of identification with a group, and all that signifies to the subject. Any overall theory that seeks to identify from the outside the differences that classify people must fail, on this view, because it excludes these active processes of group identification and the formation of subjectivity. To put it simply, there are differences we choose, and differences we do not choose. However, the active/passive tension in Derrida's original term has been lost in certain recent appropriations of *différance;* often, as in the earlier quote from Bronwyn Davies, *all* differences are regarded as mere constructions, as expressions of the subjective process of identity-formation—there are no differences that we don't choose. Christine Di Stefano terms this the "dilemma of difference": how to identify a basis for specifying which differences matter, whether we choose them or not. She asks, "Are some differences more basic than others?"[25]

The postmodern/antimodern distinction is helpful here. On the one hand, postmodernism provides strong reasons for valuing diversity, for not assuming homogeneity when it does not exist, and for avoiding modes of discursive and nondiscursive practice that implicitly or explicitly exclude subjects who do not participate in dominant modes of thought, speech, and action. This position might even be pushed a step further, to insist that, given occasions of conflict and misunderstanding, we ought to err on the side of respecting the self-identification and worldview of others, especially for members of groups who have been traditionally *told* who they are, what is true, and what is good for them.

However, at some points in the literature, this position lapses over into claims that are much more problematic. Specifically, the celebration of difference becomes a presumption of incommensurability, a denial of the possibility of intersubjective understanding, and an exaggerated critique that *any* attempt to establish reasonable and consensual discourse across difference inevitably involves the imposition of dominant groups' values, beliefs, and modes of discourse upon others. These views are antimodern in their rejection of such goals as dialogue, reasonableness, and fair treatment of alternative points of view; such legacies of the modernist tradition are not only regarded as difficult and sometimes impossible to attain—which they are—but as actually undesirable ends.

In our view, this antimodernist position is unsustainable either intellectually or practically. It derives from a deep misunderstanding of the nature of difference and has counter-educational implications for pedagogy. The literature that espouses this view is often internally contradictory, suggesting that such a severe critique is difficult to sustain consistently; many authors who advocate strong antimodern critiques later find themselves reversing direction when the time comes to offer positive recommendations. We want to analyze these inconsistencies in antimodern treatments of difference, and show how a more defensible post modern understanding of difference can support and inform a broadened conception of education.

The difficulty of sustaining a consistent antimodern analysis of difference can be seen in Ellsworth's essay. At one point, she argues a strong antimodern thesis:

> Dialogue . . . consists of ground rules for classroom interaction using language. These rules include the assumptions that all members have equal opportunity to speak, all members respect other members' right to

speak and feel safe to speak, and all ideas are tolerated and subjected to rational critical assessment against fundamental judgement and moral principles. . . . Dialogue in its conventional sense is impossible in the culture at large because at this historical moment, power relations between raced, classed, and gendered students and teachers are unjust.[26]

For Ellsworth, modernist aims such as pluralism and open discussion are considered fond illusions—or worse, actual instruments of control and dominance. Yet elsewhere in the same essay, she says:

> If you can talk to me in ways that show you understand that your knowledge of me, the world, and the "Right thing to do" will always be partial, interested, and potentially oppressive to others, and if I can do the same, then we can work together on shaping and reshaping alliances for constructing circumstances in which students of difference can thrive.[27]

Thus at times it seems that dialogue across differences is *not* possible in a nonoppressive way, and at other times that it *is* possible, but only if we conceive of dialogue differently. We agree with Ellsworth that a reconstructed conception of dialogue is achievable only when we recognize the barriers to dialogue "in its conventional [modernist] sense." But Ellsworth appears not to recognize that her latter position is a *reaffirmation* of such modernist values as "all members have equal opportunity to speak, all members respect other members' right to speak and feel safe to speak, and all ideas are tolerated. . . ." Indeed, it is not clear what "dialogue" could mean without them. This example shows how antimodern and postmodern positions are often intermingled, and how "rejected" modern concepts or principles often reappear in a new guise.[28]

The antimodern view of difference is also unsustainable practically. We can see this problem clearly in a recent essay by Iris Young. Young rejects the ideal of community, which she argues "privileges unity over difference, immediacy over mediation, sympathy over recognition of the limits of one's understanding of others from their point of view."[29] She vigorously rejects the goal of intersubjective understanding, in which "persons will cease to be opaque, other, not understood, and instead become fused, mutually sympathetic, understanding one another as they understand themselves. . . . Political theorists and activists should distrust this desire for reciprocal recognition and identification with others."[30] Instead she calls for a "politics of difference," based on the positive experiences of "modern urban life." Having criticized previous models of community as "wildly utopian and undesirable," she then posits "a vision of the good society. Our political ideal is the unoppressive city."[31]

> City life is the "being together" of strangers. Strangers encounter one another, either face to face or through media, often remaining strangers and yet acknowledging their contiguity in living and the contributions each makes to the others. In such encounters people are not "internally" re-

lated, as the community theorists would have it, and do not understand one another from within their own perspective. They are externally related, they experience each other as other, different, from different groups, histories, professions, cultures, which they do not understand.[32]

We believe that this position is fundamentally inconsistent. We do not disagree at all with "celebrating the distinctive cultures and characteristics of different groups,"[33] but merely point out that the very reason for celebrating such differences is based on the ability of different groups to (a) co-exist nonviolently and (b) interact in a way that enriches and invigorates each other's lives. These values *assume* some ability to communicate and coordinate actions across differences. *There is no reason to assume that dialogue across differences involves either eliminating those differences or imposing one group's views on others; dialogue that leads to understanding, cooperation, and accommodation can sustain differences within a broader compact of toleration and respect.* Thus what we need is not an antimodern denial of community, but a postmodern grounding of community on more flexible and less homogeneous assumptions.[34]

Does the lack of a single master metanarrative lead automatically to the conclusion that any attempt at consensus or common understanding depends on the imposition of one particularistic view over another (as Bauman, Ellsworth, and Young fear), or can a dialogical relation be established and maintained even across significant cultural or political differences?

Three important conceptual points about difference help to address these questions. First, any concrete discussion of difference also implies *sameness:* two objects, two people, two points of view, and so on, can be contrasted usefully only when there are at least some respects in which they are similar. To paraphrase Lewis Carroll, no one seriously asks the difference between a raven and a writing-desk. Two different political outlooks, or two racial groups, or two sexual orientations often have as many common elements as they do differences, although the differences are perhaps more salient to the people concerned—indeed, it is often their points of similarity that make the members all the more aware of their differences. Second, and following from this, "difference" is a relative term, depending on one's frame of reference. An essential point of difference that divides two groups or persons from each other, however crucial it may seem to them, might seem marginal, even arbitrary, seen from a third point of view; from this point of view, the similarities between the two will be much more striking than the differences. Highlighting criteria of difference across subgroups should not be allowed to obscure co-existing criteria of similarity across those groups. Third, clustering members of a larger group into subgroups of difference is the same, conceptually, as identifying similarities among each subgroup's members. Thus, an exclusive focus on difference is logically inconsistent—again, difference *implies* sameness. In general, then, we recommend a framework that regards difference and sameness as being in constant interaction with one another; whether one sees a particular cultural element as a signifier of difference or sameness is a highly dynamic and contextual judgment.

None of this is meant to deny or minimize the fact of difference, or the barriers of conflict and misunderstanding difference can create; but these observations should make us cautious about reifying difference or elevating it to the primary position in our analysis of social and political relations. It is understandable why postmodern and antimodern writers have generally emphasized points of difference as a corrective to monolithic and dominating presumptions of homogeneity, and to the imposition of one subgroup's worldview as the "neutral" or "universal" one, which forces other subgroups either to accept the imposed view as their own or to remain silent. But having stressed certain valid criticisms as a corrective it is important not to exaggerate them to the point that they become implausible and counterproductive.

Of course, much of this analysis will sound familiar to readers of John Dewey. Dewey argued that democracy was marked by two kinds of communicative diversity. While he fully understood that the existence of cultural subcommunities was a necessary, and desirable, feature of any large society, he believed that a society could be democratic only to the extent that (a) these subcommunities defined themselves over a range of common concerns, not only over single-issue identifications, and (b) these subcommunities maintained some degree of communication among them, where broader social concerns affect them all.[35]

Clearly, these subcommunities are not all equal partners in the social commonwealth; there are dimensions of power and privilege that divide them and set their interests in conflict.[36] Furthermore, communication across such subcommunities is not simply a matter of good will and persistent effort, and it is unrealistic and unfair to ask groups already put upon also to take on the burden of trying to understand, and make themselves understood by, those who harm them or benefit from their deprivation. Modernism has tended to emphasize universality over particularity and concreteness, and to overlook the ways in which power operates in dialogic relations; it has therefore been overly secure in assuming that fair and equitable consensus can be reached. By taking seriously precisely those matters glossed over in much of modernism, postmodernism makes us more sensitive to the possibility of incommensurability and radical misunderstanding. Public forums are not as open as they may appear from the modern perspective, and it would be naive to think that everyone feels (or *is*) free to speak in such contexts.

Nevertheless, there must be *some* forums in which such discussions are seriously undertaken, and there must be *some* individuals from each group who are prepared to take on the burden (and risk) of attempting some degree of communication and translation across the gulf that divides them. Our concern here is with what the benefits of such an effort might be and with how an attempt at dialogue across differences might proceed, even as we acknowledge the difficulties and the prospects for both failure and success inherent in the endeavor. The tendency to judge the outcome of dialogical encounters prior to their actual occurrence, whether optimistically or pessimistically, are the twin errors of modernism and antimodernism; neither consensus nor incommensurability can be assumed in advance.

Is Dialogue across Differences Worthwhile? Is It Possible?

Three prospective kinds of benefit can be derived from dialogue across differences: those related to the construction of identity along lines that are more flexible without becoming arbitrary; those related to broadening our understanding of others and, through this, our understanding of ourselves; and those related to fostering more reasonable and sustainable communicative practices. We would like to elaborate these areas of potential benefit in this section.

The first benefit derives from Dewey's conception of democracy. To the extent that group identification is an element in the formation of personal identity, one's identity will be more flexible, autonomous, and stable to the degree that one recognizes one's self as a member of various different subcommunities simultaneously. Such simultaneous identification can, at its extremes, produce internal conflict and a feeling of "cultural schizophrenia," but more frequently it has a beneficial effect in fostering a broader and more inclusive sense of one's self and one's relations to others. From a societal standpoint, such multiple group identifications also make possible the establishment of relations of negotiation, cooperation, and pursuit of common interests (where they exist), which tends to promote mutual tolerance and the nonviolent resolution of conflicts. Admittedly, such communicative efforts may often fail, and in some instances they may heighten rather than resolve tensions: understanding across differences does not necessarily entail agreement, and in some cases greater communication will make conflicts between groups all the more apparent. There is no reason, however, to *presume* this outcome, and weighed against this outcome are the many instances in which commonalities of interest can be, at least provisionally, identified.

Second, the anthropological categories of "emic" and "etic" perspectives (or similar categories) have often been exaggerated in discussions of dialogue across differences. Like the categories of sameness and difference, they have been too sharply dichotomized, and one perspective has been falsely prioritized over the other. The emic perspective is a group's own; the etic perspective is that of the outsider.[37] In the literature, the emic perspective has frequently been elevated to the "correct" or only legitimate interpretation of the meaning and significance of a group's beliefs and practices.[38] This view has been beneficial in some respects. It highlights the ways in which cultural meanings are internally constructed, situated in webs of signification that fully make sense only to initiates within that system. It heightens our sensitivity to the diversity of human cultures, and to how the "same" thing might look and feel quite different to members of different cultural groups. It prepares us for the possibility of radical misunderstanding, and should make us extremely modest and cautious about *imposing* an interpretive frame from one group onto another. Finally, it should make us err, if we are going to err, on the side of crediting and respecting a group's self-understanding when it seriously conflicts with our own—especially when dealing with a group already at a disadvantage in the communicative relation.[39]

Yet at the same time, these benefits should not be taken to mean that all etic perspectives are illegitimate. Sometimes an external perspective is helpful *precisely because* it is different from that of the group itself. This point has often been ignored in the literature. While it is a problem that certain privileged external groups' perspectives have tended to override other groups' internal ones so that the credibility of internal perspectives may need to be valorized as a corrective, this corrective has often been extended to the unhelpful extreme that external perspectives are inherently taken to be coercive and imperialistic. Both as individuals and groups, we can broaden and enrich our self-understanding by considering our beliefs, values, and actions from a fresh standpoint. This endeavor can yield what Walter Feinberg calls "reflective moments," opportunities for deeper self-understanding and a release from the commonsense assumptions that typically frame our daily existence.[40] This does not require embracing the other standpoint or letting it supersede our own, but it does stress the value of incorporating that perspective into a more complex and multifaceted framework of understanding.

Moreover, given the relativity of what constitutes a "difference" in the first place, the scope and limits of what we consider significant differences may change when dialogue is sustained over time; we may find a convergence of certain interests, and discover additional points of similarity or differences. All of this is to the better, if we value breadth and complexity in human understanding. Such considerations provide a second incentive for pursuing dialogue across differences.

Third, the very activity of pursuing and maintaining dialogue across differences can foster in us more general dispositions and practices of communication that help support more successful communicative relations with a variety of people over time. Attempting dialogue across difference, and persisting in the attempt even when it becomes difficult, develops such "communicative virtues" as tolerance, patience, and a willingness to listen. As a process, dialogue requires us to re-examine our own presuppositions and to compare them against quite different ones; to make us less dogmatic about the belief that the way the world appears to us is necessarily the way the world is.

However, effort and good will alone are not guarantees; dialogue is fallible. Yet even failed attempts at dialogue across differences can teach us something—that persistence does not resolve all conflicts, that some problems are not solvable but only manageable, and that a level of mystery and perplexity accompanies all attempts at human understanding. Such realizations foster in us a healthy modesty about the possibilities and limits of our communicative efforts.[41]

We have argued here for the benefits of establishing dialogue across differences where possible, and the value of pursuing it even when it turns out not to be possible. But is it ever possible?

A fascinating account of the pursuit of dialogue across differences has been offered by the Feminist Alliance Project in the Netherlands.[42] The goal of this project was to "nurture personal change, political strength, and theoretical understanding of divisions between women."[43] Parallel "alliance groups" were formed among 100 women differing in terms of race, sexual orientation, and whether or not they were Jewish. Each group originally was internally differentiated across one of these three dimensions, in order to identify "multiple interlocking identities and oppressions."[44] For example, one group emphasized Black versus White relations, although within each racial group there was diversity along other dimensions. Their paper describes the processes by which these groups attempted to develop understanding and solidarity across such similarities and differences. These efforts were not entirely successful: "In every group past experiences with oppression and domination distorted the participants' perceptions of the present and blocked their identification with people in common political situations who did not share their history."[45] Various clusters of women opted for meeting in more homogeneous subgroups: for example, some Black women chose to meet only with other Black women; then Black lesbians wanted to meet separately from *that* group in a more homogeneous subgroup of their own. (The extreme extension of this logic, which is virtually mandated by strong theories of difference, would, of course, be absurd.) Overall, however, the project was successful in improving dialogue and understanding across differences: participants concluded the project with assessments such as, "I have less of a chip on my shoulder. I used to feel 'poor me, or lucky me, nobody knows what it feels like to be me' and now I'm better able to communicate naturally about my life and to expect respect from others."[46] This example illustrates several important points about the possibilities, limits, and potential benefits of dialogue across differences. The first is that success is a partial and provisional human achievement; it is neither guaranteed by the existence of good intentions, nor precluded by the existence of serious differences. Second, the activities we might pursue to promote dialogue, such as encouraging the formation of subgroups to provide greater confidence and self-awareness when participants go back into large groups, may actually impede that goal by promoting greater separatism. Third, though, is that the greater our awareness of and sensitivity to dimensions of difference, the *stronger* the imperative to pursue means of understanding across them. The participants in the alliance groups, for example, repeatedly noted that it was through encountering women experiencing other dimensions of oppression that they gained a fuller appreciation of their own situation.

Thus the problem of "difference" poses a challenge, but not an insurmountable challenge, to the possibilities of dialogue. Antimodern arguments that rhetorically write off the very possibility of dialogue run the danger of being true, but in a self-confirming way, since if the effort to engage others across difference is never seriously made, it certainly can never succeed. And, as Nancy Hartsock has pointed out, it is exceedingly ironic that at the very time that traditionally disadvantaged groups are beginning to find their voice, an epistemological view has gained currency that legitimates relativizing their claims to credibility and respect.[47]

Earlier, we argued that there must be some forums in which such dialogue across differences is valued, and in which it is pursued by participants in good faith, even in the face of difficulty and initial misunderstanding. We believe that educational contexts potentially provide one such forum. Public schools and universities are certainly no more free from social and political conflict and patterns of domination than are any other institutions, but they do generally espouse and frequently enact a commitment—particularly at the university level—to the value of communication across difference and the benefits of encountering new and challenging points of view. All of the barriers and difficulties cited by postmodern and antimodern critics remain, but the wholesale abandonment of the possibility of overcoming them is tantamount to an abandonment of the goal of education itself. The practical questions that should concern educators are: What positive conditions make dialogue across differences possible? What can educators do to promote those conditions? What is realistic to expect from such communicative encounters? We would like to conclude by discussing several of these practical matters. Such questions are not unique to education, but they are crucial to the determination of whether education is worth the effort.[48]

Educational Aims and Hopes

The Varieties of Difference

If dialogue across difference is to succeed, sensitivity is required to the various kinds of diversity one may encounter. Differences that may not be apparent to, or salient for, others may be paramount in the minds of the individuals at hand. Difference is not simply a matter of sociological group membership, but also of the constructed worldview and subjectivity of the persons who enter a dialogical relation; thus "difference" (or its absence) cannot always be inferred or assumed from the outside. As Lisa Delpit argued, we should try to consider the elements of difference that might affect the communicative possibilities in a particular encounter from the point of view of the parties involved. We should elicit and respect their self-identifications, and admit to ourselves the limits of our ability to identify with, or make inferences about, the subjectivity of others.

Playing what Peter Elbow calls "the believing game" is one way to begin this effort. The believing game involves taking the attitude that we stand to learn from what another has to say, and that we should grant the other's claims a provisional plausibility simply based on the fact that those claims are sincerely held. This attitude does not preclude questioning the other's self-expression at some later point, but it places the priority on establishing a communicative relation of trust and openness, and of trying to err on the side of sympathy and respectfulness when discussions first begin. Mary Belenky and her coauthors term this a "connected" form of knowing, because it places the interest in forming a particular type of relation ahead of purely intellectual interests.[49]

Such efforts are necessary, but not sufficient, to insure communicative success. The situation we face might be "inherently polysemous," to use Bauman's phrase, and jumping to the conclusion that one has understood the concerns and outlooks of another may simply constitute another form of presumptuousness and arrogance. But, as we have said repeatedly, this valuable insight has sometimes been exaggerated to *assume* the impossibility of such understanding. Admittedly, there are contexts of hostility, resentment, or domination in which only further harm can be done by attempts to communicate across conflicts and gulfs of misunderstanding. We do not wish for a moment to deny that more harm can and often does occur, or to posit the naive hope that if we just keep speaking with one another all conflicts can be resolved. But neither do we want to posit, on theoretical grounds, a society of Babel that no one can seriously desire.

Incommensurability and Translation

As noted, dialogue across differences can run up against deep linguistic, cultural, or paradigmatic incommensurabilities. The frustrating experience of radical misunderstanding or non-understanding is familiar to us all. In certain cases, the gulf of misunderstanding might be so deep and wide that on specific points no meeting of the minds is possible, even at the level of mutual comprehension, let alone agreement.

But in addressing this problem, we need to keep in mind that dialogue across differences has two different aspects. On one hand, dialogue aims at the reconciliation of differences or the formation of new common meanings in pursuit of intersubjective understanding. Antimodern writers often deny the possibility of attaining intersubjectivity across differences, and regard the pursuit of such an end as threatening the elimination of differences or the domination of one particular perspective over others. This concern is supported by social and historical experiences in which the language of commonality, community, and consensus has simply masked the presumption or imposition of homogeneity, despite real diversity. But it is possible to acknowledge that threat, and work to avoid it, without giving up the hope of achieving some degree of intersubjectivity and common understanding. As Paulo Freire, Hans-Georg Gadamer, Jurgen Habermas, and numerous others have argued, dialogue can proceed in a manner that aims toward careful, respectful, non-dominating agreement.[50]

The ordinary experience of translation across natural languages tells us that the usual case is that effective common meanings *can* be established, and that sufficient equivalencies can be built over time so that speakers of any two languages can achieve a significant degree of mutual understanding and effective coordination of action. Translation does not need to be complete or perfect for this to occur. This point about natural languages can be extended to other cultural and paradigmatic systems as well.[51] The occasional experience of radical incommensurability should not obscure the much more important point that, despite enormous diversity, our ways of thinking and speaking about our world also exhibit striking commonalities. These commonalities give us some reason to pursue attempts at overcoming misunderstandings or non-understandings when they do occur, rather than abandoning the effort because it is assumed to be futile. Moreover, even where the goal of common understanding or consensus may not be achievable, a second aspect of dialogue across differences must be kept in mind.

Creating or establishing common meanings is not the only possible goal. In this second aspect, dialogue is non-convergent, directed not toward conformity and agreement but toward understanding, tolerance, and respect across difference. Even if one rejects dialogue in the first sense described above, there still remains dialogue in this second sense—and, indeed, as we have stressed, the possibility and desirability of dialogue in at least this latter sense is *assumed*, not denied, by positions that "celebrate difference." Moreover, the conflicts and tensions that exist in a complex society require more than the mere "acknowledgement of contiguity" that Young recommends. We need some way of coping with our differences and, if we are committed to a democratic form of life, a means of making discussions about such matters *more* inclusive, not less so.

Rethinking Dialogue

Dialogue, therefore, offers paths both to establishing intersubjectivity and consensus, and to creating a degree of understanding across (unresolved) differences. Recognizing this carries us beyond the conception of dialogue as a single, convergent method aimed toward Truth. Dialogue can also serve the purpose of creating partial understandings, if not agreement, across differences. Complete understanding and total incomprehensibility are not the only two alternatives—indeed, both of these are quite rare. At a deeper level, we need to realize that *understanding and misunderstanding always occur together*. No communication process is perfect; no intersubjective understanding, even among members who occupy the same category of difference, is ever complete. Moreover, it is by the very process of "misunderstanding" others—that is, interpreting their claims and beliefs in slightly different terms than they do themselves—that the process of communication actually moves forward to new understandings. This is partly why we engage in conversation. We need to be similar enough to make dialogue possible, but we also need to be different enough to make it worthwhile.

Thus, dialogue can take the form of *maintaining* difference, not trying to eliminate it. Once one embarks in a dialogical exchange, various degrees of convergent or divergent understandings might result. These can be seen along a spectrum comprising:

a. agreement and consensus, identifying beliefs or values all parties can agree to;

b. not agreement, but a common understanding in which the parties do not agree, but establish common meanings in which to discuss their differences;

c. not a common understanding, but an understanding of differences in which the parties do not entirely bridge these differences, but through analogies of experience or other indirect translations can understand, at least in part, each other's positions;

    d. little understanding, but a respect across differences, in which the parties do not fully understand one another, but by each seeing that the other has a thoughtful, conscientious position, they can come to appreciate and respect even positions they disagree with;

    e. irreconcilable and incommensurable difference.

Some antimodern writers argue as if denying the possibility of "a" leaves one only with "e" as an alternative. We have argued that a range of possibilities, of degrees of understanding and misunderstanding, can result, and that the sorts of understandings that will or will not result cannot be prejudged. We must be prepared to deal with the possibility of "e," but there is no reason to assume it.

    This discussion of dialogue across difference assumes a pragmatic, contextual, fallibilistic approach that is in our view a helpful corrective to some of the excesses of antimodern discussions. We should not allow our theoretical abstractions to obscure or override the ordinary experiences of our daily lives. It will not be evident, *a priori* and at a purely intellectual level whether dialogue in a particular circumstance will or will not be possible, or *how much* understanding will be necessary for our purposes. We may remember vividly the frustrations and pains caused by previous breakdowns of understanding, but it is in attempting to communicate across differences that we discover whether it is possible or not. As noted earlier, the presumption that incommensurability is inevitable threatens to be self-confirming, since when efforts at understanding are not made, are made half-heartedly, or are abandoned when they become difficult or discouraging, then incommensurability does indeed result—but it results as a psychological/social consequence, not because of any inherent necessity.

Context and Personal History

When possible, communicative situations of difference also need to be entered with a sense of the context and personal histories that inform the various parties' outlooks on the situation. Stereotypes about the other parties to a discussion, or degrees of skepticism that might be based on failures experienced in previous attempts, cannot be wished away. Prior experiences may have created feelings of intimidation, resentment, and hurt; an imposition of silence, or the self-imposed habit of silence, may be ingrained in some of the participants. Conversely, prior experiences may also have created feelings of superiority and a tendency to silence others.

    Such factors, especially when they become self-perpetuating, can be serious barriers to successful communication. One starting point in overcoming such barriers is eliciting and honoring the self-expressions of previously silenced partners. This effort can be self-generating: attaining some degree of successful self-expression and mutual understanding creates, in part, the conditions of confidence and trust in which future attempts might be carried further (just as failures can reinforce skepticism about the possibility of success, or the value of even trying).

Another aspect of the effects of context and personal history among the participants in a discussion is the prejudgments they might have formed about one another. Successful communication, and understanding across differences, does not in itself reconcile all differences and conflicts—indeed it may draw them all the more sharply. But it can help draw them in terms that are more accurate, and make us more cognizant of the factors and rationales that have given rise to them.

The university setting, while based on certain broad norms of tolerance and open communication, is not by any means exempt from these constraints. We see a strong contemporary illustration of these issues in recent arguments over the possibilities and limits of "free speech" on college campuses.[52] While clearly dependent on tolerance of controversial and even inflammatory points of view, universities have begun struggling with the problem of how, given the conflicts and prejudices of the broader society, the exercise of certain kinds of speech (for example, racial epithets) might actually *restrict* the freedom of others to feel secure enough to participate in the broader educational conversation. Such tensions illustrate the real social and political context in which specific educational choices need to be made; they set competing values and interests against one another, and there is no guarantee that the compromises made to further dialogue will or can serve all points of view equally. The practical choices here are rarely clear-cut, and more talking is not always the best thing.

Communicative Virtues

Such external, institutional factors, and the presumptions that the participants to a dialogical situation bring with them, provide a context that often limits the kinds and degrees of understanding that can be achieved in the discussion. But the success of dialogue across differences also depends on what we have called "communicative virtues" that help make dialogue possible and help sustain the dialogical relation over time. These virtues include tolerance, patience, respect for differences, a willingness to listen, the inclination to admit that one may be mistaken, the ability to reinterpret or translate one's own concerns in a way that makes them comprehensible to others, the self-imposition of restraint in order that others may "have a turn" to speak, and the disposition to express one's self honestly and sincerely. The possession of these virtues influences one's capacities both to express one's own beliefs, values, and feelings accurately, and to listen to and hear those of others.[53]

These virtues do not reflect a preferred linguistic style per se, but rather express an affective and intellectual stance toward partners in conversation; they promote a generous and sympathetic regard for the perspectives and self-expression of others. The point of stressing the communicative virtues is not to advance a particular educational or political agenda over others, but rather to suggest the dispositions that seem necessary for promoting any open and serious discussion about such matters. If a tentative agreement about how we ought to proceed educationally is to be inclusive in any meaningful sense, then it will require dialogue expressive of the communicative virtues. This is not to say that the communicative virtues provide a "solution" to the difficulties and inequalities that exist in many communicative situations, or that making our dialogical relations more expressive of the communicative virtues is only a matter of good will and personal effort. We wish merely to suggest that if dialogue across differences is equitable, it must be animated by such virtues.

A central question for education, then, is how such communicative virtues are developed and how they can be sustained over time. In our view, these dispositions are created, reflexively, in the kinds of communicative relations in which we are engaged, as children and into adult life. The nature of these virtues is that they are only acquired in relation to communicative partners, and improved by practice. Thus, to develop these virtues is to be drawn into certain kinds of communicative relations: one becomes tolerant, patient, and respecting of others through association with people who are similarly disposed.

Virtues require close attention to the particulars of the communicative situation at hand, and how any of them are expressed will vary according to what these situations require. Listening, for example, although generally regarded as a virtue in situations where one's partner is struggling with ideas that he or she wants to articulate, might not be so regarded in situations where urgently needed directions or information are asked for, or where silence signals acquiescence to views one does not actually hold. Similarly, tolerance and patience may be virtues when practiced by a teacher striving to understand and appreciate a student's perspective, but not so when invoked to protect racist or sexist speech that intimidates, harms, or silences others. Hence, these communicative qualities are best thought of as virtues or dispositions rather than rules, precisely because they need to be interpreted and applied thoughtfully to different situations.

Educational contexts foster some communicative virtues, but also foster habits and dispositions that interfere with effective communicative relations. The academic culture often rewards acquiring an aggressive style of communication, epitomized by an "adversary method" that assumes that the best way to evaluate another's ideas or arguments is to subject them to rigorous and severe questioning.[54] This communicative style impedes dialogue in many situations, especially given contexts of previous frustration, insecurity, or silencing. Nurturing communicative virtues in ourselves and in our students requires that we acknowledge these and other habits of speech that may work against our best intentions. While owning up to what we bring to a dialogic encounter does not ensure that we will actually practice the communicative virtues appropriate to that encounter, certainly such critical-self-awareness is a step toward changing our practices.

The value of developing and sustaining the communicative virtues in ourselves and in others provides another justification for why dialogue across differences is worthwhile, even when it is difficult. Indeed, it is precisely because of the difficulty of such situations that we stand to learn from them. There are benefits to be derived from conversations with those like us, but there are benefits also to be gained from persisting in discussions with those not like us. The communicative virtues can be enhanced by pursuing and persisting in a variety of conversations, even with reluctant partners. Yet it is also important to accept, in some contexts at least, that chosen silence can be a mode of self-expression, and that it may constitute a necessary phase of self-protection before future communication can occur.[55]

Conclusion

One of the essential communicative virtues, we believe, is a tolerance and respect across differences. There is no doubt that one of the essential personal characteristics that pre-exists and predetermines educational possibilities within a given setting is the attitude of the participants, not only to the particular differences that may divide them, but also toward the very fact of difference itself. Sometimes there are tendencies to approach opposing points of view with suspicion, fear, or scorn; these attitudes may arise from intolerance and prejudice, or from previous painful encounters with such points of view. There may be a tendency to infer from certain differences the likeliness of other kinds of conflict; to prejudge, for example, that a person will be unreasonable or insensitive to one's concerns because they are a member of a particular group. We have discussed already how these sorts of prejudgments can prevent discussion by assuming that dialogue across differences cannot occur, or will have little benefit if it does occur.

Such attitudes place a serious constraint on the possibilities of dialogue, and education generally. In this article, we have tried to present a more pragmatic view of dialogue, stressing the ways in which dialogical relations need to be formed, protected, and developed over time; specifically, in education, we often need to focus more on the formation and development of particular communicative relations, devoted to inquiry and understanding, than on specific predetermined learning outcomes. A central feature of these sorts of relations is coming to regard differences as providing educational opportunities, not as intimidating barriers. We learn by making connections between what we know and what is new to us: this cognitive process is paralleled, and fostered developmentally, by the communicative relations in which we are engaged from a very early age.

Our point in this article is that certain postmodern, and particularly antimodern, tendencies in educational theory have worked against the goal of trying to achieve understanding across differences. There is a fundamental shift in worldview between regarding difference as a problem, a threat, a nuisance, or an insurmountable barrier, and viewing difference—any difference—as an opportunity, as a challenge to our abilities to communicate and understand. In this latter view, such differences, while difficult to overcome, can benefit our understanding of ourselves and others, to say nothing of its broader social benefits in terms of promoting social concord and cooperation. If we "celebrate difference," then we also need clear positive insights into how to maintain discussion across differences; such an endeavor is crucial socially, and especially educationally. We cannot stress this final point too strongly: pursuing dialogue across differences is essential to important aims of personal development and moral conduct. We ought to help foster the disposition to work toward understanding across differences, and the communicative virtues and skills that make this possible. Yet antimodern conceptions of difference often have the effect of discouraging the exercise of such virtues.

In contrast, we have argued for the need to maintain a pragmatic stance toward framing educational problems and our methods of coping with them. Some antimodern writing has fostered an "all or nothing" attitude on these matters. If complete intersubjectivity is not possible, then it is not possible at all. If some frustrating and painful experiences have been borne in the past, this justifies future avoidance of such difficulties. If some relations have been tainted by elements of domination and inequity, they cannot be reestablished on more humane and decent grounds. If misunderstanding or non-understanding are encountered, a deep and irresolvable incommensurability is inferred. These sorts of exaggerations unnecessarily prejudge the prospects of success or failure in communicative relations, which is usually counterproductive, sometimes self-fulfilling, and nearly always oversimplifies the problem and the best way to cope with it.

As we have said, we do not wish to minimize the deep suffering, intimidation, and sense of anger that experiences of domination create. Nor do we deny the frequent failures of dialogue across differences. But our educational goal must be to learn from these, to try to avoid them in future efforts, and to move beyond them; the last thing educational theorists should be doing is exaggerating them, reifying them, and, in the process, exacerbating them. Learning and developing as a person involves incorporating painful lessons, failures, and frustrations, without being paralyzed by them; it involves living with tensions, rather than striving to mask them with oversimplifications that might make the world seem more palatable.[56] And it may be this willingness to continue the conversation without certainty of success that constitutes the basis for a fruitful postmodern outlook on education: "This is the 'postmodern' task of the critical educator—to live with courage and conviction with the understanding that knowledge is always partial and incomplete."[57]

∽

Notes

* The authors wish to credit the helpful suggestions and criticisms of Walter Feinberg, Ralph Page, and Audrey Thompson.

1. We capitalize the term here and elsewhere in the paper for a reason, to be explained.

2. Bronwyn Davies, "Education for Sexism: A Theoretical Analysis of the Sex/Gender Bias in Education," *Educational Philosophy and Theory*, 21, No. 1 (1989), 8.

3. Patti Lather, "Postmodernism and the Politics of Enlightenment," *Educational Foundations*, 3, No. 3 (1989), 8–9.

4. Todd Gitlin, "Postmodernism Defined, At Last," *Utne Reader*, July–August 1989, p. 52.

5. See M. M. Bakhtin, "Discourse in the Novel," in *The Dialogic Imagination: Four Essays* (Austin: University of Texas Press, 1981), pp. 272–282. See also Richard A. Quantz and Terence O'Connor, "Writing Critical Ethnography: Dialogue, Multivoicedness, and Carnival in Cultural Texts," *Educational Theory, 38*, No. 1 (1988), 95–109.

6. See, for example, Angela P. Harris, "Race and Essentialism in Feminist Legal Theory," *Stanford Law Review, 48* (1990), 581–616.

7. Samuel Bowles and Herbert Gintis, *Schooling in Capitalist America: Educational Reform and the Contradictions of Economic Life* (New York: Basic Books, 1977).

8. It is increasingly problematic, in fact, even to identify a coherent "Left" any longer; titles such as "What's Left?" recur in progressive publications. But two general trends are clear. One is a shift away from Marxian-flavored Leftism, which emphasized the objectivity of class, race, and gender positions as the basis for political organization and action, to a more culturalist notion of political identity, in which ethnicity, sexual orientation, body type, etc., are given at least co-equal significance with class, race, and gender—and in which even those traditional groupings are regarded more as cultural constructions than as objective "givens." The second shift, correspondingly, is a deemphasis on the traditional stakes of Left struggle, via-a-vis capitalist industry and the state, toward "new social movements" that elevate what previously might have been considered "personal" or "lifestyle" issues to the new terrain of politico-cultural struggle. Postmodernism, generally speaking, is the ideology of this new conception of political identity and activism.

9. For an extremely useful overview of the tradition, see David Harvey, *The Condition of Postmodernity: An Inquiry into the Origins of Cultural Change* (Cambridge, MA: Basil Blackwell, 1989).

10. Jean-François Lyotard, *The Postmodern Condition: A Report on Knowledge* (Minneapolis: University of Minnesota Press, 1984). For clear summaries of Lyotard's view, see Nancy Fraser and Linda Nicholson, "Social Criticism Without Philosophy: An Encounter Between Feminism and Postmodernism," in *Universal Abandon? The Politics of Postmodernism*, ed. Andrew Ross (Minneapolis: University of Minnesota Press 1989), pp. 83–104; Carol Nicholson, "Postmodernism, Feminism, and Education: The Need for Solidarity," *Educational Theory, 39*, No. 3 (1989), 197–205; and Michael Peters, "Techno-Science, Rationality, and the University: Lyotard on the 'Postmodern Condition,'" *Educational Theory, 39*, No. 2 (1989), 93–105.

11. Zygmunt Bauman, "Strangers: The Social Construction of Universality and Particularity," *Telos, 28* (1988–1989), 23.

12. The main source for these ideas, of course, is Michel Foucault. See *Power/Knowledge: Selected Interviews and Other Writings, 1972–1977* (New York: Pantheon Books, 1980), and "On Power" in *Politics, Philosophy, Culture: Selected Interviews and Other Writings, 1977–1984* (New York: Routledge, 1988), pp. 96–109. In the educational literature, a very good overview and analysis of these issues is offered by Cleo Cherryholmes, *Power and Criticism: Poststructural Investigations in Education* (New York: Teachers College Press, 1988). See also Nicholas C. Burbules, "A Theory of Power in Education," *Educational Theory, 36*, No. 2 (1986), 95–114.

13. Lather, "Postmodernism and the Politics of Enlightenment," pp. 20–21.

14. Such a strong challenge to authority in all of its forms can be found in Elizabeth Ellsworth, "Why Doesn't This Feel Empowering? Working Through the Repressive Myths of Critical Pedagogy," *Harvard Educational Review, 59* (1989), 297–324.

15. Bauman, "Strangers," pp. 39–40.

16. Maria C. Lugones and Elizabeth V. Spelman, "Have We Got a Theory for You! Feminist Theory, Cultural Imperialism, and the Demand for 'The Women's Voice,'" *Women's Studies International Forum, 6*, No. 6 (1983), 575.

17. This criticism is posed by a number of authors, including Fraser and Nicholson, "Social Criticism Without Philosophy"; Nicholson, "Postmodernism, Feminism, and Education"; Jane Flax, "Postmodernism and Gender Relations in Feminist Theory," and Christine Di Stefano, "Dilemmas of Difference: Feminism, Modernity, and Postmodernism," in *Feminism/Postmodernism*, ed. Linda J. Nicholson (New York: Routledge, 1990), pp. 39–62, 63–82; see also Peter McLaren, "Postmodernity and the Death of Politics: A Brazilian Reprieve," *Educational Theory, 36*, No. 4 (1986), 389–401.

18. To clarify our discussion, and avoid confusion, we will from now on identify postmodernism—lower case—as one particular tendency within Postmodern thought, and cease to use the global—upper case—term. We do not think that "Postmodernism" is an accurate term for describing antimodern views.

19. For a range of postmodern views, see Linda Brodkey, "Postmodern Pedagogy for Progressive Educators," *Journal of Education, 169,* No. 3 (1987), 138–145; Henry A. Giroux, "Border Pedagogy in the Age of Postmodernism," *Journal of Education, 170,* No. 5 (1988), 162–181; Douglas Kellner, "Reading Images Critically: Toward a Postmodern Pedagogy," *Journal of Education, 170,* No. 3 (1988), 231–252; Peter McLaren, "Schooling the Postmodern Body: Critical Pedagogy and the Politics of Enfleshment," *Journal of Education, 170,* No. 5 (1988), 55–99; and Peter McLaren and Rhonda Hammer, "Critical Pedagogy and the Postmodern Challenge: Toward a Critical Postmodernist Pedagogy of Liberation," *Educational Foundations, 3,* No. 3 (1989), 29–62.

20. Henry A. Giroux, "Postmodernism and the Discourse of Educational Criticism," *Journal of Education, 170,* No. 3 (1988), 26–27, and republished in his book with Stanley Aronowitz, *Postmodern Education* (Minneapolis: University of Minnesota Press, 1991).

21. For example, see McLaren, "Postmodernity and the Death of Politics," pp. 393–394.

22. Ellsworth, "Why Doesn't This Feel Empowering?," pp. 301–302.

23. Jacques Derrida, *Positions* (Chicago: University of Chicago Press, 1981), p. 27.

24. Jacques Derrida, "Difference," in *Margins of Philosophy* (Chicago: University of Chicago Press, 1982), pp. 1–27.

25. Di Stefano, "Dilemmas of Difference," pp. 77–78.

26. Ellsworth, "Why Doesn't This Feel Empowering?," pp. 314, 316.

27. Ellsworth, "Why Doesn't This Feel Empowering?," p. 324. An airing of some of the issues raised by these comments can be found in an update to that article: "Correspondence," *Harvard Educational Review, 60* (1990), 388–403.

28. Similarly, Di Stefano identifies this tendency to slide between these two theoretical perspectives in the work of Sandra Harding, who asserts: "I argue for the primacy of fragmented identities but only for those *healthy* ones constructed on a *solid and non-defensive care identity,* and only within a *unified* opposition, a solidarity against the culturally dominant forces for unitarianism" (Di Stefano's emphases). As Di Stefano points out, criteria such as "healthy," "solid," and "core," all appeal implicitly to a thoroughly modern ontology (Di Stefano, "Dilemmas of Difference," pp. 76–77).

29. Iris Marion Young, "The Ideal of Community and the Politics of Difference," in Nicholson, *Feminism/Postmodernism,* p. 300.

30. Young, "The Ideal of Community," pp. 309, 311.

31. Young, "The Ideal of Community," pp. 316–317.

32. Young, "The Ideal of Community," p. 318.

33. Young, "The Ideal of Community," p. 319.

34. Indeed, like other antimodern writers, Young exhibits postmodern elements as well; returning later in the very same essay to the topic of "community," she admits that a communitarian ideal *can* be established that respects difference (p. 320). Hence, again, having vigorously "rejected" the ideal of community, it turns out that she actually only wants to reformulate it around certain values, such as tolerance for diversity, that are every bit as much *modern* as other values she wants to deny.

35. John Dewey, *Democracy and Education* (New York: Macmillan, 1916), pp. 95–97.

36. Burbules, "A Theory of Power in Education," pp. 97–99.

37. Pertti J. Pelto, *Anthropologist Research: The Structure of Inquiry* (New York: Harper & Row, 1970), pp. 67–88.

38. See, for example, Peter Winch, *The Meaning of a Social Science and Its Relation to Philosophy* (London: Routledge & Kegan Paul, 1958), pp. 107–108.

39. Lisa Delpit, "The Silenced Dialogue: Power and Pedagogy in Educating Other People's Children," *Harvard Educational Review, 58* (1988), 280–298; Ellsworth, "Why Doesn't This Feel Empowering?"

40. Walter Feinberg. "A Role for Philosophy of Education in Intercultural Research," in *Philosophy of Education 1989: Proceedings of the Forty-fifth Annual Meeting of the Philosophy of Education Society*, ed. Ralph Page (Normal, IL: Philosophy of Education Society, 1990), pp. 2–19.
41. Nicholas C. Burbules, "The Tragic Sense of Education," *Teachers College Record, 91*, No. 4 (1990), 468–479.
42. Gail Pheterson, "Alliances between Women: Overcoming Internalized Oppression and Internalized Domination," *Signs: Journal of Women in Culture and Society, 12*, No. 11 (1986), 146–160.
43. Pheterson, "Alliances between Women," p. 146.
44. Pheterson, "Alliances between Women," p. 157.
45. Pheterson, "Alliances between Women," p. 151.
46. Pheterson, "Alliances between Women," p. 158.
47. Nancy Hartsock, "Rethinking Modernism: Minority and Majority Theories," *Cultural Critique, 7* (1987), 187–206; see also Frances E. Mascis-Lees. Patricia Sharpe, and Colleen Ballerino Cohen, "The Postmodernist Turn in Anthropology: Cautions from a Feminist Perspective," *Journal of the Steward Anthropological Society, 17*, Nos. 1, 2 (1987–1988), 251–282.
48. Peter Elbow, *Embracing Contraries: Explorations in Learning and Teaching* (New York: Oxford University Press, 1986), chap. 12.
49. Mary Field Belenky, Blythe McVicker Clinchy, Nancy Rule Goldberger, and Jill Mattuck Tarule, *Women's Ways of Knowing: The Development of Self, Voice, and Mind* (New York: Basic Books, 1986), chap. 6.
50. Paulo Freire, *Pedagogy of the Oppressed* (New York: Seabury, 1970); Ira Shor and Paulo Freire, "What Is the Dialogical Method of Teaching?" *Journal of Education, 169* (1987), 11–31; Hans-Georg Gadamer, *Truth and Method* (New York: Crossroads, 1982), pp. 273–274, 337; and Jürgen Habermas, *Communication and the Evaluation of Society* (Oxford: Polity, 1990), chap. 1, and *Theory of Communicative Action: Vol. 1. Reason and the Rationalization of Society* (Boston: Beacon Press, 1984), pp. 8–42, 286–337.
51. Nicholas C. Burbules, "Education as Translation," Paper presented at meeting of the California Association for Philosophy of Education, Davis, CA, April 1988.
52. For a good summary of these issues, see Jon Weiner, "Free Speech for Campus Bigots?," *The Nation*, February 26, 1990. pp. 272–276.
53. We are completing a separate manuscript that develops the idea of "communicative virtues" in detail.
54. Janice Moulton, "A Paradigm of Philosophy: The Adversary Method," in *Discovering Reality: Feminist Perspectives on Epistemology, Metaphysics, Methodology, and Philosophy of Science*, ed. Sandra Harding and Merrill B. Hintikka (Dordrecht, Holland: Reidel, 1984), pp. 149–164.
55. Magda Lewis, "Framing Women and Silence: Disrupting the Hierarchy of Discursive Practices," Paper presented at the annual meeting of the American Educational Research Association, Boston, April 1990.
56. See Burbules, "The Tragic Sense of Education."
57. McLaren and Hammer, "Critical Pedagogy and the Postmodern Challenge," p. 32.

Questions

1. What are some of the modernist values or ideals that Burbules and Rice refer to?

2. How do Burbules and Rice distinguish between "big P" and "little p" postmodernism? What is the distinction they draw between "postmodernism" and "antimodernism"?

3. Which of these theoretical orientations do the authors align themselves with? For what reasons?

4. Do you agree with the authors' critique of Postmodern approaches to critical education studies? Explain.

5. Why do Burbules and Rice think that "dialogue across difference" is important? Are you convinced by their argument?

6. Do Burbules and Rice do a better job of articulating a conception of "positive freedom" than the antimodernists they criticize?

7. Should public schools attempt to promote "dialogue across difference"? If so, how might they go about this project?

8. For the authors, what "communicative virtues" are central to dialogue across difference? Would you add other virtues? Explain.

9. Burbules and Rice espouse the educational goal of "trying to achieve understanding across differences." How is this different from and/or similar to other goals of multicultural education?

Culture, Subculture, Multiculturalism: Educational Options

K. Anthony Appiah

It is a truism that in the United States of America "we live in a multicultural society." But the obviousness and apparent clarity of this truism, like the apparent clarity and obviousness of most such truisms, dissolves upon inspection. To begin with what is, perhaps, the least patent difficulty, what people normally have in mind when they pronounce this slogan, is that the United States is a multicultural *nation*. This is by no means obviously the same thought, since that we in America constitute a nation is, so to speak, a juridical and constitutional fact, while our being a society requires, I should have thought, both more and less than this.

The people of Martinique, after all, are French nationals: but there is surely such a thing as Martinican society as distinct from French society—the society of the "hexagon"—and it is not obvious that Martinicans generally are participants in the latter. Similarly, many Native Americans, who live on reservations, while clearly American nationals, might be thought to live in a separate society from the rest of us; and we might also argue, less uncontroversially, that soldiers on bases, the inhabitants of Bel Air, or of South Central L.A., or of San Francisco's Chinatown, live in societies separate from those of the people whose lives go on around them.

The point is that our word "society," used in this context, means something like a group of people with probably a shared geography,[1] and certainly shared institutions and a common culture: and, granted the geographical unity of the (continental) United States and the existence, under the Constitution, of American institutions, the question whether we are a society in this sense is the same as the question whether there is such a thing, at some level, as a shared American culture.[2] To speak of American society as multicultural in this sense, as

275

composed of groups of people with distinct cultures, might seem to be, at best, confusing; at worst, actually contradictory. And the fact is that the problems of the many cultures within the boundaries of the American state are usually thought of as flowing from the yoking together of societies, groups of people with a common culture and common institutions, within a single set of political institutions and in a shared social space.

Still, to speak of America as a collection of societies, a gathering of cultures, is, in one way, rather misleading. For while some of the cultural variety of the current United States arises from the presence of people who grew up and were acculturated in other places,[3] most of America's cultures have been largely shaped by experience in the United States: if there is an overarching set of beliefs, ideas, and practices that make up an American culture, most of America's cultures were shaped by that common culture. And even if that common culture is pretty thin gruel, America's cultures have mostly been shaped by interaction with each other. America's many cultures, its various societies, have grown up together, belong in a single system of cultures; they are not the mere logical sum of a series of unrelated historically independent elements.

Question 1: Are We Really a Society?

If, as I have suggested, a society is a group of people with probably a shared geography, and certainly shared institutions and a common culture, then understanding whether we are a society will depend on both (a) whether there are American institutions and (b) whether there is an American common culture.

The first of these questions is easily enough answered: for the political institutions of the American nation are shared by all who live in the United States. (Some of us live here without being citizens, and thus without being entitled to participate in those institutions as voters, jurors, and so on; but we all have the right to participate in other politically created institutions—heterosexual marriage, for example, or property ownership—and the obligation to live under American laws.)

It is equally plain, however, that these constitutional institutions—the political structure of the American republic—take up only a small part of the lives of many who live in the United States; they have the interest and affection of a significant number of the people who live in the United States but by no means of all.

Many citizens, for example, do not vote, and their disengagement from the constitutional political process means more than that their participation in the institutions of the American nation may be minimal; more importantly, it means that they may have little investment in those institutions. (That they have no subjective investment does not, of course, mean that they have nothing at stake: the homeless may not be well enough treated in our society but they do—and they should—take advantage of their legal rights.) And this lack of investment means not sharing certain values, values that might be thought of as American.

Which brings us, then, to the second question: the question of an American culture. Suppose it is correct to speak, as many do, of American culture as centrally constituted, in part, by, for example, democratic and republican values. Then, so it seems, something central to American culture may not be held in common by all who live within the American nation. And if that is so, then, in the relevant sense, there may be no American society, nothing bound together both by American institutions and by a unitary American culture.

Question 2: What Would It Mean to Have a Common Culture?

But we will not get much further with these issues until we explore the concept of culture, an idea that immediately reveals itself to be extremely elastic. In my dictionary I find as one definition for culture "The totality of socially transmitted behavior patterns, arts, beliefs, institutions, and all other products of human work and thought."[4] This is not, I think, quite right. There is, to begin with, no obvious incoherence in the idea of a non-human culture: we can reasonably speak of the culture of some primates or imagine, in science fiction, the culture of non-terrestrial creatures.

But the definition surely picks out a familiar constellation of ideas. "Culture," in one sense, does indeed name all the "products of human work and thought." That is, in fact, the sense in which anthropologists largely use the term nowadays. The culture of the Ashanti or the Zuni, for the anthropologist, includes every object they make (clothing, pottery, houses—which, taken together, we call their "material culture") and everything they think and everything they do; or, more precisely, everything that they do that is the product of thought (which is to say, invoking a familiar philosophical distinction, not every bodily movement, but every action).

You will notice, however, that the dictionary definition could have stopped there, leaving out the talk of "socially transmitted behavior patterns, arts, beliefs, institutions," because these are all products of human work and thought. They are mentioned, of course, because they are the residue of an older idea of culture than the anthropological one. Here what the dictionary draws attention to is something more like the idea of a civilization: the "socially transmitted behavior patterns" of ritual, etiquette, religion, games, arts; the values that they engender and reflect; and the institutions—family, school, church, state—that shape and are shaped by them.

There are two tensions between the anthropologist's idea of a culture and the idea of a civilization. First, there is nothing in the anthropologist's idea that requires that the culture of a group should be a totality in any stronger sense than being what I called the mere logical sum of all the things they make and the actions they undertake.

American civilization, on the other hand, would not be just a simple logical sum of the doings and thoughts of Americans. It would have to have a certain coherence. Some of what is done in America and by Americans would not belong to American civilization because it was too individual (the particular bedtime rituals of a particular American family); some would not belong because it was not properly American, because (like a Hindi sentence, made in America) it does not properly cohere with the rest.

The second, connected, difference between what I am calling the anthropological idea of culture and the idea of a civilization, is that the latter takes values to be more central to the enterprise, in two ways. First, the civilization of a group is centrally defined by its moral and aesthetic values, and the coherence of a civilization is, primarily, the coherence of those values with each other and, then, of the group's behavior and institutions with its values. Second, civilizations are essentially to be evaluated: they can be better and worse, richer and poorer, more and less interesting. Anthropologists, on the whole, tend now to avoid the relative evaluation of cultures, adopting a sort of cultural relativism, whose coherence philosophers have tended to doubt. And they do not take values as more central to culture than, for example, beliefs, ideas, and practices.

Because there are these differences I want to reserve the word "culture" for the anthropologist's notion: henceforward I shall use the word "civilization" for the older notion I have been sketching. The habit of shaking hands at meetings belongs to culture in the anthropologist's sense; the works of Sandro Botticelli and Martin Buber and Count Basie belong to culture also, but they belong to civilization as well.

Distinguishing Between Culture and Civilization

The move from "civilization" to "culture" was the result of arguments, not a simple drift of usage. The move away from evaluation came first, once people recognized that much evaluation of other cultures by the Europeans and Americans who invented anthropology had been both ignorant and biased. Earlier criticisms of "lower" peoples turned out to involve crucial misunderstandings of their ideas (Levy-Bruhl's talk of a "pre-logical" mentality, for example); and it eventually seemed clear enough, too, that nothing more than differences of upbringing underlay the distaste of some Westerners for unfamiliar habits. It is a poor move from recognizing certain evaluations as mistaken to giving up evaluation altogether, and anthropologists who adopt cultural relativism often preach more than practice it. Still, this cultural relativism was a response to real errors. That it is the wrong response doesn't make the errors any less erroneous.

The arguments against "civilization" were in place well before the midcentury. More recently, anthropologists began to see that the idea of the coherence of a civilization got in the way of understanding important facts about other societies (and, in the end, about our own). For even in some of the "simplest" societies, there are different values and practices and beliefs and interests associated with different social groups (women as opposed to men; elders as opposed to young men; chiefs as opposed to commoners; one clan as opposed to another). To think of a civilization as coherent was to miss the fact that these different values and beliefs were not merely different but actually opposed.[5] Worse, what had been presented as the coherent unified worldview of a tribal people often turned out, on later inspection, to be merely the ideology of a dominant group or interest.

I believe there is much of value in these anthropological criticisms of the idea of a civilization.[6] I shall refer back to the idea of civilization from time to time, however, where it helps us understand some of our contemporary debates. In the meanwhile, we need another distinction within the idea of culture.

A Multicultural Society

We customarily refer to the small-scale, technologically uncomplicated, face-to-face societies, where most interactions are with people whom you know, as traditional. In many such societies every adult who is not mentally disabled speaks the same language. All share a vocabulary and a grammar and an accent. While there will be some words in the language that are not known by everybody—the names of medicinal herbs, the language of some religious rituals, the vocabulary of secret societies—most are known to all normal adults. (I shall speak loosely, from now on, of what is known to—or believed by—all who are not mentally disabled—or hugely miseducated—as universally known or believed.) To share a language is to participate in a complex set of shared expectations and understandings, but in such societies it is not only linguistic behavior that is coordinated through universally known expectations and understandings. People will share an understanding of many practices—marriages, funerals, other rites of passage—and will largely share their views about the general workings not only of the social but also of the natural world. While ethnographers in the past may sometimes have overstated the extent to which basic theories of nature are universally believed in a society, even those who are skeptical about particular elements of belief will nevertheless know what everyone is supposed to believe, and they will know it in enough detail to behave very often as if they believed it, too.

A similar point applies to many of the values of such societies. It may well be that some people, even some groups, do not share the values that are enunciated in public and taught to children. But, once more, the standard values are universally known, and even those who do not share them know what it would be to act in conformity with them and probably do so much of the time.

In such a traditional society we may speak of these shared beliefs, values, signs, and symbols, as the common culture;[7] not, to insist on a crucial point, in the sense that everyone in the group actually holds the beliefs and values, but in the sense that everybody knows what they are and everybody knows that they are widely held in the society.[8] There will be beliefs and values—those of the skeptics—in the society that are not part of its common culture, because they are the results of individual defections from a norm. There will be beliefs and values that are not socially shared, but are the property of families or other associations of social life. And there will be material culture, which is shaped by social transmission, but not the common property of all.

But even in a traditional society there will be other elements of culture that are not held in common. Skills, for example, are not beliefs or values, nor are they material culture, but hunting or singing, for example, or ritual practices are socially transmitted. These will fail to belong to the common culture not because they are the products of individual or family deviations but because they are the result of the special training associated with particular groups. I am going to call the shared beliefs, values, and practices of a socially recognized subgroup a subculture.[9] And I shall say that a nation that contains subcultures wider than the family is multicultural.

Since this definition is going to do some work later, let me point out at once some things that it does not entail. On this way of thinking of subcultures, there doesn't have to be one common culture shared by the members of all the national subcultures taken together. A subculture is "sub" because it belongs to a recognized subgroup of the nation, not because its members share the national culture plus some other more specific culture. My definition doesn't assume there is some culture in common to all the national subcultures; but it isn't meant to rule that out, either.[10]

It is also important that the overarching group is the nation, not the society. For, in the way I have been using the word "society," it is an open question whether fellow nationals share a society, because it is an open question whether there is a national common culture.

Multicultural Societies Are Not Intrinsically Problematic

No one is likely to make much fuss about the fact that a nation is multicultural in this sense. For, in this sense, many simple and all large-scale societies have been multicultural. Once you have division of labor and social stratification, there will be people who do and people who don't know about music and literature and pottery and painting; if we call all these specialized spheres together the arts, then everyone will participate in the arts to varying degrees, and there are likely to be subgroups (opera lovers, say, or dedicated moviegoers, or lovers of poetry) who share significant practices and ideas with each other that are not shared with everyone else.

If being multicultural is a problem, it is not because we have different artistic subcultures: pace those who seem preoccupied with stopping multiculturalism at the NEH or the NEA, the problems created by our many subcultures largely lie elsewhere. Since the arts were central to the idea of civilization, those who worry about the existence of artistic subcultures may be conflating the question whether there is a shared civilization in the United States with the question whether there is a common culture. If a shared culture means shared arts—a single civilization—the United States has never had a shared culture: the social meaning of the fine arts includes their not being shared; high and low are mutually constitutive categories. But, as we have seen, there is more to culture, in the sense of the term that I have chosen to focus on, than the arts.

Question 1 Answered: The United States Is Not a Society Because There Is No Common Culture

What I have called the common culture is what a social group has socially in common: it is what people teach their children in order to make them members of their social group. By definition, a common culture is shared; it is the social bottom line. It includes language and table manners, religious ideas, moral values, theories of the workings of the natural and social worlds.[11] To have a common culture, to repeat the crucial point, is to have a common language and a common vocabulary of values and theories, even if some individuals or subgroups are skeptical of the theories and reject the values. (It does not, thus, require shared commitment to the central values and theories of the natural and social world.)[12]

I associate cultures with social groups, not with nations, because I want to insist again that a group of persons living together in a common state, under common authorities, need not have a common culture. There is no single shared body of ideas and practices in India, or, to take another example, in most contemporary African states.

Thus, many, but by no means all, Ghanaians know (some) English. There is no language known to all (or even most) of us. There are Moslems and Christians and practitioners of the traditional religions of many ethnic groups. There are matrilineal and patrilineal conceptions of family; there are traditions of divine kingship and less hierarchical notions of politics. The modern constitutional order—the Presidency, the parliament, the courts—is not well understood by many and unknown to quite a few.[13]

Now I think it is fair to say that there is not now and there has never been a common culture in the United States, either. The reason is simple: the United States has always been multilingual, and has always had minorities who did not speak or understand English. It has always had a plurality of religious traditions; beginning with Native American religions and Puritans and Catholics and including now many varieties of Judaism, Islam, Buddhism, Jainism, Taoism, Bahai . . . and so on. And many of these religious traditions have been quite unknown to each other. More than this, Americans have also always differed significantly even among those who do speak English, from North to South and East to West, and from country to city, in customs of greeting, notions of civility, and a whole host of other ways.

To say this is not to deny that for significant parts of American history there has been a good deal of mutual knowledge across regional, religious, ethnic, and even linguistic barriers. My point is that the notion that what has held the United States together historically over its great geographical range is a common culture, like the common culture of a traditional society, is not sociologically plausible.

National Culture Versus National Common Culture

The notion that there is no American national culture will come as a surprise to many: observations about "American culture," taken as a whole, are common. It is, for example, held to be individualist, litigious, racially obsessed. I think each of these claims is actually true, because what I mean when I say there is no common culture of the United States is not what is denied by someone who says that there is an American culture.

Such a person is describing large-scale tendencies within American life that are not necessarily participated in by all Americans. I do not mean to deny that these exist. But for such a tendency to be part of what I am calling the common culture, they would have to derive from beliefs and values and practices (almost) universally shared and known to be so. And that they are not.

Recognizing a Dominant Culture

At the same time, it has also always been true that there was a *dominant* culture in these United States. It was Christian, it spoke English, and it identified with the high cultural traditions of Europe and, more particularly, of England. And, until recently, when people spoke of American culture, this is what they meant.

This dominant culture included the common culture of the dominant classes—the government and business and cultural elites—but it was familiar to many others who were subordinate to them. And it was not merely an effect but also an instrument of their domination. Because the dominant norms of language and behavior were those of a dominant class, their children, for example, were likely to have preferred access to the best educations—educations which themselves led to dominant positions in business, in government, and in the arts.

As public education has expanded in the United States, America's citizens, and especially those citizens educated in public elementary schools in this country, have come to share a body of historical knowledge, and an understanding—however tenuous—of the American political system. And it is increasingly true that whatever other languages children in this country speak, they speak and understand English, and they watch many of the same television programs and listen to much of the same music. Not only do they share these experiences, they know that they do; and so they can imagine themselves as a collectivity, the audience for mass culture. In that sense, most young Americans have a common culture based in a whole variety of kinds of English, but it is no longer that older, Christian, Anglo-Saxon tradition that used to be called American culture.

The outlines of this almost universal common culture, to which only very few Americans are external, are somewhat blurry. But it includes, for example, in its practices, baseball; in its ideas, democracy; in its religion, Christianity;[14] in its arts, rap music and music videos and many movies. This culture is to a large extent, as I have implied, the product of schools and of the media. But even those who share this common culture live in subcultures of language, religion, family organization, and political assumptions. And, more than this, most who are black and Hispanic have, irrespective of their incomes, radically different experiences and expectations of the state.

Multiculturalism as an Alternative to Imposing the Dominant Culture

Now I take it that multiculturalism is meant to be the name of a response to these familiar facts: that it is meant to be an approach to education and to public culture that acknowledges the diversity of cultures and subcultures in the United States and that proposes to deal with that diversity in some other way than by imposing the values and ideas of the hitherto dominant Anglo-Saxon cultural tradition. That, I think, is the common core of all the things that have been called multiculturalism.

I think this common idea is a good one. It is a good idea for a number of reasons. It is a good idea, first, because the old practice of imposing Christian, Anglo-Saxon tradition was rooted in racism and anti-Semitism (and sexism and heterosexism . . . but that is another story). But it is a good idea, second, because making the culture of one subculture the official culture of a state privileges the members of that subculture—gives them advantages in public life—in ways that are profoundly anti-egalitarian and, thus, anti-democratic.

Yet agreeing to this idea does not tell you much about what you should do in schools and in public culture. It tells you that you mustn't impose certain practices and ideas, but it doesn't tell you what you should do affirmatively. I want to suggest that one affirmative strategy in this area is a bad idea for public education and that there are other strategies that are better. And then, in closing, I want to say something about why living together in a multicultural society is bound to turn out to be difficult.

The Distinction Between Cultures and Identities

There is one final piece of apparatus I need, however. I have been talking of "subcultures" and defining what I mean by this. And it would be natural to assume that the primary subgroups to which these subcultures are attached will be ethnic and racial groups (with religious denominations conceived of as a species of ethnic group). It would be natural, too, to think that the characteristic difficulties of a multicultural society arise largely from the cultural differences between ethnic groups. I think this easy assimilation of ethnic and racial subgroups to subcultures is to be resisted.

First of all, it needs to be argued, and not simply assumed, that black Americans, taken as a group, have a common culture: values and beliefs and practices that they share and that they do not share with others. This is equally true for, say, Chinese-Americans; and it is *a fortiori* true of white Americans. What seems clear enough is that being African-American or Asian-American or White is an important social identity in the United States. Whether these are important social identities because these groups have shared common cultures is, on the other hand, quite doubtful; not least because it is doubtful whether they have common cultures at all.

With differing cultures, we might expect misunderstandings arising out of ignorance of each other's values, practices, and beliefs; we might even expect conflicts because of differing values or beliefs. The paradigms of difficulty in a society of many cultures are misunderstandings of a word or a gesture; conflicts over who should take custody of the children after a divorce; whether to go to the doctor or the priest for healing.

Once we move from talking of cultures to identities, whole new kinds of problems come into view. Racial and ethnic conflicts, for example, have to do with the ways in which some people think members of other races and ethnic groups should be treated, irrespective of their cultural accomplishments. It isn't because a black man won't understand his daughter, or because he will value her differently from a white man, or because he does not know some important facts, that Archie Bunker wouldn't want his daughter to marry one. Mr. Bunker's bigotry does not require him to differ culturally in any significant respect from black people. He would be as opposed to the marriage if the potential son-in-law had exactly the same beliefs and values (on non-race-related matters) as he had himself. Similarly, in Bosnia it is not so much that what Croats do makes them hateful to Serb bigots; or vice versa. It is rather that those things are hateful because Croats (or Serbs) do them.

These cases bring out the ways in which ethnic and racial identities are contrastive: it is central to being African-American that you are not Euro-American or Asian-American; *mutatis mutandis,* the same goes for being Euro-American or Asian-American. And these distinctions matter because (some) people think it appropriate to treat people differently depending on which of these categories they fall into; and these ways of treating people differently lead to patterns of domination and exploitation. Racial and ethnic identities are, in this way, like genders and sexualities. To be female is not to be male; to be gay is not to be straight; and these oppositions lead some to treat people differently according to their gender or sexuality, in asymmetrical ways that usually privilege men or straight people.

Now it is crucial to understanding gender and sexuality that women and men and gay and straight people grow up together in families, communities, denominations. Insofar as a common culture means common beliefs, values, and practices, gay people and straight people in most places have a common culture; and while there are societies in which the socialization of children is so structured by gender that women and men have seriously distinct cultures, this is not a feature of most "modern" societies.[15]

I take the fact that questions about feminism (gender) and gay and lesbian identity (sexuality) come up often in thinking about multiculturalism (especially in the university) as an indication that what many people are thinking about is not the multiple subcultures of the nation but its multiple identities. All I want to insist on for now is that these are not the same thing.

A Multicultural Nation's Problems with Public Education

I have been trying to explore the ways in which we are a multicultural nation, because, as I say, I want to say something about the consequences of this situation for public education.[16] But we should notice that it is not obvious what special problems the multicultural character of the American nation creates for the curriculum.

Once you have conceded what I claim is the key multiculturalist contention—that you should not use the public schools to impose the subculture of a dominant group—you might think you could proceed simply by asking what is worth teaching to American children and teaching that. This was, after all, the basis of the older curriculum; and if that curriculum confused what was worth teaching with what was valued in the subculture of the dominant class—the particular masquerading in a familiar way as the universal—the obvious correction would be to try to answer the question of what is worth teaching in a less (sub)culturally biased way.

The fact is that the older notion that we should instruct all children in "American culture" was, itself, a potentially democratic and egalitarian one. The advantages that the children of the dominant class gained by the fact that it was their home culture—their dialect of English, their table manners, the literature their parents read and admired—that was taught in schools and presupposed in public life, could be eradicated, if all children were given access to that culture through schooling. The multicultural critique might lead you to feel that it was unfair to give the dominant class a head start in this way (a fact we could deal with, for example, by refraining from preferring their dialect in official speech). But I do not see that it would require you to do anything else to reflect the multicultural character of the nation in the curriculum.

Yet if we read the National Council for the Social Studies statement on multicultural education, it is clear that this influential group of educators take it for granted that much more is required. To begin with, they move freely (as I have urged we should not) from talk of multiculturalism to talk of ethnic identities. Though they agree that not every student cares much about an ethnic identity and that children should be free not to identify themselves ethnically,[17] they also insist that ethnicity should be an important factor in shaping educational policy:

1. Personal ethnic identity and knowledge of others' ethnic identity is essential to the sense of understanding and the feeling of personal well-being that promotes intergroup understanding. . . . (278)
2. Students cannot fully understand who they are . . . until they have a solid knowledge of the groups to which they belong. (282)[18]

In the background here are widespread assumptions about what is going wrong in our "multicultural" schools: that violence between children (which is plainly a barrier to learning) often grows out of inter-group misunderstandings; that minority students (especially African-Americans and Hispanics) underachieve because they and their cultures are not respected in the school. But if the conflict in the schools is a matter of contests between identities, there is no reason to think that teaching about various cultures will eradicate it. Understanding may not help with problems that do not arise from misunderstanding. What is required, very often, is not understanding of cultures but respect for identities; and a curriculum that takes the cultural works of African-Americans seriously may be helpful here, even if it does not communicate a deepened understanding of African-American culture.

And if the "solid knowledge" of my group is to be taught as a distinct body of beliefs and ideas, then it may actually lead me to be more culturally different from my peers of other races and ethnicities (who are taught different, though, no doubt, equally solid things about "their" tradition) and thus generate more possibilities for misunderstanding. Passage (2) thus proposes a policy that increases the likelihood of the danger passage (1) seeks to avoid.

Two Rationales for Separatism

Implicit in passage (2) is the thought that the way to deal with our many cultures in public education is to teach each child the culture of "its" group. This is the strategy of some (but by no means all) Afrocentrists and of some (but by no means all) of those who have favored bilingual education for Hispanics.

This is the strategy I oppose.

To explain my first basis for objection, I need to elicit a paradox in this approach, which we can do by considering the answer that this approach—I shall call it, tendentiously, Separatism—proposes to the question, Why should we teach African-American children something different from what we teach other children? The answer will come in two parts: the first part says that we should do so because they already come from a different culture; the second part says that we should do so because we should teach all people about the traditions from which they come.

It's the first answer that is paradoxical, at least if you think that the plurality of cultures is a problem. It is paradoxical because it proposes to solve the problems created by the fact that children have different cultures by emphasizing and entrenching those differences, not by trying to reduce them.

I should make it plain that I have no problem with the argument that children's home cultures need to be taken into account in deciding how to teach them: there's no point in giving kids information in languages or dialects they don't understand, or simply punishing them—rather than dealing with their parents or guardians—for behavior that they are being taught at home. But to admit that is to admit only that culture may sometimes make a difference as to how you should teach, not that it should make a difference as to what you should teach. And defending teaching children different histories (Afrocentric history) or different forms of speech or writing (Black English) on the grounds that this is already their culture simply begs the question; if we teach African-American children different histories from other children, then, indeed, it will become true that knowing that history and not knowing any other history will be part of the culture of African-Americans.

But the fact is that if we don't enforce cultural differences of this kind in the schools, surely they will largely disappear. And what that means is that the only serious argument for Separatism that survives is the second answer I considered earlier: the claim that we must teach each child the culture of "its" group because that is the right thing to do, because we should.

Exploring the Second Rationale

That idea is much more powerful. It is presumably at the basis of the thought that many non-observant Jews share with observant Jews (who have other reasons for believing this), namely, that it is good to teach their children Jewish history and customs, because they are Jewish children. It is the argument—"we have Plato to our father"—that led to the sense of exclusion that many African-Americans felt when the history and culture of the United States were taught to them as the continuation of a white Western tradition; the argument against which so much Afrocentrism is a reaction.[19]

I myself am skeptical of all arguments of this form: my instinct is to believe that traditions are worth teaching in our public schools and colleges because they are beautiful and good and true—or, at least, interesting and important and useful—never because they are ours or yours, mine or thine. I was brought up a Protestant; but after my first seder, it struck me that this was a tradition worth knowing about for everybody, Jew or Gentile; and I have always valued the experience of family community among my Moslem cousins at Ramadan.[20]

It may be worth spending a little time reflecting on the unfashionableness of my instinctive view and insisting on some of its virtues, which may have been forgotten. I mentioned just now the "older view" that public education should teach an American culture. What was done in the name of that older view too often obscured the variety of the sources of America's cultures, as well as giving too rosy and unconflicted a view of the relations between America's various ethnic, racial, and religious subgroups. None of these mistakes needs resurrecting.

But this older view surely also held that what we should teach in public schools should be knowledge worth knowing, values worth respecting, practices useful in children's lives outside the school. Contemporary feminist, anti-racist and anti-ethnocentrist skepticisms lead us to ask, Worth knowing for whom? By whose standards? And these are fair questions. But in answering them we should take them seriously as questions about the curriculum as a practical business.

And this requires remembering some simple facts: the school curriculum contains, of necessity, an extremely small proportion of what is known; we read only the minutest sample of what has been written; and we have time to study only a fraction of the known history of the world, only the most basic scientific knowledge.

How, given these facts, can we pick from all these riches? To say we should favor truth over falsehood is to utter a truism worth holding on to; but it leaves vast decisions to be made. (It also neglects the fact that the whole truth is complicated, too complicated often to learn all at once, so that we teach children simplified versions of it, first of all—Newtonian half-truths before Einstein.) To say that in selecting what literature and art we should teach we should seek to transmit an appreciation of literary and aesthetic values is also fine enough; but to do this we need to read the mediocre and the near-great as well as the magnificent. More than this, while literary judgment can be reasoned about, it is also essentially contestable, so that part of what we need to teach is the idea that there are reasonable differences in matters of literary and artistic taste, differences that we cannot rely on argument or evidence to settle. Each of these complications makes the principle that we should teach the beautiful a poor instrument for discriminating among all the range of the arts those we should teach; and it offers little guidance as to how we should teach them.

Finally, of course, schools should teach the young what is good and evil: and also what is courageous and what foolhardy; what is compassion and what is sentimentality; where loyalty to family and friends ends and our responsibility to our fellow citizens, our fellow creatures, begins; and how to make all these moral discriminations. But there is here no easy consensus; there are too many hard cases, and we cannot expect that teaching young people to make these discriminations—which means helping them learn to think ethically—will be uncontroversial in a society where certain moral views are associated with particular group identities. For the schools will regularly be asked to recognize, say, religious identities by teaching their views.

I concede all these difficulties: indeed, thinking about them strikes me as a useful place to begin reflecting on the curriculum. But I repeat that I do not think it will help us in public education to add to our baggage of reasons for offering an element of a school curriculum to a child the thought: I teach you, this particular child, this thing because it is your tradition.

This is because I think this an inadmissible ground for the curriculum of a public school, not because I think that we should never hear such arguments. Indeed, they are among the most compelling arguments that a family or a church or temple or mosque can offer to a child. "In our family," I might tell my nephew, "we have done this for many generations. Your great-grand-uncle did it, in Asante, in the late nineteenth century; your grandfather did it when he was a boy in Kumasi." There are things and practices I value because we—my ancestors and I—have done them for generations, because I take pleasure in the sense of continuity with them as my ancestors.

If I had been to a Catholic or a Jewish or a Muslim school, I would have learned such traditions, too, not as my traditions but as somebody else's. I would have learned them not because the teachers and the school believed in them as traditions, but because they believed in them *tout court*. And because one can value them not just as traditions but as truths, I could decide to make them mine.

In the modern world many have sought to hold on to the profound pleasures of tradition even after they have left their faith behind. But, to repeat, in most Catholic or Jewish or Muslim schools, before the modern period, what was taught was taught as the truth about life, the universe, and conduct; and though people might have taken pleasure in thinking of it as a matter of the tradition of a family and a community, if they had not thought it true, they would have thought it worthless. For these schools one notion of the good and the true, a contested notion, attached to one identity, was a presupposition of the curriculum.

An Alternative View

The public schools of a multicultural, multiethnic, religiously diverse society should not operate like these older religious schools: the public schools should not propagate one faith, support the traditions of one group, celebrate the heritage of one ethnicity. They should not teach particular traditions and religions; though, of course, they should teach *about* them.

The view I am articulating here is a view about the division between public and private spheres in the education of children: on such a view, ethnicity and religion are not to be transmitted by the organs of the state. Both, rather, are created and preserved outside the state by families, and by wider communities, including religious ones. Because there are many such cultures—and identities—created outside the state, in civil society, and because for many of us they are central to our conceptions of ourselves and of our lives, the school must acknowledge them. Because they have a great deal of impact on our relations, in communities and in the political life of the state, we are all better prepared for life in this nation if we know something of the cultures and identities of others and if we learn to engage in respectful discourse with them. Outside the school, children can be preached a specific religion; within it, they can hear about their own traditions, along with others, but they should not be proselytized, even on behalf of their families.

If there is any doubt about the stability of such a view, consider the alternative: a policy in which the public schools set out to teach children according to their identities and subcultures; that not only taught about collective identities but set out to reinforce and transmit them. If carried to its ultimate, this policy would require segregation into cultural and religious groups either within or between public schools, in ways that would be plainly unconstitutional in the United States since the *Brown* decision. For if we did have unsegregated classes teaching Jewish history, and African-American history, and Anglo history and Hispanic history and Chinese history in our schools, by what right would we forbid children from going to the "wrong" classes?

Of course there are things that we surely all believe that we should teach all American children: in particular, we should teach them something of the history of the American political system. And here is a reason why we cannot hope to teach each child only "its" cultural tradition: for understanding the American constitutional system and its history requires us to know about slavery and immigration, about the Civil War and Reconstruction, the Underground Railroad and Ellis Island. If there is a sense in which each of these belongs more to the history of some social groups than others, there is also a clear sense in which they belong to us all.

And it is *that* idea that motivates the approach to dealing with our multicultural society that I favor, that undergirds my multiculturalism. For it seems to me that what is ideal in a multicultural society, whose multicultural character is created outside the state in the sphere of civil society, is that the state should seek in its educational systems to make these multiple subcultures known to each other. A multicultural education, in my view, should be one that leaves you not only knowing and loving what is good in the traditions of your subculture but also understanding and appreciating the traditions of others (and, yes, critically rejecting the worst of all traditions).[21] This approach has its practical problems also: a curriculum filled with the history of Korean-Americans and African-Americans and Anglo-Americans and Jewish Americans and so on risks being a curriculum with a shallow appreciation of all of them. But the principle of selection is clear: we should try to teach about those many traditions from around the world that have come to be important at different stages of American history. This means that we begin with Native American and Protestant Dutch and English and African and Iberian cultures, adding voices to the story as they were added to the nation. Because different elements are important to different degrees in different places today, we can assume that the balance will be and should be differently struck in different places. (All of which presupposes a general improvement, I should add, in the quality of American elementary and secondary education.)

A Final Objection to Separatism

I have a final argument against Separatism. It is that it is dangerous, for reasons that have to do with the final point I want to make, which is about the difficulty of managing multicultural—plural—societies.

I said earlier that no one is likely to be troubled by the variety of subcultures in high culture. Why is this? Because however important our participation in high culture is, it is unlikely to be at the heart of our ethnicity. High culture crosses ethnic boundaries to an extraordinary degree. (The boundaries that it crosses with less ease are those of class.) The result is that subdivisions of high culture are not so likely to become central to the organization of political life. The United States is not threatened by the cultural autonomy of the American Philosophical Association or (even) the American Medical Association. In this respect the associations of high culture are like many elements of popular culture: the next New York mayoral election is not going to be between followers of the Mets and of the Yankees.

But differences in what I have called subcultures are rather different. We pass on our language to the next generation because we care to communicate with them; we pass on religion because we share its vision and endorse its values; we pass on our folkways because we value people with those folkways.

I have insisted that we should distinguish between cultures and identities, but ethnic identities are distinctive in having cultural distinctions as one of their primary marks. Ethnic identities are created in family and community life. These—along with mass-mediated culture, the school and the college—are, for most of us, the central sites of the social transmission of culture. Distinct practices, beliefs, norms go with each ethnicity in part because people want to be ethnically distinct: because many people want the sense of solidarity that comes from being unlike others. With ethnicity in modern society, it is often the distinct identity that comes first and the cultural distinction that is created and maintained because of it, not the other way around. The distinctive common cultures of ethnic and religious identities matter not simply because of their contents but also as markers of those identities.

Culture in this sense is the home of what we care about most. If other people organize their solidarity around cultures different from ours, this makes them, to that extent, different from us in ways that matter to us deeply. The result, of course, is not just that we have difficulty understanding across cultures—this is an inevitable result of cultural difference, for much of culture consists of language and other shared modes of understanding—but that we end up preferring our own kind; and if we prefer our own kind, it is easy enough to slip into preferring to vote for our own kind, to employ our own kind, and so on.

In sum: Cultural difference undergirds loyalties. As we have seen repeatedly in recent years, from South Africa to the Balkans, from Sri Lanka to Nigeria, from South Central Los Angeles to Crown Heights, once these loyalties matter they will be mobilized in politics and the public square, except to the extent that a civic culture can be created that explicitly seeks to exclude them. And that is why my multiculturalism is so necessary: it is the only way to reduce the misunderstandings across subcultures, the only way to build bridges of loyalty across the ethnicities that have so often divided us. Multiculturalism of this sort—pluralism, to use an older word—is a way of making sure we care enough about people across ethnic divides to keep those ethnic divides from destroying us. And it must, I believe, be a central part of the function of our educational system to equip all of us to share the public space with people of multiple identities and distinct subcultures. I insisted early on the distinction between cultures and identities. It is especially important here. Teaching young people to respect those with other identities is not the same thing as teaching them some of the central practices and beliefs of a different subculture. When we teach Toni Morrison to children with serious attention, we are demonstrating respect for the cultural work of a black person in a culture where there is still pressure not to respect black people. We are showing that respect to black children; we are modelling that respect for other children. Each of these is something that a decent education can seek to do; neither is simply a matter of introducing people to a culture.

It seems to me that it will be important, too, to teach children to reflect critically on their identities, including their ethnic identities, if they care about them.

Identity as an Important Part of Education

Locke famously argued that the trans-temporal unity of the self was created through memory. Contemporary work on this question has argued that this answer to the problem of identity is at best question-begging. For if I think I did something in the past and "remember" it from the perspective of a participant, that only shows that I am remembering what happened to me if that belief is true; and its being true, if it is a belief with a first-person perspective, requires not just that some person had such experiences but that I did. The role of "memory" in constituting the trans-temporal identity of a person should more appropriately, I think, be taken another way. To be a person is to have a sense of yourself as a creature with a history. Memory here is a route into the recalled experiences whose existence, if they are veridical, certifies the story I tell of myself. But the oft-suggested parallelism between memory and history should remind us that a history of a self is not just "one damn thing after another." Our personal histories are as narratively constructed as our collective stories. For most of us the history of myself is Whig history, with a telos, or more likely, a plurality of ends, with anticipations in childhood, intimations of what is to come. Part of the function of our collective identities, of the whole repertory of them that a culture makes available to its members, is to structure possible narratives of the self.

Across cultures, people care to give a certain narrative unity to their lives: each person wants to tell a story of his or her life that makes sense. The story—my story—should cohere in the way appropriate to a person of my culture. In telling that story, how it fits into the wider story of various collectivities is, for most of us, important. It is not just that, say, gender identities give shape (through rites of passage, for example) to one's life; it is also that ethnic and national identities fit that story into a larger narrative. And some of the most "individualist" of individuals value such things. Hobbes spoke of the desire for glory as one of the dominating impulses of human beings, one that was bound to make trouble for social life. But glory can consist in fitting and being seen to fit into a collective history; and so, in the name of glory, one can end up doing the most social things of all.

Once I consciously grasp (as opposed to merely presupposing) the significance and value of my identity for me, I can see what the significance and value of their collective identities would be for others. I will also learn, from history and from social studies, both that such identities are probably humanly inevitable and that the cost of conflicts between identities can be very high, as we see now in the Balkans and in Somalia. A reasonable response to this fact is to recognize the need to accommodate others within my state with different identities. Once ethnic identities cease to be unreflective, as such a line of thought is bound to make them, I will also come to see my identity as something that can be molded, if not individually then at least as part of a common political project, or indeed as something that can be put away altogether.

What is wrong with our collective identities is not that that is what they are; it is rather that we need to restrain the persistent urge for one identity to go on the rampage against others. To do this, we may have to reshape them. Because the same "facts" can fit into many different stories, this reshaping is something we are indeed capable of. The picture I suggested earlier, in which public education simply acknowledges the ethnic identities created outside the state, is too simple. In reflecting on these identities we cannot but alter them; at least some of the children we teach about other cultures will not maintain the unreflective sense of the superiority of their own. To conceive of multicultural education in this way—as the teaching of cross-subcultural understanding and of respect for other identities—is to seek to constrain identities so that they may share a single society.

Why Not Simply Insist on a Single Culture?

Having argued that the school in our society should not simply leave everything ethnically where it is, the question of a single common culture is likely to resurface. Why not argue out democratically a common culture, making sure to learn the lesson of multiculturalism that this must not simply be the cover for a sectional interest?

My answer is, because we do not have to do so. The question presupposes that what we really need is shared values, a common culture. I think this is a mistake. What I think we really need is provided in a conjunct of our original definition of a society, something so obvious that we soon left it behind. "Common institutions and a common culture," I said, but dropped talk of the common institutions almost immediately.

But to live together in a nation what is required is that we all share a commitment to the organization of the state—the institutions that provide the overarching order of our common life. This does not require that we have the same commitment to those institutions, in the sense that the institutions must carry the same meaning for all of us.

The First Amendment separates church and state. Some of us are committed to this because we are religious: we see it as the institutionalization of a Protestant insistence on freedom of conscience. Some of us are committed to it because we are Catholics or Jews or Moslems, who do not want to be pressed into conformity by a Protestant majority. Some of us are atheists who want to be left alone. We can live together with this arrangement provided we all are committed to it, for our different reasons.

There is a useful analogy here with much mass culture and other mass-produced goods. People in London and in Lagos, in New York and New Delhi, listen to Michael Jackson and drink Coca-Cola. They exist, in part, as an audience for his work, as consumers of that drink. But nobody thinks that what either of these products means in one place must be identical with what it means in every site of its consumption. Similarly, the institutions of democracy—the election, the public debate, the protection of minority rights—have different meanings to different subcultures. Once more, there is no reason to require that we all value them in the same way, for the same reasons. All that is required is that everybody is willing to "play the game."

A shared political life in a great modern nation is not like the life of a traditional society. It can encompass a great diversity of meanings. When we teach children democratic habits, through practice in public schools, what we are creating is a shared commitment to certain forms of social behavior. We can call this a political culture, if we like. But the meanings citizens give to their lives, and to the political within their lives, in particular, will be shaped not only by the school, but by the family and church, by reading and by television, in their professional and recreational associations.

Maybe, in the end, there will be a richer American common culture; maybe it will lead to a consensus on the value of American institutions. Certainly cultural homogenization is proceeding apace. But it has not happened yet. And, so far as I can see, it doesn't have to happen in order for us to live together. Competing identities may be having a hard time living together in new democracies. But in this, the oldest democracy, so long as our institutions treat every significant identity with enough respect to gain its allegiance, we can muddle along in the meanwhile without a common culture. That, after all, is what we have been doing, lo, these many years.

Notes

1. The shared space is probably what distinguishes this sense of the term from the sense of society in the expression "international high society." We wouldn't normally speak of the latter as "a society," despite the shared institutions (Ascot, the Kentucky Derby, the fall fashions in Paris, the London season) and common culture (conventions of address).
2. My dictionary gives as the relevant sense of the word "society," "A group of human beings broadly distinguished from other groups by mutual interests, participation in characteristic relationships, shared institutions, and a common culture." *American Heritage Dictionary III for DOS*, 3d ed. (Novato, Calif.: Wordstar International Incorporated, 1993).
3. It is increasingly true, of course, that the cultures of other places are shaped by American culture—notably through the movies—so that the distinction between a culture shaped *in* the United States and one shaped *by* the United States is less sharp than it used to be.
4. *American Heritage Dictionary III for DOS.*
5. There is nothing absurd in holding that the different practices and beliefs of, say, women and men in a society cohere—not in the sense of forming a single logically consistent system, but in the sense that the reason why women engage in one practice is connected with the reason why

men engage in another different practice and that a society in which women and men engage in these different practices is, in part, held together by that fact. But even that notion came under attack when the functionalist notion that every element of practice in a society was adaptive was subjected to criticism.

6. Though, as I say, I do not think you need to react by becoming a cultural relativist.

7. I here exclude material culture—clothing, houses, pottery, weapons, and the like—from the common culture, though not the signs and symbols which adorn it.

8. Some, of course, may believe that they are universally held. This definition of the common culture excludes material culture. I believe the study of material culture is extremely important; but its relevance for debates about multiculturalism has to do with its symbolic resonance, and thus to do with language, ideas, values.

9. This is not the only way the term could be used. Some want to reserve the term for the culture of subordinate groups. I want to avoid that implication in my usage.

10. This way of defining subcultures also means that the shared beliefs and values of a subgroup of the nation need not be exclusive to them: it may be, for example, that there are some American Jewish subcultures whose shared central values and beliefs are also shared with some Jewish groups in Britain or Italy or Israel.

11. Not every society will distinguish between the natural and the social in the sort of way we do. So this formula is not meant to imply that every society has separable theories of what we call the natural and the social.

12. What I have been calling a subculture, then, consists of people who share specific practices, beliefs, and values that constitute the common culture of a subgroup of the nation.

13. Given that the constitution is about a year old as I write (it was promulgated in 1992 and came into full effect in 1993), this is not too surprising, I suppose. But much of the structure has been in place since independence with few changes.

14. This is not, remember, to claim that most Americans are Christians by belief. It is to say only that some of the central ideas and practices of Christianity are known to and understood by most Americans.

15. Men and women may have characteristically distinct experiences; but that doesn't, by itself, guarantee distinct cultures.

16. The arguments of this section are based on suggestions from Bob Fullinwider. I have taken up many suggestions he made in his helpful criticisms of my first draft. I accept full responsibility for these ideas, as I have expressed them, but I don't claim to have come to all of them myself.

17. National Council for the Social Studies, "Curriculum Guidelines for Multicultural Education," *Social Education* 55 (September 1992): 278.

18. Ibid.: "Multicultural education should stress the process of self-identification. . . ."

19. There is another problem with this way of thinking: it suggests that Western culture belongs to some American children more than others in virtue of their descent. This is doubly troubling: first, because the culture we teach in school belongs only to those who do the work to earn it; second, because it proposes to exclude certain children from certain educational experiences on what look like racial grounds.

20. Of course, I do not think—absurdly—that everyone should become both a Jew and a Moslem while holding on to Protestantism. The sort of participation in Jewish or Moslem celebrations that I am talking about is the participation of a guest, a visitor, a friend.

21. Postmodernism urges people to respond, "Worst by whose criteria?" My answer is, In the real world of intercultural moral conversation, nobody—except a postmodernist—defends his position by claiming that it follows simply from his criteria and leaves it at that. If we argue with those who practice clitoral excision and say it ought to be stopped, we need to tell those who practice it why. If we argue that it causes pain to girls and years of low-grade infections to women, and raises the risks of pregnancy; if we say that women who have not been circumcised are not, ipso facto, sexually insatiable; if we say that the practice deprives women of a source of pleasure; if we observe that the practice is not, in fact, recommended by the Koran: nobody, except in a rhetorical moment of weakness, is going to defend the practice by saying that these facts—if such they are—are relevant only by our criteria. And when they suggest to us that "we" mutilate women—through cosmetic surgery; or that "we" practice male circumci-

sion, which also reduces men's capacity for pleasure; or that an uncircumcised girl cannot get a husband: these facts—if such they are—do not strike us as relevant only by our criteria. (And, in any case, there are people here who are not so sure about the badness of the practice, and people there not so convinced of its goodness.) And this is in a hard case of intercultural disagreement. Most American subgroups share so many substantial ethical assumptions that the "Says who?" response is usually offered only by those who are losing an argument.

Questions

1. How does Appiah distinguish between nation, society, culture, and civilization?
2. How does Appiah account for the shift from use of the term *civilization* to more prevalent use of the term *culture?*
3. What is Appiah's definition of a multicultural nation?
4. Does Appiah think that Americans share a common culture? Does he think that America is "really a society"? Explain.
5. Appiah claims that there has always been a dominant culture in the United States. Do you agree with his assessment?
6. Should the concept of "identity" replace the concept of "culture" in multicultural discourse?
7. Why does Appiah object to teaching "each child the culture of 'its' group"? Do you agree with his conclusions?
8. On what grounds does Appiah object to public schools promoting the particular traditions of one group? Do you agree? Explain.
9. What does Appiah contend is an appropriate multicultural agenda for public education?
10. Should public schools in the United States teach democratic habits and cultivate a shared political culture? Why? Why not?

Excerpt from
"The Politics of Recognition"

Charles Taylor

IV

... The fact is that there are forms of [a] liberalism of equal rights that in the minds of their own proponents can give only a very restricted acknowledgment of distinct cultural identities. The notion that any of the standard schedules of rights might apply differently in one cultural context than they do in another, that their application might have to take account of different collective goals, is considered quite unacceptable. The issue, then, is whether this restrictive view of equal rights is the only possible interpretation. If it is, then it would seem that the accusation of homogenization is well founded. But perhaps it is not. I think it is not, and perhaps the best way to lay out the issue is to see it in the context of the Canadian case, where this question has played a role in the impending breakup of the country. In fact, two conceptions of rights-liberalism have confronted each other, albeit in confused fashion, throughout the long and inconclusive constitutional debates of recent years.

The issue came to the fore because of the adoption in 1982 of the Canadian Charter of Rights, which aligned our political system in this regard with the American one in having a schedule of rights offering a basis for judicial review of legislation at all levels of government. The question had to arise how to relate this schedule to the claims for distinctness put forward by French Canadians, and particularly Quebeckers, on the one hand, and aboriginal peoples on the other. Here what was at stake was the desire of these peoples for survival, and their consequent demand for certain forms of autonomy in their self-government, as well as the ability to adopt certain kinds of legislation deemed necessary for survival.

For instance, Quebec has passed a number of laws in the field of language. One regulates who can send their children to English-language schools (not francophones or immigrants); another requires that businesses with more than fifty employees be run in French; a third outlaws commercial signage in any language other than French. In other words, restrictions have been placed on Quebeckers by their government, in the name of their collective goal of survival, which in other Canadian communities might easily be disallowed by virtue of the Charter.[1] The fundamental question was: Is this variation acceptable or not?

The issue was finally raised by a proposed constitutional amendment, named after the site of the conference where it was first drafted, Meech Lake. The Meech amendment proposed to recognize Quebec as a "distinct society," and wanted to make this recognition one of the bases for judicial interpretation of the rest of the constitution, including the Charter. This seemed to open up the possibility for variation in its interpretation in different parts of the country. For many, such variation was fundamentally unacceptable. Examining why brings us to the heart of the question of how rights-liberalism is related to diversity.

The Canadian Charter follows the trend of the last half of the twentieth century, and gives a basis for judicial review on two basic scores. First, it defines a set of individual rights that are very similar to those protected in other charters and bills of rights in Western democracies, for example, in the United States and Europe. Second, it guarantees equal treatment of citizens in a variety of respects, or, alternatively put, it protects against discriminatory treatment on a number of irrelevant grounds, such as race or sex. There is a lot more in our Charter, including provisions for linguistic rights and aboriginal rights, that could be understood as according powers to collectivities, but the two themes I singled out dominate in the public consciousness.

This is no accident. These two kinds of provisions are now quite common in entrenched schedules of rights that provide the basis for judicial review. In this sense, the Western world, perhaps the world as a whole, is following American precedent. The Americans were the first to write out and entrench a bill of rights, which they did during the ratification of their Constitution and as a condition of its successful outcome. One might argue that they weren't entirely clear on judicial review as a method of securing those rights, but this rapidly became the practice. The first amendments protected individuals, and sometimes state governments,[2] against encroachment by the new federal government. It was after the Civil War, in the period of triumphant Reconstruction, and particularly with the Fourteenth Amendment, which called for "equal protection" for all citizens under the laws, that the theme of nondiscrimination became central to judicial review. But this theme is now on a par with the older norm of the defense of individual rights, and in public consciousness perhaps even ahead.

For a number of people in "English Canada," a political society's espousing certain collective goals threatens to run against both of these basic provisions of our Charter, or indeed any acceptable bill of rights. First, the collective goals may require restrictions on the behavior of individuals that may violate their rights. For many nonfrancophone Canadians, both inside and outside Quebec, this feared outcome had already materialized with Quebec's language legislation. For instance, Quebec legislation prescribes, as already mentioned, the type of school to which parents can send their children; and in the most famous instance, it forbids certain kinds of commercial signage. This latter provision was actually struck down by the Supreme Court as contrary to the Quebec Bill of Rights, as well as the Charter, and only reenacted through the invocation of a clause in the Charter that permits legislatures in certain cases to override decisions of the courts relative to the Charter for a limited period of time (the so-called notwithstanding clause).

But second, even if overriding individual rights were not possible, espousing collective goals on behalf of a national group can be thought to be inherently discriminatory. In the modern world it will always be the case that not all those living as citizens under a certain jurisdiction will belong to the national group thus favored. This in itself could be thought to provoke discrimination. But beyond this, the pursuit of the collective end will probably involve treating insiders and outsiders differently. Thus the schooling provisions of Law 101 forbid (roughly speaking) francophones and immigrants to send their children to English-language schools, but allow Canadian anglophones to do so.

This sense that the Charter clashes with basic Quebec policy was one of the grounds of opposition in the rest of Canada to the Meech Lake accord. The cause for concern was the distinct society clause, and the common demand for amendment was that the Charter be "protected" against this clause, or take precedence over it. There was undoubtedly in this opposition a certain amount of old-style anti-Quebec prejudice, but there was also a serious philosophical point, which we need to articulate here.

Those who take the view that individual rights must always come first, and, along with nondiscrimination provisions, must take precedence over collective goals, are often speaking from a liberal perspective that has become more and more widespread in the Anglo-American world. Its source is, of course, the United States, and it has recently been elaborated and defended by some of the best philosophical and legal minds in that society, including John Rawls, Ronald Dworkin, Bruce Ackerman, and others.[3] There are various formulations of the main idea, but perhaps the one that encapsulates most clearly the point that is relevant to us is the one expressed by Dworkin in his short paper entitled "Liberalism."[4]

Dworkin makes a distinction between two kinds of moral commitment. We all have views about the ends of life, about what constitutes a good life, which we and others ought to strive for. But we also acknowledge a commitment to deal fairly and equally with each other, regardless of how we conceive our ends. We might call this latter commitment "procedural," while commitments concerning the ends of life are "substantive." Dworkin claims that a liberal society is one that as a society adopts no particular substantive view about the ends of life. The society is, rather, united around a strong procedural commitment to treat people with equal respect. The reason that the polity as such can espouse no substantive view, cannot, for instance, allow that one of the goals of legislation should be to make people virtuous in one or another meaning of that term, is that this would involve a violation of its procedural norm. For, given the diversity of modern societies, it would unfailingly be the case that some people and not others would be committed to the favored conception of virtue. They might be in a majority; indeed, it is very likely that they would be, for otherwise a democratic society probably would not espouse their view. Nevertheless, this view would not be everyone's view, and in espousing this substantive outlook the society would not be treating the dissident minority with equal respect. It would be saying to them, in effect, "your view is not as valuable, in the eyes of this polity, as that of your more numerous compatriots."

There are very profound philosophical assumptions underlying this view of liberalism, which is rooted in the thought of Immanuel Kant. Among other features, this view understands human dignity to consist largely in autonomy, that is, in the ability of each person to determine for himself or herself a view of the good life. Dignity is associated less with any particular understanding of the good life, such that someone's departure from this would detract from his or her own dignity, than with the power to consider and espouse for oneself some view or other. We are not respecting this power equally in all subjects, it is claimed, if we raise the outcome of some people's deliberations officially over that of others. A liberal society must remain neutral on the good life, and restrict itself to ensuring that however they see things, citizens deal fairly with each other and the state deals equally with all.

The popularity of this view of the human agent as primarily a subject of self-determining or self-expressive choice helps to explain why this model of liberalism is so strong. But we must also consider that it has been urged with great force and intelligence by liberal thinkers in the United States, and precisely in the context of constitutional doctrines of judicial review.[5] Thus it is not surprising that the idea has become widespread, well beyond those who might subscribe to a specific Kantian philosophy, that a liberal society cannot accommodate publicly espoused notions of the good. This is the conception, as Michael Sandel has noted, of the "procedural republic," which has a very strong hold on the political agenda in the United States, and which has helped to place increasing emphasis on judicial review on the basis of constitutional texts at the expense of the ordinary political process of building majorities with a view to legislative action.[6]

But a society with collective goals like Quebec's violates this model. It is axiomatic for Quebec governments that the survival and flourishing of French culture in Quebec is a good. Political society is not neutral between those who value remaining true to the culture of our ancestors and those who might want to cut loose in the name of some individual goal of self-development. It might be argued that one could after all capture a goal like *survivance* for a proceduralist liberal society. One could consider the French language, for instance, as a collective resource that individuals might want to make use of, and act for its preservation, just as one does for clean air or green spaces. But this can't cap-

ture the full thrust of policies designed for cultural survival. It is not just a matter of having the French language available for those who might choose it. This
might be seen to be the goal of some of the measures of federal bilingualism
over the last twenty years. But it also involves making sure that there is a community of people here in the future that will want to avail itself of the opportunity to use the French language. Policies aimed at survival actively seek to *create* members of the community, for instance, in their assuring that future
generations continue to identify as French-speakers. There is no way that these
policies could be seen as just providing a facility to already existing people.

Quebeckers, therefore, and those who give similar importance to this kind
of collective goal, tend to opt for a rather different model of a liberal society. On
their view, a society can be organized around a definition of the good life, without this being seen as a depreciation of those who do not personally share this
definition. Where the nature of the good requires that it be sought in common,
this is the reason for its being a matter of public policy. According to this conception, a liberal society singles itself out as such by the way in which it treats
minorities, including those who do not share public definitions of the good,
and above all by the rights it accords to all of its members. But now the rights
in question are conceived to be the fundamental and crucial ones that have
been recognized as such from the very beginning of the liberal tradition: rights
to life, liberty, due process, free speech, free practice of religion, and so on. On
this model, there is a dangerous overlooking of an essential boundary in speaking of fundamental rights to things like commercial signage in the language of
one's choice. One has to distinguish the fundamental liberties, those that
should never be infringed and therefore ought to be unassailably entrenched,
on one hand, from privileges and immunities that are important, but that can
be revoked or restricted for reasons of public policy—although one would
need a strong reason to do this—on the other.

A society with strong collective goals can be liberal, on this view, provided
it is also capable of respecting diversity, especially when dealing with those
who do not share its common goals; and provided it can offer adequate safeguards for fundamental rights. There will undoubtedly be tensions and difficulties in pursuing these objectives together, but such a pursuit is not impossible, and the problems are not in principle greater than those encountered by
any liberal society that has to combine, for example, liberty and equality, or
prosperity and justice.

Here are two incompatible views of liberal society. One of the great sources
of our present disharmony is that the two views have squared off against each
other in the last decade. The resistance to the "distinct society" that called for
precedence to be given to the Charter came in part from a spreading procedural outlook in English Canada. From this point of view, attributing the goal
of promoting Quebec's distinct society to a government is to acknowledge a
collective goal, and this move had to be neutralized by being subordinated to
the existing Charter. From the standpoint of Quebec, this attempt to impose a
procedural model of liberalism not only would deprive the distinct society
clause of some of its force as a rule of interpretation, but bespoke a rejection of

the model of liberalism on which this society was founded. Each society mis-perceived the other throughout the Meech Lake debate. But here both per-ceived each other accurately—and didn't like what they saw. The rest of Canada saw that the distinct society clause legitimated collective goals. And Quebec saw that the move to give the Charter precedence imposed a form of liberal society that was alien to it, and to which Quebec could never accommo-date itself without surrendering its identity.[7]

I have delved deeply into this case because it seems to me to illustrate the fundamental questions. There is a form of the politics of equal respect, as en-shrined in a liberalism of rights, that is inhospitable to difference, because (a) it insists on uniform application of the rules defining these rights, without excep-tion, and (b) it is suspicious of collective goals. Of course, this doesn't mean that this model seeks to abolish cultural differences. This would be an absurd accusation. But I call it inhospitable to difference because it can't accommodate what the members of distinct societies really aspire to, which is survival. This is (b) a collective goal, which (a) almost inevitably will call for some variations in the kinds of law we deem permissible from one cultural context to another, as the Quebec case clearly shows.

I think this form of liberalism is guilty as charged by the proponents of a politics of difference. Fortunately, however, there are other models of liberal so-ciety that take a different line on (a) and (b). These forms do call for the invari-ant defense of *certain* rights, of course. There would be no question of cultural differences determining the application of *habeas corpus*, for example. But they distinguish these fundamental rights from the broad range of immunities and presumptions of uniform treatment that have sprung up in modern cultures of judicial review. They are willing to weigh the importance of certain forms of uniform treatment against the importance of cultural survival, and opt some-times in favor of the latter. They are thus in the end not procedural models of liberalism, but are grounded very much on judgments about what makes a good life—judgments in which the integrity of cultures has an important place.

Although I cannot argue it here, obviously I would endorse this kind of model. Indisputably, though, more and more societies today are turning out to be multicultural, in the sense of including more than one cultural community that wants to survive. The rigidities of procedural liberalism may rapidly be-come impractical in tomorrow's world.

V

The politics of equal respect, then, at least in this more hospitable variant, can be cleared of the charge of homogenizing difference. But there is another way of formulating the charge that is harder to rebut. In this form, however, it per-haps ought not to be rebutted, or so I want to argue.

The charge I'm thinking of here is provoked by the claim sometimes made on behalf of "difference-blind" liberalism that it can offer a neutral ground on which people of all cultures can meet and coexist. On this view, it is necessary to make a certain number of distinctions—between what is public and what is private, for instance, or between politics and religion—and only then can one relegate the contentious differences to a sphere that does not impinge on the political.

But a controversy like that over Salman Rushdie's *Satanic Verses* shows how wrong this view is. For mainstream Islam, there is no question of separating politics and religion the way we have come to expect in Western liberal society. Liberalism is not a possible meeting ground for all cultures, but is the political expression of one range of cultures, and quite incompatible with other ranges. Moreover, as many Muslims are well aware, Western liberalism is not so much an expression of the secular, postreligious outlook that happens to be popular among liberal *intellectuals* as a more organic outgrowth of Christianity—at least as seen from the alternative vantage point of Islam. The division of church and state goes back to the earliest days of Christian civilization. The early forms of the separation were very different from ours, but the basis was laid for modern developments. The very term *secular* was originally part of the Christian vocabulary.[8]

All this is to say that liberalism can't and shouldn't claim complete cultural neutrality. Liberalism is also a fighting creed. The hospitable variant I espouse, as well as the most rigid forms, has to draw the line. There will be variations when it comes to applying the schedule of rights, but not where incitement to assassination is concerned. But this should not be seen as a contradiction. Substantive distinctions of this kind are inescapable in politics, and at least the nonprocedural liberalism I was describing is fully ready to accept this.

But the controversy is nevertheless disturbing. It is so for the reason I mentioned above: that all societies are becoming increasingly multicultural, while at the same time becoming more porous. Indeed, these two developments go together. Their porousness means that they are more open to multinational migration; more of their members live the life of diaspora, whose center is elsewhere. In these circumstances, there is something awkward about replying simply, "This is how we do things here." This reply must be made in cases like the Rushdie controversy, where "how we do things" covers issues such as the right to life and to freedom of speech. The awkwardness arises from the fact that there are substantial numbers of people who are citizens and also belong to the culture that calls into question our philosophical boundaries. The challenge is to deal with their sense of marginalization without compromising our basic political principles.

This brings us to the issue of multiculturalism as it is often debated today, which has a lot to do with the imposition of some cultures on others, and with the assumed superiority that powers this imposition. Western liberal societies are thought to be supremely guilty in this regard, partly because of their colonial past, and partly because of their marginalization of segments of their populations that stem from other cultures. It is in this context that the reply "this is how we do things here" can seem crude and insensitive. Even if, in the nature of things, compromise is close to impossible here—one either forbids murder or allows it—the attitude presumed by the reply is seen as one of contempt. Often, in fact, this presumption is correct. Thus we arrive again at the issue of recognition.

Recognition of equal value was not what was at stake—at least in a strong sense—in the preceding section. There it was a question of whether cultural survival will be acknowledged as a legitimate goal, whether collective ends will be allowed as legitimate considerations in judicial review, or for other purposes of major social policy. The demand there was that we let cultures defend themselves, within reasonable bounds. But the further demand we are looking at here is that we all *recognize* the equal value of different cultures; that we not only let them survive, but acknowledge their *worth.*

What sense can be made of this demand? In a way, it has been operative in an unformulated state for some time. The politics of nationalism has been powered for well over a century in part by the sense that people have had of being despised or respected by others around them. Multinational societies can break up, in large part because of a lack of (perceived) recognition of the equal worth of one group by another. This is at present, I believe, the case in Canada—though my diagnosis will certainly be challenged by some. On the international scene, the tremendous sensitivity of certain supposedly closed societies to world opinion—as shown in their reactions to findings of, say, Amnesty International, or in their attempts through UNESCO to build a new world information order—attests to the importance of external recognition.

But all this is still *an sich,* not *für sich,* to use Hegelian jargon. The actors themselves are often the first to deny that they are moved by such considerations, and plead other factors, like inequality, exploitation, and injustice, as their motives. Very few Quebec independentists, for instance, can accept that what is mainly winning them their fight is a lack of recognition on the part of English Canada.

What is new, therefore, is that the demand for recognition is now explicit. And it has been made explicit, in the way I indicated above, by the spread of the idea that we are formed by recognition. We could say that, thanks to this idea, misrecognition has now graduated to the rank of a harm that can be hardheadedly enumerated along with the ones mentioned in the previous paragraph.

One of the key authors in this transition is undoubtedly the late Frantz Fanon, whose influential *Les Damnés de la Terre* (*The Wretched of the Earth*)[9] argued that the major weapon of the colonizers was the imposition of their image of the colonized on the subjugated people. These latter, in order to be free, must first of all purge themselves of these depreciating self-images. Fanon recommended violence as the way to this freedom, matching the original violence of the alien imposition. Not all those who have drawn from Fanon have followed him in this, but the notion that there is a struggle for a changed self-image, which takes place both within the subjugated and against the dominator, has been very widely applied. The idea has become crucial to certain strands of feminism, and is also a very important element in the contemporary debate about multiculturalism.

The main locus of this debate is the world of education in a broad sense. One important focus is university humanities departments, where demands are made to alter, enlarge, or scrap the "canon" of accredited authors on the grounds that the one presently favored consists almost entirely of "dead white males." A greater place ought to be made for women, and for people of non-European races and cultures. A second focus is the secondary schools, where an attempt is being made, for instance, to develop Afrocentric curricula for pupils in mainly black schools.

The reason for these proposed changes is not, or not mainly, that all students may be missing something important through the exclusion of a certain gender or certain races or cultures, but rather that women and students from the excluded groups are given, either directly or by omission, a demeaning picture of themselves, as though all creativity and worth inhered in males of European provenance. Enlarging and changing the curriculum is therefore essential not so much in the name of a broader culture for everyone as in order to give due recognition to the hitherto excluded. The background premise of these demands is that recognition forges identity, particularly in its Fanonist application: dominant groups tend to entrench their hegemony by inculcating an image of inferiority in the subjugated. The struggle for freedom and equality must therefore pass through a revision of these images. Multicultural curricula are meant to help in this process of revision.

Although it is not often stated clearly, the logic behind some of these demands seems to depend upon a premise that we owe equal respect to all cultures. This emerges from the nature of the reproach made to the designers of traditional curricula. The claim is that the judgments of worth on which these latter were supposedly based were in fact corrupt, were marred by narrowness or insensitivity or, even worse, a desire to downgrade the excluded. The implication seems to be that absent these distorting factors, true judgments of value of different works would place all cultures more or less on the same footing. Of course, the attack could come from a more radical, neo-Nietzschean standpoint, which questions the very status of judgments of worth as such, but short of this extreme step (whose coherence I doubt), the presumption seems to be of equal worth.

I would like to maintain that there is something valid in this presumption, but that the presumption is by no means unproblematic, and involves something like an act of faith. As a presumption, the claim is that all human cultures that have animated whole societies over some considerable stretch of time have something important to say to all human beings. I have worded it in this way to exclude partial cultural milieux within a society, as well as short phases of a major culture. There is no reason to believe that, for instance, the different art forms of a given culture should all be of equal, or even of considerable, value; and every culture can go through phases of decadence.

But when I call this claim a "presumption," I mean that it is a starting hypothesis with which we ought to approach the study of any other culture. The validity of the claim has to be demonstrated concretely in the actual study of the culture. Indeed, for a culture sufficiently different from our own, we may have only the foggiest idea *ex ante* of in what its valuable contribution might consist. Because, for a sufficiently different culture, the very understanding of what it is to be of worth will be strange and unfamiliar to us. To approach, say, a raga with the presumptions of value implicit in the well-tempered clavier would be forever to miss the point. What has to happen is what Gadamer has called a "fusion of horizons."[10] We learn to move in a broader horizon, within which what we have formerly taken for granted as the background to valuation can be situated as one possibility alongside the different background of the formerly unfamiliar culture. The "fusion of horizons" operates through our developing new vocabularies of comparison, by means of which we can articulate these contrasts.[11] So that if and when we ultimately find substantive support for our initial presumption, it is on the basis of an understanding of what constitutes worth that we couldn't possibly have had at the beginning. We have reached the judgment partly through transforming our standards.

We might want to argue that we owe all cultures a presumption of this kind. I will explain later on what I think this claim might be based. From this point of view, withholding the presumption might be seen as the fruit merely of prejudice or of ill-will. It might even be tantamount to a denial of equal status. Something like this might lie behind the accusation leveled by supporters of multiculturalism against defenders of the traditional canon. Supposing that their reluctance to enlarge the canon comes from a mixture of prejudice and ill-will, the multiculturalists charge them with the arrogance of assuming their own superiority over formerly subject peoples.

This presumption would help explain why the demands of multiculturalism build on the already established principles of the politics of equal respect. If withholding the presumption is tantamount to a denial of equality, and if important consequences flow for people's identity from the absence of recognition, then a case can be made for insisting on the universalization of the presumption as a logical extension of the politics of dignity. Just as all must have equal civil rights, and equal voting rights, regardless of race or culture, so all should enjoy the presumption that their traditional culture has value. This extension, however logically it may seem to flow from the accepted norms of equal dignity, fits uneasily within them, as described in Section II, because it challenges the "difference-blindness" that was central to them. Yet it does indeed seem to flow from them, albeit uneasily.

I am not sure about the validity of demanding this presumption as a right. But we can leave this issue aside, because the demand made seems to be much stronger. The claim seems to be that a proper respect for equality requires more than a presumption that further study will make us see things this way, but actual judgments of equal worth applied to the customs and creations of these different cultures. Such judgments seem to be implicit in the demand that certain works be included in the canon, and in the implication that these works have not been included earlier only because of prejudice or ill-will or the desire to dominate. (Of course, the demand for inclusion is *logically* separable from a claim of equal worth. The demand could be: Include these because they're ours, even though they may well be inferior. But this is not how the people making the demand talk.)

But there is something very wrong with the demand in this form. It makes sense to demand as a matter of right that we approach the study of certain cultures with a presumption of their value, as described above. But it can't make sense to demand as a matter of right that we come up with a final concluding judgment that their value is great, or equal to others'. That is, if the judgment of value is to register something independent of our own wills and desires, it cannot be dictated by a principle of ethics. On examination, either we will find something of great value in culture C, or we will not. But it makes no more sense to demand that we do so than it does to demand that we find the earth round or flat, the temperature of the air hot or cold.

I have stated this rather flatly, when as everyone knows there is a vigorous controversy over the "objectivity" of judgments in this field, and whether there is a "truth of the matter" here, as there seems to be in natural science, or indeed, whether even in natural science "objectivity" is a mirage. I do not have space to address this here. I have discussed it somewhat elsewhere.[12] I don't have much sympathy for these forms of subjectivism, which I think are shot through with confusion. But there seems to be some special confusion in invoking them in this context. The moral and political thrust of the complaint concerns unjustified judgments of inferior status allegedly made of nonhegemonic cultures. But if those judgments are ultimately a question of the human will, then the issue of justification falls away. One doesn't, properly speaking, make judgments that can be right or wrong; one expresses liking or dislike, one endorses or rejects another culture. But then the complaint must shift to address the refusal to endorse, and the validity or invalidity of judgments here has nothing to do with it.

Then, however, the act of declaring another culture's creations to be of worth and the act of declaring oneself on their side, even if their creations aren't all that impressive, become indistinguishable. The difference is only in the packaging. Yet the first is normally understood as a genuine expression of respect, the second often as unsufferable patronizing. The supposed beneficiaries of the politics of recognition, the people who might actually benefit from acknowledgment, make a crucial distinction between the two acts. They know that they want respect, not condescension. Any theory that wipes out the distinction seems at least *prima facie* to be distorting crucial facets of the reality it purports to deal with.

In fact, subjectivist, half-baked neo-Nietzschean theories are quite often invoked in this debate. Deriving frequently from Foucault or Derrida, they claim that all judgments of worth are based on standards that are ultimately imposed by and further entrench structures of power. It should be clear why these theories proliferate here. A favorable judgment on demand is nonsense, unless some such theories are valid. Moreover, the giving of such a judgment on demand is an act of breathtaking condescension. No one can really mean it as a genuine act of respect. It is more in the nature of a pretend act of respect given on the insistence of its supposed beneficiary. Objectively, such an act involves contempt for the latter's intelligence. To be an object of such an act of respect demeans. The proponents of neo-Nietzschean theories hope to escape this whole nexus of hypocrisy by turning the entire issue into one of power and counterpower. Then the question is no more one of respect, but of taking sides, of solidarity. But this is hardly a satisfactory solution, because in taking sides they miss the driving force of this kind of politics, which is precisely the search for recognition and respect.

Moreover, even if one could demand it of them, the last thing one wants at this stage from Eurocentered intellectuals is positive judgments of the worth of cultures that they have not intensively studied. For real judgments of worth suppose a fused horizon of standards, as we have seen; they suppose that we have been transformed by the study of the other, so that we are not simply judging by our original familiar standards. A favorable judgment made prematurely would be not only condescending but ethnocentric. It would praise the other for being like us.

Here is another severe problem with much of the politics of multiculturalism. The peremptory demand for favorable judgments of worth is paradoxically—perhaps one should say tragically—homogenizing. For it implies that we already have the standards to make such judgments. The standards we have, however, are those of North Atlantic civilization. And so the judgments implicitly and unconsciously will cram the others into our categories. For instance, we will think of their "artists" as creating "works," which we then can include in our canon. By implicitly invoking our standards to judge all civilizations and cultures, the politics of difference can end up making everyone the same.[13]

In this form, the demand for equal recognition is unacceptable. But the story doesn't simply end there. The enemies of multiculturalism in the American academy have perceived this weakness, and have used this as an excuse to turn their backs on the problem. But this won't do. A response like that attributed to Bellow which I quoted above, to the effect that we will be glad to read the Zulu Tolstoy when he comes along, shows the depths of ethnocentricity. First, there is the implicit assumption that excellence has to take forms familiar to us: the Zulus should produce a *Tolstoy*. Second, we are assuming that their contribution is yet to be made (*when* the Zulus produce a Tolstoy . . .). These two assumptions obviously go hand in hand. If they have to produce our kind of excellence, then obviously their only hope lies in the future. Roger Kimball puts it more crudely: "The multiculturalists notwithstanding, the choice facing us today is not between a 'repressive' Western culture and a multicultural paradise, but between culture and barbarism. Civilization is not a gift, it is an achievement—a fragile achievement that needs constantly to be shored up and defended from besiegers inside and out."[14]

There must be something midway between the inauthentic and homogenizing demand for recognition of equal worth, on the one hand, and the self-immurement within ethnocentric standards, on the other. There are other cultures, and we have to live together more and more, both on a world scale and commingled in each individual society.

What there is is the presumption of equal worth I described above: a stance we take in embarking on the study of the other. Perhaps we don't need to ask whether it's something that others can demand from us as a right. We might simply ask whether this is the way we ought to approach others.

Well, is it? How can this presumption be grounded? One ground that has been proposed is a religious one. Herder, for instance, had a view of divine providence, according to which all this variety of culture was not a mere accident but was meant to bring about a greater harmony. I can't rule out such a view. But merely on the human level, one could argue that it is reasonable to suppose that cultures that have provided the horizon of meaning for large numbers of human beings, of diverse characters and temperaments, over a long period of time—that have, in other words, articulated their sense of the good, the holy, the admirable—are almost certain to have something that deserves our admiration and respect, even if it is accompanied by much that we have to abhor and reject. Perhaps one could put it another way: it would take a supreme arrogance to discount this possibility *a priori*.

There is perhaps after all a moral issue here. We only need a sense of our own limited part in the whole human story to accept the presumption. It is only arrogance, or some analogous moral failing, that can deprive us of this. But what the presumption requires of us is not peremptory and inauthentic judgments of equal value, but a willingness to be open to comparative cultural study of the kind that must displace our horizons in the resulting fusions. What it requires above all is an admission that we are very far away from that ultimate horizon from which the relative worth of different cultures might be evident. This would mean breaking with an illusion that still holds many "multiculturalists"—as well as their most bitter opponents—in its grip.[15]

Notes

1. The Supreme Court of Canada did strike down one of these provisions, the one forbidding commercial signage in languages other than French. But in their judgment the justices agreed that it would have been quite reasonable to demand that all signs be in French, even though accompanied by another language. In other words, it was permissible in their view for Quebec to outlaw unilingual English signs. The need to protect and promote the French language in the Quebec context would have justified it. Presumably this would mean that legislative restrictions on the language of signs in another province might well be struck down for some quite other reason.

    Incidentally, the signage provisions are still in force in Quebec, because of a provision of the Charter that in certain cases allows legislatures to override judgments of the courts for a restricted period.

2. For instance, the First Amendment, which forbade Congress to establish any religion, was not originally meant to separate church and state as such. It was enacted at a time when many states had established churches, and it was plainly meant to prevent the new federal government from interfering with or overruling these local arrangements. It was only later, after the Fourteenth Amendment, following the so-called Incorporation doctrine, that these restrictions on the federal government were held to have been extended to all governments, at any level.

3. Rawls, *A Theory of Justice* and "Justice as Fairness: Political Not Metaphysical," *Philosophy & Public Affairs* 14 (1985): 223–51; Dworkin, *Taking Rights Seriously* and "Liberalism," in *Public and Private Morality*, ed. Stuart Hampshire (Cambridge: Cambridge University Press, 1978); Bruce Ackerman, *Social Justice in the Liberal State* (New Haven: Yale University Press, 1980).

4. Dworkin, "Liberalism."
5. See, for instance, the arguments deployed by Lawrence Tribe in his *Abortion: The Clash of Absolutes* (New York: Norton, 1990).
6. Michael Sandel, "The Procedural Republic and the Unencumbered Self," *Political Theory* 12 (1984): 81–96.
7. See Guy Laforest, "L'esprit de 1982," in *Le Québec et la restructuration du Canada, 1980–1992*, ed. Louis Balthasar, Guy Laforest, and Vincent Lemieux (Quebec: Septentrion, 1991).
8. The point is well argued in Larry Siedentop, "Liberalism: The Christian Connection," *Times Literary Supplement*, 24–30 March 1989, p. 308. I have also discussed these issues in "The Rushdie Controversy," in *Public Culture* 2, no. 1 (Fall 1989): 118–22.
9. (Paris: Maspero, 1961).
10. *Wahrheit und Methode* (Tübingen: Mohr, 1975), pp. 289–90.
11. I have discussed what is involved here at greater length in "Comparison, History, Truth," in *Myth and Philosophy*, ed. Frank Reynolds and David Tracy (Albany: State University of New York Press, 1990); and in "Understanding and Ethnocentricity," in *Philosophy and the Human Sciences* (Cambridge: Cambridge University Press, 1985).
12. See part 1 of *Sources of the Self*.
13. The same homogenizing assumptions underlie the negative reaction that many people have to claims to superiority in some definite respect on behalf of Western civilization, say in regard to natural science. But it is absurd to cavil at such claims in principle. If all cultures have made a contribution of worth, it cannot be that these are identical, or even embody the same kind of worth. To expect this would be to vastly underestimate the differences. In the end, the presumption of worth imagines a universe in which different cultures complement each other with quite different kinds of contribution. This picture not only is compatible with, but demands judgments of, superiority-in-a-certain-respect.
14. "Tenured Radicals," *New Criterion*, January 1991, p. 13.
15. There is a very interesting critique of both extreme camps, from which I have borrowed in this discussion, in Benjamin Lee, "Towards a Critical Internationalism" (forthcoming).

Questions

1. What form of a liberal "politics of equal respect" does Taylor find problematic?

2. According to Taylor, in multicultural societies should democratic governments be neutral toward all cultural groups?

3. Is it Taylor's position that all cultural groups have an equal right to survival? Explain.

4. Do you think Taylor would support the use of public educational resources to maximize the chances for survival of a distinct cultural group? Why? Why not?

5. What is Taylor advocating when he calls for a "presumption of equal worth" among cultures?

6. How might Taylor's "presumption of equal worth" be applied as a principle to educational practices such as curriculum design? Give specific examples.

7. Why does Taylor think that a concept like Gadamer's "fusion of horizons" is useful for a multicultural society?

8. How might educational institutions encourage a "fusion of horizons" among members of distinct cultural groups?

9. What are some possible tensions between the existence of distinct cultural groups in a society and achieving a "fusion of horizons"?

Challenges of Multiculturalism in Democratic Education

Amy Gutmann

How can a multicultural society educate its members for democracy? Many contemporary controversies about public schooling turn on the clash of two apparently competing educational aims: securing civic values and respecting cultural differences.[1] This essay argues that democratic education can integrate both civic and multicultural aims, and not merely in a pragmatic compromise, but in a genuinely principled combination. At the outset, I describe two responses that fail to do justice to one or the other of these aims. The first response sets the project of civic unity against the diversifying tendencies of multiculturalism; the second puts cultural diversity above the claims of civic education. Both responses reflect significant political impulses in the United States and throughout the world, and both contain partial insights. I try to capture the partial truth in each and integrate them into a democratic conception of a civic *and* multicultural education.

The second part of the essay develops the integration by considering a test case—a recent French controversy known as the "Affair of the Scarf" or the "chador case"—that highlights one of the deepest conflicts endemic to multicultural societies. Can a conception of democratic education accommodate religious differences that conflict with civic values? I defend a democratic response to the chador case that respects religious differences without sacrificing the aims of teaching a common set of civic values to all citizens.

The last part of the essay explores the even greater challenge that multinationalism poses for democratic education. Despite the differences between multinational and multicultural societies, there is an important similarity in the challenge they pose to democratic education. In both cases, educators must cultivate a concern for human beings, whatever their nationality, alongside a sense of civic responsibility. Integrating these two aims, and coping with conflicts between them, is perhaps the most formidable challenge for the philosophy and practice of democratic education. We shall see that there is no justifiable way of escaping this challenge by falling back on either a purely cosmopolitan or a purely civic understanding of education.

Civic Education, Cultural Differences, and Mutual Respect

Public schools in the United States once included Protestant prayers and readings from the King James Version of the Bible as central parts of the school day. Little or no effort was made to respect the diverse religious beliefs of non-Protestants. Catholic children were sometimes whipped by teachers if they refused to read from the King James Bible. In the same schools, history was taught largely without reference to, let alone understanding of, the experiences of American Indians, blacks, and women. And, perhaps more significantly, all subjects were taught to racially segregated student bodies, for whom even an inclusive, culturally respectful civics curriculum would have been overwhelmed by the civics lesson in white supremacy implicit in the way children were distributed among schools.

This traditional model illustrates the problem with a civic education unmodified by multiculturalism. The traditional model withheld respect from different ways of life, and denigrated the contributions of minority groups and women to American civic culture. It also taught morally skewed lessons in civic virtue. When history classes exalted the contributions of the founding fathers with scant discussion of the institution of slavery, the lives of slaves, the Underground Railroad, or the contributions of African-Americans to civic understandings, public schools failed, among other things, to teach students the civic values of democratic dissent and disobedience to unjust laws. In not teaching these democratic values, schools diminished the role of dissenters and restricted the range of reasonable political alternatives that children could understand and embrace.

To cite another, not atypical example, from personal experience: The world history texts in my public school devoted as much space to the heroic acts of righteous Christians in rescuing Jews during the Holocaust as to the slaughter itself of millions of Jews. These texts sent an unsubtle signal to every student who read them (which is not to say that every student did read them) that some people count for much more than others in this country. These texts also failed to convey how the historical experiences of minorities can offer American citizens a more adequate understanding of our civic values of "liberty and justice for all."

These purportedly patriotic history lessons were *repressive* and *discriminatory*. They simultaneously restricted understanding of diverse ways of life and denigrated the people who lived those lives. Repression in schooling is commonly identified with banning books and punishing teachers or students for unpopular ideas. But schooling is often repressive, and more insidiously so, by virtue of what it fails to teach. A civic education is repressive when it fails to teach appreciation and respect for the positive contributions by minorities to a society's common culture.

An antidote to this traditional civics curriculum is education that aims to appreciate the social contributions and life experiences of the various groups that constitute society. Such appreciation defines one common conception of multicultural education, a conception compatible with the principles of democratic education. We are a society constituted by many cultures. It is both morally wrong and empirically false to teach students as if it were otherwise.

Some contemporary American educators, however, defend schooling that is multicultural in a different sense. They defend schools designed primarily to cultivate the separatist cultural identities of minorities and to bolster the self-esteem of students based on their membership in a separatist culture. Afrocentrism is a currently controversial instance of such a separatist multicultural perspective, but the perspective is not unique to Afrocentrism, nor is it new to American education. Some all-white schools are designed to serve a similar if less publicly criticized purpose: to teach children a sense of racial superiority, which is taken to justify racial discrimination.

The chief problem with such segregation academies from a democratic perspective is not the inaccuracy of what they teach children about the superior accomplishments of their ancestors, but their attempt to cultivate among these children a sense of superiority based on race. These schools try to teach racial *discrimination*, albeit for differing reasons. Democratic governments cannot prevent private individuals and associations from conveying to children a sense of superiority based on race, religion, gender, or class, but they must not support schools that convey the very disrespect that democratic education should be designed to dispel.

Some educators say that teaching disadvantaged students to identify with the superior contributions of their ancestors bolsters their *self-esteem*, "the favorable appreciation or opinion of oneself." But this way of cultivating self-esteem comes at the cost of undercutting *mutual respect* among citizens, "a proper regard for the dignity of [a] person or position."[2] In a democracy, proper regard for the position of citizens includes the mutual recognition that all persons, regardless of the accomplishments of their ancestors, are entitled to equal political and civil liberties and fair equality of opportunity to live a good life.

Public schooling in a democracy should not therefore forswear the aim of increasing the self-esteem of disadvantaged students. I have argued only that schools should not try to increase self-esteem by discriminatory means, such as crediting to particular groups of students the superiority of their ancestors. This aim is to be distinguished from recognizing and respecting the identification of individuals with particular cultures. This identification is something that public schooling can support, as a way of respecting students with different cultural identifications, and also as a way of recognizing the multitude of cultural opportunities that are open to all students as members of a multicultural society. Imagine a curriculum in which the achievements of Africa and

Africans, ancient and modern, are given due place alongside the treatment of other continents and peoples, and in which the links (causal, cultural, and emotional) between the history of Africa and the history of African-Americans are made plain. Such a curriculum taught to *all* students puts multicultural education in service to democratic values, not in opposition. Such a curriculum supports rather than subverts one of the most basic lessons of democratic education: that all individuals, regardless of their cultural identifications, have equal civic standing, and are honored or dishonored by their own acts, not by the acts of their ancestors.

For schools to cultivate a sense of self-esteem in students that is sustainable alongside mutual respect among citizens, schools need to help every student succeed academically. Students learn to appreciate themselves as accomplished individuals when schools help them become accomplished learners. This educational task is a lot harder than teaching students to identify with their ancestors. Educational success entails learning something that is worthy of being publicly honored as knowledge and (moral, empirical, or analytical) understanding.[3] The fact that educational success, like self-esteem, is achieved by individuals does not mean that its attainment must be a solitary endeavor. Quite the contrary. Some of the most successful teaching occurs in cooperative and diverse learning groups. The self-esteem that is compatible with civic equality (which, in turn, is based on a commitment to treating people as equals) cannot be acquired by group identification.

We have identified two ways that schools have failed to meet the challenge of securing common values and respecting cultural differences. The traditional civics curriculum imposes a cultural singularity that is false to the pluralism of American life and disrespectful of many of its citizens. A separatist curricula also educates by exclusion by fostering a sense of superiority among some students at the cost of disparaging or degrading others. Neither response promotes mutual respect among citizens, which is still sorely lacking in our society, and many others.

Why worry about cultivating mutual respect, a positive regard for other people who are also motivated to be respectful even in the face of cultural and political differences? Why should democratic education not rest content with teaching the less ambitious virtue of toleration, simply "to live and let live" in the face of our differences? Toleration is an essential democratic virtue and a necessary but not sufficient condition of mutual respect. In a democratic society, mutual respect is a public as well as a private good. It expresses the equal standing of every person as an individual and citizen, and it also enables democratic citizens to discuss their political differences in a productive way by first understanding one another's perspectives and then by trying to find fair ways of resolving their disagreements.

Schools can teach mutual respect in at least two ways that meet the challenge of joining civic and multicultural aims to the benefit of both. Schools can create curricula that recognize the multicultural heritage of the United States as everyone's resource, belonging not only to all of us, but also to future immigrants and generations to come. In addition, schools can teach about foreign cultures in a way that is more conducive to our remaining a society of immigrants. If we are to remain a haven for political and economic refugees, we need to respect not only the diverse cultures that are already ours, but also those that are not presently represented within our borders. (This does not call for an uncritical or static approach to any culture, domestic or foreign.) Recognition of foreign cultures cannot of course be comprehensive. In any case, cultivating a relatively deep appreciation of a few foreign cultures is likely to be more educationally effective than conveying a superficial familiarity with many.

But appreciation of cultural diversity is not enough to teach students the civic virtue of mutual respect, nor is it the toughest task now facing most schools. Expanding the knowledge of students meets only half the intellectual and moral challenge of the democratic ideal that I have been defending. The second, pedagogically as well as politically more demanding, way in which schools can cultivate mutual respect is to teach students how to engage together in respectful discussions in which they strive to understand, appreciate, and, if possible, resolve political disagreements, including those that may be partly rooted in cultural differences. Mutual respect that rests only on the *recognition* of cultural diversity is an incomplete democratic virtue. Recognition needs to be accompanied by a willingness and ability to deliberate about politically relevant disagreements.

A culturally diverse citizenry dedicated to deliberation strives for reciprocity in political relationships. It seeks agreement on public policies that are (as far as possible) mutually acceptable to all citizens who are bound by them. Reciprocity is a goal which is unlikely to be fully realized. As with many valuable ends, reciprocity is an aspirational ideal, one that is constitutive of the political ideal of democracy. By teaching the skills and virtues of deliberation among citizens, schools can contribute to bringing a democracy closer to its own ideal.

Even if reciprocity may never be fully realized, we can find partial ways of approaching its educational aims of cultivating an inclusive multiculturalism and a morally informed deliberation. We can find examples of promising practices in non-elite public schools in the United States. Deborah Meier's pioneering District 4 in East Harlem and California's statewide history curriculum offer models of inclusive multicultural curricula. Neither model is perfect, but both are better than what has gone before them. Meier's school is successful both by traditional measures (increased reading and mathematical achievement scores) and non-traditional measures (integration of a multiracial student body).

Much more should be said about teaching morally-informed deliberation than this essay permits.[4] I can only point to a good illustration of teaching the virtues and skills of morally informed deliberation. The example comes from an account of an American history class in a Brooklyn high school where students were asked whether it was moral for the United States to drop the atomic bomb on Japan.

The lesson was taught in a Socratic manner. Bruckner [the teacher] did not lecture. He asked questions and kept up a rapid-fire dialogue among the students. "Why?" "How do you know?" "What does this mean?" By the time the class was finished, the students had covered a great deal of material about American foreign and domestic politics during World War II; they had argued heatedly; most of them had tried out different points of view, seeing the problem from different angles.[5]

Like this small but significant lesson in deliberation, a multicultural curriculum dedicated to teaching deliberation would encourage students to respect each other as equal citizens, regardless of the accomplishments of their ancestors, and to take different points of view seriously when thinking about politics. The practice of morally informed deliberation engages students in according each other the mutual respect and moral understanding that is too often lacking in contemporary politics.

Teaching mutual respect among citizens in these ways is a central aim of civic education in a multicultural democracy. Bolstering self-esteem by group identification is not—not because self-esteem is unimportant or insupportable by education, but because the self-esteem that is compatible with mutual respect among citizens cannot be acquired merely by means of group identification. Just as a civic education, unmodified by multiculturalism, represses cultural differences, multiculturalism, uninformed by civic values, discriminates among citizens on the basis of their group identities. Schools can meet this challenge of multiculturalism by allying common civic values with uncommon cultural appreciations.

Democratic Multicultural Education and "The Affair of the Scarf"

I have criticized two common perspectives on multiculturalism in a democratic society. One speaks in the voice of a transcendent universalism, the other in the voice of a separatist particularism. I have suggested that both speak misleadingly in that they fail to do justice to the values of universalism and particularism that they claim to represent. A civic education cannot completely transcend particular cultures, and a multicultural education should not lose sight of the universalist principles of toleration and mutual respect that inform its commitment to cultural diversity. A democratic integration of civic education and multiculturalism can capture the partial truth in the two common perspectives by refusing to divorce the aims of civic education from those of multicultural education, at the same time recognizing that there are potential tensions between these two inter-related strands of democratic education.

"Easier said than done," a critic might reply. This integration of multiculturalism and civic education has yet to confront the challenge of accommodating religious differences. To see if democratic education can meet this challenge, we should consider a controversy in which the aims of civic education are apparently at odds with religious freedom.

In 1989, three Muslim adolescent girls went to their local public high school in Creil, France wearing chadors (head coverings that are associated with religiously orthodox Muslims). French public schools are, by law and centuries-long tradition, secular. A 1937 law prohibits the wearing of religious symbols, or at least conspicuous religious symbols, in government-run schools. (Parents may send their children to private schools that teach religion, but these schools charge tuition and many families cannot afford them.) Citing the 1937 law, the principal of the high school, a Catholic of Martinican origin, told the three students that they must remove their chadors in class. When they refused, the principal, supported by the school's teachers, forbade the girls to attend class.[6]

Controversies like this one pose perhaps the toughest challenge of multiculturalism to civic education. The chador case divided not only French society, but French socialists, who consider themselves as universalist as anyone. Although the socialists could unite in criticizing reactions like those of the conservative newspaper *Le Point*, whose headline read "Should We Let Islam Colonize Our Schools?" and the right-wing politician, Le Pen, who urged the repatriation of all immigrants who had arrived in France since 1974, they were bitterly divided among themselves. Some socialists found themselves allied with conservatives in defending the 1937 law, while others proclaimed it unjust.[7] The debate among socialists helps demonstrate why transcendent universalism is inadequate as a public educational philosophy, and points us to a more defensible way of posing and provisionally resolving such problems.

Socialists who supported the 1937 law argued that the veil is "a sign of imprisonment that considers women to be subhumans under the law of Islam" and should therefore not be admitted by a public educational system committed to teaching gender equality. In opposition to the law, Prime Minister Michel Rocard argued that "tolerance must be put before principle." We might say instead that religious toleration itself is a universal principle to be considered alongside the principle of teaching gender equality.[8] Invoking universal values alone therefore does not resolve the conflict, since religious toleration and gender equality both share the status of universal principles for the social context under consideration. (To say a principle is universal in this sense does not of course mean that it *is* universally accepted or even that it should be universally accepted by all people at all times, but only that it *should* be accepted by all morally-motivated people who find themselves in relevantly similar social and political circumstances.)

Even after we reject appeals to an exclusionary nationalism, the question therefore remains: If French public schools are committed to universalist principles, which principle should take priority in the case of conflict? Should universalists agree with Mme. Mitterand who took the position that public schools should tolerate all religious symbols, even those that express gender inequality, because teaching religious toleration takes priority over teaching gender equality? Or should they side with Gisele Halimi, a founding member of a prominent anti-racist organization, *SOS-Racism*, who argued that distinctively public (or civic) values, rather than private (or personal) values, should be taught in public schools? The social equality of men and women is a public value, Halimi argued. The chador is "a humiliating form of dress" symbolizing gender subordination and therefore has no legitimate place in public schools.[9] Although each argument invokes universalist principles, they support conflicting conclusions.

The indeterminacy of universalism is not a reason to abandon it, unless particularism carries with it better moral arguments. Does particularism get the better of universalism in this conflict? Should we give up looking for mutually-acceptable values in public education, and leave education to parents or religious groups? (Might this be a more mutually-acceptable value?) One attraction of particularism is that it offers religious parents effective access to schools that reflect their religious perspectives. Divide school systems into streams, particularists argue, and give every major cultural group the effective opportunity to shape the schooling of its own children. The French government could then authorize each major community, including secularists, to run its own publicly subsidized schools. French secular schools could remain strictly secular, while orthodox Catholics, Muslims, and Jews (among other groups) could send their children to subsidized schools committed to reinforcing their particular communal values. If the government subsidizes separate schooling for each group, then no group needs to compromise its particularist values for the sake of a common civic education.

Although the particularist response would require a radical restructuring of French education, it cannot be rejected on grounds that its values are foreign to French social understandings. Asked about the situation of orthodox Jewish students in France who wish to wear yarmulkes (and might on a strict interpretation of the 1937 law be prevented from doing so in public schools), Sabine Roitman of the Representative Council of Jewish Institutions in France responded that "Jewish students have had little trouble with the issue, because those who want to wear yarmulkes generally attend private religious schools."[10] What about the fact that many parents, like those of the Muslim girls, cannot afford the private schools of their choice? Particularists can respond by defending public subsidies for all schools, religious as well as secular. Any adequate defense of this response would take us beyond particularism to the claim that subsidies of separate educational streams are more justifiable to citizens than public subsidy of a common civic education.

Something more is missing from this particularist perspective that a more democratic perspective provides. The particularist response to religious diversity neglects, or at least downplays, the government's role in regulating the schools that it subsidizes. The particularist response is radically indeterminate when it comes to specifying what governments must do to ensure that schools adequately educate future citizens. It is this aim of educating future citizens that justifies massive state subsidies of schooling. So particularism cannot escape the question that it lacks the resources to answer: What may citizens reasonably expect of schools as a condition of their receiving public funding and accreditation? The silence of particularism in response to this question sustains the worry that separatist education is not designed to promote the civic values that justify public funding in the first place.

Unless schools serve civic purposes that citizens can share, their support should be left primarily to parents and private associations. Particularists who favor public support therefore should recognize that all streams of schooling must be publicly regulated to the extent necessary to ensure that they promote civic educational purposes. This recognition opens the door to giving precedence to democratic principles (such as teaching mutual respect across cultural differences) over and alongside particularistic purposes. Particularism, so modified, is far more defensible, but it no longer can claim the attraction of avoiding controversies over the content of civic education by ceding to each religious (or ethnic) group its own autonomous sphere of schooling. Nor is this kind of particularism easy to distinguish from a universalism that recognizes the value of religious (or ethnic) diversity.

The problems of unregulated particularism are the mirror-image of those confronting a universalism that tries to transcend particularist cultures. While transcendent universalism expects too much uniformity in the content of public schooling, separatist particularism expects too little.

Public schools are the primary institution by which a democratic society educates future citizens, preparing them to share in responsible self-government. Teaching the elements of responsible self-government—which include mutual respect for basic liberty, opportunity, and a commitment to deliberate about politically relevant issues—is a major reason for mandating and publicly subsidizing schooling for all children. These lessons are constitutive of the purposes of public schooling in contemporary liberal democracies, or aspiring liberal democracies.[11]

Suppose we grant that teaching students the values of basic liberty, opportunity, and deliberation is a primary purpose of public education. We must still wonder whether any conception of education that recognizes this purpose can find a way of resolving the chador case and similar conflicts that pit civic education and cultural diversity against each other. Is there a way of resolving the conflict between religious freedom and a civic education that aims to educate children for the rights and responsibilities of citizenship, where religious beliefs apparently conflict with the aims of civic education?

We cannot defer as a matter of principle to religious freedom regardless of its claims against civic education, as does a particularism unmodified by civic values. Nor can we defer as a matter of principle to a civic education that would expel religious dissenters, regardless of the content of their claims against civic education, as would one version of the universalism represented by the French left—a transcendent universalism that is unmodified by particularist values. This kind of universalism in effect denies that religious freedom, like freedom of conscience more generally, is a basic liberty, necessary to the integrity of persons as we know them.

Public schools have a responsibility to teach and practice religious toleration as *part* of civic education. Both a universalism that respects particular values and a particularism that respects civic values can recognize this responsibility. The critical question remains: To what extent can schools teach and practice religious toleration without sacrificing civic equality and mutual respect among men and women?

We can begin to answer the question by recognizing that there are principled limits to the religious freedom that the law must respect, and therefore also limits to the religious practices that a public school must tolerate. (Insisting on wearing a chador is not the same as insisting on being taught in classes that are segregated by religion, gender, ethnicity, or race.) We need to determine the substantive limits of religious toleration in a particular context of public schooling and therefore to consider in the chador case whether the wearing of conspicuous religious symbols—especially religious symbols of gender inequality in a public school classroom—exceeds those limits.

We can locate religious practices that lie beyond the legally protected realm of religious freedom and toleration. The legally protected realm excludes religious practices that conflict with other basic democratic rights and which are themselves less valuable than the particular rights with which they conflict. Examples of religious practices that may be outlawed in order to protect more valuable rights are ritual human sacrifice and the denial of essential health care to children.

In harder cases where rights conflict, we encounter more uncertainty. These conflicts must be resolved, at least provisionally, but they cannot be even provisionally resolved without our rendering some substantive judgment, which will not be neutral, among particular ways of life. The position of deferring, either to established religious practices or established state policy, is not morally neutral, nor does liberal democracy establish a presumption in favor of either position. We have no better alternative than to assess the conflict as carefully as we can and at the most specific level that public policy can handle. We cannot legitimately counterpoise teaching gender equality against protecting religious freedom in its entirety. Instead, we need to focus on the specific aspects of gender equality and religious freedom that are at issue—that is, the school's obligation to teach students, regardless of their religion or gender, to associate as civic equals in the classroom, and the students' freedom to wear conspicuous religious symbols to school, including those that are commonly associated with gender subordination. We now must ask: Is there any way to reconcile these two apparently conflicting values? If not, which value is the more important to secure in this context?

If we recognize the school's dual responsibility—to teach the civic equality of men and women, and to respect individuals regardless of religious differences insofar as these differences are consistent with civic values—we can develop an alternative way of viewing the conflict, a principled integration of the central purposes of the two perspectives. The liberal democratic values that give public schooling its primary social purpose guide the integration. Schools should tolerate the religious difference represented by the chadors without acquiescing in the gender segregation and subordination that typically accompanies this dress in religious practice outside of schools. The French public schools could have made an educational opportunity out of the girls' wearing of the scarves in school in order to express a democratic commitment to educate all students, regardless of their gender and the religious convictions of their parents.

Schools can teach these democratic lessons in different ways, but the way in which the French government recently resolved the chador controversy is not one of them. In September 1994, the government reversed an earlier ruling by the *Conseil d'Etat* that would have allowed the wearing of chadors in public schools. Under the new policy, students are not permitted to wear "ostentatious religious signs" in the classroom, and chadors count as ostentatious signs. Crucifixes and yarmulkes, on the other hand, are considered discrete and are therefore permitted. Thus, Catholic boys and girls who wear crucifixes or Jewish boys who wear yarmulkes will be welcome within French public schools, while Muslim girls who insist on wearing chadors will not.

The previous ruling by the *Conseil d'Etat* had been more defensible on democratic grounds, though it too fell short of a fully principled integration of particularism and universalism. The wearing of religious symbols, the *Conseil* had said, is permissible so long as it does not involve one of the four Ps: "pressure on others, provocation, propaganda, or proselytism."[12] The ruling raised a critical question concerning moral responsibility in an educational context: What if the wearing of chadors provokes some students to taunt the girls? The ruling suggested that discipline may be directed to the girls rather than the taunters. Yet this way of resolving the problem of provocation would be unjust to the girls, who should not be held responsible for the uncivil behavior of students who fail to respect their right to religious freedom.

Educators should be able to distinguish such uncivil behavior from another kind of reaction among students, which would be fully consistent with democratic education. The wearing of chadors might provoke criticism among some students for being a symbol of women's second-class citizenship. This criticism, in turn, might provoke the Muslim girls to respond with a defense of their tradition. These forms of civil provocation might be discomforting to all parties, but such discomfort is not unwelcome to democratic education. While multiculturalism, informed by democratic principles, encourages us to understand the value that different ways of life have for people who live them, it also exposes every way of life to civil criticism.

The democratic rationale for opening schools to the display of religious difference, along with other kinds of cultural difference, is therefore not to protect each particular way of life from criticism or even from erosion.[13] The rationale is rather to encourage citizens to understand, appreciate, and evaluate politically relevant differences among ways of life. Because some ways of life are more open to criticism and change than others, reflection on politically relevant differences is bound to be more unsettling to some students and citizens than to others, but the non-neutrality of a democratic education is a virtue as well as a necessity. Non-neutrality is a necessity because an educational program would be empty were it to rest upon neutrality among different conceptions of the good life. Non-neutrality, more interestingly, is a virtue because citizens should support an educational system only if it is *not* neutral between those ways of life that respect basic liberty, opportunity, and deliberation, and those that do not. A liberal democracy should take its own side in arguments about teaching the skills and virtues that are constitutive of its own flourishing.

Among the various responses in France to the chador case, the one that best reflects the democratic aim of integrating particularism and universalism was that of Souad Benani, a spokesperson for *Les Nanas Beurs,* an organization of women of North African descent. "As Arab feminists of Muslim culture," Benani said,

> we believe that fundamentalism in all its forms is dangerous and the scarf is oppressive. But it should not be used as a pretext to exclude twelve- or thirteen-year-old girls from school when it is precisely these secular schools that should offer them the opportunity to learn, grow, and make their own choices.[14]

Informed by a larger conception of democratic education, this response does not simply defer to the religious beliefs of Muslim parents or students, nor does it claim to be transcendent in its universalism. Its guiding principles—which include basic liberty and opportunity for all individuals, and their effective freedom to deliberate as civic equals about collective choices—are arguably universal for our world as we now know it, but these principles are also importantly open-ended in their content. Not only will their implications vary with the facts of particular societies, but the principles themselves are also legitimately subject to interpretation by the ongoing public deliberation that democratic education ideally supports.

The principles of democratic education do not comprehensively specify what constitutes a *good* education independently of particular cultures, life projects, and democratic deliberations. Democratic education rejects the separatist strand of particularism, which would give up on the project of educating all children for the rights and responsibilities of citizenship, regardless of their familial culture. But it respects the widest range of cultural differences compatible with teaching those rights and responsibilities. These differences include cultural practices that you or I may judge wrong, or of lesser value than competing practices, but that we can still recognize as reasonable for those who adopt them.

Democratic education would not force the girls to give up wearing chadors in class, but it would expose them to a public culture of gender equality in public school. This exposure gives them reasons why women should view themselves as the civic equals of men, and it opens up opportunities (to pursue a career or hold public office, for example) that are not offered by their families and religious communities. By opening up such opportunities, democratic education may lessen the likelihood that certain kinds of cultural practices will perpetuate themselves. A democratic government should not go out of its way to perpetuate cultural practices that conflict with its constitutive principles.

Some critics suggest that this position of partial accommodation is little more than a pretense of accommodation with ways of life that dissent from liberal democratic orthodoxy. "Funny-hat liberalism," it is sometimes disparagingly called.[15] Why? Because the price paid by orthodox Muslim parents for accepting the accommodationist position of democratic education may be a serious weakening of the hold of their religious convictions and inherited way of life on their children.

The critics are correct in suggesting that democratic education does not grant illiberal ways of life nearly all that they claim for themselves, nor even all that they may need in order to perpetuate themselves in their present form. Democratic education does not claim to support any cultural way of life on its own terms, or even to the extent necessary to guarantee its survival as such. Nor should it. Cultures do not have rights to survival.[16] People have rights to religious freedom, along with other basic liberties and opportunities, that place demands on democratic education. The right to religious freedom, as we have seen, has principled limits. Among those limits is the right of children to be educated for full citizenship in a democratic society, and the responsibility of publicly-supported schools to secure that right for students, even when it conflicts with religious commitments of their parents.

Moreover, the critics' disparagement of accommodating the wearing of chadors in public schools is not true to the experience of the Muslim parents and the girls themselves. The Muslim parents and the girls in this case preferred, and had good reason to prefer, the earlier accommodation by the *Conseil d'Etat* to the more recent banning of chadors. The parents argued for the right of their children, *dressed in accordance with their religious convictions*, to be educated as future French citizens within the public schools. They did not argue for their right to be *religiously* educated, as fundamentalist Muslims, in public schools.

The critics seem to assume that religious education in publicly subsidized schools is the only consistent position available to any truly religious parents. Many religious parents reasonably believe otherwise, and it is the willingness of the vast majority of citizens to draw some line of separation between civic education and religious education that permits any religiously pluralistic democracy to pursue liberty and justice for all.

The critics are therefore correct in claiming that the earlier ruling by the *Conseil d'Etat* did not provide the Muslim girls with a public education that conformed to their religious convictions, but the critics fail to defend their presumption that public education should be judged by its conformity with the religious convictions of parents. The critics offer no reason to reject the view that publicly subsidized education should serve distinctively civic purposes, which can be shared by a diverse citizenry, not distinctively religious purposes which divide us.

Democratic education respects religious differences that are consistent with expecting all citizens, regardless of their religious beliefs, to honor a set of civic responsibilities. Those civic responsibilities include allowing one's children to be educated for democratic citizenship. Democratic education thereby integrates particularist and universalist values. A religiously diverse citizenry can honor this integration as long as they are willing to share a society together on terms that they can justify to one another.

⌒⌒⌒

Multinationalism and Education

Not all persons are so willing to share a society together. The unwillingness to share a society on mutually-justifiable terms is often rooted in a kind of cultural diversity that we have yet to consider: multinationalism as distinct from multiculturalism. While a multicultural society contains many cultures whose members typically overlap and willingly interact with each other in significant ways,[17] a multinational society is composed of two or more "peoples" who share a language, history, and territory, and either enjoy or aspire to enjoy as much political autonomy for themselves as practical circumstances permit.[18] Not every nationality has its own state, but most if not all aspire to the largest possible degree of political autonomy from other nationalities.

By this understanding, the vast majority of contemporary societies are multicultural. This is an important, although unstartling, truth. Some contemporary societies, but far from all, are also multinational. A nationality, by definition, is not morally committed to sharing a sovereign society with any other nationality on democratic terms. That aspiration would transform the nationality into a culture. (There are, to be sure, gradations between nationality and culture, but I focus here on the defining difference of multinationalism because it poses a distinct challenge for democratic education.) The United States is more distinctively multicultural than it is multinational. The former Soviet Union, in contrast, was as distinctively multinational as it was multicultural. Belgium is distinctively bi-national as well as multicultural. Thus, not all contemporary societies are multinational or multicultural to the same degree, and the degree makes a difference: the political challenges and therefore the educational challenges of multiculturalism and multinationalism are different.[19]

The distinctive challenge facing multinationalism is whether democratic education is possible in a society in which people identify as members of different nations. The logic of a nationality is to seek its own sovereign society. Out of necessity, however, nationalities sometimes seek a *modus vivendi* with other nationalities by demanding separate, semi-autonomous spaces within a sovereign multinational society. One consistently democratic resolution would be to establish separate sovereign, democratic societies for groups who are opposed to sharing a society on terms of equal citizenship with each other, but who would honor the democratic sovereignty of other societies, and do their best to make it possible for all individuals to share, as civil and political equals, in some decent democratic society.[20]

Where sovereignty for each nationality is not possible, another kind of political accommodation may be justified. Large parts of the political system, including the educational system, may be divided into national streams. Each educational stream would then be authorized to teach its own distinctive national values but also obligated to teach a universal set of civic values, including toleration and mutual respect for different national, cultural, and individual identities.

The worry about dividing schooling within a society into national streams parallels the worry that attends the more inescapable division of schooling among sovereign societies: will the division of students and curricula carry with it a message of group superiority, and a concomitant lack of concern for the interests of outsiders and disrespect for their rights? Or can the division of schooling within a society, along with the division of schooling among societies, be conceived in a way that helps to create a world combining respect for particularistic loyalties with mutual respect among persons?

Education in a multinational society, like education in a multicultural society, need not sacrifice the universal to the particular, or vice versa. All national groups within a multinational society can teach respect for a robust set of human rights—such as those articulated in the United Nations Declaration of Human Rights—that are due all people regardless of their nationality. A democratic multinational education would teach universal values as well as particular ones within an educational system that is segregated by non-antagonistic nationalities.[21] The problem with this conception is that nationalities as we know them are more often antagonistic than respectful of each other's particularities. Were they respectful of each other's particularities, they would probably feel less of a need to segregate the education of their children by nationality. (I say "probably" because there is a benign rationale for separation by nationality to perpetuate ways of life that people recognize as valuable to them, partly because it is theirs, rather than as objectively more valuable than any or all other ways of life.[22])

I have suggested that the question of whether multinationalism can be reconciled with democratic education parallels a question about multiculturalism within a single society: Must the division of schooling by a sovereign society also carry with it, implicitly if not explicitly, a message of nationalistic superiority and neglect of outsiders? The division of schooling by states more often than not carries this message, but is it because the division is inherently suspect? I think not. The problem lies elsewhere than in the division of education by sovereign societies. It lies in the nationalistic content of the education itself.

The challenge of reconciling democratic education with separate sovereign societies is importantly different from the challenge we just posed of reconciling multinationalism with democratic education. In the case of multinationalism, separate national identifications among adults create the demand for educating children in separate national streams within a single society. The demand for educating children in separate sovereign societies would exist even if all adults identified themselves not primarily as members of this or that nation or society, but as equal persons committed to the aim of establishing liberty and justice for all other persons, wherever they happen to reside. The demand for educating children within a sovereign society makes moral sense if only because each sovereign society is a major political actor in bringing about better or worse conditions for its own citizens as well as other people significantly affected by its policies. The best way we now know to bring about justice for all people on a global scale is to educate children as free and equal citizens of separate democratic societies. Our moral aim, then, should not be to abolish the sense of patriotism that attends education for democratic citizenship, but to educate children, whatever their citizenship, to be concerned with pursuing justice for all people as far as the division of moral labor among societies makes possible.

In light of the increasing interdependence of sovereign societies, democratic education must more than ever try to teach students not only about their shared citizenship, but also about their shared humanity with all individuals, regardless of their citizenship. The same values that support the commitment to using public schools to develop a shared sense of citizenship among all citizens, regardless of their more particular identities, also support a sense of our shared humanity with all individuals, regardless of their citizenship. Whereas empowering children as democratic citizens cultivates patriotism, conveying concern for all human beings, regardless of their citizenship, cultivates a kind of cosmopolitanism.[23]

Patriotism and cosmopolitanism, at their best, complement each other, both practically and morally speaking. Multicultural societies whose citizens care for each other establish the kind of social security that encourages citizens to care about people who live beyond their borders. Multicultural societies whose citizens care about people who live beyond their borders support the kind of patriotism that eschews parochialism and injustice. The aim of developing a sense of shared humanity as individuals in all citizens regardless of our particular citizenship, does not take us beyond democratic education. Quite the contrary, this educational aim follows from the most basic democratic commitment to treating all people as equals.

This aim, what might be called the cosmopolitan core of democratic education, should not be confused with the aim of educating children to be cosmopolitans in the sense of being citizens of the world. There is, after all, no world polity to be a citizen of, and were there a world polity, it would probably be a tyranny rather than a democracy. We are citizens of our own particular societies, but we should not therefore be educated to care only for members of our own societies. Quite the contrary, just democracies will educate their citizens to extend their concern to the equal liberties and opportunities of all human beings. Even in a world of just democracies, we could not assume that each society, taking care of its own citizens, would produce the most moral results. How much less can we assume that justice today will results from an education that neglects the duties of citizens to people who live beyond their country's borders.

Whereas educating children for world *citizenship* misrepresents the political aim of a democratic education, teaching children to care only for their fellow citizens misrepresents its moral content. Because there is no world polity to be a citizen of, it is all the more important that democratic education seeks to develop in all students a sense of shared humanity with concomitant responsibilities to people who live beyond their national borders. This commitment of democratic education does not presuppose either unlimited generosity or the existence (or even potential) of a democratic world polity. It presupposes only that we have moral obligations as citizens and as individuals that extend beyond national boundaries, and that we can also learn something important about our own lives by learning about the lives of culturally and geographically distant people.

Recognizing the need to teach children about foreign countries and cultures is consistent with giving greater attention to the history, cultures, and politics of our own country than we do to any other. There are at least three reasons that justify a greater (but not exclusive) focus on our own country.

The first and perhaps most basic reason is that particular cultures and politics would not thrive were people to take an equal interest in, and feel an equal commitment to, every existing culture and politics on the face of the earth. Cultures and politics are like friendship and love in this limited respect. They require particularistic commitments on the part of individuals, but those commitments—at least in the case of culture and politics—should be consistent with respecting the rights of all people and securing their capacity to enjoy similar benefits. Because most people do not enjoy the benefits of even the imperfect system of liberties and opportunities available to United States citizens, it is particularly important that we learn about foreign cultures, politics, and people.

A second reason why schools may concentrate on domestic cultures and politics, especially in the early years of schooling, is that children often learn to respect other human beings by first learning to respect people who are close and familiar to them. It is important, however, that the focus broaden over the years, and perhaps never be exclusively on one's own country, so as to begin cultivating even in young children the capacity to identify with members of other societies.

A third reason for focusing in far more detail on the politics of the students' own country is that this is primarily—but again not exclusively—the politics that they must enlist to help people not only within, but also beyond their national borders. There are of course less local forms of politics, but these are typically less effective in enlisting the political energies of ordinary people, and not primarily because education fails to familiarize people with these political possibilities. Most people want to live their lives on a local, rather than global, level. There is much that they can do to further the cause of global justice on this level, provided they learn how to be effective citizens of their own society.

These three reasons explain why public schooling in the United States, for example, may rightly focus *more* on national (including state and local) history, culture, and politics than on the history, culture, and politics of every other country. But the three reasons do not together justify the neglect of world history and politics beyond national boundaries that has characterized public schooling in the United States. If public schooling teaches respect and understanding only of already familiar people, it teaches too little to satisfy the fundamental democratic ideal of treating *all* people as equals, an ideal which informs a moral commitment to democracy at the national level. If schooling fails to familiarize students with the various means of improving the world that extend beyond their national government, it deprives citizens of a complete sense of their political power and their opportunities to create a better world for themselves and other people.

In this significant sense, multinational and multicultural education, at their democratic best, share similar aspirations, even if the means of achievement vary with local contexts and conditions. Teaching respect for basic human rights is necessary, but insufficient to satisfy either democratic ideal because democratic education also requires teaching the virtues and skills of citizenship among people who share the same sovereign society. But teaching the virtues and skills of a shared citizenship is also insufficient if schools do not count among those virtues moral responsibility toward, and intellectual curiosity about, people who happen to live in other societies. An adequate educational response to the challenges of both multiculturalism and multinationalism therefore combines respect for individuals who have particularistic identities in addition to the cultivation of common values among those individuals.

This integration is unlikely to take hold without lessons in democratic deliberation, lessons which invoke universal and particular values that are central to democratic self-government and also cross national boundaries. The history class in Brooklyn where students were asked to discuss the morality of dropping the bomb on Hiroshima is a good example of such a lesson in democratic deliberation. It demonstrates that democratic education need not be parochial or uncosmopolitan even when it is particular in its focus and provisional in its precepts. Quite the contrary, only when children are educated for a deliberative citizenship that is informed by multiculturalism and committed to treating all individuals as equals, regardless of their nationality, can we begin to reconcile civic education with cultural diversity.

Notes

1. When speaking of public education or public schooling, I include all publicly subsidized and publicly accredited institutions that satisfy a mandatory schooling requirement, whether they are actually controlled by public or private organizations. Accredited private schools in the United States and public schools in Great Britain, for example, are all part of the public education systems of those countries.
2. These definitions are taken from the Oxford English Dictionary. My discussion here draws on two more general comparisons of self-esteem and self-respect, those of David Sachs, "How to Distinguish Self-Respect from Self-Esteem," *Philosophy & Public Affairs* 10 (Fall 1981): 346–60; and Michael Walzer, *Spheres of Justice* (New York: Basic Books, 1983), 272–80.
3. What is worthy of being publicly honored is not the same as what schools have traditionally taught. Gender discrimination, for example, is not worthy of being publicly honored, despite the fact that many public schools have long taught this lesson.
4. For a detailed development and defense of deliberation as constitutive of democracy, see Amy Gutmann and Dennis Thompson, *Democracy and Disagreement* (Cambridge: The Belknap Press of Harvard University Press, forthcoming, 1995).
5. Diane Ravitch, *The Schools We Deserve: Reflections on the Educational Crises of Our Times* (New York: Basic Books, 1985), 288.
6. *New York Times*, 12 Nov. 1989 and 3 Dec. 1989. The various news stories raise an important issue: whether the parents of the adolescents gave them the option of deciding on their own whether to wear chadors in class or whether the parents decided on their behalf. According to the news accounts, the girls' fathers were committed to their wearing chadors in school. The accounts say nothing about the commitments of their mothers or the girls themselves except by implication.
7. *New Statesman and Society*, 15 Dec. 1989, 13–14. According to this report, Le Pen claimed that repatriation "would go a long way to solving . . . the problems of law and order, drugs, AIDS and the Paris traffic jams!" For a sociological interpretation of the controversy, see David Beriss, "Scarves, Schools, and Segregation: The Foulard Affair," *French Politics & Society* 8 (Winter 1990): 1–13.
8. *New York Times*, 12 Nov. 1989, 10.
9. Ibid.

10. *Washington Post,* 23 Oct. 1989, 12.

11. I discuss deliberation in the context of a conception of democratic education in *Democratic Education* (Princeton: Princeton University Press), 50–2. A detailed discussion of the values of basic liberty, opportunity, and deliberation as constitutive of deliberative democracy can be found in Amy Gutmann and Dennis Thompson, *Democracy and Disagreement* (Cambridge, Mass.: Harvard University Press, forthcoming).

12. *The Guardian,* 1 Dec. 1989, 38. For the most recent ruling of the French government, see Youssef M. Ibrahim, "France Bans Muslim Scarf in Its Schools," *New York Times,* 11 Sept. 1994, 4; and Lynn Terry, "French Girls Expelled for Wearing Islamic Head Scarves," transcript of *Morning Edition* (National Public Radio), 1 Nov. 1994.

13. Compare the perspective of Charles Taylor in *Multiculturalism and "The Politics of Recognition"* (Princeton: Princeton University Press, 1992), 25–37. Taylor suggests that democratic governments should be committed to securing the survival of cultural communities into the future insofar as their survival is consistent with respect for basic individual rights.

14. *The Guardian,* 23 Nov. 1989, 38.

15. For a critique of the disparagement of liberal toleration conveyed by the term "funny hat liberalism" and a discussion of the chador case, see Anna Elisabetta Galeotti, "Citizenship and Equality: The Place for Toleration," *Political Theory* 21 (November 1993): 585–605.

16. Compare Charles Taylor, "The Politics of Recognition," in *Multiculturalism and "The Politics of Recognition,"* esp. 58–9. For an important discussion of the ways in which individual freedom depends on membership in a culture, see Joseph Raz, "Multiculturalism: A Liberal Perspective," in *Ethics in the Public Domain: Essays in the Morality of Law and Politics* (Oxford: Clarendon Press, 1994), 155–76. Raz's essay appeared too late to be discussed in this essay.

17. For our purposes, we can consider a culture to be a human community (larger than a few families) that is historically associated with common ways of seeing, doing, and thinking about things. A culture is not only a set of behavior patterns but also a set of social standards, which can change over time. See R. LeVine, "Properties of Culture: An Ethnographic View," in *Culture Theory: Essays on Mind, Self, and Emotion,* ed. R. A. Shweder and R. A. Levine (Cambridge: Cambridge University Press, 1984), 67. See also Clifford Geertz, "The Impact of the Concept of Culture on the Concept of Man," in *The Interpretation of Cultures* (New York: Basic Books, 1973), 44. Compare Richard A. Shweder, *Thinking Through Cultures: Expeditions in Cultural Psychology* (Cambridge, Mass.: Harvard University Press, 1991).

18. This is a working definition which eschews any kind of essentialist understanding of what makes people conceive of themselves as a nation. The notion of a nation is "socially constructed," typically over a long period of time as the product of a complex history of social practices that shape people's self-understandings. The self-understanding of people as a nation, although socially constructed, is therefore not simply subject to alteration at anyone's will. It can however change over time partly as a consequence of human intentions and designs. For a more extensive discussion of nationalism and an illuminating critique of alternative understandings, see Yael Tamir, *Liberal Nationalism* (Princeton: Princeton University Press, 1993).

19. For an illuminating discussion of the political implications of multinationalism, especially in the Canadian context, see Will Kymlicka, "Three Forms of Group Differentiated Citizenship in Canada," paper presented for the Conference for the Study of Political Thought (CSPT) on "Democracy and Difference," Yale University, April 16–18, 1993. Kymlicka notes that although the United States contains national minorities, it is, with few exceptions, not a multinational state (15). He does not discuss the implications of multinationalism for educational policy, except to oppose allowing national minorities to pull their children out of school before the legally mandated age for all children (footnote 42, 22).

20. Honoring the sovereignty of other decent democratic societies is a necessary but insufficient condition for honoring the rights of all individuals. We also need to consider potentially more demanding obligations such as resource transfers to poorer societies for the sake of providing a decent life for the most disadvantaged individuals. A discussion of the source and nature of these obligations is far beyond the scope of this essay.

21. The teaching of respect for human rights is always a moral imperative, but it is also often a prudent public policy, and therefore need not be utopian in many multinational contexts. In

the absence of teaching respect for human rights, nationalist suspicions and hatreds are likely to be inflamed, preventing the establishment of even minimally peaceful and cooperative relations among national groups.

22. For an insightful defense of a similar rationale for multicultural education within a single society, see Susan Wolf's contribution to *Multiculturalism*, ed. Amy Gutmann (Princeton: Princeton University Press, 1994), 75–85.

23. The kind of cosmopolitanism that democratic education fosters is the commitment to securing liberty and justice for all individuals, regardless of their nationality. It does not claim that children can or must be educated to be "citizens of the world" above all. Compare Martha Nussbaum, "Patriotism and Cosmopolitanism," *Boston Review*, October/November 1994, 3–6. See also Anthony Appiah's comment on the compatibility of cosmopolitanism and patriotism: "We should . . . as cosmopolitans, defend the right of others to live in democratic states of which they can be patriotic citizens; and, as cosmopolitans, we can claim that right for ourselves." ("Loyalty to Humanity," *Boston Review*, October/November 1994, 10). For a more extended discussion of the issue of cosmopolitanism and patriotism in education, see the *Boston Review*, October/November 1994, 3–34.

Questions

1. According to Gutmann, what two aims of public education clash in multicultural democracies? In what ways are these aims in tension?

2. Does Gutmann think that "increasing the self-esteem of disadvantaged students" is a legitimate goal of multicultural education? Explain. What do you think?

3. On what grounds does Gutmann fault traditional civics curricula and separatist curricula?

4. Why does Gutmann endorse a principle of mutual respect, rather than simply toleration, as integral to politics and civic education in multicultural democracies? Do you agree with her argument?

5. How does Gutmann propose that schools can teach mutual respect? What might be some other ways to teach mutual respect?

6. What role does Gutmann describe for "morally-informed deliberation" in democratic politics and civic education?

7. What does Gutmann think is lacking in arguments made by particular cultural groups for state-subsidized, separatist schools?

8. For Gutmann, what are the key elements of a democratic civic education?

9. How does Gutmann defend the overt display of religious differences within public schools? Is she defending the values or survival of particular religious groups?

10. How does Gutmann distinguish between multicultural and multinational societies? What does multinationalism require of democratic education?

Section Four: Suggestions for Further Reading

Appiah, K. Anthony, and Amy Gutmann (1996). *Color Conscious.* Princeton: Princeton University Press.

Benhabib, Seyla (Ed.) (1996). *Democracy and Difference: Contesting the Boundaries of the Political.* Princeton: Princeton University Press.

Fullinwider, Robert K. (Ed.) (1996). *Public Education in a Multicultural Society: Policy, Theory, and Critique.* New York: Cambridge University Press.

Gutmann, Amy (Ed.) (1994). *Multiculturalism: Examining the Politics of Recognition.* Princeton: Princeton University Press.

Kymlicka, Will (1989). *Liberalism, Community, and Culture.* New York: Oxford University Press.

——— (1995). *Multicultural Citizenship.* Oxford: Clarendon Press5.

Rawls, John (1993). *Political Liberalism.* New York: Columbia University Press.

Smith, Stacy (1996). "Liberalism, Multiculturalism, and Education: Is There A Fit?" In *Philosophy of Education 1995,* ed. Alven Neiman, 424–433. Urbana: University of Illinois at Urbana-Champaign.

Strike, Kenneth A. (1994). "On the Construction of Public Speech: Pluralism and Public Reason." *Educational Theory* 44, no. 1 (Winter): 1–26.

Young, Iris Marion (1990). *Justice and the Politics of Difference.* Princeton: Princeton University Press.

List of Contributors

K. Anthony Appiah is Professor of Afro-American Studies and Philosophy at Harvard University. In addition to his writings in linguistic philosophy, such as *For Truth in Semantics,* he has authored many books and articles on the topics of race, culture, and multiculturalism including *Color Conscious* (with Amy Gutmann, another contributor to this volume). He is also an editor of *Transition* magazine with colleague Henry Louis Gates, Jr.

Molefi K. Asante is Professor of African Studies at Temple University. One of the leading proponents of the Afrocentric perspective, he is the author of over twenty books, including *Afrocentricity.* In addition, he edits the *Journal of Black Studies,* the *Afrocentric Review* and is a columnist for the *African Concord Magazine.*

Nicholas C. Burbules is Professor of Educational Policy Studies at the University of Illinois, Urbana-Champaign. He has continued to write on issues of dialogue and difference, as well as other topics in the philosophy of education. He completed *Dialogue in Teaching: Theory and Practice* in 1993. More recently, he co-edited *Teaching and Its Predicaments* (with David Hansen) and he continues to edit the journal *Educational Theory.*

Sucheng Chan is Professor of History and Director of Asian American Studies at the University of California, Santa Barbara. Works that she has authored or edited include *Asian Californians* and *Entry Denied: Exclusion and the Chinese Community in America.*

Ward Churchill (enrolled Keetoowah Cherokee) is Professor of American Indian Studies at the University of Colorado at Boulder. He is author of numerous books including most recently *A Little Matter of Genocide, Fantasies of the Master Race,* and *Struggle for the Land.* He has also published several writings on Indian affairs as a columnist for *Z Magazine* and as an editor of the journal *New Studies on the Left.*

Angie C. Dernersesian teaches in the Department of Chicana/Chicano Studies at the University of California, Davis. She has recently co-edited a volume of *Cultural Studies* on Chicana/o cultural representations, and has written extensively on feminism, ethnography, and criticism.

Eduardo Manuel Duarte is Assistant Professor of Philosophy of Education at Hofstra University. Duarte's work with public school teachers and administrators focuses on the interrelation among dialogue, democracy, and diversity. Recent publications include "Dialogue, Difference and the Multicultural Public Sphere," for the book *Community, Difference and Diversity: Implications for Peace* (ed. Rodopi); "Expanding the Borders of Liberal Democracy: Multicultural Education and the Struggle for Cultural Identity," for the journal *Educational Foundations;* and "Minima Moralia Redux: Reflections from a Life of Conflict," for the journal *Educational Theory.*

Henry Giroux is the Waterbury Chair Professor in Secondary Education at Pennsylvania State University. He is the author of several works including *Disturbing Pleasures: Learning Popular Culture, Border Crossings,* and *Between Borders* (with contributor Peter McLaren).

Carl A. Grant is Hoefs-Bascom Professor of Teacher Education in the Department of Curriculum and Instruction and a professor in the Department of Afro-American Studies at the University of Wisconsin–Madison. In 1997, he received the School of Education Distinguished Achievement Award. Recent publications include *Multicultural Research: A Reflective Engagement with Race, Class, Gender, and Sexual Orientation, After the School Bell Rings* (2nd ed.) (with contributor Christine Sleeter), and *Making Choices for Multicultural Education* (with Christine Sleeter).

Robin Grinter is Senior Lecturer in Education at the Didsbury School of Education, Manchester Metropolitan University.

Ramon A. Gutierrez is Professor of History, Founding Chair of the Ethnic Studies Department, and Director of the Center for the Study of Race and Ethnicity at the University of California, San Diego. Books that he has authored include *When Jesus Came the Corn Mothers Went Away: Marriage, Sexuality, and Power in New Mexico, 1500–1846.* He is also the co-editor of *Festivals and Celebrations in American Ethnic Communities, Recovering the U.S. Hispanic Literary Heritage,* and the multivolume *Encyclopedia of the North American Colonies.*

Amy Gutmann is Laurance S. Rockefeller University Professor of Politics and Dean of Faculty at Princeton University. She is the author or co-author of several works including *Democratic Education, Color Conscious* (with contributor K. Anthony Appiah), and *Democracy and Disagreement* (with Dennis Thompson). In addition, she edited and introduced the volume entitled *Multiculturalism and "The Politics of Recognition"* in which Charles Taylor's selection in this volume first appeared.

bell hooks is Distinguished Professor of English at CCNY. She is the author of many works, including *Breaking Bread: Insurgent Black Intellectual*

Life (with Cornel West), *Teaching to Transgress: Education as the Practice of Freedom, Reel to Real: Race, Sex and Class at the Movies,* and *Bone Black: Memories of Girlhood.*

Peter McLaren is Associate Professor in the Graduate School of Education at UCLA. His is the author of several books including *Life in Schools* and *Critical Pedagogy and Predatory Culture.* Among the volumes he has co-edited are: *Critical Literacy: Politics, Praxis, and the Postmodern* (with Colin Lankshear); *Between Borders* (with Henry Giroux, contributor), and *Critical Multiculturalism* (with Barry Kanpol). He is also the editor of the Internationalist Department of the *International Journal of Educational Reform.*

Suzanne Rice is Associate Professor in the Department of Teaching and Leadership at the University of Kansas. Her writings appear in several journals including *Educational Theory, Initiatives, Journal of Curriculum Studies,* and *Journal of General Education.* In 1998, she and Nick Burbules (contributor) received a Spencer Foundation Major Research Grant.

Judyth M. Sachs is Professor of Education in the School of Teaching and Curriculum Studies at the University of Sydney. She has published several works including *Control or Empowerment: Quality in Higher Education in Australia,* (AIR Annual Forum Paper), and several articles in scholarly journals such as *Australian Universities' Review, Journal of Education for Teaching,* and *Educational Training and Technology International.* Her most recent book is *Meeting the Challenges of Primary Schooling,* co-authored with Lloyd Logan.

Geoffrey Short is Reader in Educational Research at the School of Humanities and Education, University of Hertfordshire, Watford campus. He has published widely on the topics of race, ethnicity, and education. In recent years his attention has turned increasingly toward Holocaust education. Articles on this subject include "Antiracist Education and Moral Behavior: Lessons from the Holocaust" in the *Journal of Moral Education.*

Christine Sleeter is Professor and Planning Faculty Member at California State University. Among her recent works she has authored *Keepers of the American Dream* and *Multicultural Education as Social Activism.* She has also edited *Empowerment Through Multicultural Education, Making Choices for Multicultural Education* (with contributor Carl Grant) and *Multicultural Education, Critical Pedagogy, and the Politics of Difference* (with contributor Peter McLaren). She is the coeditor with Joseph M. Larkin of *Developing Multicultural Curricula.*

Stacy Smith is Assistant Professor of Education at Bates College. In addition to her work on multiculturalism she has recently authored several essays that combine her interests in the philosophy of education and public school reform. These include "School Choice: Accountability to Publics, Not Markets" for the *Journal of Maine Education* and "The Democratizing Potential of Charter Schools" for *Educational Leadership.*

Charles Taylor is Professor of Philosophy and Political Science at McGill University. He is the author of several works on the philosophy of mind, psychology, and politics including *Philosophy and the Human Sciences, The Ethics of Authenticity,* and *Sources of the Self.* He is active in politics and public life in his native Quebec and was recently appointed to the Conseil de la Langue Française.

Selected Bibliography

Adorno, T., & Horkheimer, M. (1972). *Negative Dialectics.* New York: Herder and Herder.

Appiah, A. K. (1997, October 9). "The Multiculturalist Misunderstanding" [Review of the books: *We Are All Multiculturalists Now* and *On Toleration*]. *New York Review of Books,* 1–10.

Appiah, K. Anthony, & Gutmann, Amy. (1996). *Color Conscious.* Princeton: Princeton University Press.

Arendt, H. (1958). *The Human Condition.* Chicago: University of Chicago Press.

Aronowitz, Stanley, & Giroux, Henry A. (1991). *Postmodern Education: Politics, Culture and Social Criticism.* Minneapolis: University of Minnesota Press.

Asante, M. K. (1988). *Afrocentricity.* Trenton, NJ: Africa World Press.

Banks, J. (1995). Multicultural Education: Historical Development, Dimensions, and Practice. In J. Banks & C. M. Banks (Eds.), *The Handbook of Research on Multicultural Education.* New York: Macmillan, 3–24.

Bakhtin, M. (1989). *Problems of Dostoevsky's Poetics.* Caryl Emerson, trans. Minneapolis: University of Minnesota Press.

Benhabib, Seyla, ed. (1996). *Democracy and Difference: Contesting the Boundaries of the Political.* Princeton: Princeton University Press.

Berlin, I. (1969). *Four Essays on Liberty.* Oxford: Oxford University Press.

Bernstein, R. (1988, December). "Metaphysics, Critique, and Utopia." *Review of Metaphysics,* 255–73.

Butler, J., & Walter, J. C., eds. (1991). *Transforming the Curriculum: Ethnic Studies and Women's Studies:* Albany: SUNY Press.

Carnoy, M. (1988). *Education as Cultural Imperialism.* New York: David McKay.

Cherryholmes, Cleo H. (1988). *Power and Criticism: Poststructural Investigations in Education.* New York: Teachers College Press.

Darder, Antonia. (1991). *Culture and Power in the Classroom.* South Hadley, MA: Bergin and Garvey.

Deloria, Vine. Jr. (1973). "The Rise and Fall of Ethnic Studies." In M. D. Stent, W.R. Hazard, & H.N. Rivlin (Eds.), *Cultural Pluralism In Education: A Mandate for Change.* New York: Appleton-Century-Crofts, 131–140.

Derrida, Jacques. (1982). *Margins of Philosophy.* Chicago: University of Chicago Press.

Duarte, Eduardo Manuel. (Spring 1998). "Expanding the Borders of Liberal Democracy: Multicultural Education and the Struggle for Cultural Identity." *Educational Foundations,* 12(2), 5–30.

DuBois, W. E. B. (1973[1933]). "The Field and Function of the Negro College." In H. Aptheker (Ed.), *The Education of Black People: Ten Critiques, 1906–1960.* New York: Monthly Review Press, 83–102.

Foucault, Michel. (1980). *Power/Knowledge: Selected Interviews and Other Writings 1972–1977.* Colin Gordon (ed.) New York: Pantheon.

Freire, Paulo. (1994). *Pedagogy of the Oppressed.* New York: Continuum.

Freire, P,. & Shor, I. (1987). *Pedagogy for Liberation.* New York: Bergin & Garvey.

Fullinwider, Robert K. (Ed.) (1996). *Public Education in a Multicultural Society: Policy. Theory, and Critique.* New York: Cambridge University Press.

Gadamer, H. (1990). *Truth and Method.* New York: Continuum.

Gibson, M. A. (1976). "Approaches to Multicultural Education in the United States: Some Concepts and Assumptions." *Anthropology and Education Ouarterly,* 7, 7–18.

Giroux, Henry A., & McLaren, Peter (eds.) (1994). *Between Borders: Pedagogy and the Politics of Cultural Studies.* New York: Routledge.

Glazer, N. (1997). *We Are All Multiculturalists Now.* Cambridge: Harvard University Press.

Goldberg, D. (1994). "Introduction: Multicultural Conditions." In D. T. Goldberg (Ed.), *Multiculturalism: A Critical Reader.* Oxford: Blackwell, 1–43.

Gutmann, Amy (Ed.) (1994). *Multiculturalism: Examining the Politics of Recognition.* Princeton: Princeton University Press.

Haack, Susan. (1995). "Multiculturalism and Objectivity." *Partisan Review,* Fall 1995, 397–405.

hooks, bell. (1989). *Talking Back: Thinking Feminist, Thinking Black.* Boston: South End Press.

———. (1994). *Teaching to Transgress: Education as the Practice of Freedom.* New York: Routledge.

Hu-DeHart, Evelyn. (September 1993). "The History, Development, and Future of Ethnic Studies." *Phi Delta Kappan:* 50–54.

Husserl, E. (1969). *Ideas.* New York: Humanities Press.

Kanpol, Barry, & McLaren, Peter (Eds.) (1995). *Critical Multiculturalism: Uncommon Voices in a Common Struggle.* Westport, CT: Bergin and Garvey.

Kazmi, Y. (1994). "Thinking Multi-culturalism." *Philosophy and Social Criticism,* 20 (3), 65–87.

Kuhn, T. (1970). *The Structure of Scientific Revolutions*. Chicago: University of Chicago Press.

Kymlicka, Will. (1989). *Liberalism, Community, and Culture*. New York: Oxford University Press.

———. (1995). *Multicultural Citizenship*. Oxford: Clarendon Press.

Leistyna, Pepi, Woodrum, Arlie, & Sherblom, Stephen A., (Eds.) (1996). *Breaking Free: the Transformative Power of Critical Pedagogy*. Cambridge: Harvard Education Review.

Lynch, James. (1986). *Multicultural Education: Principles and Practices*. London: Routledge.

Lynch, James, Modgil, Cecil, & Modgil, Sohan. (1992). *Cultural Diversity and the Schools Volume one: Education for Cultural Diversity: Convergence and Divergence*. Washington: Falmer.

Lyotard, Jean François. (1984). *The Postmodern Condition: A Report on Knowledge*. Minneapolis: University of Minnesota Press.

McCarthy, Cameron, & Crichlow, Warren (Eds.) (1993). *Race, Identity, and Representation in Education*. New York: Routledge.

McLaren, P. (1994). "Critical Pedagogy, Political Agency, and the Pragmatics of Justice: The Case of Lyotard." *Educational Theory*, 44 (2), 319–340.

———. (1997). *Revolutionary Multiculturalism: Pedagogies of Dissent for the New Millennium*. Boulder: Westview.

Mouffe, C. (1988). "Radical Democracy: Modern or Postmodern?" In A. Ross (Ed.), *Universal Abandon? The Politics of Postmodernism*. Minneapolis: University of Minnesota Press, 31–45.

Pratte, R. (1983). "Multicultural Education: Four Normative Arguments." *Educational Theory*, 33 (1), 21–32.

Ravitch, D. (1992). "Multiculturalism: E Pluribus Plures." In P. Berman (Ed.), *Debating P. C.* New York: Dell, 271–298.

Rawls, John. (1993). *Political Liberalism*. New York: Columbia University Press.

Rorty, Richard. (1989). *Contingency, Irony and Solidarity*. Cambridge: Cambridge University Press.

Rosaldo, R. (1993). *Culture and Truth: The Remaking of Social Analysis*. Boston: Beacon.

Ross, Andrew (Ed.) (1988). *Universal Abandon? The Politics of Postmodernism*. Minneapolis: University of Minnesota Press.

Sandoval, C. (1991). "U.S. Third World Feminism: The Theory and Method of Oppositional Consciousness in the Postmodern World." *Genders*, 10 (1), 1–24.

Schlesinger, A. (1991). *The Disuniting of America: Reflections on a Multicultural Society*. New York: Norton.

Schmitz, B. (1988). "Cultural Pluralism and Core Curricula." *New Directions for Teaching and Learning* 52: 61–69. University of Minnesota Press.

Sleeter, Christine (Ed.) (1991). *Empowerment Through Multicultural Education*. Albany: State University of New York Press.

———. (1996). *Multicultural Education as Social Activism*. Albany: State University of New York Press.

Sleeter, C. E., & Grant, C. A. (1988). *Making Choices for Multicultural Education: Five Approaches to Race, Class, and Gender.* Columbus, OH: Merrill.

Smith, Stacy. (1998). "Liberalism, Multiculturalism and Education: Is There A Fit?" In *Philosophy of Education: 1995*, Ed. Alven Neiman. Urbana: University of Illinois at Urbana-Champaign, 429–433.

Strike, Kenneth A. (Winter 1994). "On the Construction of Public Speech: Pluralism and Public Reason." *Educational Theory* 44(1), 1–26.

Suzuki, B. H. (1979). "Multicultural Education: What's It All About?" *Integrated Education, January–April*, 43–50.

Tamir, Y. (1995). "Two Concepts of Multiculturalism." In Y. Tamir (Ed.), *Democratic Education in a Multicultural State.* Oxford: Blackwell, 3–14.

Troyna, Barry. (1993). *Racism and Education.* Buckingham: Open University Press.

Troyna, Barry, & Williams, Jenny. (1986). *Racism, Education and the State.* London: Croom Helm.

Vasquez, Jesse. (January 1998). "The Co-opting of Ethnic Studies in the American University: A Critical View." *Explorations in Ethnic Studies.*

West, Cornel. (1993). *Race Matters.* New York: Vintage Books.

———. (1991). *The Ethical Dimensions of Marxist Thought.* New York: Monthly Review.

———. (1995). *Democracy in Postmodern Times.* Talk at University of Dayton, Dayton, OH: October 19, 1995.

Wittgenstein, L. (1953). *Philosophical Investigations.* Oxford: Oxford University Press.

Woodson, C. G. (1933). *The Mis-Education of the Negro.* Washington D.C: The Associated Publishers.

Young, Iris Marion. (1990). *Justice and the Politics of Difference.* Princeton: Princeton University Press.

Glossary

This volume of essays has been prepared with the belief that educators ought to engage in reflective, foundational thinking, the sort of thinking that enables us to make principled decisions about our practice. As editors, our hope is to provide resources that enable educators to interpret and understand their work in light of the multicultural condition. To that end, we have compiled a glossary of many significant terms that appear in the contributions. This glossary of terms aims to provide readers with some insights on the theoretical language that makes up the multiculturalists' vocabulary, and also to place the terms within the contexts they are used. Our strategy is to offer a thumbnail sketch. The entries are informative, without attempting to be definitive. No glossary, particularly this one, can exhaust the meaning of an important and widely used term. After all, an organizational premise of this book is that there is not one multiculturalism, but four foundational multicultural perspectives each with its own unique set of questions and answers. However, we do think it is possible, and necessary, to provide our readers with a resource that will enable them to navigate purposefully from one multicultural perspective to another.

antimodernism, antimodernist: against modernism, or, to be more precise, against the ideals of the European Enlightenment; a thoroughgoing skepticism and/or rejection of ideals such as "enlightened reason," and "inalienable rights." **Antimodernism** shares **nihilism's** extreme form of skepticism and total rejection of the established laws and institutions. However, the **antimodernist** rejection emphasizes the *realities* which have been the by-products of these *ideals*: colonialism, fascism, patriarchy, slavery, etc. **Antimodernism** suspects self-described "enlightened reason" as the culprit which "inspired" these notorious projects. So-called enlightened reason, according to the **antimodernist**, has produced mostly exploitation and oppression, rather than freedom and liberation. **Antimodernism,** as opposed to **postcolonialism,** is a reaction within the Occident. It is, essentially, a Westerner's rejection of the West. Antimodernism has found most of its exponents on the European Continent, particularly in France and Germany. In contrast to **nihilism,** which was the basis of political movements in nineteenth century Russia, **antimodernism** has been an artistic and theoretic "voice." The roots of **antimodernism** can, perhaps, be traced to the writings of the eighteenth century philosopher Jean-Jacques Rousseau (1712–1788). Rousseau's famous maxim "Man is born free, and everywhere he is in chains," (from *Of the Social Contract,* 1762) is echoed in the movement within nineteenth century art, music, and literature called *Romanticism.* These echoes are heard most loudly in the work of German philosopher Friedrich Nietzsche (1844–1900). Most **antimodernist** writers in the twentieth century have responded to the atrocities of Nazi and Communist totalitarian regimes.

Term in use: In their contribution, Burbules and Rice describe **antimodernism** as one of two **Postmodern** (see definition on page 354) reactions to modernism. Thus, in a [postmodern] description that simultaneously clarifies and confuses the meaning of these terms (because it uses the same term in two different ways in the description of the term!), Burbules and Rice write: "There seem to be two distinct trends within **Postmodernism,** which adopt fundamentally different positions relative to modernism itself. We call these two trends **postmodernism** and **antimodernism,** the first of which we see as fundamentally continuous with the modernist tradition, although it seeks to challenge and redefine it, the second of which regards itself as making a complete break from modernism" (p. 252).

axiology: the study of the nature, types, and criteria of values and of value judgments, especially in ethics. The branch of philosophy dealing with values, as those of ethics, aesthetics, or religion. Unlike the portions concerned with morality and with social justice, **axiological ethics** does not focus directly on what we should do. Instead it centers on questions of what is worth pursuing or promoting and what should be avoided, along with issues of what such questions mean and of whether and how there is any way of arriving at answers to them that constitute knowledge.

Term in use: Contributor Peter McLaren remarks, "White male confessionals simply 'induce shame' rather than convince people to change their **axiology,** yet still employ the language and shrewd methods of the overseers. It is the type of confessional that proclaims that oppressed people of color are 'as good as' white people" (p. 235). Charles Taylor states, "It is axiomatic for Quebec governments that the survival and flourishing of French culture in Quebec is a good. Political society is not neutral between those who value remaining true to the culture of our ancestors and those who might want to cut loose in the name of some individual goal of self-development" (p. 300).

border, border crossers, border cultures, border identities, borderland, borderlines (cf. Mestizo):   in the tradition of geopolitics, **borders** have signified the line that separates one country, state, province, etc. from another. Thus, the term **border cultures** signifies those hybrid or **mestizo** identities which emerge at the borders. The current usage of the term can be attributed to Gloria Anzaldúa's seminal *Borderland: La Frontera* (1987).

Term in use: The term *borderland* appears throughout the writings of multiculturalists. Critical Multiculturalists, in particular, borrow Anzaldúa's derivation of the term **borderland,** and embrace this as an ideal educational situation. They also follow her in using the term in concert with the term **mestizo.** However, Critical Multiculturalists often replace *mestizo* with the term **border identity.** For example, Peter McLaren writes: "students need to be provided with opportunities to construct **border identities. Border identities** are intersubjective spaces of cultural translation . . . spaces of intercultural dialogues . . . Especially in inner-city schools, students can be seen inhabiting what I call **border cultures**" (p. 232). Henry Giroux explains that "an insurgent multiculturalism should promote pedagogical practices that offer the possibility for schools to become places where students and teachers can become **border crossers** engaged in critical and ethical reflection about what it means to bring a wider variety of cultures into dialogue with each other, to theorize about cultures in the plural, within rather than outside 'antagonistic relations of domination and subordination'" (p. 206). Contributor Angie Dernersesian writes: "It is ironic that while we live in a period which prizes the multiplicity of identities and charts **border crossings** with **borderless critics,** there should be such a marked silence around the kinds of divergent ethnic pluralities that cross gender and classed subjects within the semantic orbit of Chicana/o." (p. 85)

critical consciousness, differential consciousness: consciousness refers to the state of being conscious; awareness of one's own existence, sensations, thoughts, surroundings, etc. In turn, **critical consciousness** signifies an heightened or magnified state of being conscious. Moreover, this heightened state enables one to recognize how one's surroundings, in particular, and one's relations fall short of one's expectations, hopes, and ideals. **Critical consciousness** signals the awareness of limitations, gaps, and contradictions. However, it also points to solutions or propositions to address these gaps, and alternatives to the present state of affairs. These alternatives are sometimes called **provisional utopias.** Within the field of education, the Brazilian philosopher Paulo Freire is responsible for the widespread use of this term, which appeared as part of the title of one his books, *Education for Critical Consciousness* (1973). Freire emphasizes that **critical consciousness** (*conscientizaçao*) involves simultaneously understanding one's world as problematic and working to transform this world. However, Freire insists, this understanding arises through dialogue with others who share the world with you. Indeed, in his widely read book, *Pedagogy of the Oppressed* (1994), Freire emphasizes that **critical consciousness** (thinking) and dialogue are mutually supporting: one cannot exist without the other. Freire writes: "true dialogue cannot exist unless the dialoguers engage in critical thinking . . . thinking which perceives reality as process, as transformation, rather than as a static entity—thinking which does not separate itself from action—dialogue creates a critical attitude" (Freire, 1973, 45).

Like **deconstruction,** which is a **postmodern** *strategy,* the term **differential consciousness** represents a strategy of **critical consciousness.** However, differential consciousness is a meta-strategy, or a strategy for using strategies of critical consciousness. Chela Sandoval (1991) writes that differential consciousness "is utilized as a theoretic model which retroactively clarifies and gives new meaning to others. **Differential consciousness** represents the strategy of another form of oppositional ideology that functions on an altogether different register. Its power can be thought of as mobile . . . a kinetic motion that maneuvers, poetically transfigures, and orchestrates" (p. 3). Indeed, it is the strategy advocated by the editor's of this volume. As we explained in the introduction, we believe the idea of **differential consciousness** is consistent with an ideal of reflective practitioners who critically reflect on each of the four multiculturalisms, and, ultimately, create their own brand of multiculturalism to serve them as a liberatory pedagogical resource.

Term in use: The term **critical consciousness** is a frequently used term within the various multicultural discourses. It is common to see the term because all multicultural discourses are stances in opposition to assimilationism (see Introduction). In one way or another, multiculturalists operate with critical consciousness. Indeed, the word "critical" in critical multiculturalism is, in fact, an abbreviated use of the term **critical consciousness.** All multiculturalists, in so far as they represent philosophies of education, are committed to explaining and identifying teaching and learning experiences that will evoke critical consciousness in learners. This commitment is expressed by contributor bell hooks when she writes "It is our collective responsibility as people of color and as white people who are committed to ending white supremacy to help one another. It is our collective responsibility to educate for **critical consciousness**" (p. 117).

culture, cultural democracy, cultural relativism, essentializing culture: culture refers to aspects of human social life including customs, rituals, habits, attitudes, beliefs, values, and norms. It centers around our symbolic representations of material reality and integrated patterns of knowledge, belief, and behavior that are transmitted from one generation to another. Culture plays a role in creating and maintaining a social order, and may be understood as a complex network of symbols. Another use of the term **culture** refers to the finest products of human thought or "civilization." **Cultural relativism** refers to the idea that the value systems that give rise to judgments about what cultural products are among the finest are themselves an aspect of culture. Thus, judgments of worth are seen as being relative to the cultural context within which they arise.

A processural understanding of **culture** has been embraced my many multiculturalists who are interested in articulating a **borderland** ideal of **culture,** and a hybrid or mestizo ideal of cultural identity. This category of **culture** accounts for the overlapping, cross-sectional experiences that occur within the multicultural condition. A processural understanding of **culture** emphasizes the importance of process and layers, rather than seeing **culture** as one fixed structure. This is believed to be more accurate in attending to the conditions under which beliefs, languages, rituals, and other cultural phenomena are constantly emerging.

Term in use: Of **culture,** Grant and Sachs write "The essentializing (e.g., the primacy of the Western canon) and popularizing of **culture** fails to comprehend that **culture** varies in status from society to society, and group to group, and that there are variations in its invocation and its very meaning" (p. 187). Christine Sleeter explains "By **'culture,'** I mean the totality of a people's experience: its history, literature, language, philosophy, religion, and so forth. The term 'culture' was probably adopted by multicultural education advocates in response to the myth of 'cultural deprivation' that was popularized during the early 1960s" (p. 127). According to contributor Anthony Appiah, "Anthropologists, on the whole, tend now to avoid the relative evaluation of cultures, adopting a sort of **cultural relativism,** whose coherence philosophers have tended to doubt" (p. 278). Appiah adds: "But we will not get much further with these issues until we explore the concept of **culture,** an idea that immediately reveals itself to be extremely elastic. In my dictionary I find as one definition for culture 'The totality of socially transmitted behaviour patterns, arts, beliefs, institutions, and all other products of human work and thought.' This is not, I think, quite right. . . . But the definition surely picks out a familiar constellation of ideas. **'Culture,'** in one sense, does indeed name all the 'products of human work and thought.' That is, in fact, the sense in which anthropologists largely use the term nowadays" (p. 277). Finally, Henry Giroux explains that "For many conservatives, the **utopian** possibility of **cultural democracy** has become dangerous at the current historical conjuncture for a number of reasons. Most important, **cultural democracy** encourages a language of critique for understanding and transforming those relations that trap people in networks of hierarchy and exploitation" (p. 201).

deconstruction, deconstructing (cf. postmodern theory): deconstruction aims to unveil the paradoxes, contradictions, and instabilities which are present in Western philosophy. The origin of this term can be located in the work of the twentieth century German philosopher Martin Heidegger (1889–1976) who called for the *Destruktion* of the mode of Occidental philosophy. This traditional mode, which Heidegger labeled "metaphysics," always aimed for exhaustive, and definitive explanations of reality, or some aspect of it. In so doing, Occidental philosophers always obscured, ignored, and/or silenced alternative explanations and experiences of reality. Philosophers were trapped, Heidegger believed, in their own way of speaking. Alternative ways of speaking and listening were needed. For Heidegger, those alternatives can be found in art, poetry, and music. The French philosopher Jacques Derrida reconceived Heidegger's *Destruktion,* and developed **deconstruction.** Derrida extended Heidegger's agenda by focusing on the language of Occidental philosophers. This language, according to Derrida, is rooted in a mistranslation of the ancient

Greek philosophical term *logos* (language). Occidental philosophers of the Middle Ages, the Enlightenment, and beyond have defined the term *logos* as the rational way of thinking. To be a philosopher in the Occident is to speak with reason. This myth of *logocentrism,* according to Derrida, resembles the **structuralists'** belief in underlying and stable cultural meanings. Following Heidegger's lead, and echoing the **poststructuralists'** critique, Derrida called for a **deconstruction** of the "official" academic language. In the wake of Derrida's work, **deconstruction** has been the most commonly embraced strategy of **postmodernists** in their attempt to create the conditions for alternative and unstable "spaces."

Term in use: Critical multiculturalists are more likely than not to use the term, and thus to embrace the agenda of **deconstruction.** They view **deconstruction** as integral to disrupting and destabilizing racist and **xenophobic** stereotypes. In most cases critical multiculturalists speak of the need to place deconstruction within a broader political project. For example, contributor Henry Giroux writes: "I want to argue that educators need to rethink the politics of multiculturalism as part of a broader attempt to engage the world of public and global politics. This suggests challenging the narratives of national identity, **culture,** and ethnicity as part of a pedagogical effort to provide dominant groups with the knowledge and histories to examine, acknowledge, and unlearn their own privilege. But more is needed in this view of **multiculturalism** than **deconstructing** the centers of colonial power and undoing **master narratives** of racism" (p. 197).

dialectic, dialectical, Hegelian dialectics: the roots of the term are located in ancient Greek philosophy. Within that context, **dialectic** signified the art of conversation, or dialogue. However, within that tradition, **dialectic** has its own history, in which it came to signify the logic or particular way of making philosophical arguments. With the philosopher Zeno (334–262 B.C.), **dialectic** represented a way of refuting hypotheses that lead to impossible conclusions. In the hands of the group of philosophers known as the Sophists, **dialectic** resembled rhetoric, or the art of making any argument sound persuasive. With Plato (427–347 B.C.), and his mentor, Socrates (470–399 B.C.), dialectic represented a particular form of dialogue, where a facilitator asks questions until the problem (or the participants) has been exhausted. This method of philosophic conversation appears to have been the established form of teaching and learning at Plato's Academy. It was there that Aristotle became acquainted with **dialectic.** Twenty years of study at Plato's Academy (367–347 B.C.) convinced Aristotle that **dialectical reasoning** was respectable, although he did not conclude that it was sufficient for acquiring theoretic or scientific knowledge. This conclusion was rejected by the nineteenth century German philosophy G. W. F. Hegel (1770–1831). It is Hegel's version of **dialectic** that defines the contemporary use of the term. According to Hegelian **dialectics,** reality is a process that evolves when ideas or thoughts encounter their opposite. For Hegel, reality was produced by minds: the minds of humans produced culture and history; the Mind of God produced reality itself (the existence of beings). The **dialectic** encounter of opposites produces something new. **Dialectic,** for Hegel, represents an evolutionary and developmental process through which human beings, and the societies they live in, become more complex. According to Hegel, the **dialectic** process is always producing a "higher unity." Hegel's belief that reality was a **dialectic** process was taken over by Karl Marx (1818–1883). However, in Marx, matter replaces mind, and God disappears. (Some years later Friedrich Nietzsche [1844–1900] declares the search for God is over, when he discovers that "God is dead!"). Within the contemporary scene, one could describe the emergence of **postmodernism** as a **dialectical** outcome.

Term in use: Multiculturalists, particularly critical and antiracist multiculturalists, incorporate **dialectical** reasoning in their work. This is due, mostly, to the great influence of the philosopher Paulo Freire whose writings are **dialectical** (see **critical consciousness** and **praxis**). Ethnic Studies Multiculturalists, however, are careful to point out the embeddedness of the concept within the European tradition. Contributor Ward Churchill describes a typical "White Studies" approach to philosophy, for instance, as one that explores the "works of the ancient Greek philosophers, the fundamentals of Cartesian logic and Spinoza, . . . dabble[s] a bit in **Hegelian dialectics,** review[s] Nietzsche's assorted rantings" (p. 51).

diaspora: any group that has been dispersed outside its traditional homeland, or any group migration or flight from a country or region. A term traditionally associated with the Jewish exile, but now used in cultural theory to cover a range of territorial displacements; either forced or voluntary emigration. This concept stresses the complex ties of memory, nostalgia, and politics that bind the exile to an original homeland, as well as the lateral axes that link **diasporic** communities across national boundaries with the other communities of the dispersed population.

Term in use: Charles Taylor states ". . . that all societies are becoming increasingly multicultural, while at the same time becoming more porous. Indeed, these two developments go together. Their porousness means that they are more open to multinational migration; more of their members live the life of **diaspora,** whose center is elsewhere" (p. 303).

discourse, dominant discourse, discursive practices: **discourse** refers to forms of expression, ranging from oral and written language to various other semiotic practices, as well as the ways in which people think about and make meaning of such forms of expression. The French **poststructuralist** theorist Michel Foucault (1926–1984) asserted that "**discourses** of truth" shape how we perceive and behave within the world. He argued that the way that ideas are presented and conveyed affects how we perceive what is true, normal, or natural. These perceptions shape our experience of reality and our sense of self within this reality. Foucault emphasized the ways in which **discourses** shift according to historical and cultural context, suggesting that meaning is socially constructed. **Postmodern** and **poststructural** theorists tend to emphasize the ways in which **discourses** that regulate what is true, natural, or normal within any given society privilege some ways of being and exclude or problematize others.

Term in use: According to McLaren, "In taking seriously the irreducible social materiality of **discourse** and the fact that the very semantics of discourse is always organized and interested, critical pedagogy has revealed how student identities are differentially constructed through social relations of schooling that promote and sustain asymmetrical relations of power and privilege between the oppressors and the oppressed" (p. 232). Contributors Grant and Sachs state, "Drawing on the work of Foucault (1978), the concept of **discourse** can be used to discuss multicultural education. **Discourse** provides the basis for understanding what people say, think and do, but also, as Ball (1990) argues, who can speak, when, and with what authority. This concept helps us to understand and interrogate the relationship between power and knowledge. For multicultural education this is significant because it provides the opportunity to further examine which **discourses** deny access to institutional structures that the dominant groups take for granted" (p. 183). As contributor Dernersesian notes, "This Chicana-Riqueña frame is a social identity constructed through any number of experiences and **discursive practices** that extend beyond what is illustrated here by way of an introduction; it intersects with Chicana/o in any number of ways implicating not only race and ethnicity but also gender and class" (p. 86).

Eurocentrism: The editors of this volume define the term in the following manner in the introduction: historically, two responses to the **multicultural condition** in the United States—racism and **Eurocentrism**—have hindered the realization of democratic ideals of individual freedom and political equality. Both of these responses are grounded in the undemocratic assumption that human beings are not equal. **Eurocentrism,** while insisting that humans are by nature equally endowed, also insists that cultural groups have used these natural endowments in more or less superior ways. Moreover, **Eurocentrism** defines commonality and worth in terms of the standards of peoples descending from the European continent, and excludes or diminishes the standards of peoples outside of this tradition.

Term in use: Ward Churchill writes, "The American educational system as a whole has been amply demonstrated to be locked firmly into a paradigm of **Eurocentrism,** not only in terms of its focus, but also its discernable heritage, methodologies, and conceptual structure. Among people of non-European cultural derivation, the kind of 'learning' inculcated through such a model is broadly seen as insulting, degrading, and functionally subordinative" (p. 50). Finally, Molefi Asante is careful to distinguish his concept of "Afrocentricity" from what he calls "**Eurocentricity.**" He says, "**Eurocentricity** is based on **White supremacist** notions whose purposes are to protect White privilege and advantage in education, economics, politics, and so forth. Unlike **Eurocentricity,** Afrocentricity does not condone ethnocentric valorization at the expense of degrading other groups' perspectives. Moreover, **Eurocentricity** presents the particular historical reality of Europeans as the sum total of human experience" (p. 40).

grand narrative, metanarrative, master narrative: a technical term developed by **postmodern** theorist Jean-François Lyotard to criticize certain forms of Occidental philosophy and science. Lyotard's critique of **grand narratives** is quite similar to Heidegger's critique of "metaphysics" (see **deconstruction**) and the **poststructuralists'** critique of **structuralism** (see **poststructuralism**). For Lyotard, the oral tradition's emphasis on narrative, or story telling, was lost when the scientific method of communicating experience was developed. The narrative possesses unique qualities: its content is tied to local experiences, memories, people and places, and its authority rests in those who listen to and/or tell the narrative. Because it is drawn from everyday life, the narrative is accessible and open. According to Lyotard, because they are grounded in "local" phenomena, narratives do not possess any universal or transcendental existence, nor do they express transhistoric meaning. Narratives exist to the degree that people of a particular place recount them, listen to them, and participate in them. On the contrary, scientific and philosophic theories are not, or at least do not claim to be, local in emphasis. These scientific "stories" are thus defined as **grand narratives, or metanarratives:** stories which attempt to speak across all peoples and places and times. Ironically, to the extent that it says something universal (e.g., human beings require oxygen to live) the **grand narrative** says very little that is meaningful, moving, or evocative. Furthermore, in explaining itself, the **grand narrative** does not speak in a language common to all peoples and places but, on the contrary, it uses an exclusive and highly technical language that refers only to itself. The **grand narrative** is incapable of reinforcing bonds of community and solidarity. It is wholly disentangled from the contexts of meaningful life experience and the specifity of local life. Thus, Lyotard's critique underlines that any narrative (grand or local) is partial, and can never rise to the status of "universal."

Term in use: Grant and Sachs explain that **postmodernism's** "project is to move beyond all totalizing discourses and to be incredulous of what Lyotard (1984) called **metanarratives.** For Lyotard the postmodern condition is one in which '**grand narratives** of legitimation' are no longer credible. Postmodernism recognizes that canons are socially constructed and always will need to be reconstructed through dialogues among and between various communities" (p. 179). According to Burbules and Rice "**Postmodernists** usually insist that there can be no single rationality, no single morality, and no ruling theoretical framework for the analysis of social and political events. The conventional language here, deriving from Jean-François Lyotard, is that there are no '**metanarratives'** that are not themselves the partial expressions of a particular point of view" (p. 249).

hegemony, hegemonic education, hegemonic Eurocentric education, hegemonic force: originally a term used in ancient Greece and Rome to describe a powerful or predominant leader. The Roman Procurator Pontius Pilate, for was called "hegemon." The current use of this term can be traced ian critical theorist Antonio Gramsci, who used it as a fundamental his *Notebooks from Prison (1971)*. **Hegemony,** according to Gramsci, represents the power which a dominant group exercises throughout a society. Hegemony produces something constructed as "consent" within the society over norms of behavior and values.

Term in use: Contributor Molefi Asante uses the term in the following way: "**Hegemonic education** can exist only so long as true and accurate information is withheld. **Hegemonic Eurocentric education** can exist only so long as Whites maintain that Africans and other non-Whites have never contributed to world civilization" (p. 46).

hermeneutic, hermeneutics: originally this term signified a distinct philosophical approach to the study of human nature which included the so-called idiosyncratic and accidental. The movement was initiated in Germany by Friedrich Schliermacher (1768–1834). In opposition to philosopher Immanuel Kant (1724–1804), who emphasized the potential of a "pure, transcendental, and universal reason," Schliermacher emphasized that reason always appeared in history as a historical personality. As such, understanding is always occurring within a tradition and historical context. **Hermeneutics's** emphasis on reason as history and tradition was extended by Wilhelm Dilthey (1833–1911) who attempted to clarify the distinct subject matter and method of **hermeneutics.** Dilthey aimed to establish a universal methodology for **hermeneutics.** This interest in articulating a "science" of historical reason was continued in the twentieth century by Hans-Georg Gadamer and others. The focus of twentieth century **hermeneutics** has placed emphasis on the meaning of interpretation and understanding. Moreover, Gadamer's work has enabled hermeneutics to recover its original emphasis on the "problem" of misunderstanding, and how one handles situations in which we encounter meanings that are not immediately comprehended, and require further interpretation. This problem, and how one handles it, is of particular interest to multiculturalists; particularly, liberal democratic multiculturalists who are interested in orchestrating a dialogue across differences.

Term in use: From the introduction to this volume, the editors emphasize the hermeneutical character of a multicultural perspective: This third characteristic signifies a foundational perspective as historically evolving. It names what the philosopher Hans Georg Gadamer (1989) would call the **hermeneutic** situation of the perspective: the determinateness of heritage coupled with the openness of current and future interpretations and uses of this past. Contributor Charles Taylor endorses **hermeneutics** when he writes: "What has to happen is what Gadamer has called a 'fusion of horizons.' We learn to move in a broader horizon, within which what we have formerly taken for granted as the background to valuation can be situated as one possibility alongside the different background of the formerly unfamiliar culture" (p. 306).

mestizaje, mestizo: **mestizaje** and **mestizo** are Spanish terms for mixed ancestry. In Latin American, **una mestiza** historically signified a person whose cultural hybrid is the meeting ground of indigenous and European peoples. Recently, the term has taken on new and often metaphorical meanings, although it continues to signify the idea of hybrid identity. The current usage of the term can be attributed to Gloria Anzaldúa's seminal *Borderland: La Frontera* (1987).

Term in use: Critical multiculturalists, in particular, borrow Anzaldúa's derivation of the term and also follow her in using **mestizo** in concert with the category of **borderland.** Contributor Peter McLaren acknowledges Anzaldúa as offering a category which emphasizes human experience as situated in specific historical and geopolitical contexts. He writes: "A **mestizaje** consciousness is linked, therefore, to the specificity of historical struggles" (p. 235). In turn, critical multiculturalists understand **mestizo consciousness** as integral to a pedagogy the name **border pedagogy,** and the critical classroom that they label **borderland.** For Giroux, the **borderland** is the site where identity is authentically expressed as **mestizo.** He writes "the interrelationship of different cultures and identities become borderlands, sites of crossing, negotiation, translation, and dialogue. At issue is the production of a border pedagogy in which the intersection of culture and identity produces self-definitions that enables teachers and students to authorize a sense of critical agency" (p. 209). However, contributor Angie Dernersesian questions whether this "new" usage has sufficiently transformed the old. She criticizes the use of the term **mestizaje** as a fetish which reinscribes a colonial framework. She writes, "This type of **mestizaje** is the age-old political embodiment of the Mexican nation who has traditionally occupied the central space and is the subject of contention by many *indígenas* for whom **mestizaje** means inequality, a concerted dilution of Indianess, and partnership with the Mexican State" (p. 84).

multicultural condition, multiculturalism: as defined by the editors of this volume in the introduction, the phrase **multicultural condition** describes the demographic presence of different ethnic groups within a population along with related factors surrounding particular groups' historical experiences, cultural beliefs and values, and social status within the society at large. By contrast, the phrase **multiculturalism** denotes a response to this condition. In other words, multiculturalism has to do with how an individual interprets or sees the world and perceives his/her place in it—the world being a place characterized by the "multicultural condition." In addition, multiculturalism has to do with how one evaluates this sense of place, for oneself and for others, and what one proposes to do in response to the multicultural condition. There is no one *"multiculturalism,"* but rather a variety of "multiculturalisms." There is no single response to the multicultural condition. Indeed, there are likely as many multiculturalisms as there are people. However, when educational theorists develop responses to the multicultural condition, the proposals are not so radically plural. Rather, the normative responses put forward by a wide variety of individual scholars and educators can be clustered into four distinguishable perspectives: Ethnic Studies Multiculturalism, Antiracist Multiculturalism, Critical Multiculturalism, and Liberal Democratic Multiculturalism.

Term in use: Some examples of the diverse uses of the terms in this volume include the following. Amy Gutmann, who represents the Liberal Democratic perspective, asserts a distinction between multiculturalism and multinationalism. She contends that "While a **multicultural** society contains many cultures whose members typically overlap and willingly interact with each other in significant ways, a multinational society is composed of two or more 'peoples' who share a language, history, and territory, and either enjoy or aspire to enjoy as much political autonomy for themselves as practical circumstances permit. . . . By this understanding, the vast majority of contemporary societies are **multicultural.** . . . The United States is more distinctively **multicultural** than it is multinational. The former Soviet Union, in contrast, was as distinctively multinational as it was multicultural" (p. 366). According to Molefi Asante, an ethnic studies multiculturalist, "[Diane] Ravitch (1990), who argues that there are two kinds of **multiculturalism**—pluralist **multiculturalism** and particularist **multiculturalism**— is the leader of those professors whom I call 'resisters' or opponents to Afrocentricity and **multiculturalism**" (p. 42). Henry Giroux says: "In [my] view, **multiculturalism** becomes more than a critical referent for interrogating the racist representations and practices of the dominant **culture,** it also provides a space in which the criticism of cultural practices is inextricably linked to the production of cultural spaces marked by the formation of new identities and pedagogical practices that offers a powerful challenge to the racist, patriarchal, and sexist principles embedded in American society and schooling" (p. 207).

nihilism: The root of this term, *nihil,* is Latin for nothing. **Nihilism,** in turn, signifies the belief in nothing, or the total rejection of the status quo institutions, particularly, laws and religions. A **nihilist** rejects conventional moral beliefs. **Nihilism,** as a movement, emerged in the nineteenth century as a result, in part, of the Industrial Revolution. The drastic changes in production and transportation, and the widespread poverty which resulted from the upheaval of agrarian life, created a ripe context for **nihilism.** The belief that nothing really exists, particularly the truths preached by religion, appeared to be confirmed by the total disruption of traditional life that occurred during the Industrial Revolution. This was precisely the situation in nineteenth century Russia, where **nihilism** was popular. **Nihilism,** as a way of life, became fashionable in Russia during the 1860s. It describes a generation of young radicals who emphasized the liberation of the individual from the social institutions and traditions that they perceived as oppressive. The classic description of the **nihilists** appears in Ivan Turgenev's (1818–1883) *Fathers and Children* (1862).

Term in use: As noted, **nihilism** expresses the thoroughgoing skepticism of antimodernism. In turn, both of these terms refer to total rejection of established laws and institutions. However, multiculturalists, such as contributors Burbules and Rice, contrast this way of life with styles of **postmodernism** they want to defend. For example, contributors Grant and Sachs endorse a postmodern multicultural project which is in contrast to forms of **postmodern** and poststructural theory which has been criticized for "its subjectivism and relativism, which often border on **nihilism**" (p. 181). Meanwhile, contributor

Henry Giroux indicates that the work of Critical Multiculturalism is to compel whites to recognize the pervasive **nihilism** that is produced by pervasive racism. Giroux writes "white America needs to address the **nihilism** that permeates black communities in the United States . . . educators must attempt to understand how white institutions, ethnicity, and public life is structured through a **nihilism** that represents another type of moral disorder, impoverishment of the spirit, and decline of public life" (pp. 197–198).

polyphony, polyvalent assemblage, polyvocal character: the term **polyphony** was originally used as a musical term to describe the artistic arrangement of music (especially choral). **Polyphonic** music emphasizes the rhythmic and melodic individuality of various parts within a composition. **Polyphony** represents music written as a combination of several simultaneous voices (parts) of a more or less pronounced individuality. **Polyphony** and **polyphonic** originally signified "many-sound" or "many-voice" music. This arrangement of music was pioneered in the sixteenth century with the choral music of Giovanni Pierluigi da Palestrina (1525–1594) and William Byrd (1542–1623). Its current use can be attributed to the Russian philosopher, linguist, and literary critic Mikhail Bakhtin (1895–1975). He is responsible for exporting the term **polyphony**. Bakhtin used the idea of polyphony to describe the novels of Fyodor Dostoevsky (1821–1881). For Bakhtin, the great gap in the study of Dostoevsky emerges with the failure of critics to "hear" the polyphony within his novels. Those who are deaf to the polyphonic composition of Dostoevsky's novels look for "fixed elements in the author's design" which "bind and combine finalized images of people in the unity of a monologically perceived and understood world; there is no presumption of a plurality of equally-valid consciousness, each with its own world" (Bakhtin, 1989, 7). Bakhtin's criticism and his alternative dialogic rendering of Dostoevsky's novels is analogous to the attempt of multiculturalists to oppose assimilationism. For multiculturalists, life in the **multicultural condition** should be understood as a **polyphony**: a world of distinct and multiple voices. The **polyphonic** dialogic encounter is based on an understanding of self and society as fluid and developing, rather than fixed and static. The idea of **polyphonic** dialogue identifies the possibility of *unifying* highly heterogenous and incompatible "voices" or a plurality of worldviews which are not reducible to a single ideological common denominator.

Term in use: The term **polyphony** is usually used, in one form or another, by multiculturalists in concert with terms like **borderland**, which express the encounter of multiple perspectives or "voices." Contributor Peter McLaren, for example, writes "**Border identities** are intersubjective spaces of cultural translation—linguistically multivalanced spaces of intercultural dialogue. It is a space where one can find an overlay of codes, a multiplicity of culturally inscribed subject positions, a displacement of normative reference codes, and a **polyvalent assemblage** of new cultural meanings" (p. 232).

postcolonial, postcolonialism, postcolonial subject: as opposed to the terms **antimodernism, postmodernism** and **poststructuralism,** that refer to movements against, yet within, the Occident, **postcolonialism** refers to the movements in art, literature, music, philosophy, etc., emerging from the tension-filled borders that separate indigenous cultures from European colonialism/imperialism. In turn, postcolonialism represents the counter-colonial moves by the colonized to disrupt the status and power of the colonial/imperial culture. These moves, expressed mostly in literature and political theory, are expressions of self-determination and liberation. **Postcolonialism** originated in Northern Africa, the Caribbean Islands, and Southern Asia. It began as a movement that both sparked and emerged within the African, Asian and Latin American struggles for liberation against the European colonial regimes (1950s and 1960s). While Aimé Césaire and Albert Memmi represent two of the most important early **postcolonial** critics, it is Frantz Fanon (1925–1961) who is considered the foundational postcolonialist. Born in Martinique in 1925, Fanon studied medicine in France, and specialized in psychiatry. Fanon was a close colleague of the French philosopher Jean-Paul Sartre. While practicing psychiatry in Algeria, Fanon witnessed firsthand the North African liberation struggles against the French colonial powers. His writings, which include *Black Skins, White Masks* (1967), *Wretched of the Earth* (1963), *A Dying Colonialism* (1965), and *Toward the African Revolution* (1967) are considered amongst the most influential writings within the worldwide civil rights, counter-colonial, and black power movements of the 1950s and 1960s. While contemporary **postcolonialism** remains wedded to the political project of liberation, the movement has evolved into a complex array of projects. This evolution has produced provocative new genres in film, literature, music and philosophy. Indeed, **postcolonialism's** current moves intersect often with experiments in **postmodernism.** A generous sampling of contemporary postcolonialism is found in *The Postcolonial Studies Reader* (1995). Contributors to the volume include such leading figures as Homi K. Bhabha, Stuart Hall, Trinh T. Minh-ha, Edward Said, and Gayatari Chakravorty Spivak.

Term in use: **Postcolonialism** has been an inspiration for many multiculturalists. Indeed, terms like **mestizo** and **borderland** are meaningful within the **discourses** of both movements. Contributor Peter McLaren demonstrates this when he writes "**border identity** . . . is, rather, an experience of deterriorilization of signification in a postnationalist cultural space—that is, in a **postcolonial,** postnational space. . . . The **postcolonial** subject that arises out of the construction of border identity is nonidentical with itself" (p. 233).

postmodernism, postmodernity, postmodern theory, postmodern lens: like the terms **multiculturalist** and **multiculturalism, postmodern** represents both a description of a social context or historical moment (**postmodernity**), and the responses to people living within that society so described (**postmodernism, postmodern theory**). As a description of a social context, the most well-known use of this term is located in the title of the French philosopher Jean-François Lyotard's book *The Post-Modern Condition* (1984). Responses to **postmodernity** have been many and diverse, but can be understood, generally, as an attempt to break from the forms and ideals of traditional academic research which, in fact, mirror the conventions of the status quo in society. **Postmodernism, in** short, is the attempt to establish the conditions for the creation of alternative and unstable "spaces" (aesthetic, existential, political, philosophical, etc.). The aim of the **postmodernist** is to create possibility in the face of conformity. The earliest developments of **postmodern theory** occurred in the field of architecture. Some noteworthy **postmodern** architects are John Burgee, Philip Johnson, and Robert Venturi. The development of **postmodern theory** within the humanities and social sciences has been widespread and has led to the development of new fields of study, which are gathered in a commitment to disrupt and **deconstruct** the old, and, thereby, to create spaces for alternatives. Among others, these new fields include cultural studies, gay and lesbian studies, gender studies, and critical multiculturalism.

Term in use: Multiculturalists of all perspectives have found it important to define their projects in relation to **postmodernism.** Although in some cases it is emphatically rejected (cf. Asante), many have endorsed some aspects of postmodernism. Critical multiculturalists, in particular, have sought to incorporate postmodernism within their projects. Contributors Grant and Sachs offer the best example of this when they write: "Multicultural education supported by a **postmodern** perspective would increase the number of critics, sharpen the critique, and better inform the teacher that the discourse they choose to espouse in their classroom will bring with it a particular ideology regarding classroom policy and practice, power and knowledge, and view of the world" (p. 185).

poststructuralism, poststructuralist, structuralism: like many of the terms in this glossary (e.g., **antimodernism** and **postmodernism**) the meaning of the term **poststructuralism** is derived, in part, from another term. In the case of poststructuralism, the term is **structuralism. Structuralism** refers to the twenti eth century French group of anthropologists who were led by Claude Lévi-Strauss. Lévi-Strauss used the term **structuralism** to describe the method for understanding whole **cultures.** This method tried to understand cultures by uncovering and analyzing the basic structures which were expressed in the culture's myths and customs. **Structuralists** believe that **cultures** are essentially structures whose basic elements, or parts, are stable and mutually supportive. In turn, structuralists strongly endorse the idea that **cultures** are autonomous and distinct, and that these differences must be recognized and respected. However, in focusing on the elements of a **culture's** structure (myths, customs), structuralism is not particularly interested in the human beings who exist within a given culture. In fact, the human being is almost an afterthought for Lévi-Strauss (*Tristes Tropiques*, 1961). **Poststructuralism** abandons the assumption that cultures are relatively stable structures, which are autonomous and unique. **Poststructuralists** suspect that "cultures" are mostly hybrid, disjointed, unsystemic and *an*-archic. **Cultures, poststructuralists** believe, are not stable structures, but unstable, and somewhat chaotic. **Poststructuralists,** such as the French thinker Michel Foucault (1926–1984), believe that the principle of difference must be applied to the cultures themselves. Foucault's emphasis on the notion of **discourses** within **cultures** suggests that structures are not stable and mutually supporting, but rather fluid and often in tension with one another. Foucault would stress that identification of the "gaps" and "fissures" within a culture's structures can serve as a strategy for resisting **hegemonic** elements within it. The so-called stable structures that one can identify represent a very limited perspective on the whole phenomenon. For a **poststructuralist**, one can never uncover completely or exhaustively interpret the basic elements of culture. The dream of doing so, **poststructuralists** say, is a myth of the Occidental anthropologist. This myth is itself unstable, and, perhaps, dangerous.

Term in use: Many critical multiculturalists have embraced poststructuralism's idea that diversity exists between and within cultures. However, many also use the term poststruturalism in concert with the distinct term **postmodernism** (see definition above). For example, contributor Peter McLaren writes: "The **poststructuralist** insight that I am relying on is located within the larger context of postmodern theory . . . and asserts that signs and significations are essentially unstable and shifting and can only be temporarily fixed, depending on how they are articulated within particular discursive historical struggles" (pp. 220–221). However, contributor Christine Sleeter identifies how the term can be used as a shield by white academics to avoid the painful process of discussing white racism. She writes: "My own discussions of racism rarely move beyond the introductory level I use with my white students. Other white academic sometimes try to close off discussions of white racism by describing such discussions as 'navel gazing,' as whites who have 'seen the light' bashing other whites, as too politically correct, or as insufficiently **poststructural** in their essentializing of whiteness" (p. 128).

praxis: Greek for practical knowledge/reasoning, or action. The term is discussed at length by the philosopher Aristotle (384–322 B.C.). In his classic *Nichomachean Ethics,* Aristotle makes a distinction between **praxis** and theoretical and technical knowledge. In doing so, he sets the stage for the modern use of the term, which distinguishes practical or political philosophy from science. The contemporary use of the term by critical theorists designates a form of practical and political reasoning that is opposed to the domination of technology and scientism. **Praxis** is contrasted with what philosopher Hans-Georg Gadamer describes as "the idolatry of scientific method and the anonymous authority of the sciences" (Gadamer cited in Bernstein, 1988, p. 44). In some ways, the term **praxis** is captured in the **local narrative.** This connection is felt in philosopher Hannah Arendt's (1958) designation of **praxis** as the highest form of human activity because it emerges in speech and is rooted in the human condition of plurality. Within the philosophy of education, Paulo Freire's (1970) discussion of **praxis** has been the most influential. **Praxis,** according to Freire, denotes the circular relation between dialogue and **critical consciousness.**

Term in use: Contributor Angie Dernesesian employs the term in her critique of Chicana/o studies: "Within Chicana/o studies it is not uncommon to hear that one of the greatest threats to this area of studies and **praxis** come from their brand of multiculturalism, the one that circulates within the institutions of dominant culture" (p. 99). Contributor Peter McLaren writes: "We need to occupy locations between our political unconscious and everyday **praxis** and struggle . . . in the form of a **provisional utopia** or contingent foundationalism" (p. 234).

solidarity: a political term signifying the unification of distinct groups who share objectives and ideals. Normally, **solidarity** signifies an intragroup struggle to oppose, subvert, and transform an institution or society. However, **solidarity** can also signify the unification of groups who seek to maintain the status quo. The latter case, however, is usually described with the term **hegemony.**

Term in Use: **solidarity** is a common term within the explicit political discourses used by antiracist and critical multiculturalists. The term is normally used to describe the unity which is necessary for opposition against racism and assimilationism. In its oppositional form, the aim of this unity is not a broad consensus. Rather, as contributor Robin Grinter explains, **solidarity** speaks to "the oppositional characteristic. . . . Its task has been and will remain that of designing an effective and subversive role within the established system" (pp. 144–145). Moreover, contributor Peter McLaren writes that a "**solidarity** has to be struggled for that is not centered around market imperatives but develops out of the imperatives of freedom, liberation, democracy, and critical citizenship" (p. 225). However, as contributor Christine Sleeter demonstrates, the term can be used to signify the actions that reinforce racism. She explains how experiencing her white students undisguised racism led her "to examine 'white racial bonding' processes white people engage in everyday, which is one of the processes by which whites attempt to maintain racial **solidarity.** By 'racial bonding,' I mean simply interactions in which whites engage that have the purpose of affirming a common stance on race-related issues, legitimating particular interpretations of groups of color, and drawing conspiratorial we–they boundaries" (p. 129).

white supremacy: this concept delineates an approach to racism that shifts the focus from individual prejudice to structural domination. Rather than emphasizing individual beliefs about race that are based on stereotypes, and then give rise to prejudiced attitudes or actions, **white supremacy** refers to systemic issues of power and domination at the structural level of society. On this view, white people are systematically privileged and advantaged within society's institutions because of their skin color and its relationship to historical patterns of oppression and exploitation. These same patterns have historically excluded, or marginalized, people of color from such structures (namely, economic and political structures within which material and social status are unequally distributed).

Term in use: Contributor bell hooks uses the term **white supremacy** "to identify the ideology that most determines how white people in this society (irrespective of their political leanings to the right or left) perceive and relate to black people and other people of color. It is the very small but highly visible liberal movement away from the perpetuation of overtly racist discrimination, exploitation, and oppression of black people which often masks how all-pervasive white supremacy is in this society, both as ideology and behavior. When liberal whites fail to understand how they can and/or do embody white-supremacist values and beliefs even though they may not embrace racism as prejudice or domination (especially domination that involves coercive control), they cannot recognize the ways their actions support and affirm the very structure of racist domination and oppression that they profess to wish to see eradicated" (pp. 111–112). According to contributor Henry A. Giroux, a Critical Multiculturalist approach to **white supremacy,** "means that a critical analysis of race must move beyond the discourse of blaming the victim in which whites view multiculturalism as a code word for black lawlessness and other 'problems' blacks create for white America. Viewing black people in this manner reveals not only **white supremacy** as the discursive and institutional face of racism, but it also presents us with the challenge of addressing racial issues not as a dilemma of black people but as a problem endemic to the legacy of colonialism rooted in 'historical inequalities and longstanding cultural stereotypes'" (p. 198). Contributor Christine Sleeter adds: "White people have developed various strategies that enable us to talk about racial issues while avoiding **white supremacy** and our own participation in it" (p. 128).

utopian, provisional utopia, critically utopian: the term **utopia** is derived from the Greek word *topos* or place. *Ou topos,* however, literally means "no place." But this literal translation does not capture the meaning of the term **utopia,** which signifies an ideal place or society. But, insofar as a **utopia** is an imaginary place or society in which everything is perfect, it is accurate to say that it does not and cannot exist. For political philosophers, then, **utopia** remains an ideal, imagined place that is held up as a contrast to the current state of affairs. This was precisely the intention of Thomas More (1477–1535) when he wrote his classic speculative political essay *Utopia* (1516). In this essay, More describes his fictional encounter with a traveller Raphael Hythloday who has discovered **Utopia,** a land with a communal sharing of property, universal education for all people, and a toleration of all religions. The ideals expressed in More's *Utopia* remain present in the current use of the term. Indeed, **utopia,** in its current use, is a term often used in concert with **critical consciousness,** because it signals the awareness of limitations, gaps, and contradictions in a society. A utopia represents solutions to address these gaps, and alternatives to the present state of affairs. These alternatives are sometimes called **provisional utopias.** Paulo Freire (1987) expresses this when he writes: "the possibility to go beyond tomorrow without being naively idealistic. This is **Utopianism** as a dialectical relationship between denouncing the present and announcing the future. To anticipate tomorrow by dreaming today" (p. 186).

Term in use: Insofar as multiculturalists promote the **multicultural condition,** and oppose assimilationism, they are all in some way utopian. Again, utopian thinking is, in essence, a way of criticizing a society by demonstrating how it falls short of its own ideals like toleration, liberty, democracy, and equality. In turn, in their defense of the **multicultural condition** multiculturalists offer **utopian** ideals. For example, contributor Peter McLaren writes: "A **border identity** is not simply an identity that is anticapitalist and **counterhegemonic** but is also **critically utopian**. . . . We need to occupy locations between our political unconscious and everyday **praxis** and struggle . . . in the form of a **provisional utopia**. . . . A **provisional utopia** is not a categorical blueprint for social change (as is fascism) but a contingent **utopia** where we anticipate the future through practices of **solidarity** and community" (p. 234).

xenophobia: pathological hatred or fear of strangers, usually accompanied by a conviction that they belong to a group that is alien. Attitudes of hatred or contempt, or negative attitudes to an outside group. **Xenophobia** arises most readily where there is a conflict of interest between the two groups. **Culturally** based fear of outsiders, often associated with the hostile reception given to immigrants into societies, but more often based on competition for jobs, or ethnic, racial, or religious prejudice.

Term in use: According to the editors of this volume: "antiracist educators work from the premise that racism is a systemic problem, and not simply the practice of bigotry, jingoism, or **xenophobia** by individuals" (p. 107).

Credits

Ramon A. Gutierrez (pp. 28–37): "Ethnic Studies: Its Evolution in American Colleges and Universities" from *Multiculturalism: A Critical Reader* edited by David Theo Goldberg. Copyright 1994 by Basil Blackwell Ltd. Reprinted by permission of Blackwell Publishers.

Molefi K. Asante (pp. 38–48): "The Afrocentric Idea in Education." *Journal of Negro Education* 60 (1991), 170–180. Copyright 1991 by Howard University. Reprinted by permission of Howard University School of Education.

Ward Churchill (pp. 50–67): "White Studies: The Intellectual Imperialism of Contemporary U.S. Higher Education." Essay reprinted by permission of Ward Churchill.

Sucheng Chan (pp. 68–79): "On the Ethnic Studies Requirement." *Amerasia Journal* 15 (1989). Copyright 1989 by Sucheng Chan. Reprinted by permission of UCLA Asian American Studies Center.

Angie C. Dernersesian (pp. 81–105): "Chicana! Rican? No, Chicana Riqueña!" from *Multiculturalism: A Critical Reader* edited by David Theo Goldberg. Copyright 1994 by Basil Blackwell Ltd. Reprinted by permission of Blackwell Publishers.

bell hooks (pp. 111–117): "Overcoming White Supremacy: A Comment" from *Talking Back: Thinking Feminist, Thinking Black* (Boston: South End Press, 1989) by bell hooks. Copyright 1989 by bell hooks. Reprinted by permission of South End Press.

Christine Sleeter (pp. 118–133): "Multicultural Education, Social Positionality, and Whiteness." Reprinted by permission of the State University of New York Press, from *Multicultural Education as Social Activism* by Christine Sleeter. 1996, State University of New York. All rights reserved.

Robin Grinter (pp. 135–153): "Multicultural or Antiracist Education? The Need to Choose" from *Education for Cultural Diversity: Convergence and Divergence,* edited by James Lynch, Celia Modgil, Sohan Modgil. Copyright 1992 by Taylor and Francis. Reprinted by permission of Taylor and Francis.

Name Index

Subject Index

affirmative action, negative criticisms of, 32

Afrocentric education, 38–48
African-American historians, 43
approach to history, 41–42, 43–46
basic principles, 39–40
challenges to, 41
connection with multicultural education, 40–41
versus Eurocentric, 40
Eurocentric notions revised by, 46–47
scholarly contributions, 47
suppression and conflict related to, 41–43

Afrocentricity
goals of, 39–40, 42–43
racist position of, 8, 218

agricultural science, Eurocentric educational approach, 53–54

alienation, cultural, 173–174

alliances, women's groups, 261–262

American history, Eurocentric educational approach, 52–53

antimodernism
aspects of, 253–254
difference, view of, 256–257
use of term, 341–342

antiracist multiculturalism, 16–18
criticisms of, 143–144
foundation of, 16–17, 142–143
historical view, 17–18

versus multicultural education, 135–137, 142–152, 166–168
multicultural education as basis for, 166–168
racism, view of, 142–143
white supremacy, overcoming, 112–117
and white teachers, 131–133

AntiRacist Teacher Education Network, 150

Asian American studies, 69–79
non-Asian students, 71, 72, 74–75, 76–78
personal elements, 70–71
reserve of Asian American students, 72–73, 75–77
student response to, 70, 74

assimilation
versus cultural pluralism, 138
multicultural positions on, 5–6, 8
and white supremacy, 113–114

Assistant Masters and Mistresses Association, 146, 151

Association for Asian-American Studies, 30

axiology, use of term, 342

bell curve, 216, 219
binarism, meaning of, 228
black, use of term, 224, 228
border cultures, meaning of, 233

deconstruction
  and postmodernism, 248
  use of term, 345–346
demagogic multiculturalism
  versus critical multiculturalism, 205
  danger of, 205
democracy
  abandonment of, 200–201
  conservatives on, 200–202
  and cultural pluralism, 5–6
  Dewey on, 259, 260
  goals of, 21
  insurgent multiculturalism on, 206
  liberal democratic multiculturalism,
    21–22
  in liberal society, 21
  multicultural position on, 5–6
  racism effects, 8
democratic multicultural education,
    316–323
  France, affair of the scarf example,
    316–323
  needs in U.S., 327–328
  particularism versus universalism,
    318–323
  religious toleration, 316–323
Department of Education and Science,
    138, 149, 157, 158
dialectical reasoning, meaning of,
    346–347
dialogue, 260–269
  across differences, 260–263
  communicative virtues, 261, 267–269
  and difference, 261–263
  to maintain difference, 265–266
  and personal history, 266–267
  translation in, 264–265
  women's alliance example, 261–262
diaspora, meaning of, 347
différance, 255–256
  meaning of, 255
difference
  antimodern view, 256–257
  and dialogue, 260–269
  emic and etic perspectives, 260–261
  mutual respect aspect, 314–316
  politics of, 257–258
  postmodern view, 250–251, 254–259
  and sameness, 258

varieties of, 263–264
  women's alliance example, 261–262
differential consciousness
  effects of, 9
  and multicultural perspectives, 22–23
  use of term, 344
*Directory of Afrikanamerican Research
    Centers*, 30
discourse
  in education, 232
  and language, 186
  meaning of, 347–348
  in multicultural education, 183–187
discrimination
  impact of, 123–124
  oppressed groups, 122–123
  sex discrimination, 123–124
dominant culture, United States, 282–283

education. *See also* Multicultural educa-
    tion
  Afrocentric, 38–48
  centricity paradigm, 39
  civic education, problems of, 312–314
  Eurocentric, 8, 40, 43
  hegemonic, 8, 42, 46
  imperialist concept, 50–51
  and multinationalism, 323–328
  and self-identity, 292–293
Education for All, 138, 141
Education Reform Act of 1986, 140
emic perspective, meaning of, 260
engineering, Eurocentric educational
    approach, 53
ethnic membership
  colorblind concept, 125
  importance of, 124–126
  involuntary minorities, 121–122
  versus race, 128
ethnic minorities, use of term, 224
ethnic studies multiculturalism, 13–16
  Afrocentric education, 38–48
  Asian American studies, 69–79
  ethnic studies as requirement, 69–79
  faculty, 31, 59, 60, 78–79
  features of, 14–15, 25
  historical development, 15–16, 28–33
  issues related to, 16